COMMUNAL JUSTICE IN SHAKESPEARE'S ENGLAND

Communal Justice in Shakespeare's England

Drama, Law, and Emotion

PENELOPE GENG

UNIVERSITY OF TORONTO PRESS
Toronto Buffalo London

ISBN 978-1-4875-0804-3 (cloth)
ISBN 978-1-4875-3744-9 (EPUB)
ISBN 978-1-4875-3743-2 (PDF)

Library and Archives Canada Cataloguing in Publication

Title: Communal justice in Shakespeare's England : drama, law, and emotion /
    Penelope Geng.
Names: Geng, Penelope, author.
Description: Includes bibliographical references and index.
Identifiers: Canadiana (print) 20200411225 | Canadiana (ebook) 20210091606 |
    ISBN 9781487508043 (hardcover) | ISBN 9781487537432 (PDF) |
    ISBN 9781487537449 (EPUB)
Subjects: LCSH: English drama – Early modern and Elizabethan, 1500–1600 –
    History and criticism. | LCSH: Law in literature. | LCSH: Lawyers in literature. |
    LCSH: Law enforcement in literature. | LCSH: Justice in literature. | LCSH:
    Justice, Administration of, in literature. | LCSH: Shakespeare, William, 1564–
    1616 – Criticism and interpretation. | LCSH: Law – Great Britain – History –
    16th century.
Classification: LCC PR658.L38 G46 2021 | DDC 822/.3093554–dc23

This book has been published with the help of a grant from the Federation for the
Humanities and Social Sciences, through the Awards to Scholarly Publications
Program, using funds provided by the Social Sciences and Humanities Research
Council of Canada.

University of Toronto Press acknowledges the financial assistance to its publishing
program of the Canada Council for the Arts and the Ontario Arts Council, an
agency of the Government of Ontario.

Canada Council   Conseil des Arts
for the Arts   du Canada

ONTARIO ARTS COUNCIL
CONSEIL DES ARTS DE L'ONTARIO
an Ontario government agency
un organisme du gouvernement de l'Ontario

Funded by the   Financé par le
Government   gouvernement
of Canada   du Canada

For my parents

Contents

Illustrations

Preface

In *Two Lamentable Tragedies* (c. 1594), an English domestic tragedy written by Robert Yarington based on an actual case of double murder, residents of a London neighbourhood awake to a scene of gruesome violence. A boy-apprentice has been attacked in his master's house, his head nearly pulverized by the repeated strokes of a hammer wielded by an unknown assailant. News of the incident flies "all about the towne," but no constable, no coroner, and no officer of the law appears to guide the investigation. Instead, it is left to the neighbours to organize themselves into a forensic party and to assume the burden of magistracy. Four neighbours assemble onstage. They vow to search "every place, where blood may be conceald ... To see if we can finde the murther out."[1] So they do. Without delay, they collect a variety of forensic evidence and pursue suspects until the murderer and his accomplice are discovered. The initial spectacle of violence resolves into a scene of communal solidarity.

The depiction of communal justice is not limited to this late Elizabethan play or indeed to the genre of domestic tragedy. Numerous texts from the early modern period – both dramatic and non-dramatic – explore the power of communal action in the prosecution of crime. Together, these texts attest to the existence of a cultural fascination with communal forms of magistracy and legal administration. Early modern English texts consistently portray witnessing, detection, arrest, and judgment as actions that are contingent on the collective action of lay magistrates. I use the term "lay magistrates" to denote those who stake their legal authority on conscience and moral feeling, not on book-based knowledge or professional legal expertise. Why did playwrights repeatedly stage scenes of communal justice highlighting the autonomous power of the community? Why did communal justice become a subject of such intense and sustained dramatic writing?

In *Communal Justice*, I theorize that popular narratives of communal justice and lay magistracy constituted a critique of the professionalization of the common law. The late sixteenth and early seventeenth centuries saw unprecedented structural changes in the common law. Among these changes, which the introduction discusses at more length, was the emergence of a professional discourse that equated legal authority with legal knowledge. For example, influential jurists such as Sir Edward Coke reserved their fullest praise for the professors of law and often chided "men of none or verie little judgement in Law" for meddling in legal business.[2] Along with this veneration of expert knowledge came a devaluation of lay legal authority and lay legal knowledge. Yet, during the period of peak professionalization, nonprofessionals continued to play an integral part in preserving the peace. Ordinary people kept the peace in their communities through a combination of surveillance, shaming, and prosecution. But these aspects of participatory justice did not fit the profession's narrative of what the law was and how it operated. The profession's withholding of recognition for, if not concerted erasure of, lay legal authority fuelled an already fraught relationship between the legal professional class and virtually everyone else whom lawyers deemed untrained or illiterate in the science of the law.

The legal profession's habits of self-promotion did not escape the notice of the sharp-eyed critics of the law who probed, tested, and resisted the authority of lawyers by issuing counter-narratives that emphasized the decentralized, incremental nature of magistracy. Early modern playwrights played a crucial role in the production of resistant narratives which depicted justice as the product of collective and communal action. They leveraged the ancient ideal of participatory and communal justice – a promise inherent in common law doctrine but sorely tested by the new reality of professionalization – and gave it a new embodied existence through staging and performance. Their efforts to entertain public audiences with stories of lay magistrates upholding the tenets of communal justice served as a pointed refusal of the law's relentless centralization and professionalization.

Just as today's audiences do not watch courtroom dramas to become educated in the art of criminal or civil pleading, surely early modern playgoers did not attend plays to learn the particular procedures behind gaol delivery or sentencing. Instead, I suggest that playgoers chiefly patronized the theatres for the pleasure of participating in fiction-making as members of an emotional community, one supported by the conditions of playgoing itself. Plays featuring ingenious nonprofessionals solving murders, grief-stricken avengers prevailing over wrongdoers, and oppressed folks exposing corrupt magistrates fed audiences' desire to see justice unfettered by legal rules and procedures. As a work of performance, a play could deliver these thrills in a quintessentially communal setting. The embodied experience of playgoing – of watching, listening, and feeling with other bodies – made the drama of communal justice that much

more meaningful. The medium augmented the message. As these dramatic narratives accumulated in the public's imagination, they helped to consolidate a
sense of civic consciousness centred on community, moulding attitudes and
norms for centuries to come.

Recent work in early modern law and literature has emphasized the inter-
dependency which existed between legal and literary enterprises. Legal practitioners and literary authors were mutually engaged in fiction-making, using
the same set of rhetorical skills learned in the humanist classroom. The Inns
of Court – England's law schools – sustained a rich tradition of playwriting
and playgoing. Theatrical (and poetic) communities benefited from a friendly
association with lawyers and judges. Some who trained in the law spurned
the demands of the profession and tried their hand at playwriting or poetry.
But while recent study of legal and literary authors' collaborations has ripened
our understanding of law and literature's intertwined histories, it has largely
neglected to address the tensions, rivalries, and antipathy that divided legal
and literary communities. That is, the shared advantages and the existence of
mutual respect among legal and literary communities did not preclude members of those communities from advocating for different values of justice and
magistracy. It is this more competitive aspect of the story of early modern law
and literature that features prominently in this book.

Throughout *Communal Justice*, I draw a distinction between "law" and
"legality" in order to register a range of nonverbal and affective legal experiences. I take the term "legality" from law and society scholarship. According
to sociologists Patricia Ewick and Susan S. Silbey, traditional legal scholarship conceives of "law" as comprising only the "formal law of the Constitution, legislative statutes, court decisions, or explicit demonstrations of state
power such as executions."[3] But Ewick and Silbey point out that this monolithic notion of law does not begin to capture the everyday experience of the
law. Hence, in place of "law," they concentrate their efforts on describing
"legality" or the "diversity of the situations out of which it [the law] emerges
and that it helps structure."[4] In response, I expand the concept of "legality" to include *imagined* legal situations. I argue that one's legality is determined as much by one's embodied legal experiences (going to court) as it is
by one's imagined legal interactions (emotionally identifying with a court
defendant, a character in a fiction). Legalities are generated from these two
complementary, mutually constitutive planes of experience – the embodied
and imagined.

Literature's role in cultural production has long been recognized. But it is only
recently that scholars have attended to early modern literature's function in the
production of legal standards, expectations, and outlooks. This book contributes
to an ongoing project in literary studies to understand the present by recovering stories and experiences from the past. It does so by exploring the responses

of literary authors who acted as reporters and eyewitnesses to the rise of the common law. It does not read literary texts as exclusively monuments of the imagination but as legal and political documents that exerted a particular power over the public imagination, shaping popular expectations on such issues as individual legal responsibility, neighbourly care, and communal response to crime.

Note on Texts

When citing, I use square brackets [ ] to indicate expansions of contractions, abbreviations, superscript letters, and tildes. I have not altered the original punctuation in early modern printed or manuscript sources. In most cases, I have kept the original spelling, replacing early modern "u," "i," and "vv" with "v," "j," and "w." Thorns are rendered "th" and yoghs "y." Early modern long esses (*s*) have also been silently modernized.

Abbreviations

Acts and Monuments	John Foxe, *The Unabridged Acts and Monuments*
BL	British Library, London
Folger	Folger Shakespeare Library, Washington DC
Huntington Library	The Huntington Library, Art Museum, and Botanical Gardens, San Marino CA
Lambeth	Lambeth Palace Library, London
ODNB	*Oxford Dictionary of National Biography*
OED	*Oxford English Dictionary*
RB	Rare Book

COMMUNAL JUSTICE IN SHAKESPEARE'S ENGLAND

Introduction: A Double Obligation

Sixteenth- and seventeenth-century English subjects were burdened by the weight of a double obligation. They were expected to obey magistrates, both "inferior" ones, like the justices of the peace, and "superior" ones, like the judges of the assize who tried felony cases.[1] As Sir Francis Bacon put it, "the law protects the people, and magistrates protect the laws."[2] At the same time, as decreed by parliamentary statutes and affirmed by centuries of custom, all individuals, working in tandem with their neighbours, were expected to play a role in the detection of crime, from the surveillance of malefactors to the presentation of forensic evidence to the judgment of the accused. When a crime occurred in a neighbourhood, for example, the local residents were legally obliged to raise hue and cry, to safeguard the corpse, to provide witness testimony, and to be willing to serve on juries.[3] Both individual and communal action shaped the course of early modern justice. In the words of Cynthia B. Herrup, "although a handful of professionals presided over the final stage of criminal prosecution, the link between justice and morality in theory made criminal law the moral inheritance of every resident."[4] Within this moral-legal universe, no person was exempt from magistracy; even the youngest member of the community was expected to do his or her part.

But beyond offering some cursory remarks about the open character of English justice and trial by jury, legal professionals gave little recognition to lay magistrates or their judgment and authority. Indeed, as common lawyers honed their professional habitus, they began to associate expert legal knowledge with legal wisdom and authority. The term "habitus" is defined by Pierre Bourdieu as "durable, transposable dispositions" that structure everyday social interactions.[5] Habitus might be manifested in one's speech, mannerism, dress, aesthetic taste, or other outward signifiers, all of which function to establish a frictionless impression of group-belonging. With respect to the common law, lawyers demonstrated their in-group credentials by mastering the law's specialized language (Law French) and its habits of thought. In *The*

Touch-Stone of Common Assurances (1648), William Sheppard of the Middle
Temple asserts:

> The subject matter of Law is somewhat transcendent, and too high for ordinary
> capacities, the manner of putting of Cases is so concise, the distinctions and dif-
> ferences of Law are so many, that it is hard for any man not well read in the Laws
> in generall, to judge or make use of any part of them in particular, and rightly and
> fully to apprehend and apply the things herein set forth.[6]

He goes on to complain of "sundry ignorant men that meddle so much in these
weighty matters."[7] The cultivation of a professional habitus occurred alongside
legislative changes that shifted the power of accusation from members of the
community to legal officeholders.

The devaluation of lay judgment, capacity, and authority was an inevitable
outgrowth of the professionalization of the law. During Elizabeth I's reign,
common lawyers began to organize themselves into a professional class on an
unprecedented scale. To quote Wilfrid R. Prest, the common law experienced a
"mushroom growth" in the late sixteenth century.[8] Based on the matriculation
records of Gray's Inn, the Inner Temple, Lincoln's Inn, and the Middle Temple –
the four Inns of Court that were central places for common law learning – Prest
calculates that the number of students called to the bar increased from 383 in
the 1580s to 510 in the 1610s, for an increase of 33.2 per cent.[9] In roughly the
same period (from 1581 to 1611), the population of England increased by
22.8 per cent.[10] The growth of the common law profession outpaced that of the
general population. Louis A. Knafla further clarifies that there were two periods
of sharp growth, the first from 1579 to 1584 and the second from 1594 to 1608.[11]
Prest and Knafla's statistical discoveries confirm what many scholars had long
thought: common lawyers boasted a new critical mass and their success as a
class of professionals had profound consequences for the political and cultural
life of Elizabeth's and James's subjects.

Communal Justice investigates the tension between professional and nonprofessional accounts of magistracy. It argues that the double obligation placed on
subjects – to be magistrates, to obey magistrates – became a source of increas-
ing contradiction as lawyers reshaped legal authority and knowledge around
the priorities of the profession. Furthermore, it argues that the tension – which
for centuries passed largely without comment – became too pronounced to be
ignored in the late sixteenth and early seventeenth centuries. This increased
tension was due to a convergence of factors, including a popular religious culture that emphasized the power of lay conscience and the rise of a robust public
theatre that profited from staging stories of inept lawyers and venal judges.

The professionalization of the common law that occurred at the tail end of
the sixteenth century triggered competing arguments about the source of legal

authority, the nature of knowledge, and the degree to which laypeople could exert legal judgment. These arguments were developed in a number of genres, for example, in epigrams, assize sermons, and character books, but they found a particularly accommodating home in London's newly established playhouses. Early modern dramatists were arguably the era's most fearless social observers, and they routinely subjected the legal profession to harsh critiques. Playwrights targeted rank-and-file members such as lawyers and scriveners, mocking them for their sophistries, venality, and general blockheadedness.[12] At the same time, dramatists invited playgoers to imagine the transformative power of lay legalism and communal legal action. For example, positive images of communal witnessing are woven into the main action of Shakespeare's *King Lear*. In the play, which I discuss in chapter 4, intersubjective witnessing forges unexpected alliances between characters of high and low status. To a public battered by the professionalization of law, the playhouse was *the* place to go to in order to feel better about being a nonprofessional.

The early modern playhouse was arguably the premier place for collective and embodied knowledge-making. As places devoted to fiction-making, theatres are in essence what Michel Foucault calls "heterotopias" or "counter-sites," in which "all the other real sites that can be found within the culture, are simultaneously represented, contested, and inverted."[13] In the heterotopic theatres of Shakespeare and his contemporaries, traditional values were represented and contested before an attentive public audience. Paul Yachnin frames early modern theatres as sites of "public making," where political, legal, and religious meaning and values were deconstructed and disseminated.[14] But they were also places for intense feeling and philosophical reflection – perhaps even emotional healing. Sarah Beckwith argues for the consolatory nature of Shakespeare's theatre within the context of the aftermath of the Reformation. Much of "Shakespeare's theater is a search for community, a community neither given nor possessed but in constant formation and deformation."[15] Shakespeare's theatre gave audiences the opportunity to understand both the tragic and comic possibilities of "human relating."[16] The collective experience that theatre fostered was dependent not only on the nature of the stories they staged – stories of human suffering and reconciliation – but on the embodied and phenomenological nature of theatrical performance. Bruce R. Smith compares Shakespeare's Globe to an "acoustic field." As the actor "projects his voice in all directions, he defines a circle. Beyond the reach of his voice stretches a horizon of silence ... [a]ctor and audience share the same field of sound."[17] Within this circle of sound, there is the possibility for fellowship and community. To these powerful insights about the participatory and communal nature of theatre I add my own about the role of the early modern theatre in shaping *legal* culture. Outside of the playhouse, lawyers increasingly policed the limits of lay judgment in law, but within it, lay legal judgment was affirmed and unabashedly celebrated, day after day, theatrical season after season. Audiences found community within the theatre, united by their passionate interest in the drama of justice. Between the 1580s and the closing of England's theatres in 1642, generations of men and women collectively exercised their capacity to imagine – and feel – the power of communal justice. This phenomenon posed a formidable challenge to those bent on legal professionalization.

Professional Distinction

Pierre Bourdieu's sociological study of cultural "distinction" serves as one of this book's theoretical touchstones. Bourdieu was fascinated by the relationship between class, consumer habits, aesthetic judgment, and public evaluation of what counted as good or beautiful or worthy of communal approbation. For Bourdieu, preference for one kind of music or art over another is never (exclusively) an expression of personal liking. It is, rather, an outgrowth of class-consciousness and class-aspiration. Taste divides a people into subcultures; it unites as well as estranges, attaches as well as repels. Taste is fundamental to community-formation. In *Distinction*, Bourdieu analyses consumer habits, which he relates to the "transmutation of an arbitrary way of living into the legitimate way of life which casts every other way of living into arbitrariness."[18]

Late in his career, Bourdieu turned to an analysis of the law. With respect to the manifestation of legal distinction, Bourdieu theorizes that the "juridical field" is "the site of a competition for the monopolistic right to determine the law" between different groups, each vying to enjoy the "capacity to *interpret* a corpus of texts sanctifying a correct or legitimized vision of the social world."[19] Upon gaining the upper hand, the dominant group begins to erase traces of competition so that the "victories over the dominated" are "converted into accepted facts."[20] In time, even the memory of a prior struggle – among different groups for the right to say what the law is, what it can achieve, and who has the capacity to ably interpret it – fades from memory. Reconstructing the origins of the competition is challenging, for it requires a wilful denial of present reality. To get back to the moment of struggle, one needs to deny the legitimacy of "accepted facts."

Today, the public largely accepts that the task of legal interpretation should be left to legal experts. It is generally taken for granted that the legal professional class, composed of lawyers, judges, and legal theorists, exercises what Bourdieu calls a "socially recognized capacity" to interpret the law.[21] Most people, having little or no professional training in the law, readily concede the law to the expert. For example, many of the people interviewed by Patricia Ewick and Susan Silbey speak of the law as having an external existence to their everyday lives.[22] Ewick and Silbey call this the "reification" of the law – "the tendency to impart to historically specific processes and behaviors a thinglike quality."[23] To the people whose legalities are shaped by a narrative of disempowerment, "the law seems transcendent," as if it existed "on a different plane," and they, the subjects of the law, are powerless before it.[24] Arguing against a legal professional's opinion flies in the face of common sense.

Recovering early modern narratives about the law goes some distance to exposing the "certainties" of modern legality as artificial and historically constructed.[25] To quote Roland Barthes, "there is no fixity in mythical concepts: they can come into being, alter, disintegrate, disappear completely. And it is precisely because they are historical that history can very easily suppress them."[26] Early modern texts, with their rich cast of lay magistrates, reveal that the attitude of uncontested submission before professional legal expertise was not always the norm but, like many learned historical gestures, a cultural "self-fashioning" that took centuries to evolve.

In the sixteenth and seventeenth centuries, popular writers and audiences actively resisted lawyers' claims about professional legal expertise. In many dramatic narratives, for example, the lawyer or advocate is consistently outsmarted by the nonprofessional whose inborn wit breaks down legal impasses. (Portia's legal triumph in Shakespeare's *The Merchant of Venice* springs to mind.) Such dramatic fictions take place in a religious culture that insisted that every person possessed the potential for magistracy on account of their faculty of conscience. Conscience, divinely implanted in the hearts of individuals, empowered them to carry out the work of the magistrate: to witness, accuse, and judge. The lay magistrate was indivisible from the broader community. Just as conscience continuously monitored the self's actions, so the community without fail guarded its members from those who sought to do them harm. The community collectively engaged in detecting sin, punishing wrong, and facilitating communal reconciliation through rituals of confession and repentance.

The Origins of Communal Justice

Communal justice denotes a form of legal remedy devised by the community rather than by the individual. Logically, communal justice opposes private remedy, such as revenge or the appeal.[27] In early English society, as Tom Lambert explains, "communality" was "[t]he most prominent ideal in the laws":

> Communities were expected to assemble regularly to consider their members' legal cases, to come to agreement about how the law applied to such cases, to issue judgements that carried their collective authority, and ... to band together in potentially violent enforcement expeditions.[28]

Preventative policing and adjudication of disputes were fundamentally communal experiences. Yet, as Lambert also observes, early English communities could often be "apathetic" to crime.[29] Indeed, historians have discovered wonderfully detailed examples of just how communities avoided their legal duties. In his important history of the medieval coroner and his jury, R.F. Hunnisett recounts tales of medieval communities dragging corpses from one vicinity to another in a game of "not it." It seems many people felt there was little to be gained from being the "first finder" of a corpse.[30] Despite the existence of laws forbidding such actions, medieval layfolk regularly shirked their inquest duties leading Hunnisett to muse, "the comfort and health of the neighbours were the least of the motives ... financial loss to the township or hundred or both was [a] far greater [concern]."[31]

Although medieval and early modern religious culture consistently emphasized the connection between justice and neighbourly love – Regina M. Schwartz locates the social model of the self, one that emphasizes the self's relation in a "network of association," in Jewish and Christian teachings[32] – much of the historical research on crime suggests that communities frequently fell short of the ideal. A number of factors could have contributed to a dampening of communal and individual enthusiasm for magistracy. For example, at a minimum, participating in an inquest meant setting aside one's daily business, which potentially affected one's economic output; those who pursued the suspect might even risk life and limb.

To promote communal justice and curb apathy, medieval and early modern English parliaments passed laws that clearly defined the legal duties of the community as well as the penalties for failing to uphold said duties. As early as the twelfth century, laws such as the Assize of Arms (1181) required that "all the men of the tithing ... bear arms when responding to the hue and cry."[33] ("Tithing" refers to the grouping of the peasantry into units of ten or more for the purpose of policing.) Hue and cry comes from the Anglo-Norman *hu e cri*, denoting the raising of alarm by members of the community.[34] This law was reinforced by the passing of the statute 27 Eliz., c. 13 (1584–5), which stated that "Inhabitauntes and Resiants [*sic*] of everie or any such Hundred (with the Franchises within the Precinct thereof)" would be subject to amercement (a financial penalty) should they fail to raise hue and cry.[35] The passages of these and similar statutes – from the twelfth to the sixteenth century (and beyond) – suggest that communal justice, a remedy based on individuals' willingness to assume legal obligations, did not occur without state supervision. The chapters that follow will make the case that drama, and to an extent, religious writing shaped collective attitudes about lay magistracy and communal justice.

Historians observe that participatory justice was integral to life in early modern England: "[t]he initial response to alleged crimes in early modern England combined communal and official participation,"[36] "the administration of the criminal law ... continued throughout the fifteenth and sixteenth centuries to depend on the participation of local people,"[37] and "[a]mateur office-holding and voluntary prosecution ... were the keystones of accusatory justice in early modern England."[38] The spirit of lay legalism was not limited to the criminal law. The same network of communal and neighbourly relations that produced communal justice also facilitated civil and ecclesiastical actions. Heresy, slander, and adultery – all falling under the jurisdiction of the church courts – operated on the exchange of local knowledge.[39] Early modern subjects actively used the civil courts to resolve disputes involving land and movables. In the sixteenth century, the Court of Common Pleas became the most trafficked common law court in the land.[40] Surveying the state of popular legal participation, James A. Sharpe comments, "practically every court, whether civil or criminal, experienced an increase in business between the mid-sixteenth and mid-seventeenth centuries."[41] Laura Gowing importantly emphasizes the role of women in initiating legal actions: "ordinary women and men knew what to sue, where to prosecute, and what to say."[42] Tim Stretton observes that it was an "intensely legal age" and that "litigation touched the lives of a greater proportion of the population than ever before, whether as suitors, jurors, witnesses or deponents."[43] Courts were positively deluged with litigation. All sorts of people, from the landed gentry to the labouring class, initiated legal grievances.[44] Christopher W. Brooks estimates that the "rate of civil litigation in 1600 was ... higher than it has been in any other period in English history before or since."[45] For these reasons, then, Steve Hindle encourages scholars to "think less of *government* as an institution or as an event, than of *governance* as a process, a series of multilateral initiatives to be negotiated across space and through the social order."[46] The many factors behind the surge in popular legalism lie beyond the scope of this project. Suffice it to say, early modern subjects were actively involved in magistracy. The enforcement of order was understood to be every person's responsibility; magistracy was imagined to be the prerogative of every individual with a God-given conscience. Likewise, the work of imagining and conceptualizing the law was shared by a dizzying array of stakeholders.

A History of Communal Justice

The scholarly study of English communal justice began in the eighteenth century – in the emergent field of legal history. In his seminal *Commentaries on the Laws of England* (1765–9), William Blackstone provided some comments on early English communal legal practices. He limited his observations to the jury system. Book 3, for example, discusses "the policy of the antient law" which required the jury "to come *de vincineto*, from the neighbourhood of the vill or place where the cause of action was laid in the declaration."[47] Similarly brief reflections appear in late nineteenth- and twentieth-century legal historiography, including Frederick Pollock and Frederic Maitland's *The History of English Law*.[48] During these years, even as antiquarian societies were bringing

little-known church and legal records to light, legal historians primarily repli-
cated the Blackstone model of narrating the story of English law from above.

Fast-forward more than a hundred years. In the 1970s, social historians subjected legal categories of "communal justice" "participatory justice," and "popular legalism" to intense archival and sociological analysis.[49] Social history is,
in the words of one of its leading practitioners, Keith Wrightson, "a history in
which a deliberate effort has been made to recover the experience of the mass
of the English people, to rediscover them as members of a distinct and vigor-
ous culture and to understand their part in the making of their history."[50] Thus,
social historians focus on describing and analysing law "from below." This
phrase, commonly seen in historiography, denotes an approach that concen-
trates on the experiences of the non-elites. Jonathan Barry and Christopher W.
Brooks explain that "'[h]istory from below,' concentrat[es] on the lower classes
and 'popular culture."[51] The "new interest in social history," Krista Kesselring
remarks, "opened the floodgates of research into the experiences and activities
of people long overlooked in accounts of the past."[52] This floodgate remains
wide open, as attested by recent publications in both legal and literary studies
on early modern legal culture.

The rise of new historicism in the 1980s brought social history and the
history of crime to the table of literary criticism, leading to a revision of the
traditional disciplinary distinctions between history and literature and their
respective archives.[53] The late 1990s and 2000s saw the establishment of law
and literature as a subfield within early modern literary studies.[54] The question
of how literature, especially drama, influenced popular legal culture became
central to many literary projects. Around the time that Julia Reinhard Lupton tilted political theology away from the body of the sovereign to that of the
citizen – "the hero of this book is not the tyrant-martyr, but the citizen-saint,
not the two bodies of the king but the many faces of the multitude"[55] – Lorna
Hutson retrained the gaze to focus on Renaissance drama's staging of participatory justice and civic participation in law. In no uncertain terms, she showed
that when critics used drama to prove the existence of a monolithic state, they
assumed that the early modern English state possessed total, hegemonic power
over its subjects' legal subjectivities and experiences. Within the body of new
historicist scholarship, in particular, "English judicial investigations are always
identified with, and administered by, the state."[56] Such a reading of the English
state was not only flawed in light of new social history, but – when it came to
the study of literature – it limited how one could read (and teach) early modern texts. Hutson's analysis of drama and law set off exciting conversations
in countless ways. Recent law and literature scholarship now begins with the
premise that law was indeed participatory and that drama absorbed that spirit
of communality into its aesthetic fabric. Derek Dunne, for example, argues that
traditional criticism of revenge tragedy places undue emphasis on the "figure

of the solitary revenger." For every hero, a Hamlet or Hieronimo, there is a community of citizens sustaining him: "the taking of revenge is rarely enacted alone ... revenge [was] ... a political, participatory act carried out by a group of citizens in opposition to the powers that be."[57] Still, despite the critical attention to the communal and the understanding that "legal judgment was, with few exceptions, a thoroughly collaborative affair,"[58] no one has yet tried to explain the cultural value of fictions and fantasies of communal justice – or to theorize the relationship between these flourishing fictions and the centralization and professionalization of law.

As I have said, communal justice was an English legal custom as well as a value sustained by the period's popular literature, especially by drama. Literature linked the act of doing communal justice to the idea of home, neighbourliness, and even civic belonging. The power of these stories, I theorize, lies in their romantic and idealistic depiction of what law could be. Playwrights understood that their audiences wanted to see a heterotopic legality, one centred on the experiences of lay magistrates. In their plays, a character's legal authority stemmed not so much from legal expertise as from conscience aided by moral feeling.

Recognizing this facet of the period's drama leads one to contemplate the role of the emotions. The field of early modern law and literature typically brings together three fields: literature, law, and history. But to understand the *affective* value of stories of communal justice, we need to add a fourth one: that of law and emotions. Susan A. Bandes points out that while law is "imbued with emotion," legal practitioners typically deny emotions a proper place in the legal field.[59] Having a background in literary studies, I was initially puzzled by her account of the legal field's resistance to emotions. *Of course* law is about the emotions. But my confusion reflected a disciplinary bias. The study of emotions (its historicity, its grammar) has always been at the heart of literary studies and literary theory. The "turn to affect" in the 2000s, advanced by the work of Eve Kosofsky Sedgwick, Sara Ahmed, Lauren Berlant, Brian Massumi, and many others carved out a vast intellectual space for the study of the emotions. The way we read, the way we teach, and the way we theorize our relationship to our writing and the academic profession – all of it – has been fundamentally shaped by affect studies.[60] And yet, in legal scholarship, it is as if the affective wave that revolutionized literary studies hit a wall and went no further. To quote Martha Nussbaum writing in 2004, "there is a popular commonplace to the effect that the law is based on reason and not passion."[61] This "antiemotion program in law," which Nussbaum connects to the English utilitarian tradition, crumbles in the face of overwhelming evidence from psychology, moral philosophy, literature, and history that points to the law as a field that both shapes and is shaped by emotions.[62] So, as Nussbaum and others have argued, the antiemotion strand in legal studies is a learned habit and, like all habits, it can be unlearned with sustained practice. Recent publications on law and emotions – such as journal special issues edited by Rachel E. Holmes and Toria Johnson (2018) and Merridee Bailey and Kimberley-Joy Knight (2017) – model ways of unlearning using early modern texts, authors, and archives.[63]

This book contributes to the law and emotions movement through its analysis of the emotional value of fictions of communal justice. Readers interested in legal emotions and the history of legal emotions will encounter in this book a chorus of voices, sourced from sermons, plays, and pamphlets, all arguing for the primacy of emotions in the law. They will become intimately familiar with the views of English preachers such as Robert Harris, who believed that "[a] judge must smite a sinner, with a weeping eie and a feeling heart,"[64] as well as with those of fictive lay magistrates such as Master James of A Warning for Fair Women, who asserts that forensic judgment is predicated on aesthetic feeling. "The passion written by a feeling pen, / And acted by a good Tragedian," he claims, can do more to uncover secrets and suppressed guilt than the law.[65]

The Profession of the Common Law

In early modern England, the "law" implied many kinds of laws, including civil law, canon law (the law used by the church), natural law, and Roman law or jus commune (the pan-European common law).[66] Urging scholars to eschew a monolithic view of the law, Wilfrid R. Prest argues:

> There was little thought out or coherent about that fragmented chaos of overlapping (and frequently conflicting) jurisdictions – national, regional and local courts, ecclesiastical and secular courts, courts occasional and permanent, courts dispensing English common law, Roman civil law, courts of considerable antiquity and courts newly erected or asserted, courts swamped with business and courts moribund for lack of suitors.[67]

In so far as the diversity of courts reflected diversity of jurisprudence, custom, and legal tradition, the Elizabethan courts exemplified "jurisdictional heterogeneity" (to borrow Bradin Cormack's useful phrase).[68] The academic study of law reflected a diversity of outlooks as well. Roman jurisprudence entered humanist classrooms through translations and commentaries. At Oxford and Cambridge, professors of civil law put their students in "contact with continental scholarship."[69] Indeed, the cosmopolitanism of English law prompted England's premier jurist Sir Edward Coke to write in 1626, "'there be divers laws within the realm of England'" and to "list sixteen different varieties, only one of which he called the common law."[70]

Yet in recognizing the superabundance of legal outlooks and jurisdictions, one should not be distracted from the fact that it was the common law that dominated sixteenth-century England. For a time, there may have been many legal traditions, but one would rule them all. The "later Tudor" period, to quote J.G.A. Pocock, saw the "great hardening and consolidation of common-law thought."[71] The primacy of common law was aided by the publication of law books, including treatises such as Coke's *The First Part of the Institutes* (his massive commentary on Sir Thomas Littleton's *Tenures*), legal manuals or "pre-paratives" for law students, handbooks for petty officeholders such as justices of the peace and constables, and the "literature of magistracy," a term of Jessica Winston's invention, which encompasses the poems, translations, and plays written by lawyers to "train current magistrates and advise them about their responsibilities, to guide the thinking of magistrates-in-training at the Inns, and also to demonstrate the authors' commitment to and ethical preparation for being legal magistrates themselves."[72] The expansion of the common law's jurisdictional presence through writing especially – from legal textbooks to legal or poetic fictions – has constituted, in Bradin Cormack's words, the "long process of centralization and rationalization through which the common law achieved interpretive hegemony" (in later centuries).[73]

The "hardening" (Pocock) or "rise" (Cormack) of common law in England goes hand in hand with its strategies of professionalization. Famous legal-ists of the period – Coke, Sir Francis Bacon, Sir William Lambarde, Sir John Davies, to name a few – were all active during what in hindsight looks to be a relatively short span of time. Together, these common law theorists, profes-sors, and practitioners built a professional society characterized, on the social front, by "clubbing" and "rituals of fellowships" (including copious consump-tion of food and alcohol and displays of "wit"),[74] on the literary front, by the aforementioned literature of magistracy (Winston), and on the jurisdictional front, by competition and antagonism with and against their legal rivals, the civil lawyers. Civil lawyers constituted a "rather small group, numbering only 200 during the period from 1603 to 1641. By contrast there may have been as many as 2,000 common law barristers at the beginning of the seventeenth century."[75] In short, the expansion of the common law societies at the Inns of Court led to a rapid accumulation of cultural and political capital which, in turn, sped up the profession's growth. J.H. Baker concludes that, by the end of the sixteenth century, "common learning of the inns was the common law."[76]

Recent Inns of Court studies have illuminated the day-to-day habits of early modern lawyers.[77] Thanks to Winston's analysis of the "literary pastimes" of writers associated with the Inns of Court, we now know that the production of magistracy literature was chiefly a phenomenon of the 1560s. Subsequent decades witnessed a steady decline in "the volumes of published verse and the performance of drama ... and this ebbing trend continued through the 1580s."[78] Playwriting, translation, and other literary experiments enabled lawyers to "raise their status and reputation" and "raise the status of the Inns and legal men."[79] In other words, the legal profession's accumulation of wealth and political power rested on its successful acquisition of cultural capital, much of it thanks to its patronage of the arts. Those who possessed the gift of eloquence published works under their own names. Those who lacked eloquence became patrons and consumers of literature.

But alongside the altruistic, commonwealth-oriented literature of magistracy existed less playful or leisurely forms of writing. The rise of the common law profession attracted many critics, triggering defensive responses from the legal profession. These responses betrayed lawyers' intense status-checking and, at times, their displays of expertise played out as attacks on lay or non-expert judgment. This aspect of the professionalization process deserves to be better understood. Lawyers invested a great deal of intellectual energy in generating the literature of magistracy. That literature, together with the kinds of texts lawyers produced for an internal audience, such as case reports, legal commentaries, readings of statutes, and yearbooks, enabled them to hone an aura of unimpeachable expertise. To promote the image of the wise, impartial, prudent expert, the lawyer asserted a difference between his knowledge and the legal knowledge and learning of the nonprofessional. Law is an art that exceeds the capacity of the ordinary "braine."[80] I focus on this aspect of the professional's rhetoric – that is, the rhetoric of expertise that divided the professional and lay practitioner.

In printed publications prepared for the wider reading public, lawyers called their métier an "art" – one whose mysteries were revealed only to the "professors of law." In *The Third Universitie of England*, a flattering account of the Inns of Court, Sir George Buck praises Coke as "not onely a most learned professor, but also a singular Antecessor, a chiefe Judge, and a principall interpreter" (figure 1).[81] Coke was widely admired by members of his profession, as well as by those tangential to the Inns, both during and after his lifetime. Ben Jonson called Coke "Solon's self" who "explat'st the knotty laws / With endless labours."[82] Coke published legal reports, commentaries, and jury charges at an astonishing pace. Even his rival, Bacon, was forced to begrudgingly admit, "had it not been for Sir Edward Coke's Reports (which though they may have errors, and some peremptory and extrajudicial resolutions more than are warranted, yet they contain infinite good decisions and rulings over of cases), the law by this time had been almost like a ship without a ballast."[83]

Coke taught other lawyers how to act the part of the professional by emphasizing the difference between expert and non-expert legal knowledge, which he boiled down to the difference between the lawyer's "artificial reason" and the layperson's "natural reason."[84] In his *Les reports* (1600), Coke insists that "reading, hearing, conference, meditation, and recordation, are necessarie … to the knowledge of the common Law, because it consisteth upon so many, & almost infinite particulers."[85] In *The First Part of the Institutes* (1628), Coke

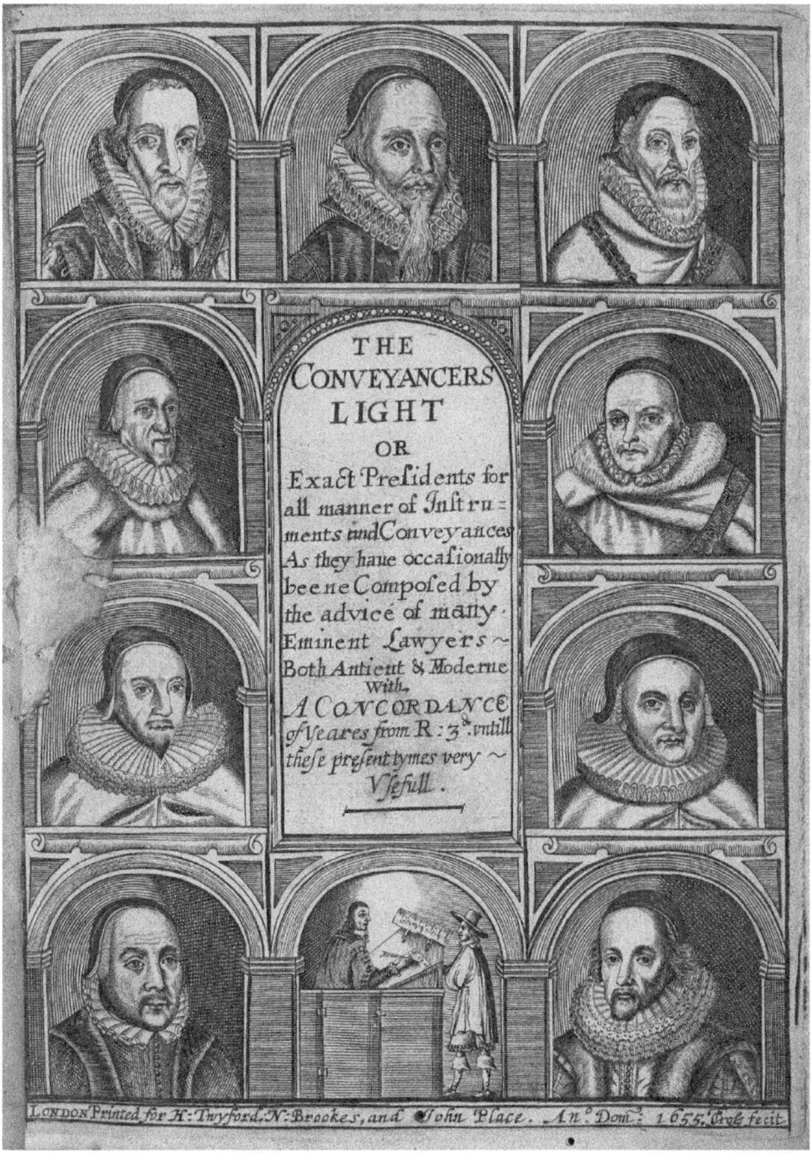
THE
CONVEYANCERS
LIGHT
OR
Exact Presidents for all manner of Instru=ments and Conveyances
As they haue occasionally beene Composed by the advice of many Eminent Lawyers
Both Antient & Moderne
With
A CONCORDANCE
of Yeares from R: 3d. untill these present tymes very Usefull.
LONDON Printed for H: Twyford, N: Brookes, and John Place. An° Dom: 1655.

Figure 1. The title page of *The compleat clark* (1655) featuring the professors of law. Note the variant title *The Conveyancers Light*.
Engraving by T[homas] Cross. The Huntington Library (RB 359209).

compares law to a "deepe well, out of which each man draweth according to the strength of his understanding." Reaching "deepest," the "Professor of Law" "seeth the amiable, and admirable secrets of the Law."[86] While not all agreed with Coke – Thomas Hobbes, following Bacon's theory of natural reason in law, commented, "'[t]hough it be true … that no man is born with the use of reason, yet all men may grow up to it as well as lawyers; and when they have applied their reason to the laws … may be as fit for and capable of judicature as Sir Edward Coke himself'" – most in the profession supported Coke's logic.[87]

Lawyers even cast doubt on the layman's intellective capabilities for legal study. In *A Direction or Preparative* (1600), William Fulbecke argues that "[m]agistrates are the ministers of Lawes, the Judges are interpreters, the people are the Servants, that they may have true libertie."[88] The idea that the people enjoyed "true libertie" while obeying magistrates was consistent with political theories of the period. Where Fulbecke strains his logic is in his attempt to undermine the layperson's capacity for legal subtlety. While he denies no one access to law books (indeed, he claims that the "prescript" of "laws" should be more widely known that "men may decline from that which is forbidden, and follow that which is commanded"), he is unable (or unwilling) to imagine nonprofessionals producing any meaningful or useful interpretation of the law.[89] Fulbecke hopes that nonprofessionals will quietly cede interpretative control to experts: "if a mans braine be no fit mould for the Law, let an other mans mouth be his teacher."[90] Some men possessed the right "braine[s]" for law and others did not.

The lawyer's criticism of lay legal authority was rarely so gently expressed. The aforementioned William Sheppard decries the meddling of "sundry ignorant men":

> And considering withall the mischief arising every where by the rash adventures of sundry ignorant men that meddle so much in these weighty matters, there being now almost in every Parish an unlearned, and yet confident Pragmaticall Atturney (not that I thinke them all to be such) or a lawlesse Scrivener, that may perhaps have some Law Books in their houses, but never read more Law then is on the backside of Littleton, or an ignorant Vicar, or it may be a Blacksmith, Carpenter, or Weaver, that have no more books of Law in their houses, then they have Law in their heads.[91]

Sheppard's denigration of the nonprofessional is itself a learned rhetorical reflex from none other than Coke. In *Le second part des reportes* (1602), Coke asserts:

> If you observe any diversities of oppinions amongst the professors of the Lawes, contende you (as it behoveth) to be learned in your profession, and you shall finde, that it is *Hominis vitium, non professionis* [it is the fault of man, not the profession]:

And to say the trueth, the greatest questions arryse not upon any of the Rules of the Common Law, but sometimes uppon Conveyances and Instruments made by men unlearned; Many times upon Willes intricately, absurdly, and repugnantly set downe, by Parsons, Scriveners, and such other Imperites: And oftentimes upon Actes of Parliament, overladen wyth provisoes, and addicions, and many times on a suddein penned or corrected by men of none or verie little judgement in Law.[92]

In this complaint, Coke downplays the legal expertise of "Parsons," "Scriveners," and other "Imperites," a now obsolete word for an "unskilled or ignorant person," even as he enumerates the extensive scale of their legal work.[93] There is a contradiction here. How ignorant could these "unlearned" men have been if they played such a prominent role in the everyday operation of the law? Coke implies that these "ignorant" amateurs were the bottom feeders of the law, but in early modern England's complex legal environment, where many courts swelled with cases, these humble legal practitioners must have played essential roles in their local communities. The last part of the passage also hints at the presence of legalists with some training but poor acumen, or, as Coke puts it, "men of none or verie little judgement in Law" who "pen" and "correct" "Actes of Parliament." These are presumably parliamentary clerks. This well-educated class of professionals also stands accused of doing shoddy legal work. Coke even faults the legislators who had "overladen" statutes with "privisoes, and addicions." These are just some of the ways Coke defined the lawyers' expertise against the non-lawyer's dilettantism.

Common law professionals routinely denigrated the work of "ignorant" scriveners. Yet their own labour was not above reproach. When Renaissance legal humanists undertook their philological study of Roman law, they revived an ancient prejudice against the legal professional. During the Roman classical period of 100 BCE to 350 CE, the work of the *juris consultus* (jurisconsult) was seen as a "gentleman's avocation."[94] Unlike the *rhetor* (advocate, lawyer),[95] the jurisconsult did not personally argue cases in court; rather, he gave counsel to advocates on points of law.[96] In the fourteenth and fifteenth centuries, during the so-called war of the faculties between humanists and scholastics, humanists nostalgically looked back on the days of the jurisconsults, the "public interpreters of the law," who combined philosophical learning with legal knowledge.[97] Guillaume Budé, for example, complained that in his time, "the study of law has degenerated from its original state. Today there are no longer jurisconsults, or philosophers, but only lawyers."[98]

English common lawyers, sensitive to the humanist complaint against the profession, did their utmost to defend their society by comparing their work to an "art," even, on occasion, to a form of divine calling. Many within the profession embraced a priestly, oracular, and sacerdotal discourse previously associated with the religious orders. They followed a precedent set by medieval canonists. In the twelfth and thirteenth centuries, James A. Brundage explains, canonists (experts versed in Romano-canonic procedures) claimed a religious institutional identity by using the term *"professio advocatorum*, familiar to them from Roman legal sources, to describe themselves and their colleagues. Medieval lawyers used related terms as well, such as *ordo* (assemblage, band, or class), *officium* (duty, office, or function), *vocatio* (calling), and *militia* (military service, employment), to describe the group to which they belonged."[99] Paul Raffield observes that the fifteenth-century common lawyer Sir John Fortescue habitually "defended the role of the judge as a minister (or messenger) of God, by asserting that 'we, who are the Ministerial Officers, who sit and preside in the Courts of Justice, are therefore not improperly called, *Sacerdotes*.'"[100] *Sacerdos* means priest, one who professes divine matters. Likewise, Virginia Lee Strain points out that sixteenth-century common lawyers, such as Sir Edward Coke, aspired to be "oracle[s] of the law."[101] Thus, just as medieval and pre-Reformation priests laid claim to the right to interpret the Bible, so lawyers to the law, evoking their artful and oracular knowledge of the field. In sum, lawyers defined legal expertise and legal authority according to the internal criteria of their society. That effort to remake law an exclusive field for just the professionals was strengthened by lawyers' vocal disdain for what they called the nonprofessionals' "meddling" – a word that implied both operational interference and, colloquially, sexual transgression.[102] Occasionally, lawyers praised nonprofessionals (such as the trial juror) for their legal participation. But they also voiced their suspicion of, if not an outright hostility toward, the limited capacity of nonprofessionals.[103] To secure their status as members of a preeminent legal and political institution, common lawyers increasingly sought to close the ranks against outsiders. It was left to those outsiders, the many who did not belong to the profession, to advocate for a more inclusive form of legal participation, one that accommodated lay judgment and communal justice.

Lay Judgment and the Liberty of Conscience

The discourse of legal judgment in popular culture could not have been more different from the actual discourse of lawyers. In the popular imagination, legal knowledge rested on moral, religious, and even emotional faculties. Legal authority was far less involved with notions of legal expertise than it was with ideas of conscience and communal care predicated on neighbourly love. Thus, abutting the common lawyer's top-down definition of legal authority was a popular model of lay magistracy that legitimized the legal judgment and labour of lay practitioners. One of the most serious conceptual impediments to the professional's attempt at controlling non-expert claims to legal authority was a Calvinist-inflected theology of conscience, popularized during and after the Reformation, which claimed that a juridical conscience was implanted in the human heart by God and endowed the human with the ability, in the words of the seventeenth-century preacher Ephraim Huit, to "discerne of good and evill, whereby he is distinguished from a beast."[104] Huit goes on to define conscience as a "power," not a socially cultivated "habit," because "wee may discerne the working of it in children, before any habits can bee acquired."[105]

During the Reformation, Martin Luther argued that every person possessed knowledge of God's law because it was written in the heart: God "will vouchsafe to write his Law in our hearts (as hee hath promised) otherwise we doe all come to confusion."[106] He and others used the theology of conscience to foment radical resistance to political "tyranny."[107] In his *Reply to King Henry VIII* (1522), Luther argues that Henry's oppression of the English Protestants was proof of his ignorance of God's law and, he reasons, being a "fool-king," Henry could not expect the obedience of any of his subjects.[108] In *Temporal Authority* (1523), Luther points out that subjects too often make the "mistake of believing that they ... are bound to obey their rulers in everything."[109] For Luther, no one ought to feel compelled to obey rulers who acted like "scoundrels ... suppressing ... the Christian faith."[110] To those rulers, Luther warns, "the common man is learning to think, and the scourge of princes ... is gathering force among the mob and with the common man."[111]

Luther's theological and political writings fanned anti-Catholic resistance across Europe. From Protestant strongholds such as Geneva and Emden, English exiles during the reign of Mary I and Philip II argued for justified resistance against the English state. Addressing English readers, the anonymous translator of Melanchthon's *A Faithfull Admonycion* (1554), reasons:

> It is not only unlawfull to obey them ... but also most lawful to stand in the defence of goddes religion and of the lawdable and awncient state of their cou[n]try against such uncircumcised tyran[t]es (thei shall never be called magistrates of me til thei shewe themselves worthy of that name) as goo abowt study devilish enterprises.[112]

Casting Catholic "magistrates" as tyrants, even devils (they "study devilish enterprises"), the text sanctions civil disobedience and resistance.[113] During the reign of Elizabeth I, the doctrine of liberty of conscience became a fundamental part of the performance of Protestant political identity. Thus, we hear in Sir Thomas Smith's political and legal treatise *De Republica Anglorum* (composed between 1562 and 1565 and published in 1583) declarations such as "[t]he Popes of *Rome*, and men of the Church" no longer "had dominion in our consciences."[114] Being a good Protestant in a reformed commonwealth meant having the power to freely exercise one's conscience in devotional, juridical, and political contexts.

In late sixteenth-century England, the popular understanding of lay magistracy was strongly shaped by John Calvin's theology of conscience. In his writings on faith, law, and devotion, Calvin consistently represented conscience as a faculty capable of forensic testimony and judgment.[115] In the English translation of *The institution of the Christian religion* (1587), Calvin defines conscience thus:

> For, as when men do with minde and understanding conceive the knowledge of thinges, they are thereby saide (*Scire*) to knowe, whereupon also is derived the name of Science: Knowledge: so when they have feeling of the judgement of God, as a witnesse joyned with them, which doth not suffer them to hide their sinnes but that they be drawne accused to the judgement seate of God, that same feeling is called Conscience. For it is a certaine meane betweene God and man, because it suffereth not man to suppresse in him selfe that which he knoweth but pursueth him so farre til it bring him to guiltines. This is it which *Paul* meaneth where he saith that conscience doth together witnes with men, when their thoughtes do accuse or acquite them in the judgement of God ... Whereupon also commeth that olde Proverbe, Conscience is a thousande witnesses ... a good conscience is nothing els but the inward purenes of the heart.[116]

Although Calvin's model of the conscience takes its cue from St. Paul's homily "conscience ... bears witness" (Rom. 2:15) – indeed, Calvin cites Paul and provides a marginal citation to that very chapter and verse – he also exceeds the biblical model in the way he emphasizes the psychosomatic effects of an afflicted conscience.[117] Conscience is the "*feeling* of the judgement of God" (my emphasis), a phrase that deposits us in the realm of the emotions. When the word "conscience" appears in the Bible, it is usually only modified by a single adjective: "good conscience" (Acts 23:1), "weak conscience" (1 Cor. 8:12), and "pure conscience" (1 Tim. 3:9).[118] But Calvin imagines a legal drama in which conscience, magistrate-like, pursues, arrests, and judges the offender. These fine rhetorical adumbrations owe much to Calvin's humanist training in forensic rhetoric.[119] Like Luther, Calvin had studied law and habitually braided the language and logic of law into his theological and religious writings.[120]

In the second half of the sixteenth century, Calvin's works were translated into English and published in both grand, folio-sized books and more modestly apportioned abridgments and books of aphorisms. As Alec Ryrie explains, "Reformed [English] Protestants" (from the 1540s to the 1640s) were de facto "Calvinists."[121] His conclusion is well supported by other scholars of the English Reformation. For example, commenting on the prevalence of Calvinist tropes in Renaissance poetry and drama, John Stachniewski ascertains that "Calvin ... was England's most published author between 1548 and 1650" and he, like Ryrie, concludes that "generally speaking ... Christianity to English people of this era meant Calvinism" for "Calvinism was, in the late decades of the sixteenth century and throughout James's reign, the orthodoxy of the Church of England."[122]

Concurring, Kristen Poole writes, "the decades on either side of 1600 witnessed the dominance of Calvinist theology in England" and that Elizabeth's successor, James, "actively promoted Calvinist theological orthodoxy."[123]

The popularity of Calvinism – particularly Calvin's writings on conscience – provided a theological basis for ideas of lay magistracy, which became anchored in the popular legal imagination by the time dramatists like Shakespeare explored themes of magistracy and communal justice. As I discuss in chapter 1, throughout the sixteenth and seventeenth centuries, English preachers instructed their auditors or readers to imagine themselves as judges sitting in the court or "assize" of their own conscience. In many assize sermons, preachers insisted that every person owed a legal obligation to the community. The assize preacher envisioned the self as a magistrate, one ruled *by* an authority – "superior" magistrates, the sovereign, God – and one who ruled *as* a legal authority over the self and others. Indeed, I argue that this model of the self as a lay magistrate empowered by the conscience became one of the defining traits of early modern English subjectivity. "I judge therefore I am" was central to the identity of early modern English personhood. Thus, unfortunately for the lawyers, the attempt to limit lay legal authority conflicted with popular Protestant culture, which celebrated the magisterial power of the conscientious individual – and the moral community.

The Drama of Communal Justice

Being principally concerned with the invention, exploration, and management of feelings, early modern drama was particularly well positioned to shape public emotions around communal justice. In my discussion of drama, I recognize two facets of "community": one, the fictional community represented by the text and, two, in a phenomenological sense, the spectating community of playgoers watching the trials and tribulations of the fictional community. Similarly, when I talk about the "people" or the layfolk engaged in the drama of communal justice, I envision both embodied and imagined communities: playgoers who watched, for example, the original performance of *A Warning for Fair Women*, townspeople who heard an assize sermon, and reading communities who imaginatively participated in the national conversation about justice and magistracy.

The staging of the first kind of community – the fictional community – was aided by a professional theatre that specialized in large casts, criss-crossing action, multiple scene changes, and dazzling spectacle. Early modern playwrights counted on playing companies to handle an ambitious cast-list through the doubling of actors or the hiring of temporary actors.[124] Playwrights also depended on professional playing companies to choreograph complex action to bring "historical events … vividly alive onstage."[125] Legal narratives, by their very nature, demanded sweeping movement: processions, courtroom scenes, trials by battle, inquests, penances – all of these necessitated a large cast of characters moving across the stage. Thanks to the resources and resourcefulness of the playing companies, early modern dramatists could confidently assume that actors would find a way to sustain the illusion of an imagined legal community.

I mention these well-known features of early modern drama in order to emphasize the formal advantage of theatre in sustaining the illusion of watching communities while being in a community as playgoers. A large cast allowed audiences to empathize with different characters, to imaginatively engage with their various conflicts, and to enter into wildly different emotional states within the span of the performance. At the same time, the phenomenological conditions of playing fostered intersubjective fellow-feeling. Playgoers could express moral outrage at the atrocious actions of the Duke of Cornwall in *King Lear*, for example, by affectively mirroring the reactions of the onstage actors and their fellow playgoers. Allison P. Hobgood observes that early modern drama "not only depended on the emotionality of audience members for its effect ... but was reciprocally reshaped and mutually constituted, sometimes in surprising and unintended ways, by those affected, and affecting, spectators."[126] Emotional contagion in the theatre ensured that what was felt by an individual was potentially reciprocated and amplified by another. This experience of being connected to others through a shared, theatrical experience fostered intersubjective empathy.[127] Thus, in theatricalizing communal justice before this affected and affecting audience, plays not only represented the power of communal justice but also depended on audiences to explore the complicated and messy emotions inherent in that communal action. This was a participatory theatre engaged in the staging of participatory justice. For this reason, I suggest that we read dramatic texts and the theatrical performances they occasioned as legal documents that shaped the public's knowledge and feelings about communal justice and lay magistracy. In a climate of professionalization in which lay participation in the law was actively discouraged and encoded as "meddling," when even the "natural reason" of the sovereign was found lacking in contrast to the "artificial reason" of the lawyer, dramatists supplied audiences with largely positive images of lay magistrates working to bring about justice. Their plays invited audiences to imaginatively occupy realities and identities that were sidelined within the professional discourse. Such was the resistant, even radical, potential of their art.

Looking back on the past, one might be tempted to say that communal justice and lay magistracy proved a "minor" or even alternative legal practice.[128] But doing so would reflect a modern bias, one that channels the legal profession's own sense of its origins. The mutually enforcing concepts of communal justice and lay magistracy were entrenched in the popular imagination of early modern authors and their audiences. Beyond their obvious appeal to playgoers' desire for escape and entertainment, the plays in question preserved a popular belief in the legitimacy of lay legal authority at precisely a time when common lawyers, in the midst of coalescing into a powerful professional class, established new limits on the degree and scope of lay involvement in the law. Early modern drama may not have invented the notion of the citizen-sleuth or the lay crime scene investigator, but it gave such characters – and their language, emotions, and actions – greater visibility as well as definition through its combination of *mimesis* and *diegesis*, imitation and description of action, the two basic ingredients of the medium. This is one of the rarely recognized political-legal legacies of early modern drama – even though it continues to impact contemporary conceptions of lay legal participation.

Chapters

The chapters explore the interactions of literary, religious, and legal writing communities as they sought to define issues of lay magistracy and communal justice for audiences seeking affirmation of their lived experiences and inspiration for how to conduct themselves in a changing society. Each chapter addresses a different aspect of the book's larger argument about the political undertow of dramatic representations of communal justice and lay magistracy – how they reveal tensions between popular and professional legal culture – while unpacking the formal and theatrical techniques involved in staging legal problems related to administration, magistracy, and judgment.

Chapter 1 examines the roots of communal justice in medieval England by focusing on the evolution of the assize from a legal process to a metaphor for the lay conscience. In the first part of the chapter, I look at communal justice in the context of the medieval assize, devoting particular attention to the role of the self-informing jury (also known as the jury of presentment) in assessing evidence. In the second part, I look at the development of the early modern assize and discuss the rise of the assize sermon. Conscience, according to assize preachers, equipped individuals with juridical authority. In the sermons of Robert Abbot, John Lightfoot, and George Closse, magistracy is described as every conscientious person's power and prerogative. The performance of magistracy determines one's membership in a godly (reformed) community. Thus, the lawyer's understanding of legal authority as an extension of book-knowledge and courtroom experience conflicted with a popular and seemingly ubiquitous discourse of lay magistracy, which rooted legal authority in conscience.

Chapters 2 to 5 trace four problems associated with communal justice: the tension between royal and communal justice, the role of neighbourliness in the criminal inquest, the power of empathetic witnessing in restoring communities on the brink of fragmentation, and the resistance of communities to legal

ceremonies and forms. The arrangement of these problems of communal justice loosely follows the rhythm of a criminal case. By using the life cycle of a case
to structure the chapters, I seek to retain the conceptual and critical flexibility
needed to examine the multifaceted condition of communal justice as it was
experienced and imagined.

Expanding on chapter 1's discussion of the tension between popular and
professional literature of magistracy, chapter 2 analyses how writers defined
the character of the judge and his work: judicature or legal administration.
Whereas religious authors emphasized the role of Christian compassion in
judgment – comparing the judge to a "loving" father – legal professionals suppressed the language of love, placing the emphasis on "logic" and reason. The
friction between the two discourses is richly recorded in Shakespeare's *Henry
IV, Part 2*. There are critics who view the Lord Chief Justice as an uncompli-
cated "symbol" of the law. But I show that in writing the character, Shakespeare
engages in a complex dialogue with his contemporaries in order to accentuate
the slippage between popular and professional legal expectations. For much of
the play, the Chief Justice patrols the streets of Eastcheap like a justice of the
peace. He involves himself in the community's affairs, settling disputes in the
marketplace through face-to-face mediation and arbitration, just as preachers
claimed biblical judges were wont to do. But in the final act, he appears in the
palace of Westminster, where the freshly crowned King Henry V embraces him
as a "father to [his] youth." This spatial dislocation, while apparently marking a symbolic victory for the Chief Justice (and the law he represents), in fact
precipitates his erasure from the narrative. The absence of the Chief Justice in
Henry V suggests that law occupies a marginal place in the Lancastrian polity, a
turn that foreshadows the political disorder to come in the reign of Henry VI.

If the solo magistracy of the Chief Justice ends in silence and erasure, what
constitutes a viable alternative? Using that as my guiding question, I examine
what English domestic tragedies have to say about communal and neighbourly
justice. Chapter 3 offers an in-depth analysis of Robert Yarington's *Two Lamentable Tragedies* and the anonymously authored *A Warning for Fair Women*. Both
plays stage narratives of communal cooperation wherein crimes are detected
and solved by members of the local community. I suggest that the plays not only
catered to audiences' desire to see their lived experience represented onstage
but also modelled the ideal of neighbourliness during a period when the economic divide between the haves and the have-nots was accentuated by failed
harvests and price inflation. Many social and economic historians understand
the 1590s to be the worst decade of the century on account of the harvest failures beginning in 1594. In the midst of the bad times, both the Privy Council and anonymous writers attacked the figure of the engrosser for hoarding
communal resources. This economic context sheds light on the ambivalent
depiction of the murder victim in *Two Lamentable Tragedies*. It helps to explain

the play's spirited depiction of neighbourly justice. The residents of the neigh-bourhood undertake the forensic labour of evidence-gathering, detection, and arrest. Indeed, in one scene, residents hailing from different parts of London gather at the site of the murder to assemble the victim's body, piece by dismem-bered piece. Officers of the law, when they belatedly appear, act as supporting characters and are given little stage time. *Two Lamentable Tragedies*' romantic depiction of communal care is augmented in *A Warning for Fair Women*. In this play, townsmen, yeomen, and even members of the labouring class (such as the watermen who ferry Londoners across the Thames) speak with moral and legal conviction. Both plays revel in the fantasy of communal justice in which lay magistrates nimbly and efficaciously close the case. Instead of lionizing the legal officers, the plays make the laypeople central to the operation of justice.

In recent years, critics have persuasively argued that *King Lear*'s depiction of bodily suffering – especially Cornwall's torturing of Gloucester – harkens back to the stories of martyrs in John Foxe's *Acts and Monuments*. Working within that critical tradition, chapter 4 begins with an analysis of the Foxean logic of communal witnessing. In Foxe's martyrology, "friends" – conscientious members of the religious community – express their collective resistance to the Catholic state by sheltering the persecuted, sustaining them in prison, and crying with them at their executions. Similar scenes of active communal wit-nessing and communal care undergird the play's action. The martyr-like suf-fering of Lear and Gloucester elicits compassionate responses from witnesses such as Kent, the Servants, and the Duke of Albany. Yet as a play, *King Lear* is capable of interrogating the dynamics of witnessing more fully than can a prose narration, even one as complex as Foxe's. The quick juxtaposition of scenes – for example, from the tempestuous heath where the delirious Lear addresses the "naked wretches" to the bloody chamber in which Gloucester is brutalized by Cornwall, Regan, and Goneril – reveals different forms of empathetic wit-nessing, both eyewitnessing of an onstage suffering and imagined witnessing of offstage horror. From the fatal exchange of empathy between the tortured Gloucester and the First Servant to the heroic mission that Albany claims with that same dead servant, *King Lear* reveals not only the ability of a ravaged com-munity to resist tyrannical power but also the ethical potential of spectatorship that theatre makes possible. What binds the surviving characters at the play's conclusion is not vassalage – an asymmetrical power relationship performed through an exchange of lands – but a shared, empathetic experience of watching and feeling with another body.

If Shakespearean drama links communal witnessing to ethical forms of polit-ical or legal repair it also, at times, associates common forms of group specta-torship with injustice. Chapter 5 looks at drama's interrogation of the public penance, a frequent punishment in the early modern disciplinary regime. In Shakespeare's *Henry VI, Part 2*, Eleanor Cobham, the Duchess of Gloucester,

is ordered to perform "open penance" to atone for her treasonous prophesy-
ing. Wrapped, as the stage direction indicates, in a "white sheet" and holding a
"taper," she fulfils the very image of a penitent. Like many early modern punishments, the public penance relied on the logic of communal judgment; the
penitential walk in the marketplace was designed to humiliate the individual
before her neighbours. Yet the text's emphasis on Eleanor's pitiful state challenges the gaze of the playhouse's audiences. The scene pricks at spectators'
empathetic nerves, inviting them to identify with the penitent rather than the
"giddy multitude." This daring theatrical exploration of the limits of communal
judgment finds an even greater theatrical articulation in *Macbeth*. Critics have
long been fascinated by the religious undercurrent in the scene of Lady Macbeth's sleepwalking; some read it as a theatricalizing of Calvin's testifying conscience. Relatively little, however, has been said of the scene's exposure of the
law's assumptions about the signifiers of remorse. Magistrates presiding over
tribunals routinely exhorted prisoners to deliver public confessions, to show
their remorse to the community through physicalized signs. Yet this legal practice was at odds with a post-Reformation religious culture that insisted on the
privacy of moral feelings. Seemingly, the attitudinal changes that swept through
the church stopped short of the legal institution. *Macbeth*, a play steeped in the
language of conscience and equivocation, problematizes the law's insistence on
making remorse legible to the community. This early modern problem persists
to this day in the criminal courts. The sleepwalking scene defines remorse as
a private experience, one that lies beyond the scrutiny of the law. Within the
larger context of Protestant polemical attacks on Catholic sacraments, Shakespeare's analysis of legal customs is at the very least provocative, if not down-
right oppositional.

   The book ends with a reflection on how the culture and literature of communal justice links the legality of the present to that of the past. In the decade
leading up to the English Civil Wars, communal justice became increasingly
politicized. During the revolutionary decades of the 1640s and 1650s, anonymous pamphleteers published utopian visions of law reform in which self-
advocacy took the place of legal mediation. While such schemes never material-
ized in the law (indeed, legal professionalization would crystallize between the
seventeenth and eighteenth centuries), elements of early modern communal
justice and lay magistracy settled in the popular consciousness. What lessons
might early modern literature offer us as we develop our uniquely individual
legalities?

Chapter One

From *Assise* to the Assize at Home

With respect to twentieth-century trials, Shoshana Felman observes that "a criminal case is always of course 'public' and 'collective' in the sense that prosecution takes place in the name of the community."[1] What happened in the past to make the "always" in that statement an "of course"? What hidden cultural processes are buried in the notion that a criminal prosecution is "always of course 'public'" – something done for the sake of, or before, the community? When did that concept originate in common law and what happened historically to render that concept both popular and obvious?

This chapter examines the important legal and theological milestones that inscribed "the name of the community" in criminal prosecution. In the early, formative centuries of the common law, the community played an accusatory role at the assize, a tribunal that brought together legal professionals and lay jurors, the former appointed by the monarch and the latter selected by the sheriff. In later centuries, the communal will was reflected not only in the persons of the jurymen but also in the language of assize sermons. Reflecting a post-Reformation fascination with the testifying conscience, assize preachers compared conscience to an "assize at home" and asked their listeners to imagine themselves as the sinner, the judge, and the communal beholder. Between these forms of communal participation, one embodied and the other imagined, early modern assizes ensured that the "name of the community" was ever present in criminal proceedings.

The assize, along with trial by jury, was established in the early medieval period. Both channelled the spirit of communal justice. The assize was arguably the most important occasion for the ritualized performance of royal justice. Early medieval assizes were intermittent events; by the sixteenth century, they had become twice-a-year affairs. At the beginning of the winter or summer assize, a pair of common law judges and one or two serjeants travelled the "circuit" (there were six in total), visiting major towns to adjudicate criminal and civil cases.[2] The assize demonstrated the vast reach of royal justice.

It was choreographed, like a theatrical scene, to remind subjects of the king's legal power, wielded by his justices, over life and death. Yet the assize was also an occasion for the community to exert their own legal judgment and authority over the proceedings. In the early days of the common law, royal justices heavily relied on lay jurors selected from the neighbourhood of the crime to "present" information against suspected persons. This jury of presentment – a precursor to the grand jury (which continues to exist in some common law jurisdictions) – articulated the community's local knowledge and attitudes in the kinds of accusations they made. In stark contrast to modern jury selection, which seeks uninformed or "ignorant" jurors (in the sense of being untainted by previous knowledge) – the United States Code, for example, states that an individual may be "excluded by the court on the ground that such person may be unable to render impartial jury service" – medieval and early modern judges relied on jurors precisely for their potential knowledge of the accused person.[3] In a custom dating from the thirteenth century, sheriffs selected jurors from the vicinity (a term derived from the Latin *vicinus* or neighbourhood) of the crime. Neighbourly knowledge was prized; only neighbours, it was thought, could shed proper light on a case.[4]

In the aftermath of the Reformation, the assize emerged as a popular metaphor for conscience. Local preachers, chosen by the sheriff to deliver a sermon at the beginning of the multi-day assize, actively drew a correspondence between the assize and conscience. Assize preachers complicated the conventional language of the testifying and accusing conscience (so frequently encountered in Calvinist theology) by wrapping a kernel of Calvinism in a shell of English common law doctrine. Their rhetorical experiments, which take part in the larger context of "the strange hybridization of political and religious thinking in the Renaissance," to quote Julia Reinhard Lupton, called into question professional definitions of legal authority.[5] To be sure, the assize sermon, and indeed all forms of conscience literature, could be read as an extension of the state's "machinery of power" used to "produce ... 'docile' bodies."[6] But I resist the familiar Foucauldian paradigm and encourage, instead, a reading that attends to assize sermons' emancipatory and empowering message of lay magistracy. The refrain of "the assize at home" that emerged in late sixteenth- and early seventeenth-century England directly challenged the vertical arrangement of legal authority. It insisted that all persons, by virtue of their divinely implanted conscience, possessed the authority to judge themselves and others. Building on the law's own native tradition of lay judgment and communal justice, the assize sermon eroded the top-down theory of legal authority that was the keystone of legal professional distinction. Hence, exploring the history of the assize and jury trial – from the twelfth century to the seventeenth – reveals some of the real and imagined forces behind the shifting role of communal justice both in law and in the popular imagination.

The First Assize

Emerging as an alternative to private retaliation, early English forms of communal justice revolved around ideas of "folk-right" (*folcricht*).[7] Eighth-century Kentish records indicate that disputes were settled at moots.[8] The word "moot" comes from the Old English word *mōt*, meaning a "meeting," and it is related to *mōtian*, meaning "to speak."[9] The moot was a public meeting where various parties aired their grievances, "settle[d] their differences or submit[ted] them to honourable arbitration."[10] For the moot to have had power, it would have needed the community to be invested in its success. That this form of conflict resolution lasted centuries indicates a strong degree of collective agreement. Later legal innovations such as the assize and trial by jury represent but an institutionalized iteration of this early form of communal justice.

Communal justice depended on a measure of goodwill and mutual trust; these values could not be assumed but had to be earned through repeated demonstrations of neighbourliness and friendship. Commenting on the importance of friendship in early English culture, Paul R. Hyams points out that the proverb "'swa on anum freondscype swa on anum feondscype' (in friendship as in feud)" emblematizes the "widely understood and shared ... instrumental view of political friendship."[11] Hyams illustrates that observation with examples taken from early English political and legal history. For present purposes, we can find a more accessible example in *Beowulf*, one of the most read and taught texts from the period in question. In the poem, political and legal personhood is determined by communal belonging. Communal inclusion is registered through rituals of friendship. In the opening lines of the poem, King Hrothgar and his warriors partake in convivial sports – drinking and storytelling – rituals which cement their political community. Queen Wealtheow plays an important role in these homosocial rites of friendship. As the hostess, she offers to the warriors the mead cup along with words of gracious welcome. Outside of this communal circle of kith and kin lurk the rebels, the strangers, the outcasts. Grendel is first presented to readers as a monster and a political exile, a creature forsaken by community and God. This "prowler through the dark" lives "among the banished monsters / Cain's clan, whom the Creator had outlawed / and condemned as outcasts."[12] Like Cain, the first murderer, Grendel "ruled in defiance of right."[13] In the poem, Grendel's exclusion from Heorot, the "hall of halls," a place of honour and justice, is paralleled by his affective distance from the merriment within.[14] Grendel experiences the warriors' laughter and singing as an acoustic assault. The sounds of community wound him to the core:

> … It harrowed him
> to hear the din of the loud banquet
> every day in the hall, the harp being struck
> and the clear song of a skilled poet
> telling with mastery of man's beginnings.[15]

Grendel's lonely existence drives home the terror of being without friends. Karl Shoemaker observes that Grendel's monstrosity is marked by his "fundamental incapacity to engage in the processes of lawful feud and concord."[16] Indeed, as the narrator of the poem makes clear, Grendel wages a "long and unrelenting feud" because he "would never / parley or make peace with any Dane / nor stop his death-dealing nor pay the death-price."[17] *Beowulf*, the longest epic poem in Old English, defines legal personhood as a state of communal belonging.

The communal spirit of early English law was assimilated into the common law by the Angevin kings who ruled England after the Norman Conquest. After the death of Henry I, civil war erupted between Henry's nephew Stephen of Blois (later, King Stephen) and the Empress Matilda, Henry's daughter and named heir.[18] Stephen and Matilda's prolonged civil war ended with the naming of Matilda's son as heir to the throne. To the new king, Henry II, "the arrangements for dealing with wrong and disorder must have looked ripe for reconstruction along with so much else."[19] Among the novel remedies he and his government devised was the assize. According to R.C. van Caenegem, "[t]he first assize was … conceived as a unique emergency measure to deal with years of violence in the aftermath of the 'Anarchy.'"[20] The assize initially denoted a court whose primary function was to adjudicate property disputes.[21] But the scope of the assize was soon expanded to include criminal prosecution. Thus, "from 1176 onwards temporary steps developed into a permanent system."[22] Seeking to bring stability to his kingdom, Henry II "claimed all homicides as violations of his peace, or as criminal pleas that belong 'to the crown of the lord king.'"[23] Certain features of the twelfth-century assize anticipated the early modern assize and even the modern criminal trial. For example, an assize gathered in one place justices, jurors, and claimants (in the instance of civil disputes) and appellees (in the case of criminal ones), as well as community members. Serving as an alternative to trial by battle, the assize obviated the violent encounter between claimants (or their designated champions) by requiring claimants to present their evidence to the court's judges.

Etymologically, "assize" derives from the Old French *asise* (or *assise*), meaning the "act of sitting down."[24] When it was first conceived, the assize simply signified the act of sitting for deliberation of an important matter. Later, the term *assise* came to include the more abstract idea of the "sittings of a court" for judgment of cases.[25] William Blackstone addresses the doubleness of the term when he writes that "the commission of *assise*" refers both to the "commission ... anciently issued to the judges" and to the action of "tak[ing] assises ... verdicts of jurors."[26] In the twelfth and thirteenth centuries, the meaning of the assize expanded to denote the jury inquest (the grand assize or *magnam assisam*), a statute, or an ordinance. For example, the Assize of Bread and Ale (*Assisa panis et cervisiae*) was a law that stipulated the price, weight, and quality of bread and beer. This assize was such a staple of English life that it was not repealed until 1863.[27] On occasion, "assize" could even signify parliament (*assisa generalis*).[28] Context was important in disambiguating what the assize denoted in medieval texts.

In the legal context, the assize came to mean one thing: an inquest or tribunal involving justices and jurors. To this day, in jurisdictions such as the Channel Islands and other former British colonies, "assize" is still the word used to denote the criminal court. The rise of the assize in England is closely connected to the development of the jury trial, which replaced the ordeal. Without going into too much detail, the ordeal was "a practice which had been an integral part of judicial procedure throughout Western Christendom" until 1215.[29] In that year, the Fourth Lateran Council banned the clergy from administering the ordeal by fire or water.[30] (Popular representations of the ordeal continued to appear in European artistic and literary culture well past the time of its formal abolition.) The abolition of the ordeal inaugurated new forms of judicial inquests across Europe. Inquisitorial justice became the dominant form of criminal prosecution on the continent; in England, it was trial by jury.[31] Instead of divine judgment governing proof, lay judges were now called on to evaluate the evidence in cases of law. By 1220, the criminal jury trial was in full swing.[32]

The writings of medieval jurists pay nominal attention to the role of lay judges. For example, in *Glanvill*, written between 1187 and 1189, toward the end of Henry II's reign, the author notes that the assize is a "royal benefit granted to the people by the goodness of the king acting on the advice of his magnates" – an enlightened and humane substitution for the limb-lopping and pate-cracking trial by battle:

> [This assize] ... takes account so effectively of both human life and civil condition that all men may preserve the rights which they have in any free tenement, while avoiding the doubtful outcome of [trial by] battle ... Moreover, in proportion as the testimony of several suitable witnesses in judicial proceedings outweighs that

of one man, so this constitution relies more on equity than does battle; for whereas battle is fought on the testimony of one witness, this constitution requires the oaths of at least twelve men.[33]

The assize promised a twofold "benefit." First, it "avoid[ed]" the "doubtful outcome of battle." By this, the author refers (euphemistically) to the possibility of one party being killed by the other. This aversion to violence is consistent with the author's horror at the prospect of such an "unexpected and untimely death," the "greatest of all punishments."[34] The second benefit is related to testimony. In trial by battle, what passes for "truth" is based on the "testimony of one witness," but at the assize, truth emerges from the "testimony of several suitable witnesses" and "oaths of at least twelve men." In that observation, one detects a glimmer of curiosity about the role of communal consensus in justice. In the absence of absolute and revealed truth, communal witnessing and judgment must suffice.

Whereas the *Glanvill* author partially acknowledges the role of lay judges, the author of *The Mirror of Justice* (*Mirroir des justices*), a thirteenth-century legal treatise once attributed to Andrew Horn, largely buries lay judges' work in favour of highlighting the labour of royal justices. The following passage is revealing:

> because some have no power to 'determine' the sins thus presented, or to punish the trespassers, and others who can do it will not, or will not duly do what law requires … it was ordained of old that the kings in person, or by their chief justices, or their general justices appointed to hear and determine all pleas, should journey every seven years throughout all counties to receive the rolls of all justices delegate, coroners, and of all stewards, containing all their judgments, inquests, presentments, and official doings, and should diligently examine these rolls, to see whether any one had erred in any point in the law, or to the damage of the king, or to the grievance of his people.[35]

The Mirror's author contrasts royal justice to local or communal justice by suggesting that all too often local peacekeepers "erred in … the law … to the grievance of his [the king's] people."[36] Without the king's justices overseeing legal administration, legal order would collapse, or so the passage implies. The author's emphasis on the assize as an extension of royal justice will be much repeated and greatly amplified in the professional literature to come. Not only does a text like *The Mirror* lay the groundwork for a professional bias against the legal authority of local inhabitants, but it also buries that bias under the unimpeachable form of factual, historical writing. Obviously, one would want the king's judges to preside over the court of justice.

Yet an alternative understanding of the relationship between royal and communal justice emerges when one consciously looks for traces of community – even in those texts that attempt to suppress them. The assize dazzlingly displayed the power of royal justice, true enough, but it also acted as the people's court. The assize opened a dialogue between the king's magistrates and the community. To appreciate this back-and-forth dynamic, we need to take a closer look at the assize's rebirth as a criminal court involving jurors.

The Early Medieval Jury

There were two kinds of early medieval juries: the jury of presentment and the trial jury. The jury of presentment, which is now obsolete, was the antecedent of the grand jury.[37] This jury decided probable cause during the pretrial phase of the inquest. The members of this jury assessed the character or "notoriety" (*fama publica*) of the accused. They decided whether there was enough evidence to formally accuse the suspect – to send the person to trial. The Assize of Clarendon of 1166 stipulated that twelve lawful men of the hundred and four of the vill "should report to the royal justices or sheriffs, those persons reputed to have committed certain serious crimes."[38] (Sir John Fortescue explains that the "kingdom of England" is divided into counties (shires), counties into hundreds, and hundreds into vills.)[39] In order to report such persons to said justices or sheriffs, however, jurors needed to be self-informing; they had to "nam[e] from their own knowledge all known rogues and villains who threatened order on their own patch."[40] Presentment took the form of a questionnaire which later came to be known as articles of the eyre.[41] The emergence of this jury, then, marks a formal, institutional recognition of the evidentiary value of local knowledge. Jurors did not and could not comprehensively represent *all* the voices in the community, yet they possessed a greater degree of local knowledge – the community's shared values and opinions – than the itinerant justices sent from London.

In cases of appeals (instances in which an individual accused another of a felonious crime – such as rape or murder), it was the jury of presentment that received the appellor's accusation, assessed the evidence against the appellee, and determined whether to formally "suspect" the appellee and send the case to trial. During this pretrial phase, the jury asked themselves whether it was probable that the accused (or appellee) could have committed the crime. Taking on the role of lay investigators, they considered the relationship between the alleged victim and the suspect and the reputation of both parties and their witnesses. They also gathered and presented the evidence.[42] In small communities, "jurors who were leading community figures (including officials) were bound to know a good deal about offenders held for trial."[43] Thus, to quote Roger D. Groot, the creation of the jury of presentment "placed the power of judgment back in the hands of ... commoners who could judge both the crime and the accused."[44] In short, knowledge of the community was essential in the early days of the jury trial. Because the presenting jury was responsible for assembling the information against the accused, it could be said to wield prosecutorial power.[45] What the jury decided communicated the "communal attitudes about the sorts of persons who ought to suffer capital punishment or the sorts of offenses for which persons ought to suffer such punishment."[46]

In the small, tightly knit communities of medieval and early modern England, reputation was paramount. In a village of a hundred or so, "everyone knew a good deal about everyone else's business."[47] Because of the greater availability of documents and records from later periods, much of the study on social credit and reputation has been done by early modern historians. Craig Muldrew explains that the sixteenth century witnessed an unprecedented proliferation of "credit networks" built on a system of trust and reputation: "reputation for fair and honest dealing of a household and its members ... became the currency for lending and borrowing."[48] In the game of reputation, women – particularly young, unmarried, women of the labouring class – were often at a disadvantage as the law's heteropatriarchal double standards held them accountable for both their own wayward actions and those of men. The scholarship on rape by Patricia Orr and Laura Gowing traces women's struggles with the law and their occasional triumphs even in the face of many legal obstacles and gross structural inequity.[49]

From a legal perspective, the intimacy of communal life in medieval and early modern England meant that, in the words of Thomas A. Green, "the role of notoriety" mattered "for both presentment and trial." "Most defendants," Green adds, "were persons whom local communities wanted to bring under some degree of embarrassment or actual punishment."[50] Bad reputation (also known as infamy) emerged over the course of countless everyday interactions over an untold period of time. The initiation of formal legal proceedings against an individual could well have signalled the community's collective decision to punish a *habitual* offender – to expel said individual from their midst after repeated offences. (That said, scapegoating, motived by prejudice or envy, was also a distinct possibility.) Medieval legal rolls, while laconic, nonetheless shed light on the power of the community to decide who was worth excusing – and who not. For example, in a set of cases from the early thirteenth century, two men appeared before a jury after being accused of theft by a woman named Alice, herself then a prisoner convicted of homicide. The rolls indicate that the men "put themselves for good and ill (*de bono et malo*) upon a verdict." After some deliberation, the jury determined that "they [were] thieves." The men were hanged. Alice issued further accusations. Three more men stood accused of theft and they too "put themselves for good and ill (*de bono et malo*) upon a verdict of the countryside." This time, the jury determined that two were thieves and the men were therefore hanged; the third man was considered lawful (*fidelis*) and was therefore spared. The assessment of *bono* or *malo* rested on the jurors' considerations of the men's local reputation.[51] For reasons that elude modern historians, the community at that moment believed that some of the men were malevolent and had no place in the community. The community killed the would-be destroyers before they could do greater harm.

Lay Judgment in Early Modern England

The status of the lay judge changed in the early modern period. In the sixteenth and seventeenth centuries, lay jurors began to share the work of presenting information against the accused with the justice of the peace (JP), a state appointee who was the chief administrator of justice within a locality. Many histories of the jury emphasize the paradigmatic shift that occurred in the late medieval period with respect to the jury's accusative role. John H. Langbein, for instance, observes the following:

> By the end of the Middle Ages ... the structure and composition of trial courts and juries had undergone significant change. As more and more jurors came to court largely ignorant of the events in dispute, trial became an instructional proceeding, at which evidence was presented to inform the jurors' verdict.[52]

Langbein's account of the jury's loss of accusative power has been challenged in recent years. For example, taking direct aim at Langbein's conclusion, Matthew Lockwood argues that "it is not at all clear that their [the jurors'] new role in considering facts and hearing testimony in any way eroded their function as suppliers of local information and knowledge."[53] The "self-informing" nature of the medieval jury of presentment, Lockwood contends, was not displaced by the introduction of new judicial processes – such as the introduction of witness testimonies (recorded by the JP). In many jurisdictions, jurors *continued* to be "responsible for detecting crime and disorder in their hundreds and for presenting the resulting criminal cases to the quarter sessions and assize."[54] Where does that leave us? Both Lockwood and Langbein make persuasive arguments. In early modern England, the juror *did* act as both neighbour and judge but *so too* did the JP, whose variegated investigative activities (including the pretrial examination of witnesses) encroached upon the legal labour of the medieval jury. To Lockwood's argument, the magistrate worked with the coroner's jury to assemble evidence and facts. At the same time, to Langbein's point, the establishment of the office of the JP meant that the jury no longer had a "monopoly" over the facts. Even though the early modern jury (as Lockwood shows) continued to wield certain powers over presentment and accusation, the early modern state had begun to take on what had previously been communal responsibilities in criminal prosecution.

Appointed to the commission of the peace by the Lord Chancellor or the Lord Keeper of the Great Seal, the Elizabethan and Jacobean JP presided over quarter sessions (also known as "sessions"), so called because it convened four times a year to try non-capital offences.[55] The statute 18 Hen. 6, c. 11 (1439) required JPs to possess a minimum annual income of £20 per year in order to be eligible for the service and this marks the rise of the JP as a socially significant public officer in the administration of justice.[56] The Marian Bail and Committal Statutes (1554–5) granted JPs additional accusatory power.[57] Although the JP is typically referred to as a "lay magistrate" in early modern historiography, I resist that label because the JP's legal training, relative wealth, and high social credit edged him closer toward the side of the assize judges than the commoners upon whom he passed judgment. This is why throughout this book I use "lay magistrate" to refer only to those who operate without an official appointment or commission to the magistracy. On the question of social standing, a tract attributed to Sir Francis Bacon, but more likely authored by Sir William Lambarde, calls JPs "gentlemen" who have the "power to preserve the peace."[58] J.H. Gleason's indispensable study of early modern JPs indicates that they "constituted an élite"; this is supported by the increased levels of formal education among the magisterial class.[59] In 1562, "only a few" of "the men who composed the commissions of the peace in the six [Kentish] counties … had been enrolled in either a university or an inn." But by 1636, the majority of those appointed as JPs had attended "a university or an inn."[60] A closer look at Gleason's tables shows that in 1608, for example, of the 97 justices who comprised the Kent commission, 48 had attended one of the Inns of Court, and of those, 12 had passed the bar. In other words, nearly half of all Kent's justices had matriculated at the Inns of Court, which suggests a fairly high degree of professionalization among early modern JPs.[61]

The state expected JPs to not only "preserve the peace," to use Lambarde's phrase, but to keep abreast of the latest changes in law. To do so, some JPs relied on justicing manuals, which were A to Z handbooks covering a variety of felonies and misdemeanours, to shore up their legal knowledge. These justicing manuals belonged to a general category of legal literature that Wilfrid R. Prest describes as "self-help manuals."[62] In his dedication to Sir Thomas Bromley, then Lord Chancellor, which prefaces his *Eirenarcha* (1581), Lambarde notes that "the more parte of the Justices of the Peace, at this day had nede of some helpe in writing for their better conduict in that office" and modestly claims that his volume might improve the legal knowledge of

England's JPs (figure 2).[63] *Eirenarcha* was a bestseller. It spawned several imitations, including *The Countrey Justice* (1618) by Michael Dalton of Lincoln's Inn, which was "[g]athered for the better helpe of such Justices of Peace as have not beene much conversant in the studie of the Lawes of this Realme" (figure 3).[64] Fortunately for the modern researcher, numerous sixteenth- and seventeenth-century justicing manuals, in both print and manuscript form, have been preserved. Readers' marks in the form of underlining, marginalia, and occasional manicules capture the particular legal interests and anxieties of their users.[65] These manuals open a window to the mental landscape of England's JPs.[66] Unlike Shakespeare's Justice Shallow, many real-life JPs were in fact capable. Some were even exemplary in the performance of their duties.

As a testament to the increased accusatory power of the magistrate, many sixteenth-century justicing manuals drew attention to the authority of the JP as well as his subordinate officer to "stay" (arrest) suspected wrongdoers. *The Duties of Constables* (1583) explains that constables should not hesitate to exert their authority when appropriate: "[n]either is it requisite, that such an Officer should daunce up and downe after the partie (as manie use to doe) untill hee can finde out sureties: but hee may lawfully stay him, untill that he can get suerties to come unto him."[67] Lambarde adds that it is "the ignorance of which point is the cause, both that many an evill man escapeth, and that manie an honest Officer is punished therefore."[68] Similarly, in Dalton's *The Countrey Justice*, the recurring phrase "upon his owne knowledge" and its variant "upon his own Discretion" draw attention to the local officer's authority.[69]

In summary, the JP was a powerful figure of moral and judicial authority within his community. He was authorized to initiate investigations and accusations. He listened to complaints, examined suspects, and granted bails. The expanded role of the JP follows a pattern of public-oriented justice under the Tudors and Stuarts. Krista Kesselring observes that between the late sixteenth century and early seventeenth century, "private vengeance … g[a]ve way to public justice" – a public justice coordinated and overseen by the state.[70] Even as members of the community acted as reporters and witnesses, these lay magistrates were no longer exclusively or even chiefly shaping the narrative of justice. Even the appeal, that lawful form of private prosecution, declined over the course of the early modern period, becoming increasingly rare in the seventeenth century. Keeping this larger structural pattern of criminal justice in mind helps us to appreciate the cultural significance of *fictions* of communal justice. The emotional appeal of those fictions must have increased during a period when the judgment of the lay magistrate came into direct competition with that of the state-appointed magistrate.

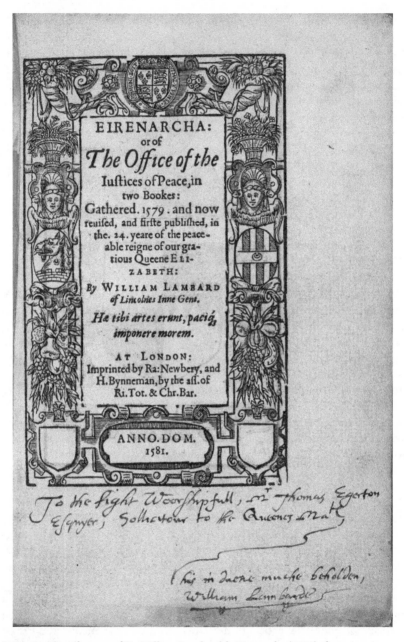

Figure 2. The title page of Sir William Lambarde's *Eirenarcha* (1581), featuring a personal dedication by the author to Sir Thomas Egerton.
The Huntington Library (RB 17273).

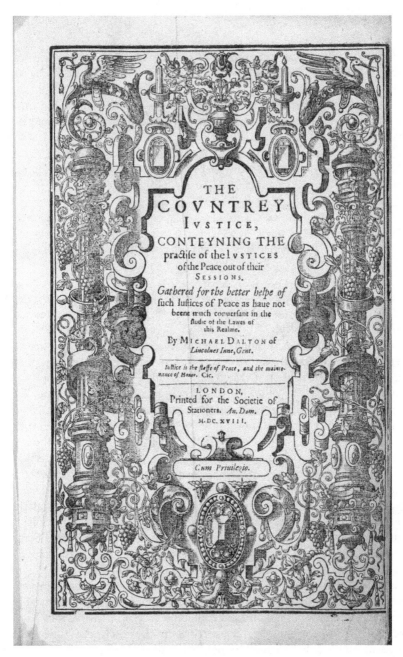

Figure 3. The title page of Michael Dalton's *The Countrey Justice* (1618).
The Huntington Library (RB 243254).

The Early Modern Assize

In the sixteenth century, judges travelled twice a year from London to cities and towns within their designated circuit to adjudicate cases.[71] Their various commissions authorized them to hear civil cases by the writ of *nisi prius* (meaning "unless before"), hear criminal cases involving "treason, felonies, and misdemeanors," and to deliver county gaols.[72] Gaol delivery was an important part of the circuit judges' work since those without bail, being denied their freedom, sometimes languished in prison for months. The plight of those awaiting gaol delivery is vividly recounted in the diary of the German traveller Philip Julius, the Duke of Stettin-Pomerania:

> When we entered the suburb [of London], the prisoners with petulant cries beseeched us for alms, this being the custom throughout England ... the poor fellows can scarcely be blamed, for time must wag rather slowly with them. For only twice a year is justitia [justice] administered in the kingdom.[73]

In dramatic texts, legal time passes with blinding speed. When, in *Measure for Measure*, Angelo informs Isabella that her brother is scheduled to be executed "to-morrow," she protests, "To-morrow! O, that's sudden!"[74] That was not the reality that Philip Julius encountered during his travels – nor the one that contemporary legal records bear witness to. While awaiting gaol delivery, prisoners routinely depended on the goodwill of family and friends to supply them with nourishing meals and other basic necessities, lest they grow too "low / And crestfall'n with [their] wants," as the imprisoned Palamon does in *The Two Noble Kinsmen*.[75]

Before sitting for the multi-day assize, judges and members of the assize court went to the local church to hear an assize sermon by a preacher selected by the sheriff.[76] According to Barbara J. Shapiro, the first printed assize sermon appeared in 1571 and "by 1610 they were quite common."[77] By the early seventeenth century, printers were publishing assize sermons with some regularity – one or two different titles every year. By the end of the seventeenth century, the number of printed assize sermons had swelled to 200 with an untold number in manuscript. Some sermons were rushed into production and, like Shakespeare's "bad quartos," printed without the author's permission. For example, one "M.M." published William Overton's *A godlye, and pithie exhortation, made to the judges and justices of Sussex* and defended his actions thus: "I maye perhappes have blame of the Authour to put it foorth in printe without his knowledge ... I trust he will not be offended, if by my meanes he doe more good to a greate number that hearde him not, but shall reade him."[78] (If the apology rationalizes the injury, does it still count as an apology?) More often, however, the preacher carefully edited his sermon notes for publication. The existence of such a large corpus of assize sermons testifies to the genre's enduring popularity. Evidently, many readers, not just the godly, collected printed sermons for their personal enjoyment.

According to a mid-seventeenth-century sheriff's manual, the preacher of the assize sermon was typically an "able person" hand-picked by the sheriff to "say grace [at] every dinner" and to "preach before the judges."[79] Preaching at the assize was an honour as well as a professional opportunity. A well-delivered sermon could impress not only those in the community and but also the august visitors. Many assize sermons focused on the theme of the accusing and testifying conscience. Typically, the preacher began by defining what conscience was before exploring its psychosomatic effects on the mind and body. The definitions of conscience tend to sound formulaic to modern ears. For example, in his assize sermon preached at Chard, Somerset, George Macey spoke of the "pricking" of conscience: "your accuser is within you, every mans owne conscience. Whosoever therefore shall feele any inward pricking, let him acknowledge the power of the word of GOD, which is mightie in operation and sharper then any two edged sword."[80] Anthony Cade, who delivered his sermon before the judges Sir Henry Hobart and Sir Edward Bromley, added a flourish to his definition of conscience without breaking from the formula: *"[c]onscience is ... Gods leager Embassador, to put man in mind of his duty, observe what he doth, & to be a witnes unto God either with Man, or against him."*[81]

But some assize preachers broke the mould. Addressing professional magistrates, jurymen, and members of the community, some called their listeners to account – to see themselves as magistrates and judges by virtue of their inborn conscience. Legal administration, in other words, was not the exclusive work of officeholders; it was every person's duty. That discourse of godly, lay magistracy was consistent with the program of religious reform begun much earlier. Early Protestant reformers during the reign of Mary I had called on English subjects to resist Catholic authority by harkening to their free and sovereign conscience. For example, the English translator of Wolfgang Musculus's *The Temporysour* (1555) reminds the "gentle Reader" that "after thou hast diligently perused the same [the text], and examined it with the touchstone of Gods word, and thyne owne conscience, thou wilt search no more excuses to cover thy dissimulation and impiete withall."[82] This resistant strand of reformist polemics found its way into the literature of conscientious magistracy. Like the mid-sixteenth-century reformists, assize preachers invented increasingly elaborate accounts of the magisterial power of conscience. They insisted that the power to judge was not limited to magistrates, but that it was the birthright of all conscientious individuals. Borrowing images and phrases from the occasion of the assize, these preachers emphasized the communal component of the judicial proceedings while underscoring the power of individual judgment. The model of the self that assize preachers espoused and their celebration of lay magistracy interrupted the logic of professional distinction. Whereas lawyers were in the habit of disparaging lay judgment, assize preachers praised lay judgment, offering a theological grounding for the participatory promise of the common law.

What follows is a close reading of three assize sermons by Robert Abbot, John Lightfoot, and George Closse. I attend to the way each author shifts the balance of legal authority from the professional judge to the lay magistrate. Associated with Black Torrington, Devon, Closse was active from the mid-1580s to the mid-1610s. Following the discovery of the Gunpowder Plot, Closse rushed into print a murder pamphlet about a "papist" son who bludgeoned his devoutly Protestant father with an iron bar.[83] A "turbulent priest" who boldly challenged the authority of common law judges, Closse's preaching career was terminated by the High Commission in 1615.[84] Unlike Closse, Robert Abbot of Cranbrook, Kent, was well connected to the local gentry and achieved a modicum of fame in his lifetime.[85] Six of his sermons were printed in 1623 in an octavo edition under the title *A Hand of Fellowship to Helpe Keepe out Sinne and Antichrist*. His sermon, *The Assize at Home*, which I discuss in detail shortly, is part of this volume. John Lightfoot was the master of St. Catharine's College, Cambridge and a deeply respected scholar of Hebrew. Some of Lightfoot's writings were collected and printed after his death in a handsome, folio-sized, two-volume edition adorned with a grand portrait of Lightfoot by the celebrated engraver Robert White. Whatever renown these authors enjoyed when they were alive, today they are now largely forgotten except by a handful of specialists. Their sermons, however, are worth reading for they capture popular sentiments about lay judgment and magistracy. Their rhetorical choices tell modern scholars what was available in the popular legal imaginary. All three exploited the occasion of the assize and jury trial to level the notion of legal hierarchy and difference between professional and lay judges. All three instructed their auditors and readers to be humble and to accept that all people possessed magisterial powers on account of their conscience.

The Assize at Home

In his sermon, Robert Abbot compares conscience to an "assize":

> God hath established an assize for judgement within our selves. Hence is it that we are said to be Judges. To conceive therefore aright of it, consider that there is the Judgement seat, or Court Hall, within a mans selfe; the partie to be tried, man himselfe; the Judge, witnesse, Jurie, the conscience which shall proceed according to true allegations and proofes; and all these sweetly inwrapped in these reasoning thoughtes. Yea and that all things may be carried the more fairely, there is the law impose upon the reasonable creature, as apprehended by him to be the rule and records.[86] (figure 4)

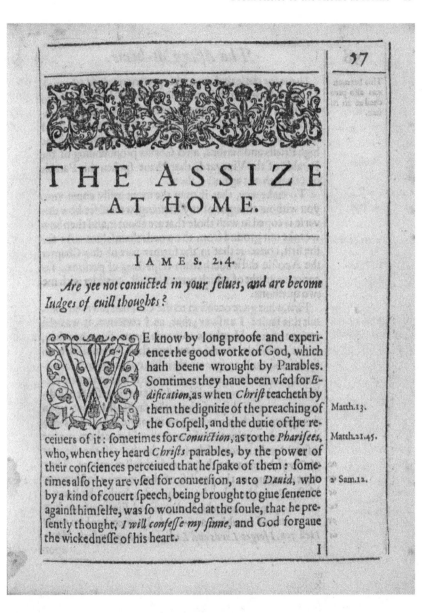

57

THE ASSIZE
AT HOME.

IAMES. 2.4.

Are yee not conuicted in your selues, and are become Iudges of euill thoughts?

E know by long proofe and experience the good worke of God, which hath beene wrought by Parables. Somtimes they haue been vsed for *Edification*, as when *Christ* teacheth by them the dignitie of the preaching of the Gospell, and the dutie of the receiuers of it: sometimes for *Conuiction*, as to the *Pharisees*, who, when they heard *Christs* parables, by the power of their consciences perceiued that he spake of them: sometimes also they are vsed for conuersion, as to *Dauid*, who by a kind of couert speech, being brought to giue sentence against himselfe, was so wounded at the soule, that he presently thought, *I will confesse my sinne*, and God forgaue the wickednesse of his heart.

Matth.13.

Matth.21.45.

2 Sam.12.

I

Figure 4. Robert Abbot, *The Assize at Home* (1623), sig. E5r.
The Huntington Library (RB 389220).

The title of the sermon, *The Assize at Home*, demands from its audience a fluid understanding of the meaning of "home." "Home," in this context, could be the invisible, internal "home" that is the individual's heart, the external "home" of the parish, or the jurisdiction of the Home Circuit, one of the established judicial circuits that included the counties of Essex, Kent, Sussex, Surrey, and Hertfordshire.[87] Abbot was the resident preacher of Cranbrook, Kent, making him and his original audience all subjects of the Home Circuit. Abbot assumes that all individuals possess knowledge of God's law. He emphasizes the ability of every "reasonable creature" to recognize justice: "our understandings, either by the light of reason, or by the light of faith, should have the law of God presented unto them."[88] The day of the assize becomes an opportunity to celebrate every person's ability to "give judgement according to reason."

Warming to his theme of universal magistracy, Abbot continues: "[t]hus we have heard these reasoning thoughts as a witnesse propounding the truth: next we shall heare them as a Jurie applying the truth to the parties to be tried. And this it doth as an Assumption: whence we note that *In our selves there is a Jurie which will bring in a verdict concerning us, either of guilty or not guilty.*"[89] Throughout his text, Abbot employs the first person plural "we" to reinforce his central theme: "we are said to be Judges." The pronoun "we" commonly features in Protestant conscience literature. Martha Tuck Rozett explains that it was especially common among Puritan preachers to refer to "the elect as 'we' … this usage effectively took for granted the election of all present." For Puritan preachers, "the 'I-you' distinction is consistently deemphasized; instead, the audience is drawn into the community of the elect and made to feel no different from the preacher."[90] What Rozett describes is precisely what we see in Abbot's evocation of "we." Through this inclusive form of address, Abbot asserts the godliness of the entire assembled community. He reinforces the assembly's collective capacity for moral evaluation, exhorting them to attend to the jury "*[i]n our selves*" before attending to matters in the community. The phrase "the assize at home," then, configures the lay subject as (simultaneously) one who is ruled *by* an authority (magistrate, king, God) and one who rules *as* a legal authority.

In a near-parallel example, John Lightfoot informs "every one here present" and "every one of you" to hold "Assises of conscience" before they proceed to the actual assize:

I doe bouldly & resolutelie, call to every one here present, hold up your hand, you are here indited by the name of wicked at the barre of my text: God holdeth here the Assisses of conscience upon every one of you, that are by & by to hold an Assisse of law upon others. let St Paul be the Clarke, & read your inditement. You are here every one indited by the name of wicked, for that thou, that Judgest an other Judgest not thy selfe; Thou that hangest a murtherer, doest thou beare malice? Thou that accusest a theafe, doest thou take bribes? Thou that art sworne to the Law, doest thou transgresse the Law? Thou that castest the wicked, art thou wicked thy selfe? Go, & your owne conscience be Jurie, Evidence, & Judge, whether ye be guiltie, or not gultie. I am onelie the voyce of a cryer to tell all this court, that let every man first Rise up in Judgment against himselfe, before he Rise up in Judgment against an other.[91]

This passage (so reminiscent of Isabella's admonishment of Angelo) contains an impassioned call to recognize the spiritual equality among the members of the court. Like a biblical prophet, Lightfoot declares, "God holdeth here the Assisses of conscience upon every one of you." Lightfoot uses the legal terms that are part of the assize to chisel away at the idea of a spiritual separation between the saved and the damned, the judge and the sinner. Keeping in mind Rozett's discussion of pronouns, one observes that Lightfoot uses pronouns to develop an argument about legal and moral inclusion and exclusion. Initially, he addresses the audience, one comprising judges, jurors, and other members of the legal community, with the formal "you." Midway through the passage, however, after he assumes the voice of the "cryer" who announces the "inditement," he switches to the familiar pronoun "thou," asking, "Thou that castest the wicked, art thou wicked thy selfe?" The use of "thou" is particularly interesting for it is a pronoun that is used either to suggest the speaker's emotional closeness to the addressee – or social superiority over a perceived subordinate. It is as if Lightfoot uses "thou" to momentarily deflate the aura of the justices. Only in the final lines does he turn, once again, to using the formal "ye." This text was never published. The fact that it exists only as a manuscript copy possibly indicates that Lightfoot's emphasis on spiritual equality was seen by the author (or his literary editor) as too controversial for a general readership.

In *A looking Glasse for lawers, & lawiers*, an incendiary assize sermon, George Closse dismisses the learning of the legal profession by telling a series of increasingly satirical anecdotes.[92] Initially, Closse repeats a common complaint about jurors: "[s]ome ... had rather have one Ulisses than ten Ajaxes ... one wise judge that can scanne an evidence, rather then 12. unlearned Jurors that cannot read, much lesse understand the recordes."[93] To support his claim that juries are often packed with "10 fooles, & .2. knaves," Closse recounts the following anecdote, which he heard from a "gentleman ... an aunciant at Innes of court":

a co[m]mon juror, requested by greater man to appeare for a frend of his, w[hi]ch he redily p[ro]missed, he began to instruct him in the case: tush saith the juror tell not me of the case, but tell me whether you will have me be for the plaintiffe, or def[endan]t. & that being entred upon his note he was sufficiently instructed; so quick conceited are some jurors to understand the case before they heare it.[94]

Closse's faulting of jurors as those prone to favouring the "greater man" over the lesser one recalls a common critique of juries. But Closse is as harsh, if not harsher, in his indictment of the legal professional – both the lawyer and the judge. Citing the popular view that lawyers are motivated less by a love for justice than by naked avarice, Closse reminds his auditors that "in olde time, that the practise of the law was numbred amongst other illiberall sciences of merchantes & craftesmen, whereof yet they retaine the denominations."[95] Closse mocks the legal professional's learning, reporting that "I well know that two reverend Judges of the lande ... to that effect told a preacher, that he might know divinity but he knew no law." But how could a preacher not know the law when he, a minister of God, understands better than most, certainly better than the lawyer, God's laws? To expose the absurdity in the legal professional's reasoning, Closse adopts the voice of a faux naïf:

> the assertion semed strange ... For not only devines, but allso their law booke of the Doctor & Student doth hold, that all lawes being devine & humaine the devine law is prædominant (because in gods wisdom is no error, uncertainty or alteration) are beneficiall to mankind, & direct us to eternall blessednes: & that humaine lawes are subject to the lawe eternall.[96]

In the margins of this passage is recorded "cap:2:3:etc.," a reference to the opening chapters of Christopher St. German's *Doctor and Student* (1530), which celebrates – and equates – the "lawe of reason" with the "lawe of nature" and the "lawe of God."[97] By alluding to these passages in St. German, Closse exposes an inconsistency in the judges' conviction about the pre-eminence of their legal authority by citing one of their own learned professors.

Evidently, Closse was not the only assize preacher to make a public spectacle of criticizing members of the judiciary to their faces. In his diary entry for 8 March 1629, John Rous mentions that at the Thetford assizes, he heard a certain "Mr. Ramsey, whom Sir Roger Townsend, high sheriffe, had preferred to an impropriation" – that is, been given a benefice – "preac[h] ... upon Isaiah i. 26 ... He had many touches upon the corruptions of judges and councellors."[98] Rous adds that the preacher developed a "similitude" between the commonwealth and the body, cautioning his auditors to heed the following lesson: just as "the head receiving all the nourishment" will "caus[e] the other members to faile and the whole man to die," so in the case of the "commonwealth, where all is sucked upwards and the commons left without nourishment." Next, the preacher Ramsey

> touched upon the favouring of causes, and making all sound well on the favoured side and so on the contrary extenuating the greatest proofes on the side not favoured, &c.; he touched the Councell also for taking fees to be silent. He apologised *(ut dicitur)* before and after, saying that judges and all must learne at the lips of the priest.[99]

Rous does not say how the judges reacted, but he records his own response: the sermon was "wonderous pithy; full of all good words and all learning." Another example from 1630 captures both the gist of the sermon and the reaction of the sitting judge: "Mr. Scot ... made a sore sermon in discovery of corruptions of judges and others" to which the presiding justice, Sir Francis Harvey, retorted, "[i]t seems by the sermon that we are corrupt, but know that we can use conscience in our places, as well as the best clergyman of all."[100]

What larger lessons might we draw from looking at these sources of popular theology and jurisprudence? While many sermons rehearsed formulaic statements about the divinity of judges, the importance of conscience, the virtue of obedience to the state, and so on, some deviated from the rule to voice popular complaints about the judiciary and to shore up a strong theological foundation for lay magistracy. The assize sermon could be a political whip used by some preachers to scare congregations into obedience. But it could also be an organ to sound out popular frustrations about the law or legal administration. Abbot, Lightfoot, Closse, and others echoed popular ideas about the law and they informed the state's legal officers, the judges of the assize and the justices of the peace who accompanied them, of uncomfortable truths that they might not wish to hear. On occasion, they chastised the magistracy for falling short of the ideal. The assize sermon was therefore one of the few state-sanctioned avenues for communicating public opinion from below. After all, who better than the local preacher to assess the mood of the local community? To report *up* to the judges the people's desires for them and for the law? The assize sermon reminds us that even a prescriptive text could serve as a vehicle for popular protest. Upon publication, assize sermons travelled far and wide. Like other printed texts, assize sermons were shared widely, ventriloquized, read communally, and excerpted into commonplace books.

In time, the idea of conscience as an "assize at home" entered the popular lexicon. In George Wither's plague poem, for example, the author uses the assize to excoriate the wayward self. In a dialogue between Reason and the poet's Conscience, Reason reveals that it was "[i]n this City [London]" that "thou hast laught and sung ... Abus'd thy Christian-liberty, and trod / That Maze, which brings forgetfulnesse of God":

Here, thou hast moved thy Creators wrath:
Here, thou hast sinned; and thy sinnes they were,
Which holpe to bring this Plague now raging here.
. . . .
Here, therefore, doe thou *fast*: here, doe thou mourne,
And, into sighes, and teares, thy laughter turne.
Here, yeeld thy selfe to prison, till thou see
At this *Assize*, how God will deale by thee:

Ev'n here, the time redeeme thou: here, restore
By good examples, these whom heretofore
Thou hast offended: here, thyselfe apply
Gods just incensed wrath to pacifie.[101]

Wither draws on the idea of the assize to illustrate his message of penitence. Just as prisoners must wait for their gaol delivery by the assize judges, so the self must patiently submit to God's judgment at the time of the appointed "*Assize.*"

To give another example, in William Drummond's "A Translation," part of his *Poems* (1656), the poet reflects on the sacrifices of "sweet Jesus," earnestly praying, "Thou supreame Judge, most just and wise, / Purge me from guilt which on me lies / Before that day of thine Assize."[102] Similarly, the final pages of Sir Thomas Browne's *Religio Medici* evoke the assize to dramatize the trial of the soul. Form and feeling mingle and cohere as Browne closes the final chapter with a meditation on the lifecycle of man:

> Let us call to assize the lives of our parents, the affection of our wives and children, and they are all dumbe showes, and dreames without reality, truth, or constancy; for first thereis [*sic*] a strong bond of affection between us and our parents, yet how easily dissolved we betake our selves to a woman, forgetting our mothers in a wife.[103]

At the "assize," the individual discovers treason within the family. The "strong bond of affection" between members of the same family is broken as new "affections" supplant old ones. Thus, the young man loves his parents – until he enters into marriage. Whereas human love is fickle, the love that God offers is strong and enduring. Human love and affection are merely "dumbe shows, and dreames without reality," for "[a]ll that is truly amiable is God."[104] Echoing the comparisons between the conscience and assize, so commonly heard in assize sermons, these imaginative texts helped to expand the popular vocabulary for lay magistracy beyond the purely legal context. And like certain assize sermons, they interrupted the logic of legal professionalization by emphasizing the law's promise of popular participation.[105]

Conclusion

As a point of entry into the complex history of communal justice, I have focused on the assize, which evolved alongside the institution of trial by jury. My goal in covering roughly six hundred years of legal history and post-Reformation religious writing has been to foreground an important fact: from its inception, English common law revolved around the idea and custom of communal justice.

   In the early days of the assize, jurors extended protection to those who were deemed to be a part of its fold and punished outcasts by exposing them to the rigours of the law. Royal justices of the assize relied on the willingness of neighbours to provide testimony and evaluate evidence. From the very beginnings of the common law, the community played a powerful role in determining the course of justice. The intertwined histories of the jury and the assize show just how deeply embedded concepts of communal justice and lay magistracy were in everyday legalities. In the sixteenth and seventeenth centuries, the assize became attached to a *juridical feeling* – a feeling of self-evaluation, of self-directed magistracy, grounded in the testifying and accusing conscience. This feeling played a role in shaping a model of the godly self and in defining the nature of the spiritual community. In the early modern period, claiming magistracy for oneself became synonymous with being a conscientious, reformed English subject. Conscience literature, like the assize sermon, helped to develop a baseline level of knowledge about lay magistracy. In the next four chapters, I discuss how dramatists critiqued professional magistracy while constructing elaborate narratives of communal witnessing, neighbourly justice, and lay adjudication both to entertain and to challenge their law-savvy audiences.

Chapter Two

Judicature in Crisis: *Henry IV, Part 2*

The figure of the judge loomed large in the early modern English imagination. Popular writers idealized the judge, crowning him with the same virtues – prudence, fairness, justice – that the citizens in Aristotle's *Nicomachean Ethics* attribute to the Athenian magistrate: "[t]o go to a judge is to go to justice, for the ideal judge is so to speak justice personified."[1] This chapter traces the key differences between professional and popular representations of judges and their relationship to the community. It looks at the popular writing of legal character – the depiction of the figure of the "good judge" – frequently found in the assize sermon and the character book. The former has already been discussed in the previous chapter; the latter refers to a genre of satirical writing that enumerates the virtues and vices of common social types, including legal ones such as the good magistrate, the pettifogging attorney, and the honest lawyer. As Christy Desmet explains, the genre was "introduced to Shakespearean England by Isaac Casaubon's Latin translation of Theophrastus's *Characters* (1592–9) and Joseph Hall's *Characters of Vertues and Vices* (1608)" and enjoyed relative popularity "well into the eighteenth century."[2] In these popular genres, authors imagined scenes of direct contact between a loving judge and his community, fuelling a fantasy of intimate, compassionate, and local justice. But the language of love and the narrative of direct contact were absent in the professional literature on judicature. On the whole, lawyers and judges emphasized the necessity of emotional and physical distance in law.

The tension between popular and professional opinions on judicature, or legal administration, sustained Shakespeare's theatrical imagination. In *Henry IV, Part 2*, the gradual transformation of the Lord Chief Justice – a character loosely based on Sir William Gascoigne (c. 1350–1419) – from a local mediator to a royal justice who stands between the sovereign and his subjects captures the dissonance and irresolution within the cultural discourse on legal administration.[3] By emphasizing the dual nature of the character, my analysis revises a standard interpretation of the Chief Justice that views him as an emblem of the law – a "symbol, not man."[4] Such an identification suggests that he embodies a monolithic or coherent vision of the law. But this is not the case. The Chief Justice exemplifies the excesses and contradictions found in both popular and professional legal ideology. Like the idealized magistrates in popular and moral-legal writing, the Chief Justice establishes a paternalistic relationship with those who petition him for help. He dispenses ad hoc justice without middlemen or documentation. Yet his personal, intimate style of justice, while emotionally satisfying, is ephemeral. In the play's final act, the Chief Justice abandons the community, leaving its members without remedy. Then, in the final scene, the Chief Justice mirrors the remoteness of Henry V's majesty and participates in the latter's public shaming of Falstaff. The tragic mood of this scene exposes a paradox in judicature: by acting on the King's orders, the Chief Justice enforces royal justice at the expense of communal justice.

During the late sixteenth and early seventeenth centuries, the English common law gained historic strength. The number of legal officers tasked with legal administration grew steadily, as did the rate of matriculation at the Inns of Court. Although contemporaries lacked access to the numerical data of modern historians, they were acutely aware and deeply sceptical of the structural transformation of the law, especially with respect to the exponential growth of the legal profession in a relatively short span of time.

A comparison of how legal professionals and nonprofessionals witnessed the rise of the common law reveals starkly different worldviews. Lawyers took pride in the growth of their profession. "The posterity of Lawyers hath more flourished then that either of the Clergy or Citisens," remarked the lawyer and diarist John Manningham.[5] But the phenomenal growth of the legal profession also provoked a wave of deeply critical responses. Indeed, it was generally suspected that lawyers enriched themselves by entrapping their clients in legal intricacies. In his 1603 assize sermon, George Closse (whom I introduced in the previous chapter) sharply rebukes lawyers for their unethical practices. Closse recounts the following story: a man of the cloth asks a lawyer what "law is," and the lawyer replies that law is "a pretty tricke to catche mony w[i]t[h]all." Closse quips, "and indeed a man may beleve it to be a principall point in the p[ro]fession."[6] He reminds his audience that "our lawes are not cobwebbes to catche flyes, & let great birdes breake theron them."[7] The image of the spider's web comes from Plutarch's biography of Solon, which numerous moral and religious writers used "to illustrate inequitable judicial procedure."[8] Guillaume Guéroult's emblem, for example, features a spider, a fly, and a wasp; as the accompanying verse makes clear, the web of law ensnares those who are feeble ("[l]'homme foible"), leaving those of high rank ("l'homme opulent") unharmed (figure 5).

Figure 5. Guillaume Guéroult, *Le Premier livre des Emblèmes* (1550), sig. B6r, detail.
Bibliothèque nationale de France.

People used the courts – and depended on the counsel of lawyers – but they complained bitterly about the necessity of both courts and lawyers.

And even as lawyers fashioned themselves as the guardians of the law, others, not bound by personal or institutional loyalty, attacked the legal profession in print and performance.[9] The explosion of anti-lawyer complaints, however, did not amount to a mass protest against the law itself. Few disputed the professional's claim about the superior character of English law. As Sir Edward Coke put it, in "other Nations," people are oppressed by the "tyranny" of monarchs' "powerfull will and pleasure."[10] Rather, complaints about the law were directed at the administrators or officers of the law, especially those lower-ranked in the legal hierarchy.

Lay legal commentators, devoid of modern-day notions of institutional or systemic injustice, attributed injustices to human moral failings. They reasoned that if the law was the perfection of reason, and humans (by nature) were weak and fallible, then injustice had to be the result of human negligence or corruption. In early modern England, those who had the ability to reflect and comment on the law (and print those comments for public consumption) defined justice as a form of moral character, of individual virtue or vice. This reading of justice resonated with popular audiences and, on occasion, professional ones as well. In his essay "Of Judicature," Sir Francis Bacon complains of the "Unjust Judge" whose "Foule Sentence … Corrupteth the Fountaine" of justice.[11] Bacon raises the spectre of the partial judge in order to preserve the integrity of the profession: blame the lawman but spare the law.

As law came to occupy an ever-greater share of the cultural imagination, writers from different social and professional backgrounds made a concerted effort to define the character of the judge. These prescriptive comments touched on the magistrate's moral wisdom, his ethical character, and even on his decorum and affective demeanour.[12] Preachers exhorted judges to be loving fathers to the people and to practise mercy in judgment. As Robert Harris put it, "you [magistrates] are tearmed *Fathers*: direct you must, correct you may, but all in love" because a "judge must smite a sinner, with a weeping eie and a feeling heart."[13] Just as a father strives to create harmony within his household, so the judge ought to try to cultivate a sense of fellowship and belonging within the community. Yet the professional class's response to judicature was quite different. Lawyers emphasized the role of reason, knowledge, and Stoic disavowal of the passions. The word "love" rarely appears in the professional's vocabulary. Indeed, lawyers typically associated love with judicial corruption. When judges and lawyers reflected on the duties of their office, they emphasized the intellectual demands of their work: reading, pleading, and commentary. Professional and nonprofessional writers thus competed for discursive space, producing narratives about legal administration that, on the surface, seemed to share a common agenda (shaping good magistracy), but upon closer examination, plucked at different thematic chords, producing different affective responses in their intended audiences.

Judges in the Popular Imagination

In England, face-to-face encounters between superior magistrates and ordinary petitioners occurred – for the most part – in court. People pleaded before judges in prerogative courts such as the Court of Requests and Star Chamber. Both courts attracted relatively humble petitioners.[14] On very rare occasions, an individual appeared before a justice in an intimate, informal setting. For example, John Levermore, an Exeter trader, managed to make his case before Sir John Popham (who was then the Lord Chief Justice) while the latter sat at dinner with a friend.[15] Stories like Levermore's survive, in part, because of their exceptional nature. What people expected, and what they got for the most part, was a highly mediated experience of the law.[16] Instead of addressing judges directly, many were forced to seek lawyers and other legal intermediaries.

The very remoteness of these judges paradoxically fuelled a popular fantasy about direct contact in law. In his character book, Joseph Hall imagines that the "good magistrate ... knows himself made for a public servant of peace and justice" and that as a "public servant," he willingly allows his "meals" to be "short and interrupted" by petitioners.[17] Hall was not alone in keeping that fantasy alive in the popular legal imagination. Preachers and moral writers combed the Bible (especially the Old Testament) to find examples of judges renowned for both their accessibility and impartiality.[18] David, Solomon, Josiah, Hezekiah, and Job emerged as exemplars. The popular London preacher Henry Smith, whose sermons saw multiple printings in the 1590s, praises David for establishing a "seate for judgment ... set in the gate, wher[e] through men might have passage to and from the judgement seat."[19] Samuel Garey, another preacher, reminds his readers that Samuel travelled "about yeare by yeare, (as it were in circuite) to *Bethel, Gilgal,* and *Mizpeth,* and judged Israel in all those places."[20] For these writers, the chief value of direct contact was the preservation of unmediated truth. By hearing the facts of the case from the people themselves, judges were able to deliver just decisions.

Job's compassionate magistracy earned particular attention from preachers. As Kim Hedlin explains, early modern writers followed the medieval patristic tradition in celebrating Job as a loving judge.[21] Hence, Richard Carpenter in his 1620 assize sermon saves his highest praise for Job:

> And as for his publike government, you shall finde him lively described and char-actered in the 29. Chapter, to be the Oracle of Wisedome, the Guardian of Justice, the Refuge of Innocency, the Comet of the guilty, the Champion and defender of the fatherlesse, poore and needy, the Patron of peace, and the perfect Myr-rour and paterne for all Magistrates, to direct them in the wise managing of all publike affaires of Judgement and Mercy: in performing of all which duties, *Job* shewed himselfe very sedulous and sollicitous; yea, most studious he was of doing well, and most timorous of doing evill, because he was assured, that God himselfe would one day come to visit all his doings; and then, *Quid faciam,* saith he, vers. 14. What shall I doe, when God shall rise up to judge me? when he shall visit me, what shall I answere?[22]

Be a new Job, Carpenter intones, be a loving judge who loves and cares for the dispossessed and afflicted, be a "Champion" and "defender of the fatherlesse, poore, and needy." Likewise, the aforementioned Robert Harris instructs the "Reverend Judges" in his audience to attend to the "poor brother['s]" plight "as *Job* did":

> Your office is to plucke the spoile out of the teeth of the mighty, as *Job* did; and to bestride your poore brother, when hee is stricken downe. Alas, Justice will fall in

the streets, swound at the barre, if you doe not support her; a poore man cannot be a constant Tearmer, and retaine halfe a dozen Lawyers at once: hee can buy beggery with as little cost, and lesse paines at home, and therefore heeds his people; Husband (saith the wife) father (saith the child) let all goe, let us live together tho wee starve together.[23]

Harris's Dickensian portrait of the suffering husband, wife, and child reinforces the point about the importance of compassionate magistracy. Both preachers recall Job's testimony: "I put on righteousness, and it clothed me: my judgment was as a robe and a diademe. / I was eyes to the blind, and feet was I to the lame. / I was a father to the poore: and the cause which I knewe not I searched out. / And I brake the jawes of the wicked, and pluckt the spoile out of his teeth."[24]

Although preachers advocated a program of loving magistracy, they were sensitive to the all-too-easy slippage between affection and favouritism. Thus, Harris reminds judges to "smite a sinner, with a weeping eie and a feeling heart" – but as soon as "Magistrates ... discover ... [the] passions, partialities of men, they grow into contempt even with their friends."[25] "Passion and unruly affections," Harris's fellow preacher Samuel Ward affirms, have no place in judicature.[26] Few navigated the complicated discourse of love in law better than Henry Smith. In his assize sermon, Smith explains that when judges sit "upon the Bench," they "should forget themselves to be men, which are lead [*sic*] by the armes betweene favour and feare, and thinke themselves *Gods*, which feare nothing."[27] However, Smith insists that judges should blend that "feare nothing" attitude with compassion. When common people petition them for protection, judges should respond with sympathy, not contempt. Smith tells the following story to illustrate his point:

When *Phillip* the king of Macedonia did cast of the earnest sute of a poore widowe, with this slender answere; go thy way, for I have no leasure to heare thee now. She replied thus, and why hast thou leasure to be a King: as if shee should have said, God hath given thee time to raigne, and power to govern, that thou mightest applie them both unto that end wherefore they are given thee: for mercie and truth preserveth a King, and with loving kindnes his seat is upholden. Prov. 20.[28]

There are two details here that are relevant to the present discussion. The first concerns the nature of the suppliant. The "poor widow" (or her cognates, the poor man or orphan) is a stock character in religious literature. She represents a subordinate subject who is particularly deserving of judicial regard. Lacking money and male protection, she occupies a vulnerable and marginalized position. Regina M. Schwartz explains that in the Judaeo-Christian tradition, "the widow, the orphan, and the stranger are singled out in the account of those to whom we owe ... love." Thus, "the injunction, 'Thou shalt love thy neighbour as thyself' (Lev. 19:18)" means that to "love one's fellow is to comprehend his needs and respond to them." Those who are "hungry, dispossessed, lonely, mourning, lacking protection" emblematize a universal condition and draw attention to the care and love that we owe to each other as social beings.[29] Seen in this religious context, the poor widow may be said to be an archetypal character whom Smith evokes in order to trigger a meditation on the part of the auditor on the value of neighbourly compassion. The second detail concerns the magistrate. Smith frames the themes of kingship and magistracy in the affective language of care. For Smith, the end of kingship ought to be the preservation of "mercie and truth." By refusing to hear the widow's "truth" in the form of her "earnest suit," the king fails his duty as a ruler. To Smith's audiences, the attack on Philip would have carried an extra layer of political resonance, for the name "Philip" had become associated with Spanish aggression. Thomas Wilson's translation of Demosthenes's *Philippics* (1570) explicitly connected Philip of Macedon's military aggression with that of Philip II of Spain.[30] The lesson that Smith seeks to impart is that kingship and magistracy do not lie in grand performances of "majesty" but rather in small, nearly unseen acts of "loving kindnes," such as those that Philip might have bestowed upon the widow.

For these writers, the ability to achieve equitable judgment is dependent on a judge's ability to forge an emotional bond with the people. To practise "right judgemente" and "equitye," judges must first see themselves as loving fathers.[31] They must themselves be moved by the people's suffering. The ideal judge opens his heart to the people; he also makes himself available to them by journeying into their midst and by adopting an approachable, as opposed to haughty, deportment. Patience, fairness, and sympathy are the moral virtues of good judges. Hence, religious and moral writings on magistracy tend to equate moral feelings (religious piety, Christian love, even empathy) with judicial power, action, ability. This writing of legal character, reflecting popular notions of magistracy, posits a link between a judge's capacity for fellow-feeling and his power to do justice. Real justice does not stem from legal bureaucracy or legal force but from direct contact: the face-to-face encounter between magistrates and petitioners. Love has everything to do with magistracy.

Judges According to the Judges

The popular opinion on magistracy was conceptually at odds with the emergent antiemotion prejudice in law. Whereas religious and moral authors habitually emphasized love and familiar contact in judgment, legal professionals largely argued for the need to suspend all "passions" in judgment in order to achieve judicial distance. This mismatch of expectations is amply illustrated by lawyers' and judges' discussions of judicial character. On the qualities of the excellent lawyer, the judge Sir John Dodderidge stated, "[t]he first and chiefest Natural gift is sharpenesse, and dexterity of wit."[32] Lesser authorities concurred. The judge and law reporter George Croke praised Sir Christopher Wray, his contemporary and a Chief Justice of the Queen's Bench, as that "most revered Judge, of profound and judicial knowledge."[33]

The question of legal knowledge and its importance for legal judgment dominated Sir Edward Coke's jurisprudence. Coke habitually emphasized the challenges (and pleasures) of legal study. He celebrated "Judges of the Law" who addressed "matters of difficultie."[34] Coke was especially in awe of Sir Thomas Littleton, who, according to Coke, exemplified "certaintie and knowledge of the Lawe."[35] Justices such as Littleton devoted their lives to honing the "[a]rt" of law:

> He [Littleton] was learned also in that Art, which is so necessary to a compleat Lawyer (I mean) Logicke, as you shal perceive by reading of these Institutes, wherein are observed his Sillogismes, Inductions, and other arguments; & his Definitions, Descriptions, Divisions, Etymologies, Derivations, Significations, & the like.[36]

When professionals such as Coke talked about themselves or their colleagues, they invariably mentioned their "Logicke" and "wit." The standards by which Coke evaluated his peers – past, present, and future – were textual or academic.

Sounding not unlike a modern-day university professor, Coke instructs readers to work their way through the complete text before resorting to abridgments and commentaries:

> Myne advice to the Student is, That ... hee read againe and againe our Author himselfe [Littleton] in that Section, and doe his best endeavours, first of himselfe, and then by conference with others, (which is the life of Studie) to understand it, and then to read our Commentarie thereupon, and no more at any one time, than hee is able with delight to beare away, and after to meditate thereon, which is the life of reading.[37]

To "read againe and againe" and then "meditate thereon" constitute Coke's understanding of the legal method. Coke was fundamentally interested in the intellective aspects of legal study: how lawyers acquired, developed, and ultimately perfected what he called "artificial reason."[38]

Despite their political differences, Bacon agreed with Coke (and fellow lawyers) on the nature and practice of judicature. In his address to the circuit judges before the summer assize of 1617, Bacon states that "[a] popular Judge is a deformed thing: and *plaudites* [applause] are fitter for players than for magistrates." While Bacon encourages judges to "[d]o good to the people, love them and give them justice," he warns them against courting popularity: "let it be, as the Psalm saith, *nihil inde expectantes*; looking for nothing, neither praise nor profit."[39] Bacon's statement reflects an ongoing concern among early modern statesmen with what Jeffrey S. Doty calls the "problem of popularity."[40] Public figures who courted popular opinion, whether in the legal, political, or religious sphere, attracted suspicion and envy.

Closely related to the question of popularity in law was that of friendship in judgment. In *Archeion*, Sir William Lambarde identifies "friendship" as one of the leading causes of judicial corruption in the courts. Too often, judges, justices of the peace, and "other Commissioners or Delegates ... will dip their owne fingers in the *Suits* that depend before them; and will be seene more like to affectionate *Advocates*, or *Parties*, than to sincere and indifferent *Judges*."[41] The pitfalls of friendship in law are recounted in Coke's 1607 charge to the grand jury. Coke tells the story of a virtuous young Roman who foreswears friendship shortly before he assumes his senatorial duties. The young man invites his friends and family to a banquet and, at the end of the meal, makes the following announcement:

> It is true that I purpose as I must, to take my leave of you all, and to be a stranger to my dearest friends, and nearest Allies: I must forget all former friendships, and my most familiar Acquaintance, I must accompt as greatest stra[n]gers unto me; Thus must I depart from you, & yet continue amongst you, for by the love, power & authoritie of the *Senate*, I am appointed to be a Judge, and in the seate of Justice, I must forget the remembrance of your former friendships and acquaintance, and onely in the person of a Judge, with respect to keepe my conscience cleare, must with equitie & uprightnes, justly administer justice unto you all.[42]

For Coke, the "person of a Judge" is one who relinquishes the pleasures of friendship to pursue the right but lonely path of judicial impartiality. To be a good judge, one must in effect act contrary to the dominant customs and rituals surrounding communal belonging: drinking, feasting, and conversation. Seeking popularity and cultivating friendship go hand in hand, but neither has a place in the law. To resist temptation, judges must adopt Stoic self-reserve, perfected through devotion to legal study. According to legal professionals, it is better for magistrates to stand apart from the people than with them. The young Roman from Coke's fable who "forget[s] all former friendships" is held as an example for all judges to emulate.

Henry IV, Part 2

The two sections above offer a taste of popular and professional discourses concerning the character of the judge. Sampling these discourses prepares us for an examination of the complex and ambivalent depiction of judges and judicature in Shakespeare's *Henry IV, Part 2*. The character of the Lord Chief Justice has generally been viewed by critics as a symbolic figure. Deploying a structuralist reading inspired by Mikhail Bakhtin's analysis of carnival, C.L. Barber argues that – like a pair from a morality play – Falstaff epitomizes the gluttonous extravagance of "Vice" and the Chief Justice exemplifies the sobriety and good counsel of "Virtue": where the one character goes, so goes the other.[43] After the rise of new historicism in the late twentieth century, critics adjusted to account for the Chief Justice's political role in the play. Like many of the history plays, *Henry IV, Part 2* explores the tension between royal authority and the rule of law. Some critics see the humble pledge by the newly crowned Henry V to the Chief Justice in act 5, scene 2, as the play's subversive critique of royal absolutism and affirmation of "limited monarchy."[44]

But that conclusion obscures Shakespeare's complex portrait of the judge. When one takes into account the character's actions in the scenes that lead up to and follow from the scene of reconciliation between Henry and the Chief Justice, one becomes less certain that the play stages a triumph of law. In a way, Barber was right to point out that the Chief Justice seems tethered to Falstaff throughout the play. By dogging Falstaff like a village constable, the Chief Justice accrues substantial stage time and, at least initially, much of that time is spent in the company of the tavern riff-raff and Mistress Nell Quickly, the hostess of Boar's Head. These minor characters belong to the interstitial scenes. Their quarrels with each other – and Mistress Quickly's ongoing lawsuit against Falstaff – form an amusing, comedic subplot to the serious, and at times tragic, politics of the main plot. Into their orbit the Chief Justice is drawn. These early scenes, then, reproduce the accessible and loving form of judgment that comes from popular religious literature. But, later in the play, after the Chief Justice is called back to Westminster and after he assumes his duties as Henry's symbolic "father," he adheres to an aloof and antiemotional form of judicature found in legal professional literature. The duality inherent in the character reveals the play's active engagement with both popular and professional legal literature.

The Walkabout of the Lord Chief Justice

In the opening of the play, the Chief Justice patrols the streets like an inferior officer of the law: a justice of the peace, a sheriff, or even a constable. Falstaff's greeting to the Chief Justice – "I am glad to see your lordship abroad" (1.2.92) – establishes the signature difference between this judge and his textual predecessors. Shakespeare's Chief Justice bumps into Falstaff in the streets, a notable departure from his literary antecedents. In Sir Thomas Elyot's *The Boke Named the Governour* (1531), the figure of the Chief Justice is found in his natural environment, the King's Bench, as the following passage makes clear:

The moste renomed prince kynge Henry the fifte / late kynge of Englande ... was noted to be fierce and of wanton courage : it hapned that one of his serva[n]tes

/ whom he well favored / for felony by hym co[m]mitted / was arrayned *at the kynges benche*: … [the prince] in furious rage came hastily *to the barre* … & in a terrible maner / came up *to the place of judgeme[n]t* / men thinkyng that he wolde have slayne the juge / or have done to hym some damage : but the juge *sittyng styll* without movynge / declarynge the majestie of the kynges place of jugement / And with an assured and bolde countenance / hadde to the prince these words folowyng. Sir reme[m]bre your selfe: *I kepe here the place* of the king your soveraigne lorde and father.[45]

As my emphases indicate, Elyot's description of the Chief Justice locates him at the King's Bench, seated behind the bar separating the judge from the rest of the court. Elyot's juxtaposition of the two men's emotional states – the prince's "furious rage" and the judge's "assured and bolde" composure – reinforces the sense of the latter's stoic immovability. In the anonymously authored *The Famous Victories of Henry the Fifth* – a play performed before 1588 and published in 1598 and one that likely served as one of Shakespeare's inspirations for his second tetralogy – the character of the judge is similarly bench-bound. Flanked by two legal officers, a jailer and a clerk, the judge calls out, "[j]ailer, bring the prisoner to the bar," thereby establishing the judge's physical stillness.[46]

Unlike those judges, Shakespeare's Chief Justice walks the streets of Eastcheap, keeping the peace using a combination of wit, compassion, and legal reason. Upon hearing Fang and Mistress Quickly's cries – "A rescue, a rescue!" and "Good people, bring a rescue or two" (2.1.54–5) – the Chief Justice materializes and lends an ear to Mistress Quickly's complaint that Falstaff "hath eaten [her] out of house and home" (2.1.72) and cheated her of a sum of "thirty shillings" (2.1.100).[47] The knight has also broken his promise of marriage to make her his "lady … wife" (2.1.91) – a contract that was witnessed by "goodwife Keech the butcher's wife" (2.1.92). Hearing the complaint and evidence, the Chief Justice decides the case in her favour. He bases his decision on his prior knowledge of Falstaff's "great infamy" (1.2.133). He knows all too well Falstaff's "manner of wrenching the true cause the false way" (2.1.108–9). Chiding Falstaff for "practis[ing] upon the easy-yielding spirit of this woman, and ma[king] her serve your uses both in purse and in person" (2.1.112–14), the Chief Justice orders Falstaff to compensate her: "[p]ay her the debt you owe her, and unpay the villainy you have done with her. The one you may do with sterling money, and the other with current repentance" (2.1.116–19). Attentive readers and auditors will smile at the judge's double entendre since "purse" signifies both "money bag" and "scrotum."[48] Like Hal of *Henry IV, Part 1*, the Chief Justice can speak the language of the taverns. In this moment, the lawman is not the binary opposite of Falstaff but rather shares with the knight a bawdy sense of humour while still maintaining the law's spirit of equity.

The Chief Justice's judicial style, as the scene reveals, is personal and leavened with humour. In these close encounters with the people, he practises a form of restorative justice – a process of legal reconciliation and forgiveness premised on the face-to-face encounter between victim and offender.[49] In restorative justice, the mediator tries to persuade the offender to repair the harm done to the victim either "materially" or "symbolically."[50] Despite his lofty rank, he mingles with members of the Eastcheap community like a JP or village constable. He hears the complaints of the low-born petitioner, Mistress Quickly, and he is willing to pass summary judgment on the spot. He does not rely on clerks to transcribe the evidence. In short, he fulfils the fantasy of unmediated magistracy. He acts as the ideal magistrate, the "defender of the fatherlesse, poore and needy" as prescribed in the religious and moral literature.[51] Embodying the archetypal, biblical image of the good judge, the Chief Justice addresses the needs of Mistress Quickly and gives her a just and immediate solution.

The play's reduction of distance between the judge and the people he oversees is paralleled in the play's topographical foreshortening. The urban landscape of the play, ostensibly the streets and taverns of fifteenth-century London, is limited to a few landmarks. In her study of metropolitan tragedies, Marissa Greenberg observes that certain plays in the period, such as domestic tragedies, exploited the public's anxiety concerning urban growth by "rendering London epistemologically secure" through an obsessive naming of London streets, boroughs, docks, markets, churches, and other topographical features.[52] *Henry IV, Part 2* experiments with spatial semiotics as well, although not in the same way as the tragedies. Shakespeare not only domesticates the urban landscape by mapping the imagined space with place names, but also by deleting spatial markers. Audiences come to see London as only "Smithfield" and "Paul's" (1.2.48, 49) and "Pie Corner," "Lombard Street," and "Eastcheap" (2.1.26, 28, 69). The vastness of the city is tamed; the city is shrunk to the size of just a few locations. This is the London that the Chief Justice patrols.

The intimate style of the Chief Justice is thrown into relief by his foils, two actual justices of the peace, Justice Shallow and Justice Silent. Unlike the Chief Justice, who involves himself personally in legal disputes, Justice Shallow relies on an underling, Davy, for information, a decision that spells legal uncertainty, even injustice, for the community.[53] As discussed in chapter 1, the justice of the peace was a local administrator. Appointed to the office on account of their social prominence or political connections, JPs constituted an elite class of semi-professionals. They were responsible for settling everyday disputes between bickering neighbours, overseeing poor relief, investigating recusancy, regulating alehouses and inns, and, if the occasion called for it, making inquiries into felony cases and deposing witnesses. In theory, only those who were "wise and learned in the law ('*sages et apris de la leye*')" could be appointed to the office.[54] The "keepers of the Peace" were, ideally, "[m]en of the beste reputation (*Meultz vailantz*)."[55]

Elizabethan magistrates were expected to possess moral integrity, legal competency, and physical endurance. J.H. Gleason explains that Norfolk JPs in 1562 "were entrusted with [the care of] 120 square miles and 10,000 people ... a characteristic Norfolk JP, working in harness with colleagues, might have been concerned with as many as 50,000 people scattered over a roughly circular area of which the perimeter was twenty-five miles from his residence."[56] The inquest books of Sir William Lambarde, Bostock Fuller, and William Dove – three unusually well-preserved examples from the period – offer tantalizing details of the everyday burdens of the magistracy.[57] These justices investigated injuries, physical assaults, thefts, recusancy, and accidental and suspicious deaths. In an entry dated 23 February 1583, for example, Lambarde and his fellow magistrate Sir Christopher Alleyn "examined sundry persons at Sevenoaks concerning the suspicion of willful poisoning of William Brightrede by Thomas Heyward and Parnel, his now wife, then wife of the said William."[58] Many, if not most, of the cases involved common but non-life-threatening grievances between quarrelling neighbours. In late spring of 1618, for example, Fuller records that "Abraham Alford [was] brought before me for cutting & caryeing awaye certayne small ashes in wydow Cowpers ground he confessed one and I judged him to pay ij[s] [two shillings] to her which he presentlye performed."[59]

The records of the labours of diligent JPs offer a startling correction to Shakespeare's depiction of the obtuse Justice Shallow. Robert Shallow, as we learn when he reappears in *The Merry Wives of Windsor*, is a "Justice of Peace and Coram ... and *Custa-lorum*."[60] And just as his judicial efforts never bear fruit in *The Merry Wives* so in this play he (happily) wiles away the time with Falstaff. Riding across the shire to hear a dispute in person holds no appeal for Shallow. Whereas the Chief Justice listens to Mistress Quickly's complaint in person, Shallow gleans his information from his servant Davy. From Davy, Shallow learns of a conflict between one "William Visor of Won'cot" and one "Clement Perks o'th'Hill" (the nature of the dispute is never made clear).[61] Davy pleads with Shallow to "countenance" or favour Visor over Perks, even though Davy acknowledges the latter's good reputation (5.1.33). Initially, Shallow resists, remarking that "Visor is an arrant knave, on my knowledge" (5.1.35). But Davy asserts that an "honest man ... is able to speak for himself, when a knave is not ... I beseech you let him be countenanced" (5.1.38–9, 43–4). Here, Davy juggles two meanings of the word "knave." Derived from the Old English word *cnafa*, "knave" could signify both "boy" and "rogue."[62] In a linguistic sleight of hand, Davy transposes a more innocent meaning of the word ("boy") for a more insidious one ("rogue"), as when he argues that a "knave" ("boy") is unable to deliver his own defence. The silver-tongued Davy also hoodwinks his master by confusing the universal category with the particular. Even if a knave is unable to "speak for himself," it does not follow logically that all knaves lack eloquence. But Shallow is too dull to detect the logical fallacy. Finally, Davy wraps his argument in the sweet words of friendship. He tells Shallow that Visor is "mine honest friend" and reminds his master, "I have served your worship truly … this eight years" (5.1.40). The evocation of friendship and loyalty proves irresistible to Shallow. Even though "Visor" signifies the "front part of a helmet" and a "mask to conceal the face," meanings which instantly connect the character to the play's recurring scenes of nighttime violence and military aggression, and "Clement" suggests Christian mercy, mildness, kindness, humility, and perhaps wisdom, Shallow abides by Davy's request to favour the former.[63] Witnessing the episode from his place at the dinner table, Falstaff concludes his host is ruled by his servants: "by conversing with them, [he] is turn'd into a justice-like servingman" (5.1.59–60). This breakdown in justice, stemming from both Justice Shallow's misplaced notion of friendship and his reliance on hearsay, is precisely what writers decried in sermons and moral essays. Shallow does not actively subvert justice, but his pursuit of small gains, companionable dinners, and easy entertainment culminates in his failure to dispense justice to his community.

While Justice Shallow's failure to administer justice is easy to spot, it is important to recognize also that his foil, the Chief Justice, is no less compromised as a legal administrator. The Chief Justice's approach to judicature or the administration of justice seems equitable, intimate, personal, and perhaps emotionally satisfying – but it is unsustainable. Instead of keeping the peace and establishing order once and for all, the Chief Justice facilitates Falstaff's continued exploitation of Mistress Quickly. When presented with the chance to investigate Falstaff's part in the robbery at Gad's Hill, the Chief Justice decides to overlook Falstaff's transgression for, in his words, the knight has done a "day's service at Shrewsbury" which has "a little gilded over [his] night's exploit on Gad's Hill" (1.2.143–6). The Chief Justice's comment reflects a willingness to set aside the strict demands of the law in favour of an equitable solution. His decision exemplifies a form of equity in which the letter of the law is bent to accommodate the spirit of the law.[64] But act 2 reveals the consequences of the Chief Justice's decision to maintain the status quo. At the precise moment when he appears to have successfully pressed Falstaff into "satisfy[ing] the poor woman" (2.1.129), Gower enters bearing a message for the judge. As he becomes immersed in reading the latest "news" (the allocation of the royal troops), the Chief Justice misses Falstaff's new trick: conning Mistress Quickly out of £10, which is a greater sum than the original one cited in her suit. At the end of the scene, Mistress Quickly, who has, in her words, "borne, and borne, and borne, and have been fobbed off, and fobbed off, from this day to that day," is left to bear her burdens for another day (2.1.33–4). In short, while full of good intentions, the Chief Justice fails to produce tangible results. His legal interventions fail to advance the cause of justice in a lasting way.

Thus, a later scene overwrites the logic of an earlier one. Taken together, they form a palimpsest. Initially, the familiar contact between the Chief Justice and the people fulfils the popular notion that justice depends on the absence of legal intermediaries. Unlike Justice Shallow, who allows his servant Davy to mediate the dispute between William Visor and Clement Perks, the Chief Justice does not rely on hearsay but investigates cases in person. During his walk through Eastcheap, he nips street violence in the bud and, demonstrating his humanity, he soothes Mistress Quickly by acknowledging her right to become Falstaff's wife. In these scenes, the Chief Justice is the very image of a loving, public-oriented magistrate as posited in the popular literature on judges and magistracy. But even as the play invites audiences to commend the Chief Justice's employment of summary justice, it leaves them in doubt of the practicality of that model. The Chief Justice lacks the means to enforce his judgment. He remains an outsider to this community.

By leaving the bench and making his way through the city, the Chief Justice comes in contact with the commoners. Yet in so doing, he relinquishes the power to correct their transgressions and to enforce the law. The Chief Justice's inability to make a lasting change, coupled with his unimpeachable moral rectitude, recalls the toothless "old lord of the Council," briefly mentioned in *Henry IV, Part 1*. In that play, Falstaff reports to Hal that this councillor "rated" him "in the street" about his pernicious influence over the Prince.[65] (The character of the old lord does not actually appear in the play.) When Falstaff boasts that he "marked him not ... and yet he talked wisely, and in the streets, too" (1.2.86–7), Hal compares the old lord to the figure of Wisdom: "[t]hou didst well, for wisdom cries out in the streets and no man regards it" (1.2.88–9). In Proverbs, Wisdom, personified and gendered female, is ignored by the people: "Wisdome cryeth without, and putteth forth her voice in the stretes ... I have called, and ye refused it: I have stretched out my hande, and no man regarded it."[66] In an unmistakable intertextual allusion to this scene, *Henry IV, Part 2* stages the initial encounter between Falstaff and the Chief Justice to evoke the clash between two old men, one wise and the other foolish, one scolding, the other scorning. Yet the chain of comparison that connects the Chief Justice to the "old lord of the Council" and to Wisdom does not presage a triumphant arc for the character. Wisdom "cries out in the streets" but is not heard – and the same could be said of the Chief Justice. He casts a magisterial presence in the scenes that he is in, but his legal judgments are largely ignored.

The inability of the Chief Justice to produce lasting change is one of the ways the play punctures the romantic image of loving magistracy. However, its reduction of one fantasy does not amount to an unambiguous support of another: the professional or institutional ideal of the judge. The play reproduces, yet at the same time denies, the popular as well as the professional discourse. The Chief Justice's final scenes demonstrate the paradox of legal authority. In order to embody the splendour of the law, the Chief Justice has little choice but to sever his relationship with the people, resulting in the permanent rupture of the merry world.

In act 5, scene 2, the Chief Justice appears before Hal, now Henry V, at Westminster. Before their meeting, the Chief Justice frets that the death of the old King has left him "open to all injuries" (5.2.8). Courtiers concur with his grim assessment. Warwick informs him, "[i]ndeed I think the young King loves you not" (5.2.9) and Prince John agrees, "[y]ou stand in coldest expectation" (5.2.31). Seemingly abandoned by his former allies, the Chief Justice, for the first time in the play, expresses fear: "O God, I fear all will be overturned" (5.2.19). When he meets the new King, the Chief Justice launches into an eloquent defence of his actions and of the necessity of his office. The speech effectively disassociates the man from the judicial office:

> I then did use the person of your father.
> The image of his power lay then in me;
> And in th'administration of his law,
> Whiles I was busy for the commonwealth,
> Your highness pleasèd to forget my place,
> The majesty and power of law and justice,
> The image of the King whom I presented,
> And struck me in my very seat of judgement. (5.2.72–9)

In this speech, the Chief Justice tries to downplay a sense of his own agency: he claims that he did not punish the Prince for physically assaulting him, the private individual, but for attacking the king, the commonwealth, and the "majesty and power of law and justice" (5.2.77). Not unlike a conjurer who arranges his charms, tokens, and talismans before casting a spell, the Chief Justice enumerates the objects that bespeak his authority, such as the "seat of judgement" (5.2.79), the "awe-full bench" (5.2.85), and "the sword / That guards the peace and safety of your [the King's] person" (5.2.86–7). Through such a layering of legal language, he tries to recreate the symbolic parts of the law. At the same time, the attempt is evasive, for he hides behind the scrim of judicial symbols. In this speech, then, he engages in a linguistic act of self-fashioning through self-effacement. In order to establish his own authority, the Chief Justice develops a parallel between legal and royal authority. Yet this is potentially problematic, for it jeopardizes the independence of the judiciary and endangers the common lawyer's vision of English mixed government. In response to this rousing speech, Henry promises to honour the Chief Justice, to make him his symbolic "father" and the chief administrator of the law:

> You shall be as a father to my youth;
> My voice shall sound as you do prompt mine ear,

And I will stoop and humble my intents
To your well-practised wise directions. (5.2.117–20)

In recent criticism, this scene has been read as a triumph of common law doctrine over royal absolutism. Henry's meek submission before the "wise directions" of the Chief Justice fulfils, it is argued, a common law fantasy of English
kingship, what the fifteenth-century common lawyer Sir John Fortescue called
"*dominium politicum et regale*, a limited monarchy."[67] In adopting the Chief
Justice as his "father," Henry seemingly proclaims a new form of royal justice,
one that promises to conform to the law that the Chief Justice represents, one
that finds within it a place for communal or local justice.

Yet the alliance between Henry and his Chief Justice comes at a cost to the
community. Following the agreement to act as Henry's "father," the Chief Justice is shorn of his previous role as a local mediator. By assuming his place
at the royal council, the Chief Justice becomes leashed to the royal will, leaving the community in Eastcheap without a justice. In a scene that has been
unjustly overlooked in criticism, a pair of beadles (warrant officers) accuse Doll
Tearsheet of causing a man's death. They drag her out for a flogging:

> FIRST BEADLE: The constables have delivered her [Doll] over to me, and she shall
> have a whipping-cheer, I warrant her. There hath been a man or two killed
> about her.
> DOLL TEARSHEET: Nut-hook, nut-hook, you lie! Come on, I'll tell thee what, thou
> damned tripe-visaged rascal, an the child I go with do miscarry, thou wert better
> hadst struck thy mother, thou paper-faced villain.
> . . . .
> MISTRESS QUICKLY: O God, that right should thus overcome might! Well, of
> sufferance comes ease.
> DOLL TEARSHEET: Come, you rogue, come, bring me to a justice. (5.4.4–10, 23–5)

The identity of the dead man (or two), the means by which he came to be in
Doll's company, her motives for allegedly beating the man to death (the First
Beadle states "the man is dead that you and Pistol beat amongst you" [5.4.16]) –
these are all left as open-ended questions. Doll demands a fair hearing, "bring
me to a justice," she declares, but her request is ignored by the beadles. Prone
to tripping over words, the agitated Mistress Quickly accidentally inverts the
proverb "might overcomes right," adding an element of painful comedy to an
already confusing scene. In all this, "justice" – the Chief Justice – is conspicu-
ously absent and so too the form of intimate, loving justice he had previously
represented. Shakespeare trusts his audience to supply Doll's punishment. Middlesex County Records contain graphic descriptions of whippings of female
offenders. One Joan Lea, for example, for bearing "a bastard child begotten on

her by Thomas Bates," was "openly whipped at a cart's tail in St. John Street upon Saturday next until her body be all bloody."[68] This is the implied punishment awaiting Doll. Of course, audiences cannot be sure that she will be judged guilty and the ambiguity could well be the point. The legal resolution hinges on the Chief Justice but it must be deferred because he is preoccupied with royal affairs.

The end of the play sees the establishment of a new political order – yet this comes at an emotional cost to the community. Shakespeare has prepared audiences for this moment of rupture ever since Henry's first soliloquy in *Henry IV, Part 1*: "I know you all, and will a while uphold / The unyok'd humor of your idleness" (1.2.195–6). But no amount of foreshadowing can really soften the blow of Henry's public shaming of Falstaff. The impact of the scene on audiences hardly needs to be rehearsed. A.C. Bradley comments, "we feel … during the King's speech, a good deal of pain and some resentment."[69] Following the exits of Henry and his retinue, Falstaff turns to Justice Shallow and acknowledges reality: "Master Shallow, I owe you a thousand pound" (5.5.71). It is an impossibly large sum as befitting a larger-than-life swindler.

The rejection of Falstaff is a dramatic and tragic moment and the Chief Justice plays a prominent role in it (figure 6). Coldly, Henry charges the Chief Justice to "see performed the tenor of my word" (5.5.70). In the footnote of the Oxford edition, "tenure" has been modernized to "tenor." Although this emendation makes perfect grammatical sense, that editorial choice flattens the semantic richness contained in the original spelling. The 1600 quarto editions (known as QA and QB) and the 1623 first folio edition consistently spell the word as "tenure," not "tenor."[70] "Tenor" is the "course of meaning which holds on or continues through something written or spoken; the general sense or meaning of a document, speech, etc.; substance, purport, import, effect, drift."[71] Yet there is a secondary, legal meaning. In English common law, "tenure" signifies the "name given to the relationship whereby a tenant holds land of a lord."[72] Henry's wordplay recasts his relationship with the judge as that between a lord and his tenant.

In this moment, the Chief Justice executes his duties as an arm of royal justice. His efficiency serves as a notable contrast to his previous efforts at communal mediation. Following the King's exit, he orders his officers to "[g]o carry Sir John Falstaff to the Fleet / Take all his company along with him" (5.5.89–90). The Chief Justice cuts off Falstaff's beseeching "My lord, my lord –" and defers the conversation: "I cannot now speak. I will hear you soon. Take them away" (5.5.92–3). These simple lines seem transparent, yet they jangle with extra significance. "I cannot now speak" expresses the Chief Justice's desire to follow the King. But the line also suggests his lack of agency. As a royal councillor representing the living "image" of the sovereign, the Chief Justice must form his words and actions according to the sovereign's will. "I will hear you soon" is the Chief Justice's

Figure 6. Robert Smirke, *Falstaff Rebuked* (1795). The Lord Chief Justice, dressed in black, divides Henry V and Falstaff.
Oil on canvas. The Folger Shakespeare Library.

promise to listen to Falstaff. Yet the line also signals the Chief Justice's participation in the game of deferral and mediation that so often leads to judicial neglect. Finally, his line, "take them away," foreshadows the death of Falstaff and of the joyful world for which he stood. Indeed, the sentence presages the quiet erasure of the Chief Justice himself, for he, like Falstaff, plays no part in *Henry V*.

The Chief Justice's absence in *Henry V* empties out Henry's promise to "stoop and humble my intents / To your well-practised wise directions" (5.2.119–20). In *Henry V*, it is the King and his bishops who resolve thorny legal questions such as the historical origins of the "Salique law" and the punishment of the traitors

Scroop, Grey, and Cambridge.[73] The absence of the Chief Justice deprives the royal court of his "wise directions" and paves the way for the King to rule with near-absolute freedom. In *Henry V*, Henry epitomizes the charismatic king who acts as accuser, judge, executioner, and conqueror. But this dilation of royal justice is also haunted by the historical memory of the turbulent reign of Henry's heir, Henry VI. Shakespeare's original audiences, having already seen the unravelling of Henry VI's authority in his dramatizations of the Wars of the Roses (the *Henry VI* plays were completed before *Henry IV, Part 2* and *Henry V*), would have been in a position to anticipate the tragic outcome of the kind of charismatic kingship that Henry V embodies. In the *Henry VI* plays, the pious yet unready Henry VI is undermined by Queen Margaret as well as backbiting royal advisers, counsellors, bishops, and courtiers, all plotting for control. Legal truths are not decided by a formal legal process, but by force. For example, when Henry VI hears that Horner, the armourer, has been accused of treason by Peter Thump, his apprentice, he defers judgment to Duke Humphrey who decrees a trial by battle:

> And let these [men] have a day appointed them
> For single combat in convenient place,
> For he (*indicating Horner*) hath witness of his servant's malice.
> This is the law.[74]

There is no investigation and no interrogation of witnesses and no room for human judgment. Instead, proof is decided by the judgment of God, *judicium Dei*.[75] Perhaps the scene recalls a purer form of justice from a bygone day. Or, as I read it, the scene underscores the total absence of an independent judiciary in the Lancastrian court.

Conclusion

Reflecting on the panoply of legal jurisdictions and interactions in *Henry IV, Part 2*, Richard Strier concludes that Shakespeare's representation of the law shows off "the great advantages" of literary texts: they "do not have to resolve the problems that they raise; they just have to raise them in interesting and provocative ways."[76] This play takes full advantage of drama's open-endedness by exploring fundamental questions related to royal and communal justice while evoking the voices of multiple communities, multiple cultures, and subcultures. In *Henry IV, Part 2*, as indeed in many of his plays, Shakespeare displays an omnivorous appetite for legal discourses. This play embraces the contradiction between legal discourses – those expressed in assize sermons and moral literature and those produced by and for legal professionals. Like his fellow playwrights, Shakespeare occupied a middle realm between the eloquent but few – the professors of the law – and the silent but many – the playgoers who attended performances of his plays and the congregations who attended sermons where they learned and internalized a grammar of lay magistracy. For this broad audience, Shakespeare reflected back popular yearnings for immediacy in judicature even as he explored the contradictions inherent in those fantasies.

The play refracts a monolithic sense of law into multiple legalities.[77] The Chief Justice possesses many of the moral qualities of a good judge as defined by preachers and moral authors: "deepe understanding," "boldnesse and courage," "honesty of conscience," "uprightnesse of justice," and "equitie of sentence."[78] But these moral qualities do not equip him to administer the law. The Chief Justice mingles with the people, yet that personal contact does not lead to the people's lasting happiness. True, the people gain a measure of recognition in the eyes of the law. However, this in itself does not appear to accomplish the "end" of justice. "Happy are those Com[m]on wealthes where men may injoy their owne according to the Law," Sir John Dodderidge declares in his 1620 jury charge.[79] We can trace this maxim back to classical and post-classical era jurisprudential texts. For Aristotle, the end, objective, or *telos* of justice is the "attainment of ... happiness" and "'the good life.'"[80] Justinian's *Institutes* begins with the often quoted definition of justice as "the continual desire of always rendering to each one that which is his due."[81] With these values in mind, we might ask, do the actions of the Chief Justice produce the conditions for justice and the "good life"? It seems not. His judgments are not enforced. He leaves the inhabitants of Eastcheap in various states of irresolution and even suffering at the end of the play.

Yet the failure of the familiar model of magistracy does not function as an endorsement of the professional discourse that views legal administration as a performance of majesty and imagines legal distance to be a crucial part of the law. When the Chief Justice acts as a royal justice, he becomes an instrument for a kind of poetic injustice, and for that breach he appears to be condemned to dramatic oblivion. Thus, the play problematizes both institutional and popular visions of the character of the judge. What we are left with is a character constructed out of the clashing desires and anxieties of multiple communities: common lawyers, preachers, and satirists – perhaps audiences themselves. Shakespeare's legal character both arises from and magnifies conflicting legal ideologies. A judge should strive to be accessible but not common. A judge should be with the people but maintain his distance, for he risks subjecting himself to the people's rule if he is seen to be too accessible. A judge should be loving – but also severe. A judge should listen to his "feeling heart" – but control his feelings with reason. What a bewildering set of contradictions.

Henry IV, Part 2 depicts the interwoven histories of many worlds, elite and common, urban and rural, and develops the most urgent social, political, and legal questions of the day. The play functions as a heuristic, an instrument of investigation, in the way it exposes the internal contradictions in commonly held logics about legal administration. To be effective, should judges strive to be removed from the people? Should they privilege legal reason over human compassion – what preachers and others called "love"? The play provides no easy answers. In withholding a resolution to a persistent problem, and in resisting the affective logic of preachers and other moral writers, the play breaks free from its popular roots. Yet even as the play seems to criticize popular sentiments, it draws audiences toward an unspoken, perhaps unspeakable, conclusion: the ascension of law comes at the expense of justice. The appointment (or reappointment) of the Chief Justice promises the beginning of a golden age of legal administration in England. Yet the final scenes hint that the remove of the judge from the community paves the way for the eventual demise of Lancastrian rule. When he abandons face-to-face mediation, the Chief Justice achieves not so much judicial independence as feudal servitude to the new king. The word that Henry uses to describe the Chief Justice's service to him is "tenure," which hints at the crown's new claim on the judiciary. The reduction of the Chief Justice to the King's retainer, coupled with the Chief Justice's total absence in *Henry V*, raises questions about the nature of legal administration: what kind of a legality does a nation like England deserve? What is lost in the march toward state formation, of bureaucratic expansion, and the centralization of the law? Is the community better or worse off without magistrates judging at the city gates and intervening in the marketplace? These are some of the questions that *Henry IV, Part 2* considers, at times with tremendous compassion and insight, but ultimately leaves unresolved.

Chapter Three

Neighbourliness and the Coroner's Inquest in English Domestic Tragedies

On 23 August 1594, a London tavern keeper by the name Thomas Merry murdered his neighbour Robert Beech and Beech's apprentice Thomas Winchester. In a matter of days, Merry and his sister Rachel were apprehended, tried, and executed. To capitalize on the news of the double murder, printers entered five ballads and a pamphlet in the Stationers' Register. These publications, regrettably, are lost, and so too are the court documents related to the case. At least the titles of the lost ephemera have survived. The title of one of the ballads announces the "*wofull murder of ROBERT BEECHE*" and likewise the title of the pamphlet emphasizes the "*most cruell and barbarous murther committed by one Thomas Merrey, on the persons of Roberte Beeche and Thomas Winchester.*"[1] There is a record of a performance of "The Tragedy of Merry" by William Haughton and John Day in 1600 (at the Rose Theatre) – but the play text, like the pamphlet and ballads, is lost.[2] Against this pattern of loss stands a single, extant text: Robert Yarington's *Two Lamentable Tragedies*. Although the play was published in 1601, Yarington's play was likely written immediately after the execution of the Merry siblings.[3] As suggested by the play's title, the action flits between two plots. The first plot, also known as "The Tragedy of Merry," or the Merry plot, centres on the 1594 case.[4] The second plot, also known as the Italian plot or the Italian tragedy, is set in Padua and tells the story of a rich orphan who is eventually murdered by his avaricious uncle. Very little is known of Robert Yarington. Several Yaringtons were alive and working in London in the 1590s.[5] Critics wonder whether the play was ever performed.[6] Whoever he was, and whatever source texts he worked with, one thing is clear about the play text: as a dramatic adaptation, it contains one of the most detailed and entertaining representations of communal justice.

Of the handful of surviving examples of domestic tragedies, *Two Lamentable Tragedies* arguably stands out as the goriest.[7] Its spectacular violence anticipates today's body horror films which specialize in the depiction of broken bones and torn flesh.[8] In conveying a "graphic sense of physicality," such films test the boundaries of everyday respectability.[9] They enthral audiences by giving them a glimpse of what is, under normal viewing conditions, unobservable or not appropriate for extended viewing. Body horror indulges audiences' desire to stare at what is conventionally off-limits. *Two Lamentable Tragedies* luxuriates in horror and excess—at least, in its initial scenes. One stage direction indicates that Merry "*strike[s] him [Beech] in the head fifteen times*" (sig. B4r).[10] This shocking act of violence challenges audiences to closely observe the abject body – to identify with and be nauseated by the body in pain. Merry's attack on Beech's boy-apprentice, Thomas Winchester, is no less extreme: "*When the boy goeth into the shoppe* Merrie *striketh six blowes on his head & with the seaventh [sic] leaves the hammer sticking in his head*" (sig. C4r). And if this were not graphic enough, another stage direction indicates that the actor playing Merry is to dismember Beech's body in plain view of the playgoer: "Merry *begins to cut the body, and bindes the armes behind his backe with* Beeches *garters, leaves out the body, covers the head and legs againe*" (sig. E2r).[11] (In performance, if indeed the play was ever staged, a dummy would have been used.) At the end of the play, the executions of Merry and his sister Rachel seem anticlimatic in comparison to the actions that precipitated them.

Yet these Goya-worthy scenes of brutal violence – which one early twentieth-century critic scorned as "gruesome and crude beyond redemption" – are counter-balanced by wholesome images of orderly, procedurally correct communal justice.[12] The inquest of the murders eventually comes to involve all of Beech's neighbours: the regular residents of the Lambeth Hill neighbourhood and those who pass through its streets and corridors.[13] These amateur investigators include Loney (Beech's landlord), Master Cowley, Neighbour 1, Neighbour 2, Neighbour 3, a Maid, a Gentleman, a Salter's man, Waterman 1, Waterman 2, and others. Alongside the initial impression of bodily violence, then, is a countervailing image of communal and neighbourly justice.

As discussed in the introduction, communal justice was the jewel in the crown of common law jurisprudence. Medieval and early modern jurists asserted that what gave English law its essential character was the jury trial. Unlike the inquisitorial system, English accusatory justice was conducted openly before the community.[14] Yet no matter how consistently English jurists proclaimed the wonders of participatory justice, the real experience could (and did) fall short of the ideal. Domestic tragedies such as *Two Lamentable Tragedies* flourished in the gap between legal fantasy and embodied reality. Lena Cowen Orlin has argued that "just as archives can be fiction, fiction, too, can be an archive … In this case, the domestic tragedy can be a resource for understanding the private matters of its period."[15] As proven by Orlin's research, as well as that of Catherine Richardson, Frances E. Dolan, Marissa Greenberg, Emma Whipday, and others, the English domestic tragedy is an endlessly rich archive for studying the values, ethos, and imagination of the "middling sort."[16] In what follows, I analyse the contributions of two domestic tragedies, *Two Lamentable Tragedies* and *A Warning for Fair Women*, to the ongoing debate about the source of legal authority and the capacity of laypeople for legal labour.

In both of the domestic tragedies that I consider, the lay magistrate is featured as a heroic figure who brings law and order to a fractured community. In the plays, the victims' neighbours enter and exit the stage in a flurry of excitement, stealing the spotlight from the appointed magistrates. These neighbours are amateur sleuths and, as the texts make clear, it is precisely because they are nonprofessionals that they are able to harness their intimate knowledge of the neighbourhood to quickly narrow the circle of suspects. While legal officers appear – in *A Warning for Fair Women*, for example, four lords of the "Council" help to coordinate the investigation and, similarly, in *Two Lamentable Tragedies*, a "Constable" and "three watchmen" arrest Merry and Rachel – these officers of the law are relegated to the play's spatial and textual periphery. They enter, make official-sounding pronouncements, and exit. The bulk of the dramatic interest, and audiences' attention, rests on the citizen-detectives. In his comments on the sixth commandment "thou shalt not kill," John Calvin states that "we watch to keepe them [our neighbours] from hurt, & if they be in any danger, that we give them our helping hand."[17] In *A Warning for Fair Women* and *Two Lamentable Tragedies*, the neighbours are not able to prevent the murders – but they do the next best thing. Capably and collectively, they carry out the coroner's inquest.

The Murder of George Sanders

To appreciate the theatrical representation of participatory justice, it is instructive to look at how legal authority is depicted in Arthur Golding's *A briefe discourse of the late murther of master George Saunders* (1573, hereafter abbreviated to *A briefe discourse*), the key source text for *A Warning for Fair Women*.[18] Golding composed one of the first murder pamphlets to be published in England. In it, he provides a detailed account of the murder of George Sanders, a London merchant, by his wife's lover, George Browne. Golding's literary reputation now largely rests on his translation of Ovid's *Metamorphoses*. But during his lifetime, he was also admired for his translations of the writings of John Calvin and Theodore Beza.[19] It was likely on account of his sterling reputation as a promoter of religious reform – as well as his personal connection to William Cecil, Lord Burghley, his relative through marriage – that he was commissioned by Elizabeth's Privy Council to compose the official account of the murder of George Sanders and the arrest and execution of the conspirators.[20]

George Sanders's murder attracted the attention of the Privy Council from the very start. In a letter to Sir Francis Walsingham written shortly after the incident, Cecil notes, "[h]ere hath been a murther committed about Shooters-hill, somewhat to the reproof of this place, and herein I have used such care, as the party is taken, being one Brown an Irishman, who had served, and is put from my Lord of Oxford's service."[21] The Privy Council's special interest in the case likely stemmed from the fact that George Sanders was related to high-ranking members of the government.[22] The women, Anne Sanders and Anne Drury, had court or governmental ties as well.[23] The Sanders were well connected to the upper echelons of Elizabethan society. It is not surprising, then, to find Golding actively striving to cast the state and its legal and religious agents in the best possible light.

Literary historians have carefully reconstructed the facts of the case: on 25 March 1573, George Browne ambushed George Sanders and his companion, John Bean, near Shooter's Hill in Kent. Sanders was "striken quite and cleane through at the first blowe" (217).[24] Later that day, two locals found the bodies of Sanders and Bean. Bean was alive despite his "ten or eleven deadly wounds" (218). They raised hue and cry and London officials promptly issued an arrest warrant for Browne. Browne sought help from his lover and their go-between. The women provided Browne with £20 that day and an additional £6 the next day (218). On 28 March, however, before he was able to "shifte ... by flight," Browne was arrested "by the Mayor of the towne" of Rochester, Kent (218).[25] Three days later, he was executed at Smithfield and his body was carried to the scene of the crime and left there to rot in chains (219). Gibbeting was a particularly grisly form of spectacular justice.[26] On 14 April, Anne Sanders and Anne Drury were arrested. Drury was taken to the Tower of London and interrogated.[27] On 6 May, the women were arraigned at Guildhall (219). Two days later, Roger Clement, Drury's servant, was arraigned at Newgate (220).[28] Found guilty, all three were hanged at Smithfield on 13 May. According to Golding, "so great a number of people" gathered to watch their executions that "windows & walles were ... beaten down" for better viewing (220).

In *A briefe discourse*, Golding uses the Sanders case to advance a strictly top-down model of legal authority. He does this initially by admonishing the public for its unwholesome reaction to the tragedy: "many delight to heare and tell newes, without respect of the certentie of the truth" (216). To the reader, he promises not only to disseminate the true facts of the case but also to model the appropriate emotional responses. Golding's opening gambit sets the stage for his subsequent intervention as a gatekeeper of information and emotions. For example, he reserves his highest praise for the professional judges and the clergy; he writes movingly about the work of those who heard the prisoners' confession and counselled them before their executions, lavishing praise on "Mr. Macwilliams," "Mr. Cole," the "Dean of St. Paul" (Alexander Nowell), "Mr. Charke" (likely the preacher William Charke), and "Mr. Yong" (Matthew Yonge).[29] Whereas the anonymous playwright of *A Warning for Fair Women* would concentrate on exploring Anne Sanders's emotional and psychological states, Golding devotes his narrative to the feelings of the religious attendants.

For example, the "Dean of Paules" was overcome by a "great griefe and indigna-
tion of mind" when he found Anne Sanders proclaiming her innocence despite
her conviction (228), and Mr. Cole "laboured very earnestly with hir to bring
hir to repentance" (229). Each "laboured very painfully to instruct them [Anne
Sanders and Anne Drury] aright" (230).

After itemizing the work of the clergy, Golding shifts to a celebration of the
work of the judges. First, he declares that people should not question the wisdom of the judges; by virtue of their office, judges possess superior knowledge
of the law and of fact. As Golding puts it, "[w]hen lawe hath once passed upon
them [the guilty ones] … christian charitie willeth men eyther to burie the
faults with the offendours in perpetual silence, or else so to speak of them, as
the vices and not the parties themselves may seeme to be any more touched"
(217). Further public legal chatter constitutes unchristian conduct. Golding's
emphasis on "perpetual silence" dovetails with the professional legal discourse
on legal knowledge and authority. I have already mentioned in the introduction the opinion of common lawyers such as William Fulbecke, who argued
that "magistrates are the ministers of laws, the judges are interpretors [sic], the
people are the servants."[30] By characterizing the people as "servants," Fulbecke
suggests they lack the authority (and knowledge) to offer useful legal analysis. This is Golding's message as well. Because the judges have already decided
the case, any further discussion of the "parties themselves" would be shameful
and transgressive. Golding exhorts "all persons to refrayne from any devises or
practises to deface or discredite the honorable proceedings of Counsellors, and
publike and lawfull forme of trialles and judgementes according to Justice, or to
hinder the beneficiall course of so good examples" (222).

To illustrate his point, Golding recounts the fate of George Mell, a minister
of Newgate prison. This "foolish" man "f[e]ll in love wyth hir [Anne Sanders]"
(221). Believing her "solemne asseverations and protestations of innocencie"
(222), he sought to exonerate her.[31] Mell asked Anne Drury to "take the whole
guilt upon hir selfe" (221). When she refused, he petitioned "an honest Gentleman," perhaps a lawyer, to take up Anne Sanders's case, even going so far as to
offer that man a bribe (221). The unnamed gentleman, however, spurned Mell's
money and turned him in to the authorities. For his punishment, the

> Lordes of the Counsell … adjudged him [Mell] to stand upon the pillorie, with
> apparent notes and significations of his lewde and foolishe demeanour … a paper
> pinned upon hys breast, wherein were written certain wordes in great Letters con-
> teyning the effecte of his fact, to his open shame: videlicet, *For practising to colour
> the detestable factes of George Sanders wife.* (222, original emphasis)

The pillory was used to publicly shame offenders for their "aggravated" offences.[32]
With a "paper pinned upon hys breast" containing "wordes in great Letters"

decrying his foul deed, Mell was made a laughingstock of his community. As Golding tells it, Mell's "doting affections" blurred his judgment, causing him to challenge the authority of the magistrates, leading him straight to his ruin (222).

In *A briefe discourse*, Golding uses the Sanders case to highlight the limitless capacity of the state to detect, investigate, and punish murder. Judges and clergymen emerge as the heroes of the story. This is not to say that Golding erases all signs of lay magistracy. He duly informs his reader that an "old man and his mayden" raised the initial hue and cry upon their discovery of the bodies (218). Yet on the whole, layfolk appear as background figures in Golding's account. As for the public at large, they are depicted as gossipmongers and thrill-seekers.

Participatory Justice in *A Warning for Fair Women*

Whereas Golding's text imagines a top-down model of legal authority – justice is something that is set by the judges or "Lordes of the Counsell" – *A Warning for Fair Women*'s theatrical adaptation of the case allocates legal and moral authority to the various residents of the vicinity of the crime.[33] Laypeople undertake the criminal investigation with utmost diligence. While they go about their legal labour, these lay magistrates supply a steady stream of moral, social, and legal commentary. Upon the discovery of John Bean's body, Old John, a character based on the "old man" of Golding's text, laments the decline of civility:

> What an age live we in? When men have no mercy of men more than of dogges, bloudier than beasts? This is the deed of some swaggering, swearing, drunken desperate Dicke. Call we them Cabbaleers? Mass they be Canniballes, that have the stabbe readyer in their handes than a penny in their purse: Shames death be their share. (sig. F2r)

This bite-sized sermon is sprinkled with rhetorical flourishes; the alliteration of "swaggering, swearing, drunken desperate Dicke" slides into "Cabbaleers" (an anglicization of *caballeros*, Spanish for gentlemen) and "Canniballes." The countryman speaks with the lofty cadence of the best of London's preachers and moralists. He sounds like Richard Brathwaite, William Prynne, and a host of other popular moralists who associated drunkenness with political disorder.[34] Imbuing the countryman with poetic grace and moral seriousness is one of the ways the play accentuates the power of the lay magistrate.

So aggressively does *A Warning for Fair Women* pursue its romantic vision of communal justice that it creates a world of frictionless jurisdictional transfer. Take, for example, the play's representation of how information passes between the hands of the lords of the Queen's Council and local authorities. In one scene, several "Lords" receive letters from local authorities informing them of the murder. The first letter contains a brief mention of the "very bloudy act" (sig. G1r).[35]

The second details the "manner, and the marks of him, / (By likelihoode) that did the impious deede" (sig. G1v). One of the lords declares, "[w]e shal not need to send these Messengers, / For hew and cry may take the murtherers" (sig. G1r). That prediction proves true. In the play, as in Golding's pamphlet, Browne attacks Sanders and Bean near Shooter's Hill in Kent.[36] The first to arrive at the scene are Old John and Joan, Bean's sweetheart. Lamenting Bean's wounds and the death of his companion, Old John promises to "rayse all Wolwich to fetch home this man [the murderer], and make search" (sig. F2r). The raising of hue and cry fulfils one of the ideals of participatory justice: that every person will do the right thing by following their "natural" instinct for justice (an instinct which is honed through custom and powered by conscience). Further diverging from Golding's narrative, the play carefully enumerates the people's legal labour. For instance, one of the lords declares that the Waterman who had transported him had also "row'd him [Browne] up" (sig. G1v). Testifying before the lords, the Waterman states that Browne had tried to hide his "bloody" "hose" with his "hat" and that he had "sigh'd and star'd as one that was afraide." Acting on this information, the lords issue "warrants" for Browne's arrest (sig. G1v).

In the play, the people work closely with the authorities to resolve the case; they do not appear in the capacity of the law's "servants" (in Fulbecke's sense) but as its stewards. Master James's shaming of the "Minister" (a character based on Golding's George Mell) offers a striking example of this narrative pattern. As his character's name suggests, Master James is neither a judge nor a justice of the peace. Yet, he assumes the role of the magistrate when he sentences the meddler to a sound public shaming:

> Now let me tell ye, that I am ashamde [sic],
> A man of your profession should appeare
> So far from grace, and touch of conscience,
> As making no respect of his owne soule,
> He should with such audaciousnes presume
> To baffle Justice, and abuse the seate,
> With your fond over-weening and slie fetch.
> . . . .
> Well sir, since you have so forgot your selfe,
> And (shamelesse) blush not at so bold offence:
> Upon their day of execution,
> And at the selfe same place, upon a pillorie,
> There shall you stand, that al the world may see,
> A just desert for such impietie. (sig. I4v)

Like Old John in the previous scene, Master James is a layman in both the legal and religious sense of the word. Yet he speaks with the diction and conviction of a seasoned magistrate and preacher. The lay magistrate uses the language of conscience and salvation to shame the errant clergyman. In presenting scenes of laypeople efficaciously engaged in legal work – from the "wise and speedie search" for the suspected Browne (sig. G2r) to the sanctioning of detractors who seek to "baffle Justice" (sig. I4v) – *A Warning for Fair Women* accomplishes a degree of ideological compromise that is as sophisticated as it is subtle: it accommodates both an official version of events, as told by Golding's pamphlet, and it utilizes its scenes of participatory justice to celebrate the ability of laypeople for various aspects of legal work, including the preliminary investigation, witnessing, and even judgment.

Neighbourliness in *Two Lamentable Tragedies*

The scenes of communal justice in *A Warning for Fair Women* find a fuller expression in *Two Lamentable Tragedies*. When Merry attacks the boy Winchester, the stage direction indicates that the boy *"groaning must be heard by a maide who must crye to her maister"* (sig. C4r). The maid's instinctive "crye" at the noise, an echo of the boy's groans, triggers a chain reaction that ends with the arrest of Merry and Rachel. In the play, murder ruptures the peace, yet the peace is eventually restored through the actions of the victims' neighbours, who spontaneously cohere to form a coroner's jury. The neighbours gather evidence, tend to the dying boy, and knock on doors in search of witnesses and suspects. At one point, a nervous Merry exclaims, "[w]hy go the neighbours round about the streete / to every house?" (sig. G3v). His neighbours walk the street, I suggest, because they are characters in a play intent on showcasing the capacity of citizens to restore law and order through their own collective initiative.

As previously mentioned, in order to dispose of Beech's body, Merry cuts it into "peece-meale" chunks (sig. E2r). He places the head and legs in one bag and the "mangled rest" in another (sig. E2r). He deposits one bag in an alley near Baynard's Castle and the other in a ditch near Paris Garden. Before long, residents find Beech's scattered remains. One scene, in particular, is freighted with symbolic and political meaning. It begins with the arrival of the Gentleman and the Porter carrying a sack. After a brief exchange of greetings, Beech's landlord, Loney, breaks into a lament: his tenant Beech is "dead indeed, but yet we cannot finde, / What is become of halfe his hopelesse bodie … No man can tell what is become of it." At this point the Gentleman exclaims:

> Then I doe thinke I can resolve your doubt,
> And bring you certaine tydings of the rest,
> . . . .
> Walking betime by Paris-garden ditch,
> Having my Water Spaniell by my side

. . . .
When we approach'd unto that haplesse place
. . . .
My Spaniell gan to sent [scent], to barke, to plunge,
Into the water, and came foorth againe,
And fawnd on me, as if a man should say,
Helpe out a man that here lyes murthered.
. . . .
I gan to rate and beate the harmlesse Cur,
Thinking to make him leave to follow me,
But words, nor blowes, could move the dog away,
But still he plung'd, he div'd, he barkt, he ran
Still to my side, as if it were for helpe:
I seeing this, did make the ditch be dragd,
Where then was found this body as you see,
With great amazement to the lookers on. (sig. G2r–v)

When the Gentleman says that he was "[w]alking betime by Paris-garden ditch," he reveals himself as a particular social type: a London gallant. Located on the south bank of the Thames near today's Blackfriars Bridge, the manor of Paris Garden was known for its bear-baiting and other blood sports and was associated with a subculture of idle young men.[37] John Davies (before his knighthood and appointment to the judiciary) wrote an epigram satirizing the pleasure-seeking habits of "Publius, a student at the Common-law," who neglects "old Ployden [Plowden], Dyer, Brooke" for "recreation": "To Paris Garden doth himself withdraw / To see old Harry Huns and Sackerson."[38] (Harry Huns and Sackerson were two celebrity bears.) The Gentleman is a stranger to the neighbourhood. His presence would be unwarranted under normal circumstances. He belongs to a world of pleasure and sport while the humble neighbours occupy one of industry and manual labour. Despite their differences, the Gentleman conducts himself courteously and amiably toward the Lambeth Hill residents. He addresses a group of them as "Gentlemen" and calls one of them his "friend" (sig. G2v, G3r). The play naturalizes the collaboration between people of differing status. Such an erasure of status consciousness again draws attention to the ideological inner workings of the play as it tries to promote a wholesome image of social belonging against a backdrop of competition. The Gentleman's presence therefore reveals another side to the play's logic of communal justice. Differences in wealth and degree that *ought* to have separated the classes are ignored in the play in the pursuit of staging participatory justice. In the play, once the action gets past the initial conflict between Merry and Beech, social distinctions are relegated to the periphery of the narrative.

The Coroner and His Jurors

The everyday residents who participate in the criminal inquest in *A Warning for Fair Women* and *Two Lamentable Tragedies* bear a striking resemblance to the coroner's jury – a medieval and early modern jury that no longer exists today. The early modern coroner's jury, working in tandem with the coroner, effectively performed the duties of today's medical examiner. They determined the cause of death and collected forensic evidence. Legal historians emphasize that, unlike trial juries, "coroners' juries typically deliberated much more closely to the events in question and may thus have better reflected community concerns."[39] What interests me is how both plays – in the course of staging communal justice – collapse the then-standard distinction between the coroner and his jury.

Legal formularies, justice of the peace manuals, legal glossaries, and other related genres stressed the separation of duties between the coroner, also known as a "conserver of the peace," and his jurors.[40] The office of the coroner was established in 1194. Early coroners "helped in running the county and acted as a check on the sheriff."[41] They were essentially the king's tax collectors. Throughout the medieval and early modern periods, the coroner was also called the crowner because he kept in his safekeeping the rolls containing the pleas of the crown (*custos placitorum corona*) from the time of the discovery of the body to the time of the assize, at which he was obliged to present the pleas to the judges.[42] In theory, every shire was staffed by two coroners; they were chosen, in the words of Sir John Dodderidge, "by the Free-holders of the Shire."[43]

Medieval statutes required that the coroner be a man of significant socio-economic standing – a knight or, failing that, a substantial landowner.[44] Thus, the Statute of Westminster I of 1275 (3 Edw., c. 10) stipulated that "through all Shires sufficient Men shall be chosen to be Coroners, of the most wise and discreet Knights [*leal e plus sages Chivalers*], which know, will, and may best attend upon such Offices, and which lawfully shall attach and present Pleas of the Crown."[45] But the knighthood requirement proved to be an impossible ideal. As R.F. Hunnisett explains, there were simply not enough knights to fill all the vacancies. As a result, by the early fourteenth century, the law had to be amended.[46] Lower-status men could now be appointed coroners.

The downgrading of the coroner's status continued in the sixteenth century. In Edward Aston's translation of Johann Boemus's *The Manners, Lawes, and Customes of All Nations* (1611, originally published in 1520 as *Omnium gentium mores, leges, et ritus*), we learn:

> ... there be ordained in every countie, certaine of the worthiest and wisest sort of Gentlemen, who are called Justices or conservators of the peace; *under whom* high Constables, *Coroners*, petty co[n]stables, headboroughs, and tything-men have every one their severall offices.[47]

This passage indicates that by the early sixteenth century, coroners had become subordinated to JPs. They served "under" the "worthiest ... Gentlemen ... Justices." Sir Thomas Smith echoes that point when he calls the coroner "a meaner sort of gentleman."[48] Likewise, Michael Dalton in *The Countrey Justice* states that "[c]oroners also (by the Common Law) are conservators of the peace, within the County where they be Coroners: but they have power for the keeping of the peace, onely as the Constables have."[49] While the mid-sixteenth-century Marian Committal and Bail Statutes mention the sharing of inquest duties by coroners and JPs – both are "responsible for examining witnesses and liable to the same fines for negligence" – by the end of the sixteenth century, it was the JP who possessed the far greater share of legal authority.[50] According to Matthew Lockwood, early modern "coroners were ... usually of a slightly lower social status than JPs and thus closer in status to the people with whom they interacted."[51] Nonetheless, in spite of the diminishment of the social prestige of the coroner's office, the original spirit of the early medieval statutory requirement that the coroner be a man of noble qualities – that he be elected from the "most wise" men of the neighbourhood – persisted in late Tudor legal literature. In his glossary of law terms, for example, John Rastell informs his readers that the coroner occupies an "[o]ffice of trust and of great authoritie" and that he is "a principall conservator, or keeper of [th]e peace to beare record of [th]e Plees of the crown."[52]

The coroner's most important task was to hold a public inquest involving a jury. According to the Statute of Marlborough (52 Hen. 3, c. 24, 1267), the coroner's jury ought to be composed of all males over the age of twelve residing in the four vills adjacent to the vicinity of the crime.[53] In the fourteenth and fifteenth centuries, the coroner's inquest regularly came to "consist of from twelve to twenty-four men, who were sometimes described as men of the four neighbouring townships"[54] On account of the shortage of available bodies, however, certain men participated as both coroner's jurors and trial jurors. Legal historians have recently taken a strong interest in the agency of the coroner's jury. Sara Butler, for example, argues that the coroner's jurors were "were self-informing 'hearsay witnesses' or 'neighbor-witnesses.'"[55] Likewise, Matthew Lockwood emphasizes that "coroners' jurors were suppliers and seekers of evidence as well as assessors of evidence."[56] This jury was, effectively, a body of lay judges. Holger Schott Syme surmises that the "coroner's inquest ... produced a collective second-level witness statement whose oath-bolstered narrative authority explicitly positioned itself against whatever defence the prisoner could mount."[57] In other words, because the coroner's jury was composed of members of the local community – and, at least in theory, all adult males of the four neighbouring vills – their verdict amounted to a communal judgment against the suspected person even before the individual was tried at the assize.

According to Sir Thomas Smith, the essential difference between the coroner's jury and the trial jury was the former's ability to "goe at large" – to traverse communities – in their "search":

> He [the coroner] doth empanell an enquest of xij men or mo, of those which come next by, be they strangers or inhabitantes, which upon their othes, and by the sight or viewe of the bodie, and by such informations as they can take, must search howe the person slaine came to his death, and by whome as the doer or causer thereof. These are not inclosed into a streit place, (as I tolde before of other enquests) but are suffered to goe at large, and take a day, sometime of xx or xxx daies, more or lesse, as the fact is more evident, or more kept close, to give their evidence, at which day they must appeare there againe before the saide Coroner to give their verdict.[58]

Smith recognizes that the public perception of justice hinges not only on the work of the "knightly" coroner but also on his jury. Smith allows the reader to equate the work of the coroner's jury with the spirit of English justice, wherein communal judgment is equated with judicial transparency and procedural orderliness. Members of the coroner's jury give "their verdict" – a communal judgment – to the coroner. Smith envisions the coroner in the more passive position; he receives the jurors' verdict after they have "take[n] a day, sometime of xx [twenty] or xxx [thirty] daies" to speak with witnesses and gather the evidence. Unlike trial jurors who are "inclosed into a streit place," the coroner's jurors move about freely.

Because the coroner's jury conducts its inquests in an "open" and public space, Smith points out that some people, not knowing any better, believe that the term "coroner" evolved from the official's presentation of the body before a "circle" of people. "Coroner," Smith clarifies, bears no etymological relation to *corona populi*, or a circle (assembly) of people:

> The empanelling of this enquest, and the viewe of the bodie, and the giving of the verdict, is commonly in the streete in an open place, and in *Corona populi*: but I take rather that this name commeth because that the death of everie subject by violence is accounted to touch the crowne of the Prince, and to be a detriment unto it, the Prince accounting that his strength, power, and crowne doth stande and consist in the force of his people, and the maintenaunce of them in securitie and peace.[59]

Smith's explanation, while etymologically sound, found resistance in the wider legal community. Writing in the early seventeenth century, Sir John Dodderidge trots out the same mistaken definition: coroners "are called Coroners or Crowners, as one hath written, because their enquiries ought to be publique,

& in corona populi."[60] The persistence of the "wrong" etymology – even in the works of professionals – speaks to the popular desire to associate community with consensus and justice.[61]

To summarize, sixteenth-century legal texts posited that the office of the coroner was critical to the health of local justice. Though his status had fallen since late medieval times, the early modern coroner retained an aura of moral credibility. He had two main duties: to assemble a coroner's jury and to keep the rolls for the assize. Domestic tragedies like *A Warning for Fair Women* and *Two Lamentable Tragedies* absorb the figure of the "wise" coroner into the collective body of the neighbours.[62] The role of the coroner is assumed by multiple individuals, ordinary folks like the innkeeper Loney, the Watermen, and the yeoman Old John.

This is not to say that the laypeople carry out an effortless investigation. In fact, those in *Two Lamentable Tragedies* initially struggle to narrow the search to Merry's house. Upon discovering a Salter's mark on the bag containing Beech's remains, they question the "Salters man" (sig. G3r), who assures them that he would recognize the woman to whom he sold the bag: "if I saw her I should know her sure" (sig. G3r). Yet when they take the man to Rachel (who was, indeed, the purchaser of the bag), the Salter's man draws a blank. One of the neighbours asks him, "This is not she?" to which the man replies, "No truly." Notwithstanding this failure, the neighbours ultimately solve the case with the help of one of their own, a "maister Cowley." This character befriends Harry Williams, Merry's man.[63] In a previous scene, Merry tells Harry that he has murdered Beech and asks Harry to "conceal" the knowledge; Harry reluctantly agrees: "Ile never utter it, / Assure yourself of that" (sig. C1r). But the secret wears at Harry's conscience. After Master Cowley questions Harry – "Why go you not unto your maisters house?" "Why fell you out? Why did you part so soone?" "What accident begot your mutuall feare?" (sig. H3r–v) – Harry lets slip the truth. Master Cowley urges him to "Confesse the truth unto the officers, / And thou shalt finde the favour of the lawe" (sig. H4r).

In these scenes involving the neighbours, the official distinction between the coroner and the coroner's jury is blurred. No single person directs the inquest: rather, the investigation proceeds through communal action. Various neighbours contribute a clue, a piece of evidence, or, in Master Cowley's case, an interrogator's deft touch to advance the inquest. Medico-legal authority is scattered and decentralized among these minor characters. If we recall that these minor parts would likely have been "played by apprentices and hirelings," as was the Elizabethan repertory norm, then the reversal of orthodox legal authority assumes an even more surprising turn.[64] The gathering of so many bodies onstage, each standing in for a different profession and class, a truly eclectic cast of characters, generates an irrefutable narrative of communal justice. Communal justice bridges social divides – even as the plays make a point of preserving and indeed emphasizing citizens' distinctiveness. In the pursuit of social cohesion, the plays arrange gentlemen, lords, watermen, and neighbours – the people who occupy London's many publics – onstage as one body.

Neighbourly Justice as Neighbourly Care

Two Lamentable Tragedies was likely written in the mid-1590s, possibly in late 1594 or early 1595, in the aftermath of the double murders. This is significant because the 1590s was "the worst decade sixteenth-century Londoners experienced."[65] The year 1594 marked the beginning of the dearth period.[66] While harvest failures had occurred before the 1590s – for example, in the late 1580s – the consecutive harvest failures of 1594, 1595, 1596, and 1597 placed a severe strain on everyday hospitality and neighbourliness.[67] Steve Hindle describes the mid-1590s as a "time of social dislocation" as the culture of Christian hospitality was fractured by food insecurity and interpersonal conflict.[68] The strain on social and economic relations threatened traditional communal (Christian) values such as charity, good fellowship, compassion, and neighbourly love. In London, where the disparity between rich and poor had always been pronounced, the economic pressure would have been felt by those immediately impacted, especially the destitute, as well as those who were precariously balanced between poverty and solvency. Against this backdrop of scarcity and competition, the image of citizen-detectives working together to bring malefactors to account registers as a deeply aspirational fiction.

In this section, I focus on *Two Lamentable Tragedies* because of its more certain date of composition, but my conclusion could be applied to a reading of *A Warning for Fair Women* and other domestic tragedies. Although *Two Lamentable Tragedies* in no way sanctions murder, it takes pains to establish a credible motive for Merry's violence. Merry's fear of losing his livelihood fuels his resentment against Beech. That sense of precarity must have been shared by some in the theatre. The play begins with Merry welcoming Beech and a neighbour to his tavern for a drink. Although the Neighbour praises Merry for brewing the "best" and "strongest beare" "in all this towne," he acknowledges that Londoners have developed a taste for French wine:

> Tis good indeed and I had rather drinke,
> Such beare as this as any Gascoine wine:
> But its our English manner to affect
> Strange things, and price them at a greater rate,
> Then home-bred things of better consequence. (sig. A4r)

The Neighbour declares he would "rather drinke" Merry's locally made beer than "any Gascoine wine," which he associates with "[s]trange things."

He concedes, however, that his is a minority opinion. Others, carried away by fashion, prefer French wine despite its "greater rate" (price) and lesser "consequence" (quality). To this, Merry replies, "if all were of your minde, / My poore estate would sooner be advanc'd: / And our French Marchants seeke some other trade" (sig. A4r). This opening scene quickly yet efficiently situates the play in the context of London's competitive market. By disparaging "[s]trange things" – in the sense of foreign or non-native – the Neighbour evokes an anti-alien discourse and sets up an affective expectation that the third man in the scene, Beech, will speak up in solidarity with them.[69]

But Beech's sympathy is not forthcoming. Instead of commiserating with Merry or participating in the Neighbour's xenophobia, Beech enumerates his blessings:

> Thankes be to God I live contendedlie,
> And yet I cannot boast of mightie wealth:
> But yet Gods blessings have beene infinit,
> And farre beyond my expectations,
> My shop is stor'd, I am not much in debt;
> And here I speake it where I may be bold,
> I have a score of poundes to helpe my neede,
> If God should stretch his hand to visit me,
> With sicknesse, or such like adversity. (sig. A4v).

Beech echoes the words of a dutiful Christian, giving thanks for "Gods blessings" while acknowledging the possibility of a reversal of fortune. Yet in the context of the others' conversation, Beech displays a glaring lack of fellow-feeling. While Merry complains about his "poore estate," Beech congratulates himself on his good fortune. The scene raises a fundamental question about Beech's capacity for compassion. Just what kind of a neighbour is he?

To some in the audience, Beech's reply could have brought to mind the biblical parable of the Pharisee and the Publican. Jesus tells the parable as a warning against self-righteousness (Luke 18:9). In the Temple, the Pharisee "stoode and prayed … God, I thanke thee, that I am not as other men, extortioners, unjust, adulterers, or even as this Publicane. I fast twise in the weeke: I give tithe of all that I possess" (Luke 18:11–12).[70] Meanwhile, the Publican standing to the side "would not lift up so much as his eyes unto heaven: but smote upon his brest, saying, O God, be mercifull to me a sinner" (Luke 18:13).[71] Between the two, Jesus concludes, the Publican "departed to his house justified rather then [sic] the other: for every man that exalteth himselfe, shall be brought lowe, and he that humbleth himselfe shal be exalted" (Luke 18:14).[72] Like the outwardly righteous Pharisee, Beech relishes his good fortune just a little too loudly.

Truth, the chorus-like presenter of the action, insists that only Merry is to be blamed for Beech's murder: his "selfe devouring sinne" drove him to it (sig. K3r). Yet the certainty of that reading is called into question by the Neighbour's report of economic competition and Merry's own sense of financial trouble. Thus, the play encourages its audiences (and readers) to take seriously Merry's fear of destitution. While it is true that Merry is far from poor – he states that he possesses a "pretty house," is aided by his "loving sister" Rachel, and entertains "many guests and honest passengers" – following his conversation with the Neighbour and Beech, he spirals into an existential terror at the prospect of losing it all (sig. A3v). After biding goodbye to Beech and the neighbour, Merry glumly states:

> I cannot buy my beare, my bread, my meates:
> My fagots, coals, and such like necessaries,
> At the best hand, because I want the coine,
> That manie misers coafer up in bagges. (sig. A4v)

In this passage, people are divided into two sorts: those who "want" and those who "coafer up." He associates Beech with the hoarders, the "manie misers" who keep their gold in storage because they have "enough to serve their turnes" (sig. A4v). He imagines Beech to be so much wealthier than him, so much more able to indulge in a life of leisure. In Merry's mind, Beech has the power to buy the best goods. Beech is a chandler by trade – a trader or maker of candles, a commodity for which there will always be demand. In contrast, Merry is a tapster or innkeeper. In the stratified world of London's mercantile society, Beech, a member of a guild, enjoys more economic status and social capital than Merry. Adding insult to injury, in none of the scenes does Beech actually discuss his trade, cementing the impression that he truly does live a carefree and blessed life. The only visible work that Beech does in the opening scene is to drink at Merry's establishment. Merry's tighter circumstances means he must serve, host, and be on the lookout for foreign competitors.[73]

"Orders against Ingrossers"

The initial encounter between Beech and Merry establishes a resemblance between Beech and the much-vilified character of the engrosser. As already mentioned, the 1590s was one of the worst decades in English economic history on account of the "unseasonableness" of the weather – a euphemistic term found in official documents that barely captures the scale of the crisis.[74] Even before the 1590s, the public had witnessed an inexorable "rise in the prices of basic commodities."[75] Wheat, an English staple, doubled in price between 1570 and 1630.[76] To be more exact, in December 1596, 16 per cent of London householders found themselves "in want of relief."[77] Hardship, poverty, and hunger were not limited to London but were widespread in many parts of the country.[78] Evidence of the crisis may be found in Sir William Lambarde's September 1596 jury charge: "[n]ow that we have been a long while together tossed in the waves of war, dearth, and dissension, there is no man so simple but he seeth, no man so safe but he partly feeleth, nor so hard and stony but he sometimes melteth to behold the long train of innumerable evil manners that are stert up and grown by them."[79]

During the crisis of the 1590s, both popular and official literature attacked the figure of the engrosser. The *OED* defines "engrosser" as "one who buys in large quantities, especially with the view of being able to secure a monopoly."[80] In the period in question, however, engrossment was synonymous with food monopoly. For example, in *The Office of the Clerk* (1676), the engrosser is defined as "he that hath bought Corn, Grain, or other Provision of Victual, with intent to sell the same again."[81] A pair of royal proclamations from 1596 shed light on the government's anti-engrossment policy. The first one, issued on 31 July, blames "the sellers of Corne, as rich Farmers, and Ingrossers" for "rais[ing] the prices by colour of the unseasonablenesse of this Sommer." The proclamation orders sheriffs and JPs to "assemble themselves in their places accustomed" and "diligently … peruse the said Orders published" in the previous year.[82] A second proclamation dated 2 November renews the attack on "Ingrossers, Forestallers, and Regraters of Corne." This two-page proclamation takes aim at "rich Owners of corne [who] would keepe their store from common Markets, thereby to increase the prices thereof," and it calls on such "offenders … to be severely punished, to the terror of others" by JPs.[83] The proclamation also reminds "officers … that have … naturall care of their Christian brethren & Countreymen, being in need" to follow the Privy Council's orders, and to warn those "sundry persons of abilitie" who might be thinking of abandoning the countryside for the city – "thereby leaving the reliefe of their poore neighbours, as well for foode, as for good rule" – to remain in place. "Her Majestie chargeth all maner of persons … not to breake up their households, nor to come to the said Citie."[84]

In addition to these public declarations against engrossment, the Privy Council sent harshly worded chastisements to local officeholders for their failure to suppress the "insatiable avarice of some Corn Maisters, that take holde of the late unseasonabless of the Weather":

And therefore, there can be none other reason rendered of this so great an innundatio[n] of evils, saving this only that the Magistrates be more than remisse in the things w[i]thin theire charge, and eyther for sloughte, feare or favour, doe stand w[i]th theire handes in theire Bosome, w[hi]ch ought to be extended for redresse and remedie.[85]

The Privy Council relied on established channels of communication to keep an eye on local operations. In his letter to Lord Burghley dated 25 July 1594, Sir Henry Cocke reports, "[i]t is verie lyke that it will at this time doe verie muche good" if "some order may be sett downe for … the restrayninge of Farmers, Myllers, Bakers, Brewers, & others allso, w[hi]ch contrary to the One Course of lawe doe buye uppe great quantityes of Corne and grayne in the markette."[86] Cocke's second letter, dated 13 September of the same year, discusses the "unseasonable wett weather" and the resulting "verye great losse in this kynde of grayness." He predicts a disaster for the "poore people" in the coming winter for "[m]oney they have verie little and the onely meanes w[hi]ch they have for the obteyninge thereof is by their worke and laboure, and that is very hard to be gotten, and in the winter it wilbe a great deale worse."[87] The letter ends with a familiar distinction between the deserving and undeserving poor.[88]

By October 1594, enterprising printers had begun to enter pamphlets and ballads in the Stationers' Register on the topic of scarcity and dearth. These texts bear titles like "*Newes from JACK BEGGER UNDER THE BUSHE, with the advise of GREGORY GADDESMAN his fellowe begger touchineg the deare prizes of corne and hardnes of this present yere*" (entered on 15 October 1594) and "*The poores lamentac[i]on for the price of corne with GODes [sic] Justice shewed uppon a cruell horder of corne*" (entered on 16 October 1594).[89] The texts do not survive; ballads, especially, were often the first material texts to be recycled.[90] Other texts (also lost) are more indirect in their reference to the crisis. Their titles – "*The poore widowe of Copthall in Kent and her Seaven children how wonderfullie the LORD fed them in their wante*" (entered on 31 October 1594) and "*The poore mans Complaint against the hard world*" (entered on 15 November 1595) – allude to a world defined by hunger, scarcity, and hardship.

The distinction between these licensed texts and those printed illicitly is very likely a function of the degree to which they explicitly discussed the government's efforts at regulating food prices. It was dangerous to speak about the harvest failures. For example, in a letter dated 26 July 1596, Sir Stephen Slany, the mayor of London, informs Lord Burghley and the Council of the confiscation of a satirical ballad by Thomas Deloney, "an idle fellowe," and the arrest of Deloney's printer. According to Slany, the ballad was written in a language "very fond and undecent," and it took the form of a "dialogue" between Queen Elizabeth and her "people" in which the Queen promises to publish the Lord Treasurer's "orders for [th]e remedying of the dearth of corn." The intent of the ballad, Slany surmises, was to stoke popular discontent so that "the poor may aggravate their grief & take occasion of some discontentment."[91] He ends his letter by noting that while he has committed the printer to the Compter (one of London's prisons), he has not been able to find the author.

Between the ravages of time and the Elizabethan censorship apparatus, only a few printed pamphlets addressing the harvest crisis have survived, and these contain messages of self-reliance and Christian charity that more or less restate the status quo. In *Sundrye newe and artificiall Remedies against famine* (1596), the polymathic Sir Hugh Plat offers recipes for making unappealing food palatable. For example, he recommends that one "[b]oile ... beanes, pease, beechmast [nut of beech trees], &c. in faire water, and if they be not yet pleasing inough, change your water againe ... till the taste please you." He also shares the gracious wisdom of the ancients: "good Authors" such as Paracelsus recommended applying a "fresh turfe or clod of earth ... every daie unto the stomach of a man" to "preserve him from famishing for some smal number of daies."[92] The anonymous author of *A Solace for This Hard Season* (1595) offers few remedies but much grievance. In the opening pages, the author laments the sharp rise in the price of corn in a single year and vehemently attacks wealthy "Cornmasters" for their unconscionable hoarding:

> The Corne-master, who hath (and I feare me doth still) hoord up corne to the hindrance of his brethren, should now bring it foorth to further the poore. You know what *Salomon* saith, *He that withdraweth the corne, the people will curse him: but blessing shall be upon the head of him that selleth corne. Pro.* II.26. If you have deserved the curse before, now labour to get the blessing.[93]

Such commentaries build on the official suspicion that certain selfish and greedy individuals, under the guise of prudent stewardship, have exploited communal resources, preyed on the vulnerable, and subverted the government's efforts at crisis management.

The context of dearth and scarcity extends the present analysis of the emotional work of the domestic tragedy. Merry's attack on Beech and his grotesque dismemberment of Beech's corpse enact the discursive violence against the type of person Beech stands for: the engrosser. When Beech announces that he keeps his stock well-"stor'd," he sounds like a hoarder. The proclamation of 2 November 1596 threatened to "severely punish" hoarders and engrossers "to the terror of others" and the anonymous author of *A Solace* intimated that the "people will curse" the engrosser. Merry's destruction of Beech's body literalizes the metaphorical violence inherent in official anti-hoarding literature. Beech's dismembered body recalls the state's punishment of the traitor wherein "his body, lands, goods, posterity, etc. should be torn, pulled asunder, and destroyed, that intended to tear, and destroy the majesty of government."[94] In a fleeting scene, the second Waterman explains that it is the job of the hangman to "set [the] head upon the bridge, and the legs upon the gates" (sig. G1r). Merry applies that ritual of punishment to Beech's remains. Thus, arguably, Merry undertakes the work that the state should be doing, but will not do, because it tolerates engrossers and hoarders in spite of its harsh rhetoric of retribution.

Alive, Beech spent little money and therefore made little positive impact on the local economy; indeed, his habit of keeping his goods "stor'd" implies a negative contribution to the economy – a withholding of coin at a time when the circulation of it was needed. But his death shocks his community into action. Beech's destroyed, dismembered, and desecrated body becomes the site of communal knowledge-making. When the Gentleman and the neighbours reconstitute Beech's body onstage, they form a circle, a *corona populi*. Yet the scene also exceeds the legal parameters of the coroner's inquest. Not only is the corpse forensically examined *within* a circle of the people but it has been assembled *by* the people. Furthermore, the play's metatheatrical addresses to playgoers dilate the impression of a "circle" of people; the spectators who occupy the "round" of the playhouse are welcomed into the circle of lay magistrates onstage. As the fictional lay magistrates busily assemble the clues, gather the forensic evidence, and question the witnesses, they set in motion a narrative of political reformation. By re-forming Beech's body, they also re-form their community. This dramatic spectacle paves over the sense of economic competition with more wholesome neighbourly examples of conscionable magistracy. Through the image of communal initiative, the play resuscitates the doctrine of participatory justice articulated in legal treatises, tantalizing spectators with a triumphant vision of what neighbourly care could look like even as it acknowledges interpersonal conflict and struggle.

Judges of (Aesthetic) Fact

The impression of neighbourly and communal cohesion in domestic tragedy extends beyond the plot. Both *A Warning for Fair Women* and *Two Lamentable Tragedies* use the threshold-breaking opportunity afforded by prologues and choric interludes to actively inscribe audiences into their fantasy of communal justice. A domestic tragedy based on a real-life case of murder is an adaptation in that it dramatizes a story first reported in a murder ballad or pamphlet. Like the modern adaptations that Linda Hutcheon examines, adaptations which "shift" the very "ontology" of a story "from the real to the fictional," a domestic tragedy self-consciously shifts from a presentation of legal facts (typically found in a murder pamphlet) to a representation of imagined conflicts.[95] In between these shifts, the play engenders "knowing" audiences. These are audiences who know the original story and their foreknowledge empowers them to compare what they remember about the case with the dramatic retelling – a hermeneutical game that contains limitless aesthetic pleasures.[96]

In *A Warning for Fair Women* and *Two Lamentable Tragedies*, the game of interpretation is set in motion by the metatheatrical prologue (or induction). Elizabethan prologues acted as "threshold devices" that facilitated a "transition … between the somewhat turbulent world of the playhouse and the equally energized but more focused representational world of the performed play."[97] The induction scenes of both plays do precisely that. In exceptionally forceful ways, they situate their audiences as both judges of legal facts and of dramatic quality. In *A Warning for Fair Women*, Lady Tragedy addresses the audience in the "faire circuite" with the following words: "All you spectators, turne your chearfull eye ... My Sceane is London, native and your owne ... my subject too well knowne" (sig. A3r). Employing a rhetoric of supplication – a standard feature of Elizabethan prologues – she announces that although the "subject [is] too well knowne," patient and forbearing playgoers will be rewarded with a transformative tragic experience (sig. A3r).[98] Likewise, in the induction scene of *Two Lamentable Tragedies*, the presenter Truth notes that many people in the audience are already familiar with the story and the characters: "[t]he most here present know this to be true" (sig. A3r). Toward the end of the play, Truth once more declares that there are some in the audience who have been eyewitnesses to the recent executions of Merry and Rachel at Smithfield: "Your eyes shall witness of their [Merry and Rachel's] shaded tipes, / Which many heere did see perform'd indeed" (sig. I2v). These direct addresses by Lady Tragedy and Truth to their respective audiences celebrate communal memory and witnessing. Drawing on the collective memory of the audience, the presenters of the scene confer forensic authority to "you."

But to be a truly knowing and judicious spectator, the playgoer is also required to feel the fullness of tragic storytelling. Even as Lady Tragedy and Truth call audiences to attention, they also demand playgoers' emotional surrender.[99] In *A Warning for Fair Women*, Lady Tragedy challenges playgoers to deny the transformative power of her art:

> I must have passions that must move the soul,
> Make the heart heavie, and throb within the bosome,
> Extorting teares out of the strictest eyes,
> To racke a thought and straine it to his forme,
> Until I rap the sences [senses] from their course;
> This is my office. (sig. A2v)

Extort, rack, strain, rap. This is the language of affliction and torture. This language is both descriptive and prescriptive. She claims that a tragic play, acted well, has the power to "straine" thought and feeling, to "rap" (or knock) the senses from their normal "course."[100] At the same time, Tragedy tells her audience – especially those less experienced in the ways of the playhouse – how to feel about the play they are about to see. Emotional ambivalence is not an option. "I must have passions that must move the soul," she declares.

Lady Tragedy's speech foregrounds a bold claim about the rightful place of tragic drama in a post-Reformation spiritual economy. Early modern Protestants embraced strong emotions. As Alec Ryrie explains, what Protestants feared was "dullness, hardness, heaviness, dryness, coldness, drowsiness, or deadness" – a *lack* of feeling.[101] The godly associated powerful emotions like fear and sorrow with the workings of conscience. This is the important religious context behind Lady Tragedy's speech. In essence, her statement places drama on the same level as devotional texts; both quicken godly feelings. The playwright revisits the idea of his genre's spiritual potential toward the end of the play. As the plot winds down, a member of the community, the civilian Master James, whose measured speech and pious nature mark him as an exemplary figure, steps forward as a judge of both forensic and aesthetic fact.

The scene in question comes after the arrest of George Browne. Having failed to elude his searchers, Browne is detained and brought into the presence of the victim, John Beane. In an aside, Browne worries that his victim's "very eies will speake … And will accuse me" (sig. H1v). Sure enough, Beane awakens and accuses Browne with the following words: "this is he that murdred me and M. Sanders" (sig. H1v). (Following this accusation, Browne is led away by the officers.) Having eyewitnessed this "wondrous worke of God" (sig. H1v), Master James, Master Barnes, and the Mayor of Rochester begin to place the shocking turn of events within a larger pattern of providentialism.[102] "In the case of blood," Master James muses, "Gods justice hath bin stil miraculous" (sig. H2r). Taking turns, each man tells a story of the miraculous discovery of murder, culminating in Master James's story of a woman at King's Lynn who confesses to the murder of her husband upon seeing a domestic tragedy:

> Ile tell you (sir) one more to quite your tale,
> A woman that had made away her husband,
> And sitting to behold a tragedy
> At Linne [King's Lynn] a town in Norffolke,
> Acted by Players travelling that way,
> Wherein a woman that had murtherd hers
> Was ever haunted with her husbands ghost:
> The passion written by a feeling pen,
> And acted by a good Tragedian,
> She was so mooved with the sight thereof,
> As she cryed out, the Play was made by her,
> And openly confesst her husbands murder. (sig. H2r)

The play in question was almost certainly Thomas Heywood's *Friar Francis*, a lost play.[103] Master James's story asserts the forensic and aesthetic power of theater. Domestic tragedy functions as a moral-legal instrument, not unlike a sermon, which pricks at the conscience of its audiences. In its true-to-life depiction of the crimes committed by ordinary people (characters that closely resemble the audience in dress, action, and speech), a domestic tragedy momentarily erases the audience's sense of fiction and reality. This confusion is catastrophic for those who harbour or try to suppress guilt – as proven by the example of the woman at King's Lynn. In its ability to "moov[e]" playgoers "with the sight thereof," even to self-incrimination, the domestic tragedy exceeds the law in its ability to unravel deeply buried secrets. Theatre possesses what Ellen MacKay calls a "persecutorial poetics" that shreds the composure of the guilty, leaving them exposed to the judging eyes of the community.[104] There is a great deal more to say about the importance of Master James's speech and its place in a history of Renaissance tragic poetics. Hamlet's decision to use a play "to catch the conscience of the King" may have been directly inspired by *A Warning for Fair Women*.[105] And both texts may have been on Thomas Rymer's mind when he theorized the concept of poetic justice: "Poetry discover'd crimes, the Law could never find out; and punish'd those the Law had acquitted."[106] What matters for the present discussion is that in assigning this speech about the power of theatre to a lay magistrate, our anonymous playwright celebrates the lay magistrate's capacity for both legal and aesthetic judgment and the audience is part of that celebration.

The stage direction in *Two Lamentable Tragedies* emphasizes that it is the "groaning" of the boy Winchester that triggers a maid's "crye." This is a moment of sensational and affective drama. One character echoes the verbalized pain of another, amplifying perhaps the spectator's own experience of intense empathy as he or she bears witness to the suffering of the boy. These moments of recognition and empathy soften the hearts of audiences toward godly reform. Toward the end of *Two Lamentable Tragedies*, Truth affirms audiences' tragic emotions: "I see your sorrowes flowe up to the brim / And overflowe your cheeks with the brinish teares" (sig. E2v). This is an explicit challenge to the authority of magistrates. Instead of a judge occupying the centre of the legal-cosmic order, it is the tragic playwright, the actor, and the playgoer.

Conclusion

In *Two Lamentable Tragedies* and *A Warning for Fair Women*, communities – comprising townsmen, merchants, yeomen, labourers, and servants – demonstrate a striking capacity for investigation and detection. By vividly enacting communal justice, the plays affirm citizens' participation in the legal order. In this respect, the plays could be said to be intervening in the institutional narrative of the law. To audiences of the 1590s, to those who grappled with economic instability, rapid urbanization, price inflation, and acute immiseration, such narratives would surely have held appeal. In the plays, the victims' neighbours, acting as "first finders," not only raise hue and cry but also conduct the coroner's inquest, leading to the suspecting and arresting of the murderers and their accomplices. Legal officials appear, but always at the margins. The main action of neighbours hurrying to and from the scene of the crime conjures an indelible image of participatory justice. The play presents a legality built on an idea of communal justice at the precise moment when a feeling of community is threatened by acute dearth and competition. Both plays stage participatory justice, and in so doing they offer an idealized image of society as it might have been, not as it was.

A Warning for Fair Women and *Two Lamentable Tragedies* show that drama can do the work of not only modelling communal justice but also of helping audiences to shape the meaning of it within the communal present that theatrical performance makes possible. Audiences are invited to be co-authors of legal knowledge. The invitation to collaborate directly challenges the logic of professionalization, which insists on a hierarchy of legal authority and a storehouse of legal knowledge passed down from one generation of the law's "professors" to another. The drama of communal justice was long-lasting not simply because it was enforced by legal praxis. It endured because it was embedded in the public imagination. Domestic tragedy fortified this exercise of the imagination. Being an adaptation in more ways than one, domestic tragedy straddled two distinctive ontologies, "the real" and "the fictional," and it used a variety of representational strategies to create a frictionless transition between the two states of being.[107] It trusted audiences to be committed to the fiction. Just as audiences needed to see the fleshy body of the victim in a mannequin, so they had to make a similar leap of faith in seeing the triumph of communal justice. Domestic tragedy recognized that communal justice was not just a legal practice forced upon the people by magistrates, but a fiction whose persuasiveness rested in the eyes of the public.

Chapter Four

Repairing Community: Empathetic Witnessing in *King Lear*

"Witnessing" and "testimony" describe different aspects of seeing. In law, testimony is synonymous with evidence. The word derives from the Latin *testimonium*, which refers to the "evidence of a witness or witnesses; evidence given by a witness, under oath or affirmation."[1] Law courts in Shakespeare's England recognized two forms of testimony: the deposition, taken of witnesses by a justice of the peace or a coroner before the trial and delivered at a session or an assize, and the *viva voce* report spoken in person by the witness in open court. Lawyers and judges silently treated the voices contained in depositions as evidence of real "presence."[2] While depositions were generally accepted by legal practitioners, they were viewed with suspicion by those untrained in the law. Laypeople placed greater value on the oral delivery of evidence. J.H. Baker points out that while the practice of reading depositions to a jury was becoming increasingly the standard in Tudor England, "it does seem to have been an accepted principle that testimony *ought normally* to be given in person in the presence of the accused."[3] Popular demand for oral testimony reflected centuries of juristic investment in accusatory justice. As Jamie K. Taylor explains, medieval canonists insisted that "witnesses offering vocal testimony were the best mode of proof, better than … written documents."[4] Sara M. Butler agrees, noting that fourteenth-century forensic investigators believed that "oral testimony garnered a confidence that written documents could not evoke."[5]

Because testimony is a form of legal storytelling, it has been and continues to be a speech act that privileges the seeing "I." In many modern courts, for example, a witness is asked to share their "personal knowledge" of the facts. Rule 602 of the United States Federal Rules of Evidence stipulates, "[a] witness may testify to a matter only if evidence is introduced sufficient to support a finding that the witness has personal knowledge of the matter."[6] The emphasis on the individual's "personal knowledge" is echoed in the form of the court's question to the witness: "do *you* swear to tell the truth, the whole truth, and nothing but the truth?" to which the witness is expected to affirm, "*I do*."[7]

In contrast to the egocentrism of testimony, "witnessing" – which derives from the Old English word *witan*, meaning "to wit, know, have knowledge, be aware"[8] – presumes the presence of a communal "we." The linking of witnessing with community came about through the Christian rewriting of the Greek concept of the "witness." The English word "martyr" is a loan word from the Greek noun *martyr* (μάρτυς), which is chiefly a forensic term to describe a legal witness. The Greek verb *martyromai* means "to be a witness to."[9] In the classical Greek literature of Aeschylus, Sophocles, and Plato, for example, *martyr* was used in the forensic sense to refer to a witness in a legal case. By the tenth century, after Christianity had become solidly established in England, "martyr" came to be thought of in the religious sense of "a person who chooses to suffer death than renounce faith in Christ."[10] The religious martyr bears witness to a transcendent, spiritual truth – an act accomplished before a crowd of beholders. Over time, "martyr" and "witness" became interchangeable through repeated usage by English Christian communities. Early modern texts reflected that usage. In *Leviathan*, for example, Thomas Hobbes writes, "nor is it the Death of the Witnesse, but the Testimony itself that makes the Martyr: for the word signifieth nothing else, but the man that beareth Witnesse."[11] Today, the sense of a witness as a religious martyr has largely faded from popular usage.[12] Yet in medieval and early modern England, witnessing was commonly linked with martyrdom – and martyrdom, in turn, evoked images of bystanders and spectators who communally witnessed the martyr's self-sacrifice for their religious truth. Numerous medieval and early modern texts bear the stamp of what Jamie K. Taylor calls the "logic of communal witnessing."[13]

This chapter explores the logic of communal witnessing through John Foxe's *Acts and Monuments* (1563) and Shakespeare's *King Lear* (1606). Both texts depict communal witnessing as catalysts for political repair. Foxe's *Acts and Monuments*, popularly known as *The Book of Martyrs*, was styled at the time of its publication as a history of the persecution of Protestants from the time of the early church to the reign of Mary I and Philip II. Second only to the Bible in importance in the Elizabethan era,[14] Foxe's massive Protestant hagiography gave common readers stories that reflected the role of local communities (and the friendship networks within those communities) in reforming a political and religious polity.[15] The book contoured the English literary imagination in ways that we are still only beginning to understand despite decades of intensive study. Recently, building on Richard Strier's influential analysis of conscientious non-obedience in *King Lear* and Protestant resistance theory, John D. Staines and David K. Anderson persuasively argue that just as Foxe's text repeatedly emphasizes the illegality of the Catholic church and state (under Mary I and Philip II) to persecute Protestants, so *King Lear* depicts the tyranny of unchecked state authority and stages scenes of communal witnessing in order to strengthen audiences' capacity for what Staines calls "radical pity" and what Anderson calls "proper recognition," both of which have the power to disrupt the state's ability to obliterate the humanity of the persecuted subject.[16]

This chapter picks up where these scholars have left off by using Foxe's depiction of communal witnessing to illuminate Shakespeare's writing of testimony and witnessing in *King Lear*. I agree that Shakespeare's scenes of witnessing – true and false, embodied and imagined – unmistakably bear the Foxean stamp. But I also suggest that the play's debt to Foxe only goes so far. Because *King Lear* was composed for the stage, by definition it exceeds Foxe's prose narrative in its complex exploration of the relationship between what I call *embodied* witnessing and *imagined* witnessing. The First Servant's eyewitnessing of Gloucester's torture by the sadistic Duke of Cornwall is an example of embodied witnessing. Edgar's use of vivid description (or *enargeia*) to conjure up both images and feelings of the communal for the now blind Gloucester in the Dover cliff scene is an example of imagined witnessing. The Dover cliff scene, which will be discussed in the final section of this chapter, reveals what it means to simultaneously "see with" and "see for" the other. In *A Midsummer Night's Dream*, Duke Theseus muses that "imagination bodies forth / The forms of things unknown."[17] Many characters in *King Lear*, like the poet in Theseus's account, use their imagination to invent novel states of being and feeling. The back-and-forth cuts between scenes of embodied and imagined witnessing reinforce the overall idea that communal witnessing brings about spiritual and political renewal. In this way, the very conditions of participatory theatre – the audience's participation in these scenes of communal witnessing – deepen the promise of participatory justice.

Communal Witnessing in Foxe's *Acts and Monuments*

First published in English in 1563, just five years after the ascension of Elizabeth I, Foxe's *Acts and Monuments* chronicles the suffering of the "godly" from the time of the early Christian church to the reign of Mary I and Philip II.[18] On 20 January 1555, Mary I and Philip II passed the statute against heresy (1 & 2 Phil. & M., c. 6, "An Acte for the renueng of three Estatutes made for the punishement of Heresies"), leading to the arrest and execution of hundreds of Protestant subjects.[19] In *Acts and Monuments*, legislative documents appear alongside transcriptions of heresy trials; such a formal arrangement illustrates the impact of heresy legislation on English communities. The stories in Foxe's book follow a predictable pattern: adhering to their conscience, or the "law of the heart," the martyrs break traditional bonds that define family and social relations to find solace and comfort among their co-religionists.[20] New communities, sparked into existence by witnessing, contest old ones. A communal logic of witnessing – spiritually feeling with the martyr and acting on those feelings through political action – is repeatedly featured in the text.

Foxe enumerates the suffering of individual martyrs as well as records the emotions experienced by those who witnessed the burnings or heard about them days or months later. Documenting the collective response was a political necessity. He and his collaborators needed to prove to both the English at home and Catholic detractors abroad that English Protestantism was a popular movement embraced by all people at all levels of society.[21] Thus, he opens his book with a roll call of the persecuted:

> ... men and wemen, both old, yonge, chyldren, infantes, new borne, maryed, unmaryed, wyves, wydowes, maydes, blynde men, lame men, whole men, *of all sortes, of al ages, of al degrees*. Lordes, Knightes, Gentlemen, Lawyers, Merchauntes, Archbishops, Bishops, Priestes, Ministers, Deacons, Lay men, Artificers, yea whole householdes, and whole kyndredes together, Father, Mother and Daughter, Grandmother, Mother, Aunt, and Chylde. &c. (Foxe [1563] 12, my emphasis)

The book mostly lived up to its ambitious promise.[22] Examinations of poor labourers – such as the illiterate colporteur Elizabeth Young, who defied authorities by smuggling and distributing Protestant polemics – occupy the same textual space as those of elites, such as Lady Jane Grey and archbishop Thomas Cranmer.[23] In its inclusivity with respect to the "godly" community, the text delivers on the radical promise of the Reformation: conscience creates a fellowship of believers. Conscience, combined with faith, obviates the need for priestly mediation between the believer and God.

Heresy Detection and Legal Testimony

While technically a spiritual crime, heresy detection exploited the well-established system of criminal justice that operated by local or communal participation. As discussed in chapter 1, medieval kings established a nested system of legal administration by dividing the realm into shires, shires into hundreds, and hundreds into vills. From hue and cry to pretrial inquests to the jury trial, English criminal law relied on communal participation. Heresy detection depended on the same network of state and local policing. In theory, heresy detection fell under the jurisdiction of ecclesiastical officials. In practice, however, it was jointly pursued by church and temporal authorities.[24] Religious authorities, forbidden to participate in the execution of heretics, acted as interrogators and jailors. Upon finding the defendant "obdurate" or "stubborn" (terms that signified the defendant's refusal to recant despite multiple offers of clemency), church officials transferred the prisoner to the secular authorities for punishment. The Marian Bail and Committal Statutes "stipulated that justices of the peace should examine suspects and witnesses, transcribe their testimony, and certify the record to the trial court."[25] While justices of the peaces' examinations could not be used as evidence at trials – a point that John H. Langbein makes clear when he observes that while "genuine deposition evidence ... was preserved ... JPs' examinations were not"[26] – the expansion of the JPs' responsibilities meant that they were forced to be heresy detectors. Ralph Houlbrooke estimates that "nearly 60 per cent of the arrests described in Foxe's account were due to the initiatives of justices of the peace and constables."[27] Local church and state authorities (including lay legal officers) collaborated to root out heresy in their respective communities.

Local authorities such as JPs depended on the community – neighbours and family members – to inform on and expose suspected heretics. But the same intimate betrayals that fuelled heresy persecution – the willingness of neighbours and, in some cases, family members, to observe, eavesdrop, and spy on each other – could just as quickly be reversed. The case of Joyce Lewes of Lichfield offers a particularly salient (and understudied) example of communal witnessing.[28] Women like Lewes did not often travel beyond their immediate communities. They had limited contact with the politically active London-based evangelicals. Their stories illuminate the affective nature of testimony and witnessing.

Foxe introduces Lewes as a "ge[n]tle woma[n] ... delicatly brought up in the pleasurs of the world" (Foxe [1563] 1700) who converts to Protestantism after she learns of the execution of the Protestant Laurence Saunders (figure 7). (His story is notable for its gruesomeness: officials had built Saunders's pyre with green wood, which needlessly prolonged his suffering at the stake.) When Lewes "heard of the burning of that most godly & learned maister Laurence Sanders," she "begonne to take more hede to the matter" (Foxe [1563] 1700). John Glover, a neighbour, "dilige[n]tly instructed her in the ways of the Lord" (Foxe [1563] 1700).[29] "And because she had learned the masse to be evil & abhominable, she began to hate it ... whe[n] the holy water was cast, she turned her back towards it, and shewed her self to be displeased with their blasphemous holy water" (ibid.).

Initially, Lewes's husband tries to protect her from the local authorities. When the bishop's apparitor delivers a "Citatio[n]" to the husband following her public rejection of mass, her husband in "a[n]ger ... se[t] a dagger to his hart," forcing the man to eat the document.[30] Yet the husband's loyalty wanes when Lewes refuses to abandon her newfound faith. In the end, it is he who delivers her to the bishop's house because "he would not lose or forfet anye

The burnyng of Laurence Saunders.

Figure 7. John Foxe, *Acts and Monuments* (1563), sig. BBB2v, detail. Laurence
Saunders is executed before a large crowd of witnesses.
The Huntington Library (RB 59840).

thinge for her sake." In an editorial aside, Foxe tersely comments that this
man was "lyke a murtherer of his own wife" (ibid.). The husband's transformation from his wife's protector to her betrayer, from a dagger-wielding
paterfamilias to an English Judas choosing material rewards over his conscience, illustrates the unpredictable nature of shifting loyalties in a single
household.

Foxe's description of the husband's actions takes up a paragraph in the original text. The narrative focuses on Lewes's experiences, her imprisonment, and
her eventual execution. In prison, Lewes welcomes a steady stream of "frendes"
who give her spiritual "co[m]fort" (Foxe [1563] 1701). According to the *OED*,
"friend in Christian use with reference to God or Christ" means "a comforter
or supporter."[31] Lewes's friends, then, demonstrate their spiritual kinship with
her by maintaining former practices of neighbourliness: paying her visits and
engaging her in conversation. These friends support her to the last. On the day
of her execution:

> When she was brought through the town ... a great multitude of people beinge
> present, she beyng led by her frendes (of the which M. Michael Renigar was one) ...
> the place was farre of, and the throng of the people great ... she ... prayed th[e]re
> several times ... the moste part of the people cried Amen, yea, even the sherife that
> stode hard by her. (Foxe [1563] 1701)[32]

Foxe describes a remarkable scene. Lewes, in her final moments, performs an
ad hoc religious service for the townspeople. She gets the townspeople to cry
"amen," thereby usurping the power of the priest; she also inspires them to participate in her version of a holy communion.[33] As Foxe tells it:

> ... she toke the cup into her hands, saying. I drinke to all them that unfainedly
> love the gospell ... when she had dronken, they that were her frendes, dranke also.
> After that a great nomber, especially the weome[n] of the town, did drinke with
> her ... When she was tied to the stake with the chayn, she shewed such a chere-
> fulnes that it passed mans reason, being so well colored in her face, & so pacient,
> that the most part of them that had honest hartes did lament, and even with teares
> bewayle the tyranny of the papistes. (Foxe [1563] 1701)[34]

Gender plays a role in the transmission of religious feeling. Those who drink
the most heartily are the "weome[n] of the town." By raising their cups to Lewes,
the townspeople – without verbally incriminating themselves – signal their fellowship with her. Foxe draws the reader's attention to the crowd's extraordinary
size: "a great multitude of people," "the throng of the people great," "the moste
part of the people," "a great nomber, especially the weome[n]," "the most part of
them" (Foxe [1563] 1701). The repetition here recalls his roll call in the preface
of the book.

The state's attempt at shock and awe backfires. Instead of deterring the community, the execution of Lewes emboldens it to act as a collective witness,
to claim her as its spiritual leader. Gilles Deleuze and Félix Guattari theorize
that "weapons are affects and affects weapons," wherein "affect is the active
discharge of emotion."[35] In this story, we find a historical instance of weapon-
ized affect. Just as St. Paul praised fellow-feeling – "Rejoice with them that do
rejoice, and weep with them that weep" (Rom. 12:15) – so the townspeople
weep for Joyce Lewes.[36] Foxe describes Lewes in her final moments as exhibit-
ing "such a cherefulnes that it passed mans reason, being so well colored in
her face, & so pacient, that the most part of them that had honest hartes did
lament, and even with teares bewayle the tyranny of the papistes" (Foxe [1563]
1702).[37] The emotions of these witnesses – horror, pity, anger, fear – are "dis-
charged" into the communal space. The spectacle of her execution produces
a cascade of intersubjectivity that destabilizes traditional bonds of loyalty and
fealty.[38]

Lewes's initial witnessing occurred in her mind's eye – in the place of her imagination – outside of the jurisdiction of the authorities. A report of Saunders's agonizing death stirred her conscience. She was not there, in Coventry, on the day of his execution, and yet she placed herself there retroactively using her imagination. As the account of Saunders's execution worked on her mind, Lewes cast off her former political and religious affiliations and embraced those espoused by the martyred Saunders. Her shunning of Catholic ceremonies, and her courage in the face of imprisonment and execution, in turn inspired a communal rejection of the status quo. These mysterious, affective processes of empathetic witnessing find a powerful dramatic response in *King Lear*.

Testimony and Witnessing in *King Lear*

Readers of *King Lear* are often struck by the number of words pertaining to eyes, sight, and seeing. Indeed, the word "see" occurs over forty times in the folio.[39] In the early and mid-twentieth century, critics interpreted the proliferation of sight-related words as a manifestation of the moral confusion or "blindness" of Lear.[40] From the moment that Lear ignores Kent's warning to "see better" and to "let me still remain / The true blank of thine eye" (1.1.156), Lear marks himself as one who suffers from emotional and political blindness.[41] Fearing diminishment, both Lear and Gloucester fall prey to the emotional manipulation of their children. When Regan comments that Lear "hath ever but slenderly known himself" (1.1.290–1), it is difficult not to agree. The characters themselves anticipate such scrutiny. As the fourth act draws to a close, Lear asks forgiveness of Cordelia and acknowledges that he has grown "old / and foolish" (4.6.76–7). Gloucester, too, admits, "I stumbled when I saw" (4.1.19).

While the play's repeated allusions to seeing and sight have generated enduring readings about the importance of *anagnorisis* (recognition) and acknowledgment, less attention has been paid to seeing as witnessing. The many references to eyes and seeing foreground the dynamic of witnessing, both in the legal sense of giving testimony and in the spiritual sense of bearing witness to one's faith. Whereas testimony plays a role in destroying familial and social relations, witnessing becomes the basis by which political regeneration occurs. Like a pair of Old Testament patriarchs who rashly cast off their devoted children, Lear and Gloucester perform parallel acts of disinheritance and banishment against Cordelia and Edgar based on the false testimony of their other children.[42] Shakespeare complicates the biblical parallelism, however, by layering the narrative with early modern concepts of testimony and magistracy. As their initial decisions bear out, both fathers contaminate the protocols surrounding testimony. For their mishandling of magistracy, Lear and Gloucester find themselves abused *by* the law. Stripped of legal protections, they suffer physical and psychological abuse at the hands of the Duke of Cornwall, Goneril, and Regan.

False Testimony

Lear abuses his sovereign and legal powers in the opening scene when he puts his daughters through a trial-like contest. Lear declares, "'tis our fast intent / To shake all cares and business from our age, / Conferring them on younger strengths" (1.1.37–9). "Conferring" is a legal term that means to "grant" a title to someone, and the word establishes the trial-like conditions of the occasion: the daughters are required to plead for their patrimony. Lyrical phrases such as "shadowy forests," "champaigns riched," "plenteous rivers," and "wide-skirted meads" (1.1.63) inadequately hide the troubling logic of Lear's desire to convert a child's love for a parent into something that could be quantified, mapped – and once mapped, divided. Goneril and Regan agree to Lear's terms. Each offers an account of feelings beyond not just what she feels, but beyond what anyone can feel. The kind of love-testimony that they correctly perceive that Lear desires to hear traffics in the realm of poetic hyperbole. It is a love that, to quote Goneril, "makes breath poor and speech unable" (1.1.59).

The opening scene thus establishes a crisis of magistracy as Lear fails to distinguish truth from fiction. A second instance of failed judgment occurs in Gloucester's treatment of Edgar. In the entirety of the play, the word "testimony" appears only once – in Edmund's speech to Gloucester in which he convinces his father to withhold his judgment against Edgar until he has stronger proof of his brother's villainy:

> If it shall please you to suspend your indignation against my brother till you can derive from him better *testimony* of his intent, you should run a certain course; where, if you violently proceed against him, mistaking his purpose, it would make a great gap in your own honour and shake in pieces the heart of his obedience. (1.2.75–81, my emphasis)

Edmund's evocation of "better testimony" is, needless to say, disingenuous. He speaks of "testimony" in the very process of hollowing it out of its rightful meaning. Gloucester is too enraged by Edmund's story to reflect on the flimsiness of the evidence. Edmund has masterfully manipulated his father's emotions by reminding him of his age: "I have heard him [Edgar] oft maintain it to be fit that, sons at perfect age and fathers declined, the father should be as ward to the son, and the son manage his revenue" (1.2.67–70). At the same time, Edmund exploits his father's inflated sense of authority by convincing

Gloucester that he is indeed the decision-maker. In that passage quoted above, not only does Edmund evoke "you" and "your" six times, a repetition that positions Gloucester as the magistrate, but he also assures his father that he will soon come in possession of "auricular assurance" of Edgar's treason (1.2.86). Throughout, Edmund highlights Gloucester's personal judgment: "If your honor judge it meet, I will place you where you shall hear us confer of this" (1.2.85–6).

Lear's trial of his daughters introduces the theme of botched judgment; Gloucester's hasty and procedurally flawed conviction of Edgar amplifies that theme.[43] Initially, Gloucester agrees to withhold his judgment until he comes to possess more substantive proof. He consents to Edmund's suggestion that he wait in concealment. But upon hearing details of the plot, Gloucester cries, "O villain, villain, his very opinion in the letter. Abhorred villain, unnatural, detested, brutish villain – worse than brutish" (1.2.71–3). "Abhorred" comes from the Latin "ab" (away from) and "*horrēre*" (to bristle, to shudder). The word could also be heard as "ab-whored." "Whore" derives from the Old English "*hóre*," meaning a harlot, prostitute, or adulterer.[44] In describing Edgar as "[a]bhorred," Gloucester verbally diminishes and disinherits Edgar, marking him unworthy of his name and estate. The language of abuse (and disinheritance) signals that Gloucester has already decided against Edgar, proof or no proof, and has found him guilty based on a verbal report and a letter, both produced by Edmund – a single witness. Thus, while the scene permits audiences to feel some sympathy for Gloucester – how could he have suspected his meekly obedient younger son? – it also positions audiences to critically assess Gloucester and to fault him on the basis of his mishandling of forensic evidence.

Parricide and the Two-Witness Rule

The proof that Edmund manufactures (a forged letter, a report of a conversation, and, finally, a struggle in the dark) is weak by early modern evidentiary standards.[45] Edmund has essentially accused his brother of a conspiracy to commit parricide. English common law prosecuted parricide "under regular homicide law" although jurists were sensitive to the Roman tradition of treating parricide as a special category of murder.[46] Lawyers debated the question of whether parricide was a species of petty treason. Some resisted the equivalency; Ferdinando Pulton "noted that 'the Treason should be in respect of the duty of service broken, and not of duty of nature violated.'"[47] Others, like Michael Dalton, insisted that parricide was a form of petty treason; for Dalton, it was a "[t]reason in the child, in respect of the duty of nature violated."[48] This was closer to the popular legal understanding of parricide. Edmund calls his brother's transgression an "unnatural purpose" hated by the "revenging

gods" (2.1.49, 44). In *An/The Old Law*, a play attributed to Thomas Middleton and William Rowley (later revised by Thomas Heywood), a mash-up of
Sophocles's *Antigone*, Shakespeare's *Measure for Measure*, and Plato's *Cratylus*,
the good son Cleanthes accuses his avaricious brother Simonides of parricide,
calling the offence one of the "[t]he heaviest crimes that ever made up / Unnatu-
ralness in humanity."[49]

Because of the heinous nature of the crime (premeditated parricide) of
which Edgar stands accused, Gloucester should have applied a higher evidentiary standard. According to both legal theory and custom, Gloucester
should have tried to find at least two credible witnesses before condemning
his son. Both English common and civil law recognized the validity of the
two-witness rule, also known as *testis unus, testis nullus*.[50] The two-witness
rule derived from Deuteronomy 19:15: "the mouth of two witnesses or at
[th]e mouth of three witnesses, shall the matter bee [e]stablished."[51] In cases
of treason and petty treason, Tudor statutes required the testimony of two
lawful witnesses:

> no p[er]son ... shalbe endited arrayned condempned convicted or attaynted for
> any of the Treasons or offenc[es] aforesaide ... unlesse the same Offendor or
> Offendors be thereof accused by two laufull accusars, w[hi]ch said Accusars ...
> yf they be then livinge, shalbe brought in p[er]son before the partie soe accused,
> and avowe and maynteyne that they have to saye against the saide partie to prove
> him giltie of the Treasons or offenc[es] conteyned in the bill of Inditement layed
> againste the Partie arrayned.[52]

This is commensurate with continental norms. As Andrea Frisch explains,
across European jurisdictions, legal witnesses were summoned "at the minimum in pairs, if not in even larger groups" because of magistrates' adherence
to "the repeated citation in the Middle Ages and Renaissance of the Old Testament Book of Deuteronomy's prohibition on the testimony of a lone witness,
together with its Roman analogue (*testis unus, testis nullus*)."[53] Although not
without exceptions, convictions of treason in the sixteenth century did (in general) require the testimony of two corroborating and sworn witnesses.[54] The
requirement was standardized, once and for all, during the reign of William III
with the passing of 7 & 8 Wil. 3, c. 3 (1695–6).[55] It is highly likely that Shakespeare's audiences were aware of the rule – and its purpose in cases of treason –
from their legal experience with the law. This was, after all, a generation that
had a front-row seat to a series of highly publicized treason trials.[56] It is equally
likely that those unfamiliar with the statutory requirement remembered the
rule from the Bible, which mentions the rule in several places.[57] And, finally, it is
worth pointing out that the two-witness rule was not limited to treason. Lesser
crimes required two or more witnesses to arraign and convict. For example, in

his personal copy of *Vade Mecum*, a justicing manual, Thomas Birch notes that "two witnesses" were needed to convict anyone caught "hawk[ing] between the first of *July*, and last of *August*" according to "7. Jac. I. 1."[58]

In medieval and early modern England, the two-witness rule was related to another important legal concept: infamy or *fama publica*. *Fama* "served the function 'probable cause' does in modern criminal law, or (perhaps more accurately) the function a grand jury presentment served in the early common law," and it was "both a means of initiating a criminal trial and a protection against abusive prosecution."[59] To establish a person's infamy, a "sufficient number of people, not just a small group" had to be found to hold the same opinion; these community members "must have been creditable persons, not *ribaldi*, habitual perjurers, or persons of no credit in the community."[60] This practice had an antecedent in the early English "notion of the '*tihtbysig* man,' the untrustworthy man of bad repute."[61]

The two-witness rule existed to protect the rights of the accused, to prevent a *ribaldus* from gaining the upper hand. The harm done to Edgar affirms – in a roundabout way – the necessity of procedural safeguards against false conviction. In light of this context, Gloucester's failure to hold Edmund's evidence to the established evidentiary standard becomes glaringly obvious. Edgar is twice victimized – by his brother, who accuses him falsely, and by his father, who denies him due process. Had Gloucester followed the standard legal practice, would he have been spared his ensuing grief? Had he shared his suspicion with the wider community – as legal protocol dictated – would he have come to a different conclusion about his son?[62] These are some of the questions that the play raises. To be clear, I am not arguing that the play straightforwardly endorses the two-witness rule or the common law's reliance on local knowledge. Instead, I suggest that the play actively involves audiences in the unfolding legal drama by giving them the opportunity to use their own legal and religious knowledge (and their practical experience with the law) to examine and assess Gloucester's instinct for magistracy.

Shakespeare was interested in the dramatic potential of staging the two-witness rule from the outset of his career. Some of his plays test the validity of the rule. In *Much Ado about Nothing*, the rule is maliciously misused by Don John to slander Hero. "I will disparage her no farther till you [Claudio and Don Pedro] are my witnesses," Don John declares, before positioning them as eye-witnesses to her supposed sexual transgression.[63] In *Othello*, the rule is implicit in Othello's demand to see the "ocular proof"; Iago places him as a second eye-witness to Desdemona's supposed infidelity.[64] But other plays, like *King Lear*, affirm its existence. Confused by false testimony, Lear and Gloucester banish the truth-speakers and raise perjurers to positions of power, thus introducing chaos into their households and, by extension, into the realm. Yet their actions also set in motion new forms of political consciousness and organization. Like iron filings aligning around a powerful magnetic field, characters begin to arrange themselves around a common desire for justice. For some characters, like the Duke of Albany, that justice is framed in the language of divine retribution. For others, such as the Servants (First, Second, and Third of the quarto *King Lear*), justice is as conscience dictates. In the second half of the play, scenes of false legal testimony, proven to be so destructive to the community, are replaced by scenes of communal witnessing in which characters bear witness to each other's suffering.

Witnessing and Empathy

The web of witnessing begins in the play's electrifying third act when Lear, staggering between madness and lucidity, takes notice of "poor naked wretches." Throughout the scene, Lear shifts between states of sympathy (pity for) and empathy (feeling with). In distinguishing empathy from sympathy, I follow Suzanne Keen who defines "empathy" as "a spontaneous sharing of feelings, including physical sensations in the body, provoked by witnessing or hearing about another's condition." Keen observes that "most people ... can recall times when they felt *with* another (as opposed to feeling *for* another, or sympathy)."[65] In acts 3 and 4, interlinked scenes of painful and empathetic witnessing mark a turning point in the play as the action tilts from a persecutory and lawless imaginary to one grounded in the power of individual conscience and justice.

"*Storm still. Enter Lear and Fool*" (3.2). Lashed by the rain, Lear sways between states of self-pity and empathy. Initially, Lear rages against the elements:

> ... Here I stand your slave,
> A poor, infirm, weak and despised old man,
> But yet I call you servile ministers,
> That will with two pernicious daughters join
> Your high-engendered battles 'gainst a head
> So old and white as this. O, ho, 'tis foul! (3.2.19–24)

Lear pictures himself as the victim of several assaults. He is reduced to being a "poor, infirm, weak, and despised" man by the force of the storm and the antipathy of his "two pernicious daughters." He is a lonely self at war with nature and his children. His gaze is turned inward: "I am a man / More sinned against than sinning," he insists (3.2.58–9). Yet Lear's feeling of isolation recedes, a little, when he perceives his shivering Fool. "My wits begin to turn ... How dost, my boy? Art cold? / I am cold myself ... I have one part in my heart / That's sorry yet for thee" (3.2.67–9, 72–3). Lear expresses sympathy for his Fool: he is "sorry."

Soon, this sympathy evolves into empathy, and Lear begins to feel with those who are dispossessed:

> Poor naked wretches, wheresoe'r you are,
> That bide the pelting of this pitiless storm,
> How shall your houseless heads and unfed sides,
> Your looped and windowed raggedness, defend you
> From seasons such as these? O, I have ta'en
> Too little care of this. Take physic, pomp,
> Expose thyself to feel what wretches feel,
> That thou may'st shake the superflux to them
> And show the heavens more just. (3.4.28–36)

What a tangle of perspectives! Initially, Lear sees a vision of abject poverty: "naked wretches" without shelter ("houseless heads") and without food ("unfed sides"). Moved by this mental image of elemental poverty, Lear's language takes on strange, metaphorical possibilities. The image of the house with windows is a reminder of the lost home but also of clothes that are ragged and ripped, of "windowed raggedness." Lear's outward-looking perspective, however, takes a turn in the second half of the speech, as the more formal second-person pronoun "you" (which may be singular or plural in the lines in question) jostles with the introduction of the egocentric "I" and the ambiguous "thou." The shift from "you" to "I" to "thyself" and "thou" presents a syntactical puzzle. The "I" clearly refers to Lear. But what of "thy"? Does Lear address himself in the third person, making "thyself" Lear? Or does "thyself" refer to another person in the abstract? Or to the other characters who are present, namely the Fool, Edgar (disguised as Poor Tom), and Kent (disguised as Caius), or perhaps the audience? Is Lear saying that *he* should "expose thyself to feel what wretches feel" or that the onstage characters should – or that *we* should? The uncertainty concerning the identity of the subject produces a moment of ontological confusion between self and other, a moment that resembles intersubjective witnessing. This scene is followed by others of seeing and witnessing, each one hastening the process of political resistance against Cornwall, Regan, and Goneril's authority.

"*Enter Gloucester and servants*" (3.7.26.1). In the moment just before his gruesome blinding, Gloucester declares, "I am tied to th'stake, and I must stand the course" (3.7.51). Strictly speaking, he is "tied" (bound) because moments earlier the Duke of Cornwall had commanded his servants to "[p]inion him like a thief" (3.7.22). But some editors gloss the line as a reference to bear-baiting.[66] (In *Macbeth*, for example, the battle-wearied Macbeth declares, "They have tied me to a stake. I cannot fly, / But bearlike I must fight the course.")[67] Promising spectacles of blood, guts, and viscera, the sport of bear-baiting pitted a bear against attacking mastiffs.[68] Gloucester's self-comparison to a bear uncannily anticipates the spectacle of his gory blinding.

Yet the allusion to the "stake" also brings to mind the martyr's stake. David K. Anderson observes that "Gloucester ... characterizes himself as a sacrificial victim ... the image of being tied to a stake also suggests martyr burnings."[69] To build on Anderson's suggestion, Gloucester's resemblance to a religious martyr is accentuated by the religious cadence of his language. When Regan asks why Lear has gone to Dover, Gloucester defiantly replies:

> Because I would not see thy cruel nails
> Pluck out his poor old eyes, nor thy fierce sister
> In his anointed flesh stick boarish fangs.
> The sea, with such a storm as his bare head
> In hell-black night endured, would have buoyed up
> And quenched the stellèd fires.
> Yet, poor old heart, he holp the heavens to rain.
> If wolves had at thy gate howled that stern time,
> Thou shouldst have said 'Good porter, turn the key;
> All cruels else subscribe.' But I shall see
> The wingèd vengeance overtake such children. (3.7.52–63)

Gloucester positions himself as a martyr-witness to profane violence. He sees Regan and Goneril attacking "his" (Lear's) "anointed flesh" with "cruel nails" and "boarish fangs." The image is freighted with theological and legal meaning. It recalls the Roman punishment of *damnatio ad bestias* (exposure to wild beasts), a form of capital punishment typically reserved for "non-citizens, prisoners of war, and slaves."[70] For Shakespeare's audience, the image could well have reminded them of the martyrdom of the Christians in Rome. Echoing Eusebius's chronicle of the early church, Foxe records that in Phoenicia during the reign of the Emperor Diocletian, martyrs were "geven to most cruell wylde beastes" (Foxe [1570] 123). In the moment before his torture, Gloucester imagines Lear's misery and humiliation, not his own pitiful condition. His refusal to acknowledge his imminent torture, and his projection of empathy outward to another, subverts the empathy-closing strategy of his torturers. Even as they hurl abuses at him – "traitor," "thief," and "ingrateful fox"[71] – Gloucester performs his allegiance to Lear through the description of the imagined scene. In other words, Gloucester asserts his authority – at a perilous moment – by choosing to witness certain scenes and refusing to see others, including his own terrorized condition. Witnessing functions as both a political instrument of resistance and a psychological barrier against reality.

Gloucester's speech contains a bevy of religious tropes. He conjures a scene of apocalyptic destruction: "the sea ... would have buoyed up / And quenched the stellèd fires" – the stars, providential light. The image of a rising sea dousing the celestial lights brings to mind Jude's prophecy that those who spurn God's commands shall be destroyed by "raging waves of the sea, foaming out their own shame; wandering starres, to whom is reserved the blacknesse of darknesse for ever" (Jude 1:13).[72] Like a prophet, Gloucester foretells utter destruction: "I shall see / The winged vengeance overtake such children." By the end of this speech, he has verbally disavowed his former identity and has remade himself in the image of a prophetic witness.

Gloucester's resemblance to a martyr is grounded in his capacity to envision and feel Lear's suffering. His torture, meanwhile, sets off a chain of witnessing that eventually culminates in political action. Various household retainers watch Cornwall, Regan, and Goneril interrogate Gloucester. One of them refuses to be a silent spectator. Designated First Servant according to the cast list, one of Cornwall's servants challenges his master's authority:

> Hold your hand, my lord
> I have served you ever since I was a child,
> But better service have I never done you
> Than now to bid you hold. (3.7.69–72)

What would have been more shocking conceptually to early modern audiences: the torture of a host by a guest or the murder of a master by his servant? According to English common law, it was the second action that was more reprehensible. The servant killing his master was petty treason.[73] Yet the First Servant's resistance is unambiguously depicted as a justified act.[74] Listening to his conscience and performing an act of heroic non-obedience, the Servant breaks out of the household in which he was "bred," severing his feudal (and emotional) ties of obligation and obedience. It binds him to another community, one dictated by an ineffable revulsion at sadism and cruelty. When he instructs Cornwall to "hold your hand," the Servant neither declares a political agenda nor hints at his political allegiance to Gloucester or to Lear. Furthermore, he does not express, as perhaps one might expect, some abstract claim about justice and morality. In a later scene, Albany will indeed interpret the Servant's action as an extension of divine justice: "[t]his shows you are above / You justicers" (4.2.45–6). But this is a posthumous interpretation of the action, and it does not quite match the scene. As the text makes clear, the Servant's action is not primarily driven by a sense of divine retribution. It is, instead, seemingly prompted by an emotional reaction – outrage – at the sight of the extraordinary violence inflicted upon Gloucester. The Servant becomes a lay magistrate the moment he acts virtuously, yet instinctively. The form of witnessing that emerges echoes the image of the politically engaged, witnessing community in *Acts and Monuments*, in which spiritual renewal brings about a political transformation as individuals harken to their enflamed conscience.

For the First Servant, witnessing prompts action – one that ends in his death but also in the destruction of the tyrant and abuser. The heroism of the First Servant is repeated (albeit in less spectacular fashion) by the Second Servant and Third Servant in a scene that appears only in the quarto *King Lear*:

> SECOND SERVANT: I'll never care what wickedness I do
> If this man come to good.
> THIRD SERVANT: If she live long
> And in the end meet the old course of death,
> Women will all turn monsters.
> SECOND SERVANT: Let's follow the old Earl and get the bedlam
> To lead him where he would. His roguish madness
> Allows itself to anything.
> THIRD SERVANT: Go thou. I'll fetch some flax and whites of eggs
> To apply to his bleeding face. Now heaven help him! (3.7.96–103)

This brief scene underscores the play's entrenched interest in the people's response to injustice. The Second Servant's conditional statement "I'll never care … If this man" works as a moral wager: *if* Cornwall survives the play, then it would be time to abandon all notions of moral conduct. When it is later revealed that Cornwall does *not* survive his wounds, the moral wager becomes null and void. Similarly, echoing the same conditional construction, the Third Servant's line establishes a second premise: *if* Regan lives to a ripe old age and "meet the old course of death," then all women will be turned to "monsters." This starkly misogynistic line, which equates Regan with all women and all women with monsters, is somewhat blunted by Regan's death in the final act.

The final exchange between the Servants is also striking. Concerned for his safe passage through Cornwall's realm, they pair him with Poor Tom, counting on the "bedlam's" "roguish madness" to ensure that others will keep their distance. Unbeknownst to them, their solution facilitates the reunification of father and son. Thus, their decision, inspired by sympathy, strengthens familial and communal ties. Their positive action is reinforced by their care of Gloucester's wounds. To stanch Gloucester's bleeding eyes, they affix "some flax and whites of eggs to apply to his bleeding face" (Q1, 3.7.100–1), a poultice made from notably common, household ingredients.[75] These everyday ingredients bring to mind a world of communal custom and local knowledge, of collective wisdom gained over generations. The servants' act of kindness in the face of Gloucester's excruciating pain echoes the neighbourliness of the "friends" in *Acts and Monuments*.[76]

These interstitial scenes involving nameless, household servants emphasize the political agency of ordinary people to create new forms of association, one based on conscience, empathy, and neighbourliness. By extending political and legal consciousness to those engaged in service and husbandry, the play invites a comparison between individual heroic actions (such as Kent's defiance in the play's opening and the First Servant's defence of Gloucester) and communal ones.

The Duke of Albany

The political tide decisively turns against Cornwall, Regan, and Goneril when Albany enters the fray. Just as many Protestants in Foxe's account were inspired to defy Catholic authorities via verbal report – for example, Joyce Lewes's stricken reaction to the news of Laurence Saunders's execution – so Albany is shocked into action when the Messenger reports that

> A servant that he [Cornwall] bred, thrilled with remorse,
> Opposed against the act, bending his sword
> To his great master, who thereat enraged
> Flew on him, and amongst them felled him dead,
> But not without that harmful stroke which since
> Hath plucked him after. (4.2.40–4)

Upon hearing this, Albany proclaims, "This shows you are above, / You justicers, that these our nether crimes / So speedily can venge" (4.2.45–7). Note Albany's rhetorical embellishments. Whereas the Messenger emphasizes the servant's active opposition to his "great master," Albany turns his self-sacrificing agency into a symbol of divine justice. The gods, or "justicers," punish Cornwall. The erasure of individual agency allows Albany to imagine himself as a divine instrument:

> Gloucester, I live
> To thank thee for the love thou show'dst the King,
> And to revenge thine eyes. Come hither, friend,
> Tell me what more thou knowest. (4.2.61–4)

Albany's evocation of friendship verbally links him to the community of friends that Gloucester had earlier alluded to.

After establishing himself on the side of divine justice, Albany shapes up to be a watchful, cautious, and patient magistrate – the kind of magistrate that Lear and Gloucester could have been. For example, he bides his time in charging Edmund with treason. He observes Regan's amorous pursuit of Edmund and guards the information, provided in Edgar's letter, concerning his wife's adulterous desire for Edmund. Only when Regan declares, "take thou my soldiers, prisoners, patrimony … Witness the world that I create thee here / My lord and master" (5.3.68, 70–1) does Albany strike:

> For your claim, fair sister,
> I bar it in the interest of my wife.
> 'Tis she is subcontracted to this lord,
> And I, her husband, contradict your banns.
> If you will marry, make your loves to me.
> My lady is bespoke. (5.3.77–82)

So many legal words ("claim," "bar," "interest," "subcontracted," "contradict," and "banns") compressed into so few lines make Albany sound like a supercilious attorney, which could be construed as subtly undermining the authority of the character – especially in light of the anti-lawyer discourse discussed in chapter 2.[77] Yet a barrister's shrewdness, arguably, signals the narrative's turn toward lawfulness, order, and good rule. Albany's legalism is not merely for show but serves a tactical function; his accusation of bigamy and annulment delegitimizes Regan's "banns" and opens up the possibility of his divorce from Goneril and her lawful arrest. His precise legal diction is therefore in keeping with his overall transformation, in the latter half of the play, into a conscientious magistrate: a judge whose legal wisdom is grounded in an understanding of due process.

Albany is cautious, investigative, and, when the occasion demands it, battle-ready. In the final act, he even shows an unexpected degree of personal courage. He risks life and limb when he charges Edmund with treason, challenging the latter to battle when he believes that the promised "champion" would not appear (5.2.32); "[l]et the trumpet sound … There is my pledge" (5.3.83, 86). And, as one critic has noted, he comes through the play morally and politically intact.[78] It has been theorized that this character was written to appeal to King James and his courtiers.[79] Whatever the case, dramatic or political, Shakespeare – particularly in the quarto *King Lear* – expends considerable dramatic energy on developing Albany's character, by showing his transformation from a passive observer to an active agent – and this choice has a direct impact on the question of succession at the end of the play.[80] Albany speaks the final lines in the quarto text (Edgar in the folio):

> The weight of this sad time we must obey,
> Speak what we feel, not what we ought to say.
> The oldest have borne most; we that are young,
> Shall never see so much, nor live so long. (Q1, 5.3.315–18)

For Nina Taunton and Valerie Hart, regardless of who utters the lines, the speech constitutes an "enigmatic plea for a society where freedom of expression (and perhaps liberty of conscience?) is every subject's right" – a plea that could have been especially poignant to audiences following the discovery of the Gunpowder Plot in 1605.[81] Placed in the wider context of English Protestant culture, the "plea" is no less stirring. It asks subjects to exercise their witnessing capacity – to see, know, and feel – and to give expression to "what [they] feel." Formally, the lines succinctly capture some of the play's inciting conflicts, including Goneril and Regan's insincere pledges of love, Cordelia's tortured relationship to language ("[w]hat shall Cordelia speak? Love and be silent" [1.1.61]), and Edmund's false accusation against Edgar. For those who remain onstage, their survival and the realm's political repair depend on the continuation of truthful witnessing.

On the "Verge" of Witnessing

The discussion of communal witnessing cannot conclude without a comment about the Dover cliff scene. In it, Edgar, occupying the position of the poet, uses description to convince his blind father that they have arrived at the edge of a cliff. Feigning another's voice, Edgar tells his father that he now stands at "th'extreme verge" of a cliff (4.5.26). In most editions of the play, "verge" is glossed as an edge. That is certainly the most commonsensical meaning, but "verge" also signifies "xii. miles of the chiefest Tunnell of the Court" – the twelve miles surrounding the king's person.[82] As Doug Eskew points out, medieval and early modern law imagined the sovereign to be the "point of authority ... the most local and most sacred point in the kingdom, the ground-zero of ideological geography."[83] Thus, if we pause here and savour the legal sense of "verge," we gain an appreciation of our position within this scene, a scene of legal judgment. We are witnesses to Gloucester's self-imposed sentence of death.

   In medieval and early modern legal geography, Dover was the port from which felons, having been granted mercy by the authorities, entered into exile. This process, known as abjuration, was completed when the abjurer "reached the port" and took "the first ship available overseas, never to return."[84] According to legal tradition, if no ships were available, the abjurer was to wade into the water and wait for either rescue or death. In other words, Gloucester's chosen method of suicide could have been understood by Shakespeare's audiences as the completion of a legal circuit in which the flawed magistrate, in atonement for his crime of faulty judgment, condemns himself to a felon's punishment. Dover is a place of exile, of crossing over, where the abjurer of the realm becomes a legal nonbeing. Gloucester tries to embody this state of being nothing. Lear speaks of a world turned upside down: "change places, and handy-dandy, which is the justice, which is the thief?" (4.6.146–7). This is Gloucester at the "cliff" – and the legal motif effectively empowers audiences to occupy, and not for the first time, the perspective of both witness and jury.

For a number of critics, Edgar's verge speech stands out as a "poetic tour de force" of "highly wrought topographia."[85] It is that and more. Edgar imagines for his father several scenes, each crafted with a draughtsman's precision and replete with feeling that stretches the emotional and imaginative faculties of Gloucester and the spectator. Here is Edgar's speech in full:

> Come on, sir, here's the place. Stand still. How fearful
> And dizzy 'tis to cast one's eyes so low!
> The crows and choughs that wing the midway air
> Show scarce so gross as beetles. Halfway down
> Hangs one that gathers samphire, dreadful trade!
> Methinks he seems no bigger than his head.
> The fishermen that walk upon the beach
> Appear like mice, and yond tall anchoring bark
> Diminished to her cock, her cock a buoy
> Almost too small for sight. The murmuring surge
> That on th'unnumbered idle pebble chafes
> Cannot be heard so high. I'll look no more,
> Lest my brain turn and the deficient sight
> Topple down headlong. (4.5.10–24)

The form of the lines is sinuous. Enjambments create a rushing, hurtling, and vertiginous sensation for the reader as well as for the blind Gloucester. It is as if the very arrangement of the verse creates a shape poem. Simon Palfrey aptly captures the phenomenology of reading this passage: "the end of each line is a precipice; the words stop, the eyes look over, the head swoons."[86] In performance, the actor can recreate the dizzying enjambments by using modulations in the voice – breaths, pauses, pitch – to suggest movement.

Samuel Johnson judged the verge speech as not being "wrought to the utmost excellence of poetry" because the description of the cliff is "enfeebled from the instant that the mind can restore itself to the observation of particulars and diffuse its attention to distinct objects." For Johnson, the "enumeration of the choughs and crows, the samphire-man and the fishers, counteracts the great effect of the prospect ... and stops the mind in the rapidity of its descent through emptiness and horror."[87] But in a wonderful rejoinder to Johnson, Bert O. States argues that it is precisely the "enumeration" of humans, animals, and sea that imbues the scene with illusionistic power. He says that, like a Brueghel painting in which "each event has its own visual and energetic integrity," "everything" in the scene that Edgar imagines for his father, and by extension for audiences, "behav[es] naturally. The fishermen and the samphire man move to a strictly occupational rhythm, turning their backs on the disaster at the verge."[88] States recognizes that the Dover cliff scene is suspended somewhere between the comic and the tragic vein and it is this beautiful tension that gives the scene its lasting power. I agree.

Like States, I am mesmerized by Edgar's painterly details of the existence of a life beyond the play's tragic frame. But these details mean something different to me. Viewed through the lens of intersubjective witnessing, I find in the famous passage a meditation on the power of theatre to create a sense of community among playgoers – a sense of intersubjectivity achieved through language and the imagination that vibrates at a different frequency than is seemingly available to the characters onstage. The scene bestows upon audiences the gift of a shared experience of communal witnessing at the expense of the characters who struggle in vain to overcome their tragic circumstances.

In his verge speech, Edgar uses description to see signs of communal life in his attempt to cure his father of his despair. While his efforts do not bear fruit – Gloucester cannot be cured of his suicidal thoughts – nonetheless, the attempt transforms audiences into a collective, witnessing community. We can appreciate Edgar's description of everyday labour – a labour that intimates the domestic and the communal, one whose everydayness stands as a symbolic bulwark against the horror of the main action. The description of the cliff is not only an aesthetic experience but also, crucially, an emotional and political one. The image of the sea recalls Gloucester's empathetic witnessing the moment before his blinding. Confronting the prospect of being tortured by Cornwall, Gloucester had prophetically declared, "[t]he sea, with such a storm as his bare head / In hell-black night endured, would have buoyed up / And quenched the stellèd fires" (3.7.56–8). Whereas Gloucester's description makes the sea a force of cosmic destruction – the sea sweeping away stars, purging and cleansing the universe of its ills – Edgar's description casts the sea as a "murmuring surge / That on th'unnumbered idle pebble chafes." This elemental image is closer to the natural than the supernatural; the internal rhyme in "murmuring" and "th'unnumbered" creates the sonic equivalent of waves pushing and pulling small pebbles along the beach. Lacking any animating force, the pebbles must follow the water even as it wears them down.[89]

In the midst of that description is a discovery of life, labour, and community. Nearly "halfway down" both the passage and the imagined cliff appears a human figure, "one that gathers samphire." Samphire is an anglicized version of *sampere* or *herbe de Saint Pierre* (St. Peter's herb). It was (and still is) a popular root commonly employed in pickling.[90] In John Gerard's *The Herball* (1597), it is said that "Rocke Sampier groweth on the rock cliffes at Dover ... and most rockes about the west and north west parts of England ... Rocke Sampier flourisheth in May and June, and must be gathered to be kept in pickell in the beginning of August" (figure 8).[91] The evocation of everyday life is reinforced a line later

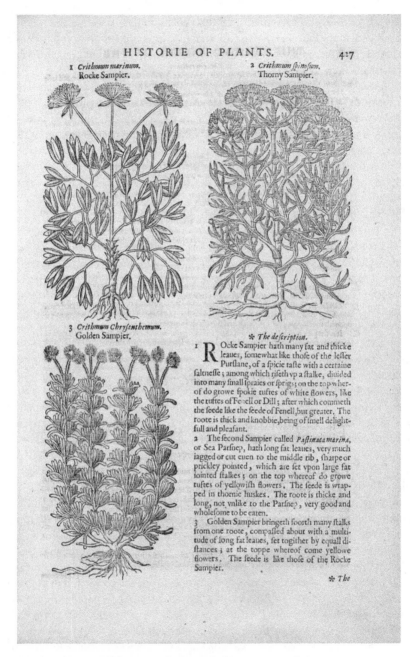

Figure 8. John Gerard, "Samphire," *The Herball* (1597), sig. Dd6r.
The Huntington Library (RB 61079).

when Edgar sees further signs of communal routine: "The fishermen that walk upon the beach / Appear like mice." Edgar's description of the cliffs of Dover asks his father, and likewise audiences, to imagine signs of human industry and to intuit the latent hospitality behind that labour. Why pick samphire if not to feed someone with it – or sell it at the market? Images of fishermen going about their business and locals picking herbs serve to remind Gloucester – and, by implication, audiences – of the way life continues in the face of monumental tragedy. As long as fish continue to inhabit the sea and herbs sprout from the rocks, this community will go on as it always has. This is a philosophy that is grounded in the image of community and oriented toward the future.

In their essay on description, Sharon Marcus, Heather Love, and Stephen Best argue that finely wrought description – often encountered in poetry – constitutes a form of loving, human attention:

> Why describe? Because describing and descriptions can produce pleasure – granular, slow, compressed, attentive, appreciative – as when Roland Barthes reproduces, codes, and interprets every sentence of a Balzac novella in *S/Z*, then reproduces the text again in its entirety … Because description can allow us both to see more and to look more attentively, more fully, *and* more selectively. Because description can take us out of ourselves, as when we try to see a mite or to see like a mite. Because description connects us to others – to those described, to the makers of what we describe, to other describers.[92]

In other words, describing is a highly concentrated, and potentially pleasurable, form of psychic attachment and sociality. Description facilitates community as well as self-discovery; it enables us to "see more and to look more attentively" as well as to "take us out of ourselves … connect us to others." The poet Mark Doty goes a step further. He connects description to ethical witnessing: "Description is an ART to the degree that it gives us not just the world but the inner life of the witness."[93] After exploring instances of "anti-simile" in the poetry of Pablo Neruda and Wisława Szymborska, Doty argues that the poet's refusal to over-embellish the description of "unbearable" death – of massacred children, of the September 11 "jumpers" – constitutes a "MORALITY of description," guided by "generosity and respect."[94] Within the "art" of description lies the possibility of witnessing and community: a marriage of minds between the critic who closely reads the poem, the poet who describes the world, and the reader of the criticism (you) who grasps both experiences at once. Poet, critic, reader: reader, critic, poet. Communities have been built on far less.

This is why the Dover cliff scene matters for thinking about communal witnessing. It expands the already multitudinous forms of witnessing in the play. We have already seen instances of eyewitnessing producing immediate political action (the First Servant's cry of "hold your hand") and empathetic witnessing connecting characters across space and time (Lear to the "poor naked wretches" and Gloucester to Lear's "anointed flesh"). Now, through Edgar, Shakespeare gives us witnessing as a form of both *seeing with* and *seeing for* – a kind of witnessing that exists in the tension between outward sight and inward feeling. Edgar's description then is an attempt at communication and world-building. His description of the cliff cannot be cleanly disentangled from love. But to what extent can poetic description stand in for love? In spite of Edgar's effort to purge his father of despair, Gloucester remains hopeless. "I ... saved him from despair," Edgar tells Albany, but in Gloucester's final onstage appearance, he prays, "You ever gentle gods, take my breath from me. / Let not my worser spirit tempt me again / To die before you please" (4.5.211–13). Fearing that his "worser spirit" or despair will "tempt" him to suicide again, Gloucester begs for a quick death.

Conclusion

Communal, intersubjective, and empathetic witnessing frame the scenes of spectacular violence in *King Lear*. Through the fleeting sense of community between Lear and the nameless wretches, the spontaneous transference of allegiance by the First Servant from Cornwall to Gloucester, and finally to the common mission that links Albany and the self-sacrificing First Servant, the play repeatedly demonstrates the ability of characters to find fellowship through witnessing. The play's community might therefore be said to be a sovereign community; its very existence is a challenge to the traditional definition of sovereign power. In *The Trew Law of Free Monarchies*, King James declares, "the King is over-Lord of the whole land: so is he Master over every person that inhabiteth the same, having power over the life and death of every one of them."[95] By this tenet, only the monarch possesses the power to decide life and death – to exercise sovereignty.[96] In the play, however, sovereign power is distributed among the wider political community. Every character is a potential foe or friend, a killer or a saviour.

My emphasis on witnessing as a communal phenomenon complicates readings that nominate *King Lear* for the title of Shakespeare's bleakest tragedy.[97] "Shakespeare imagines a dark, pitiless world without God or gods in an age in which providential thinking dominated religious culture."[98] I do sympathize with that pessimism. It is true that in the play, "[l]ove cools, friendship falls off, brothers divide; in cities mutinies, in countries discord, in palaces treason, and the bond cracked 'twixt son and father" (1.2.98–100). Yet the play does not preclude a reparative reading, particularly with respect to the question of the political self-governing power of the community. At the end of the play, even as playgoers and readers are confronted by the dead, a community remains. It is a ragged group, but they represent human survival. Crucially, they form the beginnings of a new political order created through empathetic witnessing. Thus, even though certain characters struggle for and never quite find personal redemption, the ones who bear witness to their suffering participate in a project of political repair.

The bonds that arise between characters are not exclusively the ones imposed by traditional patriarchal and legal concepts of bondage, that is, oaths of allegiance or fealty. Blind adherence to those traditional bonds sets off the disastrous events in the initial acts. After act 3, the play pursues a different argument: that bonds may be created from empathetic witnessing. These bonds are forged through a highly theatrical mode of witnessing: seeing, imagining, and feeling – seeing with the mind's eye to seeing with actual eyes and feeling with the other bodies in the playhouse.

The community at the end of *King Lear*, it must be emphasized, is bereft of women. The deaths of Goneril, Regan, and Cordelia imply that this society of men will have no genetic future. The survivors possess greater wisdom, and an awakened conscience, but cannot pass it to the next generation.[99] But this makes the audience even more privileged judges, since they do have a genetic and political future. The audience has learned to see better – using their imagination as well as their senses. Again and again, the play challenges the audience on the ethics of theatrical spectatorship. For the characters, watching *is* feeling – empathetic witnessing – and this blurring of embodiment and imagination foments ethical, political action that cuts across class, status, and gender. Through watching, a web of consciousness spans time and space to connect characters to characters. The audience is implicated in this web. The audience is incorporated into the play's landscape of witnessing and community. The play closes with a prophetic vision: "We that are young / Shall never see so much, nor live so long." The "we" in that line is an invitation to audiences to join the community of witnesses-survivors-sovereigns in the time that remains before us.

Chapter Five

Communal Shaming and the Limitations of Legal Forms: *Henry VI, Part 2* and *Macbeth*

Time after time, Shakespeare's plays advance the interrogatory potential of theatre to destabilize law's hallowed traditions, and two scenes in particular exemplify that power: the penance of Eleanor Cobham, the Duchess of Gloucester in *Henry VI, Part 2* (c. 1591–2), and the sleepwalking of Lady Macbeth in *Macbeth* (c. 1606). Both scenes upend expectations about law's reliance on codified forms – the performance of the penance and remorse – and in so doing, they cast doubt on law's avowed ability to detect and punish sin. The scenes were written at very different moments in Shakespeare's career yet they cohere as a type of "rhyming action," a concept I borrow from Charles Baxter, who writes that readers encounter in poetry

> … an image that we half-remember. We hear a voice that we think we have heard before. We watch as someone performs an action that someone else did very much that way years ago … These are the stories that poets often like to tell, but most stories have some elements of time-reversal, of what I'd call stutter-memories, or rhyming action.[1]

Eleanor's public penance and Lady Macbeth's sleepwalking produce that very sense of "rhyming action," of déjà vu. Both scenes use the particular affordances of theatrical performance – costumes, props, theatrical space, and movement – to underscore the legal community's complex, even contradictory, desires about seeing shame and remorse within a communal setting.

Various elements of an early modern trial depended on the performance of magisterial power. Take, for example, the assize. Upon their arrival at a town, the visiting judges and their clerks were formally welcomed by the local grandees.[2] The ensuing ceremonies served to heighten the difference between the jurisdictional power of the judges and the local authorities. This initial welcome emphasized the social as well as legal distance between the visitors and the locals. But soon after the party's arrival, a process of integration took place that brought the visiting judges into the communal fold. The judges dined with the locals at a banquet on the night of their arrival, and the next day they and other members of the local community heard a sermon by a specially appointed preacher.[3] As discussed in chapter 1, the preacher of the assize sermon used the occasion to examine the theological basis for lay magistracy and lay conscience. Finally, at the assize, the reading of witness depositions, the *viva voce* testimonies of neighbours against the offender, and the work of the jury all added to the sense of communal justice at work. Under ideal circumstances, the assize successfully integrated royal and professional legal administration with local and communal justice.

But what form did communal justice take in the final phase of the trial, after the verdict had been delivered? While documents like indictments, witness testimonies, and juries' verdicts fill gaps in our understanding of pretrial and trial procedures, they do little to answer my question. How did communal justice operate at the nonverbal and the nontextual level – at the level of communal emotions? Early modern reporting on the post-sentencing phase of the trial tends to be sparse and fragmentary, nonetheless, it is possible to glean some sense of the emotions that magistrates deemed essential by reading legal formularies like magistracy manuals.[4] "An Exhortacion to Prisoners Condemned," written in the neat italic hand of the lawyer Nathaniel Rogers, is one such example. This two-page document reads like a theatrical script:

> Bee not therefore ashamed to Caste up yo[u]r eyes, and hold upp yo[u]r handes w[hi]ch have bene beholders & doers of Iniquitie unto Almightie god, humbly Confessing yo[u]r offences and Crave of him p[ar]don for yo[u]r sinnes with true repentance, And let the sighes and sorrowes of yo[u]r hartes soe openly appeare before the beholders as they may judge well of the same and Rejoyce asmuche of yo[u]r Convert[i]on as they were greived w[i]th yo[u]r Iniquities. Feare not deathe for that is Common to all living Creatures and this is gods appointm[en]t[.] And now for asmuch as the lawe requireth the punishm[en]t of yo[u]r bodies for yo[u]r offences, By yo[u]r deathes give such example as his Ma[jes]t[i]es subjectes may be ware to Committe the like, And thincke that the first stepp [that] yo[u] goe from this Barr is the highe way to heaven.[5]

Much like a preacher leading a congregation in a communal act of expiation, the magistrate counsels his prisoners to seek salvation and crave God's pardon for "sinnes with true repentance." He does that by telling the prisoners how to gesture and how to breathe: "[c]aste up yo[u]r eyes, and hold upp yo[u]r handes" and let out the "sighes and sorrowes of yo[u]r hartes," for these are the outward signifiers of remorse. The specificity of the desired gestures, and the assumed correspondence between a gesture and a feeling, recall John Bulwer's *Chirologia* (1644). Bulwer states that "with our *Hands* we Sue, intreat, beseech, solicite, call, allure, intice, dismisse, graunt, denie, reprove, are suppliant, feare, threaten, abhor" and that the arrangement of the hand serves as "an outward helpe unto devotion, appointed by the ordinance of Nature to expresse the holy fervour of our affections" (figure 9).[6] Rogers's text parallels Bulwer's advice. Demonstrating the majesty of his office is no longer the magistrate's primary concern; it is, rather, his management of communal emotions. To shift the emotions of the "beholders" from a state of sadness to one of "rejoice[ment]," the magistrate first needs to convince his prisoners to welcome death as the "first stepp" in "the highe way to heaven."

Reading "An Exhortacion" reveals the lengths to which an early modern magistrate was expected to go in cultivating the right emotions in the courtroom during the post-sentencing phase of the trial. It reinforces the uncanny resemblance, which scholars have previously observed, between the courtroom and the playhouse. Rogers's text assumes that it is within the power of an experienced magistrate to manage the emotions of the prisoners and the spectators, that he can model godly compassion and grief, inspiring reciprocal feelings in the breasts of the onlookers. What it ignores is the possibility of failure. The text's silence on that front is conspicuous particularly when one recalls the standard form of the early modern English criminal trial. As J.S. Cockburn pithily explains, "criminal trials on circuit appear nasty, brutish, and essentially short."[7] The uncompromising form of the criminal trial could never adequately accommodate the emotions of those present at the trial, the trauma of the victim's kin, for instance, or the shame and remorse experienced by the criminal. But drama did have more capacity to investigate powerful legal emotions. Theatre could take on the emotional labour that the law could not.

This closing chapter focuses on shame and remorse, and considers theatre's ability to draw out the communal dynamics of these powerful emotions. It begins with a discussion of the "open penance," a form of public humiliation deployed by both secular and church authorities during the "reformation of manners."[8] The open penance, which the offender performed in a white sheet, occurred in the "external forum," a public space – in or near the church or in the marketplace – where the offender's sin could be published before the community.[9] Shakespeare's *Henry VI, Part 2* critiques the disciplinary logic of penance and the public's role in this ancient ritual of shaming through a deeply sympathetic portrayal of the female penitent. His bold theatrical challenge is surpassed, years later, by his writing of the sleepwalking scene in *Macbeth*. In this iconic scene, the somnambulant Lady Macbeth reveals her role in the regicide to the horror of the Doctor and Gentlewoman. Lady Macbeth's confession, expressed in the total absence of a legal infrastructure, sets in motion the play's interrogation of law's preoccupation with ceremonies. As the scene makes clear, remorse is a private emotion that eludes

Figure 9. John Bulwer, *Chirologia* (1644), sig. L6r. Letter "Q" shows the gesture for
"*pœnitentiā ostendi* [show penance, regret]."
The Huntington Library (RB 113590).

legal detection. The scene advances popular Protestant notions about the secret workings of conscience in the "assize" of the heart. But it goes beyond merely repeating the logics of conscience literature. It renders the *spectating* of remorse a problem, and it articulates this problem through theatrical means: although the actor performing the role of Lady Macbeth uses theatrical gestures to counterfeit the expression of remorse, audiences – actively participating in the fiction – must choose to imagine that what they see is authentic, genuine remorse. Yet because an actor has successfully mimicked the gestural grammar of remorse, audiences are also reminded that it is possible to feign this emotion. The sleepwalking scene forces audiences, then, to grapple with the following questions. How should they understand remorse beyond the playhouse – in legal spaces like the courtroom? Are prisoners' expressions of remorse simply performances designed to satisfy legal or communal expectations? What does this suggest about the law's ability to gain access to the inner sanctum of the prisoner's heart? The sleepwalking scene generates such questions and, in so doing, it destabilizes legal assumptions about the ability of magistrates to facilitate the expression of genuine remorse and true repentance.

The Public Penance

In medieval and early modern England, the open or public penance took a number of forms. Some offenders were sentenced to walk the streets or the marketplace (on market days) in a white sheet, holding a burning taper in their hand, a requirement that was largely abandoned in the sixteenth century following the Reformation.[10] Some penitents were made to stand in the parish church, "making an open confession of guilt" before a congregation on a Sunday or several Sundays.[11] In addition, the ever "creative" Tudor authorities sentenced transgressors to carting, riding backwards, and the stocks.[12] Public penance was meted out for a range of offences from slander to adultery. In theory, church courts adjudicated cases and fashioned appropriate penances, but in practice, as Martin Ingram explains, there was a good deal of collaboration between secular and ecclesiastical authorities. The "secular appropriation of the notion of 'penance'" was especially prominent in London where common law courts freely adapted the penance to punish offenders for a variety of offences.[13] Ingram cites a case from 1529 in which a man, having spoken discourteously to a sheriff, was made to do penance through the streets, and another from 1561 in which an apprentice did penance after "spending his master's goods."[14]

Medieval canon law prescribed a division between the internal and external courts or *fora*. The internal forum was the "confessional court of the conscience," one predicated on the individual's participation in the sacrament of penance.[15] In the privacy of the confessional, the sinner confesses their sins to the priest, who, in turn, like a judge, pronounces absolution and imposes an appropriate penance suited to the sin.[16] Scenes of auricular confession appear throughout medieval literature. In *Sir Gawain and the Green Knight* (c. 1375–1400), Gawain confesses "fully and frankly" to a household priest before his meeting with his foe. The priest "declares him so clean and so pure / that the Day of Doom could dawn in the morning."[17] In 1563, the Church of England passed the Thirty-Nine Articles (revised in 1571), thereby abolishing the sacrament of penance.[18] So began the official "Protestant de-sacramentalization of penance."[19] The impact of this doctrinal shift on early modern English society has been richly documented, analysed, and debated in recent scholarship. Curiously, the most common form of the late medieval public penance – walking the streets or the marketplace in a white sheet – remained unchanged despite the various religious reforms instituted by the Elizabethan church.[20] It seems that the Protestant attack on religious ceremonies and on the Catholic sacraments, including the sacrament of penance, did little to alter the public performance of penance as it was played out in the external forum.

Historians of crime date the disappearance of the public penance in England to sometime in the late eighteenth century or early nineteenth century.[21] This is supported by anecdotal evidence. One of William Wordsworth's earliest childhood memories, from the mid or late 1770s, was of seeing "a woman doing penance in the church in a white sheet."[22] Robert Shoemaker attributes the decline of the penance to the rise of a new culture of "impersonality" in the eighteenth century. According to Shoemaker, "changes in economic and social life caused by … the growth of independent wage labour, together with high levels of migration, weakened the social ties which facilitated community-based punishments."[23] To contextualize that point, sixteenth- and seventeenth-century English society relied on what Craig Muldrew calls "credit networks."[24] Up and down the social ladder, early modern men and women engaged in competitive performances of godliness in pursuit of good credit.[25] Women had to work harder than men at preserving their reputation and women toiling away in domestic service, Laura Gowing emphasizes, had to work harder still to safeguard their household and social reputation.[26] The public penance was a punishment designed to maximally damage one's social reputation. The harm done to that reputation by the penance could be irreversible. A blighted reputation could have serious ramifications for an individual's employability, marriage prospects, or access to economic or political resources (loans, patronage, etc.). Shakespeare's *Othello* lays bare the relationship between reputation, gender, and death. After Othello strips Cassio of his military office, Cassio grieves the loss of his reputation, that "immortal part of myself" – yet by the end of the play, that loss is shown to be only a temporary setback. Cassio fails up. For Desdemona, however, the loss of her reputation leads inexorably to her death.[27] To return to Shoemaker's argument, cosmopolitan eighteenth-century London proved to be unaccommodating to traditional forms of communal shaming, which were predicated on communal memory and social credit. Demographic change, triggered by the growth of wage labour and urbanization, meant that neighbourhoods were always in the process of forming and fragmenting. The rise of the modern city killed the public penance.

Shoemaker's account of penance's obsolescence is fascinating. But his emphasis on material factors – how streets were reshaped in response to the growth of London's urban population of itinerant workers – marginalizes the non-material factors that played a role in the disappearance of the public penance. I argue that a history of the penance should also take into account the cultural impact of the arts on the public's moral and legal imaginations. Doing so not only expands our understanding of early modern penance, humiliation, and communal shaming, but it also addresses the question of the legislative role of the makers and consumers of imaginative texts. If one believes, as I do, that stories and storytellers have some power in shaping legalities, the constellation of beliefs, experiences, and feelings that comprise a subject's understanding of the law, then one may also give some thought to the shaping influence of a popular literary event (such as a successful theatrical run), a literary fad (such as the rise of a new genre), or a literary sensibility (such as a turn toward inwardness) on the legal imagination and attitudes of audiences. Shakespeare's chronicle history *Henry VI, Part 2* – and to a more limited extent, Thomas Heywood's *Edward IV, Part 2* (c. 1599) – created just that ripple in early modern legality.[28] These 1590s plays contributed to the rewriting of the public meaning of penance through their overtly sympathetic, even sentimental, portrayal of female penitents.

As plays about the Wars of the Roses, Shakespeare's and Heywood's chronicle histories placed their action in what the Elizabethans saw as the "bloudy" civil wars of the recent past. In the imagination of late sixteenth-century playgoers, the fifteenth century was a time of rebellion, judicial irregularities, and, at times, senseless violence. Samuel Daniel's influential *Civil Wars* (1595, expanded in 1609) characterizes that period of England's history as one of "tumultuous broyles, / and bloudy factions ... Bowes against bowes, the Crowne against the crowne, / Whil'st all pretending right, all right throwen downe."[29] Set against that Elizabethan perception of the fifteenth century, Shakespeare's and Heywood's staged penances serve as graphic reminders of that violent and uncivilized age. By associating the public penance with the excesses of the past, a period of gothic horror that was positioned in direct opposition to "the quiet calme" and "blisse" of the age of "ELIZA," the plays helped to revise the history of the penance.[30] Never mind that penances were still very much enforced in London and elsewhere, albeit with decreased frequency.[31] Shakespeare's and Heywood's drama insisted on imagining the public penance as a *historical* artefact. These imaginative experiments arguably laid the groundwork for a reshaping of penance's cultural and symbolic meaning. In the plays, penance becomes a spectacle of injustice rather than an incontrovertibly just solution.

In writing the scenes, Shakespeare and Heywood borrowed deeply from the female complaint literature that flourished in the mid to late sixteenth century, particularly in narrative poetry. Mid-century poets found rich poetic material in the stories of the rise and fall of Eleanor Cobham and Jane Shore.[32] George Ferrers's *Elianor Cobham's Lament*, published in the 1578 edition of *A Mirror for Magistrates*,[33] refreshes older material, such as the anonymously authored "The Lament of the Duchess of Gloucester" (1441).[34] The story of Jane Shore was commemorated in Thomas Churchyard's *Shore's Wife*, composed sometime during the reign of Edward VI and published in the 1563 edition of *A Mirror for Magistrates*. Richard Helgerson observes that "no poem in the *Mirror* was more influential than *Shore's Wife*," as indicated by the existence of numerous admiring comments, from 1563 to the 1590s, for Churchyard's poem.[35] The various poems drew on English confessional literature and classical poetry such as Ovid's *Heroides*.[36] The literature of female complaint shaped subsequent dramatic representations of penitential women, including that of Shakespeare's Eleanor and Heywood's Jane.

When Shakespeare and Heywood revisited the women's stories, they heightened the tragic emotions in the poems using the theatrical benefits of staging. In act 2, scene 4, Eleanor, her husband Humphrey, and the sheriff and his officers occupy different spatial and affective zones on the stage. Their movements – recorded in the dialogue and the text's unusually rich stage directions – force playgoers to repeatedly experience penance from Eleanor's perspective as well as from that of the spectators onstage. Hence, audiences are given the chance to calibrate their emotional reactions to the spectating characters: who among the characters (citizens, legal officers, courtiers, etc.) are attuned to her suffering?[37] These opportunities for emotional appraisal, which the form of theatrical performance makes urgently possible, test audiences' capacity for empathy. At the same time, the scene encourages audiences to feel antipathy toward the moblike citizens who spurn Eleanor. Thus, the scene brings into existence what Lauren Berlant calls "intimate publics": "There are lots of ways of inhabiting these intimate publics: a tiny point of identification can open up a field of fantasy and de-isolation, of vague continuity, or of ambivalence."[38]

The Woman in White

In 1441, the Duchess of Gloucester was tried and convicted by an ecclesiastical tribunal for necromancy, witchcraft, and treason. Four of her associates were arrested, including members of her household. Prior to her disgrace, Eleanor Cobham had enjoyed a life of power and luxury. At the peak of their influence, the Duke and Duchess of Gloucester held court at their Greenwich estate, La Plesaunce.[39] The trial of the Duchess for treasonous conjuring reversed their fortunes.[40] Because parliament at the time did not have a law to try a peeress for treason, her case was relegated to an ecclesiastical court. This ecclesiastical tribunal, composed of high-ranking bishops and other officials, found her guilty and sentenced her to perform public penance over the course of three market days "when London's population would be swollen to its maximum by visiting tradesmen and shoppers."[41] On 13, 15, and 17 November 1441, the disgraced Duchess – in a white sheet – walked from Westminster to a church in London holding a taper in her hand.[42]

Fifteenth-century chronicles documenting the Duchess of Gloucester's penance stuck mainly to the legal facts.[43] The *London Chronicles* records the following:

> The lady of Gloucester had confessid her wichcraft … sche whas joyned be all the spirituell assent to Penaunce to com to london frro Westmynster on the monday nexte sewyng, and londid at the Temple bryge oute of her barge … and went so thorow fflet strete on her feete and hoodeles un to Poulys [Paul's]; and ther sche offeryd up her taper at the high auter … and att eche of the tymes the meyer with the sherves and the craftes of London were redy at [th]e placys ther sche shuld lond.[44]

Gregory's Chronicle, another fifteenth-century source, offers a similarly laconic account, noting briefly that "the Lady of Gloucester" did penance at "iij sondry or dyvers placys."[45] These factual reports form the basis of a more florid Elizabethan historiography. In the second edition of *Acts and Monuments* (1570), John Foxe "conjectures" that Eleanor Cobham had been the victim of a Catholic conspiracy: "the Lady Eleanor, & Onley [one of her clerks] semed then to favour and savour of that religio[n], set forth by Wickleffe, and therefore lyke enough, that they were hated of [th]e clergy."[46] So went the Elizabethan (sympathetic) rewriting of her character. No longer exclusively remembered as a political upstart, in the Elizabethan imagination, she had gained the gravitas of a tragic heroine: a proto-Protestant martyr brought down by Catholic prelates who were in cahoots with the enemies of the crown. Shakespeare's construction of Eleanor reflects aspects of Foxe's sympathetic interpretation as well as the tragic lyricism of female complaint literature.

Shakespeare stages the penance because it was part of the collective, communal memory. The story had become too famous not to be staged. As indicated by the stage direction, Eleanor enters *"barefoot, with a white sheet about her, written verses pinned on her back, and a wax taper burning in her hand, with the Sheriff of London, and Sir John Stanley, and officers with bills and halberds"* (2.4.17.1–5).[47] At first glance, the scene seems to legitimize the convergence of popular and royal justice. Yet the tragic structure of the scene resists that interpretation. The scene of Eleanor's penitential walk begins with Duke Humphrey instructing his followers (and hence audiences) to watch "the coming of my punish'd duchess. / Uneath may she endure the flinty streets, / To tread them with her tender-feeling feet" (2.4.7–9). These lines prepare audiences to see her penance as a physical trial. "Flinty streets" emphasizes the roughness of the pavement upon which Eleanor must tread. As the scene unfolds, it becomes obvious that it is not only the cutting surface of the streets that hurts her but also the people's derisive laughter. Thus, "flinty streets" comes to signify the emotional stoniness of the London citizens. Humphrey worries that the shame of communal judgment will break Eleanor's "mind":

> Sweet Nell, ill can thy noble mind abrook
> The abject people gazing on thy face
> With envious looks, laughing at thy shame,
> That erst did follow thy proud chariot wheels
> When thou didst ride in triumph through the streets. (2.4.10–15)

His sympathy, wrapped in a husband's tender rhetoric – "Sweet Nell," "thy noble mind" – invites audiences to feel as he feels: pity and sorrow for the Duchess, who had hitherto travelled the streets on "proud chariot-wheels."

When Eleanor appears several lines later, her anguish seemingly justifies his fears and further encourages audiences to feel even more pity. She repeatedly acknowledges her "shame" – but not guilt, it should be noted – while compulsively enumerating the casual cruelty of the citizens:

> Come you, my lord, to see my open shame?
> Now thou dost penance too. Look how they gaze,
> See how the giddy multitude do point
> And nod their heads, and throw their eyes on thee.
> . . . .
> Ah Gloucester, teach me to forget myself;
> For whilst I think I am thy married wife,
> And thou a prince, Protector of this land,
> Methinks I should not thus be led along,
> Mailed up in shame, with papers on my back,
> And followed with a rabble that rejoice
> To see my tears and hear my deep-fet [fetched] groans.
> The ruthless flint doth cut my tender feet,
> And when I start, the envious people laugh,
> And bid me be advisèd how I tread.
> . . . .
> As he [Humphrey] stood by whilst I, his forlorn Duchess,
> Was made a wonder and a pointing stock
> To every idle rascal follower. (2.4.20–3, 28–48)

Each iteration of the word "shame" creates the possibility of a "tiny point of identification" (Berlant) between Eleanor and the offstage spectator. Eleanor catalogues the many ways she is objectified by the watchers, her husband included: "Come you, my Lord, *to see* my open shame? … a rabble that rejoice / To *see* my tears" (my emphasis). Edwin Austin Abbey's painting *The Penance of Eleanor, Duchess of Gloucester,* first exhibited in 1900, vividly supplies the expressions of the "envious" and "idle" people. But Eleanor's description of how it feels to be made the "pointing stock" – an archaic expression that signifies being an object of scorn of the community – also serves to encourage playgoers to appraise (and condemn) the behaviour of the citizens.

Nowhere in the stage direction does it indicate that actors playing the citizens are to share the stage with Eleanor, Humphrey, or the officers. Instead, going by the stage direction alone, one assumes that the actor playing Eleanor is meant to turn to the theatrical audience when addressing the "giddy multitude." In that moment, the playgoer is given the opportunity to resist being grouped with the implied mob by recognizing that anyone who does "gaze," "point," "nod," and "laugh" at her reveals himself or herself to be one with the London citizens alluded to in her speech. Does any playgoer want to be grouped with that uncouth "rabble"? The staging of Eleanor's penance offers audiences a chance to use their emotions to differentiate themselves from the fictive masses. Those pitying Eleanor can actively resist the excitement of the (implied) London mob. Theatrical pleasure lies with identifying more with the disgraced penitent than with the legal and spiritual authorities that condemned her.

Unlike the theatrical audience, the characters onstage do not have a full view of the facts of Eleanor's case. In an earlier scene, Eleanor, while not entirely blameless, is shown to be the victim of political circumstances beyond her control.[48] Seeking to ruin the Duke, her husband's enemies plot her disgrace. Sir John Hum, whom she trusts as a go-between, reveals to audiences in an aside that he has in fact been "hired" by her enemies (Cardinal Beaufort and the Duke of Suffolk) to "undermine the Duchess, / And buzz these conjurations in her brain" (1.2.98– 9). Through Hum, Eleanor employs Margery Jourdayne, a "cunning witch," and Roger Bolingbroke, a "conjuror," to prophesy the future of the King and his chief counsellors (1.2.75–6). In a spectacular set piece, Margery and Roger raise a spirit, Asmodeus, while Eleanor and Hum watch from "*aloft*" (1.4.12.1). The spirit prophesies the deaths of the King, the Duke of Suffolk, and the Duke of Somerset. Upon the sound of "*Thunder and lightning*" (1.4.39.1), it descends and the conspirators are burst upon by "*the Dukes of York and Buckingham with Sir Humphrey Stafford and their guard*" (1.4.39.2–3). In the face of the overwhelming evidence, the King has no choice but to exile his aunt – but not before sentencing her to do "open penance" (2.3.11), punishment for her role in the "devilish practices" (3.1.46). Eleanor's co-conspirators – Margery, Roger, and Southwell (a third conspirator) – are hanged and burned offstage.

In the wake of Shakespeare's history plays, Thomas Heywood adapted for the stage another well-known episode from the Wars of the Roses: the penance of Jane Shore, Edward's mistress, an event that occurred in 1483 and was commemorated by Sir Thomas More in *The History of King Richard III*.[49] Heywood does not stage a confrontation between Jane and the London citizens.[50] This choice is perhaps connected to his civic orientation and the play's consistently sympathetic depiction of the citizens of London. Rebecca Tomlin observes that throughout the play, "Heywood positions the city against the court, offering honesty, openness and stability as the city's enduring virtues, and showing its citizens as morally superior to ... Edward IV and Richard of Gloucester."[51] Whatever the reason, the decision to obscure citizens creates an entirely different – and arguably less participatory – theatrical experience.

Following King Edward's death, Brakenbury warns Jane that the newly ascendant King Richard III has publicly "proclaimed" her punishment: "having first done shameful penance here, / You shall be then thrust forth the city gates / Into the naked, cold, forsaken field" (18.104–6). Later in the scene, two of the "bishop's 'parritors" (18.190) – historically, an apparitor was an ecclesiastical officer who delivered summons or citations – appear with further details of the expected penance:

> This day, it is commanded by the King [Richard III],
> You must be stripped out of your rich attire,
> And in a white sheet go from Temple Bar
> Until you come to Aldgate, bare-footed,
> Your hair about your ears, and in your hand
> A burning taper. Therefore, go with us. (18.192–7)

These double pronouncements, Brakenbury's "repor[t] of this news" (18.118) followed immediately by the apparitor's speech, heighten audiences' suspense. But instead of delivering on expectations – giving audiences the spectacle of Jane's penance – the action ricochets to another part of London, a room in Doctor Shaw's house where he is visited by the ghost of Friar Anselm. By the time the play catches up to Jane in scene 20, she has already completed her penance. The stage direction indicates that the actor is to appear in the traditional costume of the penitent: "*in a white sheet, with her hair loose, and a wax taper in her hand*" (20.20.1–3). Accompanied by the same two apparitors who had pronounced her penance, Jane delivers a moving speech dressed in what she calls her "robe of shame" (20.4). By deciding to forgo staging the full penance – Jane's walk from Temple Bar to Aldgate – Heywood accentuates her pitiful isolation: she is only accompanied by the apparitors. This decision means that while audiences are free to imagine her penitential scene, their emotional responses cannot be easily disentangled from Jane's own perspective. Both Shakespeare and Heywood demand emotional effort on the part of playgoers; playgoers are given every opportunity to feel with the female penitent. But in the particular way the penance of Eleanor forces playgoers to choose sides, prompting them to actively resist the ugly emotions of the "giddy multitude," Shakespeare can be said to be more fully exploiting the participatory potential of theatre and performance.

Shakespeare's and Heywood's dramatizations of the female character's open penance upended traditional legal expectations, altering the very hermeneutics by which penance could be read. From the law's perspective, the penance served chiefly to emphasize the error of the sinner and to reconcile the penitent to the community. "Public penance simultaneously promised salvation in the next world and public order in this."[52] That certainty is missing in the play texts. In the case of *Henry VI, Part 2*, it is the community that errs by unwittingly facilitating a political power struggle it knows nothing about. Eleanor's defiance in the face of this communal scorn underscores the wrongheadedness of the citizens. Even as she is reduced to an abject spectacle, Eleanor pointedly questions the people's right to judge her. The citizens stare at Eleanor, but she looks back at them. She views them as an uncouth, uncivil, and perhaps even unchristian "giddy multitude." Strictly speaking, the citizens occupy the moral high ground in comparison to Eleanor – after all, *they* are not the ones who have raised a demonic spirit and who are being punished with a public penance – yet their unthinking participation in communal shaming arguably debases them in the eyes of the knowing audience.[53] Eleanor meets her social death like a martyr going to an execution. Those who laugh and point at her are exposed to the critical judgment of the audience. The overwhelmingly tragic feeling that the scene produces, lifted by the lyricism of Eleanor's final speech, suggests that "good" playgoers – the ones who have the capacity to feel compassion, pity, and sorrow for suffering characters – must reject the "bad" emotions of the crowd.

Emotional Contagion

Affect theory emphasizes the transmittable, sociable, and "contagious" nature of public emotions.[54] Challenging the longstanding Cartesian model of the self that sees the body as a closed and coherent vessel, Eve Kosofsky Sedgwick argues that shame, in particular, is "contagious from one person to another."[55] Sara Ahmed agrees: "[t]hinking of affects as contagious does help us to challenge what I have called an 'inside out' model of affect ... by showing how we are affected by what is around us."[56] Yet Ahmed also wonders "whether the concept of affective contagion might underestimate the extent to which affects are contingent (involving the 'hap' of happening): to be affected by another does not mean that an affect simply passes or 'leaps' from one body to another."[57] Ahmed's critique, as I understand it, is not so much a rejection of the contagiousness of emotions, but a reminder of the *choices* available to individuals when they participate in or resist contagious and powerful group feelings. In other words, the epidemiological connotation of "contagion" implies a one-note response to a stimulus. But emotions do not actually behave like viruses and individuals' emotional responses can fluctuate a good deal. Ahmed insists that individuals have some measure of control over the intensity of their responses. In the case of theatre, the ability of playgoers to control their affective commitment to the fiction can vary widely. The ending of *King Lear* leaves some members of the audience sobbing and others dry-eyed.

The theatricalized penance may indeed have moved the hearts and bodies of spectators to empathize with the female penitent's suffering. Or perhaps audiences discovered the limits of their pity. With Ahmed in mind, we can also imagine that instead of compassion, audiences experienced schadenfreude, "enjoyment of the misfortunes of others" – that they were entertained to see the public humiliation of Eleanor or Jane.[58] Tiffany Watt Smith explains that while schadenfreude is often understood as a form of "malicious joy," it is in fact a feeling that expresses a sense of justice or "moral balance":

> Schadenfreude may appear antisocial … It may seem misanthropic, yet it is enmeshed in so much of what is distinctly human about how we live: the instinct for justice and fairness; a need for hierarchies and the quest for status within them; the desire to belong to and protect the groups that keep us safe.[59]

Schadenfreude, in other words, contains at its core a judicial logic. Indeed, it could be said to be an extension of the very human instinct to appraise actions based on an intuitive sense of "deservingness."[60] Thus far I have emphasized spectatorial pity at Eleanor's penance, but I also want to acknowledge the possibility of other emotional reactions.

In the play, Eleanor is depicted as proud and ambitious. She says to her husband, "[p]ut forth thy hand, reach at the glorious gold [the crown]"; Humphrey rebukes her for these "ambitious thoughts" (1.2.11, 18). When she takes up the theme again, he reprimands her: "wilt thou still be hammering treachery / To tumble down thy husband and thyself / From top of honour to disgrace's feet?" (1.2.47–9). As Jean E. Howard has pointed out, female characters in Shakespearean drama who transgress the "sexual hierarchy" and the patriarchal order are often disciplined, policed, and "tamed" in the text.[61] Eleanor's ambition certainly positions her as potentially deserving punishment; not only does she attempt to upset the political order but also the gender hierarchy of the household. Conceivably, audiences might have taken satisfaction in seeing the humbling of the upstart Duchess.

While a number of "haps" (Ahmed) may impede and interrupt the transmission of pity from body to body, I argue nonetheless that the scene of Eleanor's penance – its language, mood, and movement – all encourage playgoers to harbour fellow-feeling and compassion for Eleanor. Indeed, it is possible for audiences to believe that Eleanor deserved her comeuppance while still pitying her. Shakespeare's audiences were immersed in a Christian value system that emphasized compassion and mutual feeling. Furthermore, Calvinism encouraged an acceptance of one's own depravity. To quote the physician Timothy Bright, "all men are sinners, and being culpable of the breach of God [*sic*] lawes, incurre the punishment of condemnation."[62] Like a portrait of a saint whose suffering aids lay devotion, the afflicted Eleanor could have reminded audiences of their own moral shortcomings. Any emotional reaction is, of course, possible. Yet, I argue, only one is probable: that audiences reject membership in one emotional community – that of the heartless rabble – for another – that of the intimate circle whose members include Humphrey, epitomizing husbandly compassion, and Eleanor, caught in the throes of agonizing humiliation.

Macbeth and the Limits of Law's Forms

The scenes of penance in the history plays examined above defamiliarized play-goers from law's disciplinary logic. *Macbeth* ventured beyond defamiliarization to an outright interrogation of law's forms and assumptions by troubling the very notion that an officer of the law, a magistrate, could adequately examine and judge the heart of an individual. In the sleepwalking scene – the moneymaker in any performance of *Macbeth* – Lady Macbeth is observed by a pair of newly introduced characters, the Doctor and the Gentlewoman.[63] These minor characters are clearly layfolk. Their nobody-status marks them as outsiders. They are not courtiers, thanes, or witches, but ordinary people who happen to come across an extraordinary and haunting spectacle. Like the nameless man gathering samphire in Edgar's verge speech, they represent life outside of the tragic narrative. Thus identified, the Doctor and the Gentlewoman become potential surrogates for the audience. Their emotional distress, wonder, shock, and revulsion shape our emotional reactions. The scene creates a frictionless intersubjectivity that binds the spellbound spectator to the equally mesmerized Doctor and Gentlewoman. I am interested in how this affective binding, achieved through the juxtaposition of two overlapping circles of spectators – we watch the Doctor and Gentlewoman watching Lady Macbeth – challenges the rules of spectatorship.

Watchfulness opens the sleepwalking scene. The Doctor begins by commenting, indeed, complaining, that he has these "two nights watch'd" with the Gentlewoman yet "can perceive no truth in your report" (5.1.1).[64] His frustration is abruptly curtailed by the appearance of Lady Macbeth. He diagnoses her condition as one of sleepwalking, a "great perturbation in nature, to receive at once the benefit of sleep and do the effects of watching" (5.1.10). "Lo you, here she comes ... Observe her, stand close" (5.1.20), he instructs the Gentlewoman as they arrange themselves as witnesses, as her observers. The language of surveillance immediately situates the dramatic action in the forensic field. Lady Macbeth, the criminal, is under surveillance. She is trapped by the evaluative gazes of the Doctor and the Gentlewoman, who embody twin realms of institutional knowledge: the medical and the moral.

Yet these characters, so newly introduced and so devoid of even the sem-blance of inwardness or psychological depth, prove quite hapless. They derive little satisfaction in being the Queen's witnesses. They display none of the self-confidence, the weighty, ennobling instinct for justice, of the neighbours in chapter 3's domestic tragedies. They hover at the periphery of the stage and evince timidity and furtiveness, even going so far as to undercut their author-ity as judges. The Doctor suggests that perhaps an innocent explanation lies behind Lady Macbeth's strange behaviour: "yet I have known those which have walk'd in their sleep who have died holily in their beds" (5.1.61). He expresses uncertainty in his parting line, "I think but dare not speak" (5.1.79). The Gen-tlewoman is a little less circumspect – she declares Lady Macbeth "has spoke what she should not" – yet even she cannot find the courage to articulate an outright accusation against the Queen. She leaves it to God to judge, saying "Heaven knows what she has known" (5.1.39), adding, "I would not have such a heart in my bosom for the dignity of the whole body" (5.1.55), meaning, she would not trade her clean conscience for any promise of "dignity" (worthiness, rank).[65] Her parting line brings to mind commonplace ideas about godliness and humility. Commenting on the final hours of a "great man" who had pur-sued "the credit and current of the times," the preacher Robert Bolton argues, "I tell you true, I would not endure an houres horrour of His wofull heart, for His present Paradise to the worlds end."[66] Alarmed by what they have seen, the Doctor and the Gentlewoman defer legal judgment to a dateless future, but this moment of legal restoration never comes. Lady Macbeth dies before the end of the play. Before the arrival of Malcolm, Macduff, and the others, she has taken her life, or so Malcolm reports in the closing of the play.

The gap between what the Doctor and the Gentlewoman suspect but cannot fully articulate positions the spectator as the ultimate arbitrator of truth. As audiences, we have already played the role of silent witnesses to the murder of Duncan. Now we serve as a self-informing jury of presentment, holding truths about Lady Macbeth that the Doctor and the Gentlewoman cannot access. Yet even as the scene empowers audiences to supply the accusation against Lady Macbeth, it implicates them in an intimate circuit of shame. Like Claudius's confession in *Hamlet*, Lady Macbeth's sleepwalking takes place in a room of the castle; in some productions, it is her very bedchamber. "I have seen her rise from her bed, throw her nightgown upon her," according to the Gentlewoman (5.1.3–4). The reference to the "nightgown," which early modern women wore for intimate occasions, creates an indelible impression of trespass on the part of the onlookers – those onstage and offstage. By gazing on the female figure in her nightgown, we join the Doctor and the Gentlewoman in a collective act of voyeurism. Thus, the uncomfortable spectating performed by the Doctor and the Gentlewoman – and by implication, our spectating as audiences – differs from the sanctioned watching of Eleanor in *Henry VI, Part 2*. Recall that in that scene, Humphrey's opening speech summons our gazes. He tells all present to "look" on the spectacle of his wife. But the sleepwalking scene lacks that explicit, verbalized permission to look. We look at Lady Macbeth, along with the Doctor and the Gentlewoman, but our looking is unsummoned. Affectively bound to these surrogates by the rules of the *mise en abyme*, we watch, unable to peel our eyes away from the morbid spectacle, yet the moral high ground we might have been able to claim is undercut by an identification with the surrogates, the Doctor and the Gentlewoman, who encircle the body of Lady Macbeth like a pair of voyeurs. Contagiously, shame connects the onstage and offstage spectators. Watching is marked as illicit, dangerous, even shameful.

The erotic nature of looking has been brilliantly explained by film scholar Laura Mulvey. According to Mulvey,

> The cinema offers a number of possible pleasures. One is scopophilia. There are circumstances in which looking itself is a source of pleasure, just as, in the reverse formation, there is pleasure in being looked at ... in his *Three Essays on Sexuality*, Freud ... associated scopophilia with taking other people as objects, subjecting them to a controlling and curious gaze.[67]

The erotics of looking is arguably implicit in the sleepwalking scene. Yet even as the scene satisfies audiences' desire to look – specifically, to catch sight of the guilty party in a moment of unfeigned remorse – it also demands that audiences pay an emotional tax for the privilege of looking. By looking, audiences assume part of the burden of guilt, shame, and remorse. We must accept that the Doctor and the Gentlewoman's unfolding sense of shame is also our shame. Whatever theatrical pleasure we seek in watching the play, in this scene, becomes tainted (or perhaps excitingly heightened as in voyeurism?) by the addition of shame – a painful, involuntary, and *conscious* reaction to the knowledge of a potential transgression. Echoing the experience of Leontius of Plato's *Republic*, who, in spite of his inhibitions, cannot help but stare at the corpses of the recently executed criminals, or that of the modern connoisseur of body horror films, who accepts that the "pleasure of the text is, in fact, getting the shit scared out of you – and loving it," we gaze on Lady Macbeth with horror, pleasure, and shame.[68] This looking affectively displaces us from the law, which endorses a more limited set of emotions such as righteous anger and perhaps sadness for the accused (as evinced in Nathaniel Rogers's manual).

Lady Macbeth's unconscious state forecloses the possibility that she experiences shame. Although her sleepwalking and unconscious confessions result from her irrepressible feelings of remorse, because she is unconsciousness throughout the scene, she cannot be said to actually *experience* shame. So shame hangs over the scene on account of the voyeuristic Doctor and Gentlewoman, and arguably the playgoers. Like the lay characters, we cannot look away from the spectacle. This unforeseen reversal of shame from the body of the sinner to the legally guiltless, but emotionally complicit, community – both the two-person onstage community and the far larger one in the theatre – unleashes the scene's interrogation of law's forms.

The Gunpowder Plot

The sleepwalking scene, and its intense meditation on the conditions of watching remorse, highlights the problem of interpreting this elusive emotion, which was (and continues to be) a feature of criminal trials. In the year of *Macbeth's* first performance, this interpretative dilemma posed an epistemological and legal crisis following the discovery of the Gunpowder Plot in November of 1605 and the trials and executions of the conspirators in late 1605 and spring of 1606. The Gunpowder Plot was, to quote Rebecca Lemon, the "most sensational treason plot in English history."[69] Its political and legal ramifications, including the harsh, legislative crackdown on the Catholic community and the eruption of fresh fears about Catholic recusancy, have been extremely well studied by scholars.[70] In sermons and pamphlets, the favoured media for Jacobean political communication, writers replayed the near-disaster in order to offer information and consolation to the public as well as to demonize the conspirators.[71] Anne James's study of the textual afterlives of the Gunpowder Plot has revealed the high level of engagement by dramatists, preachers, and pamphleteers following the discovery of the plot.[72] To quote the prosecuting attorney, Sir Edward Coke, the plot was "*Sine exemplo*, beyond all examples, whether in fact or fiction, even of the tragique Poets, who did beate their wits to represent the most fearefull and horrible murthers."[73] The public's fascination with the near-disaster produced, in Allison P. Hobgood's words, a "culture of terror," one that firmly established a "collective national paranoia associated with that treasonous act."[74]

During the investigation of the Gunpowder Plot, the conspirator's remorse became synonymous with equivocation. In *A True and Perfect Relation of the Whole Proceedings against the Late Most Barbarous Traitors* (1606), an anonymously authored, government-sanctioned account of the trial of Father Henry Garnet, the state accuses the Jesuit priest of penning "A Treatise of Equivocation" (c. 1598) in order to justify "amphibology, or mixed speeches."[75] For the magistrate, the giving of truthful testimony was the bedrock of legal proceedings. To quote Chief Justice Sir John Popham (who presided over the trial of Garnet's fellow priest Father Robert Southwell in 1595), "yf this Doctrine [of equivocation] should be allowed, it would supplant all Justice, for we are men, and no Gods, *and cane* judge but according to theire [to men's] outward actiones *and* speeches, *and* not according to there secrete *and* inward intentions."[76]

In the minds of judges and lawyers, then, the doctrine of equivocation attacked fundamental legal principles. During Garnet's trial, Coke was at pains to establish the heinous nature of equivocation: "perfidious and perjurious Equivocating" sanctioned subjects to "not onely simply to conceale or denie an open trueth, but Religiously to averre … to swear that which themselves know to be most false, and all this by reserving a secret and private sense inwardly to themselves."[77] Those who practised equivocation, such as Garnet, had "no faith, no bond of Religion or civilitie, no conscience of trueth."[78] They transgressed both law and nature: "The law and Sanction of Nature, hath (as it were) married the heart & tongue, by joyning and knitting of them together in a certaine kinde of marriage; and therefore when there is discorde betweene them two, the speech that proceedes from them, is said to be conceived in Adulterie, & he that breedes such bastard children offends against Chastitie."[79]

In the detailed reporting of Coke's prosecution of Garnet, the author of *A True and Perfect Relation* clearly wanted to convey to readers the demonic allure of Garnet. Yet, from a modern perspective, one gleans a different lesson: that Garnet's trial reveals just how dependent remorse and repentance are on the willingness of the spectating audience to see (and believe) them. Faced with a hostile audience, there was nothing Garnet could have done to convince them that he was capable of remorse. At one point in the proceedings, Garnet, exhausted by rounds of interrogations, reportedly broke down in "remorse." Hearing the Earl of Salisbury's remark "that Jesuits were condemned by Jesuits" – that Garnet's confession had exposed and condemned his fellow conspirators – "*Garnet (as it should seeme) being here mightily touched with remorse of his offence, prayed God and the King, that other Catholickes might not fare the worse for his sake.*"[80] That parenthetical remark, "*as it should seeme*," carries the suggestion that Garnet's remorse was inauthentic, counterfeited, rehearsed. Because Garnet was an equivocator, his remorse must be fake. In his final address to the court, Coke doubted Garnet's capacity for remorse:

> But *Pœnitentia vera nunquam sera, sed pœnitentia sera rarò vera.* True repentance is indeed never too late: but late repentance is seldome found true, which yet I pray the mercifull Lord to grant unto them, that having a sense of their offences, they may make a true and sincere Confession both for their soules health, and for the good and safty [*sic*] of the King and this State.[81]

When Coke says that he "pray[s] the mercifull Lord to grant unto them … a true and sincere Confession," he all but implies that it is impossible to believe such a miracle could happen.

The sensational reporting of the conspiracy, the publication of Coke's examination of Garnet, made the problem of remorse a matter of public interest, and this is one of the historical contexts of *Macbeth*. If nothing else, Lady Macbeth's unconscious confession reveals the powerlessness of legal or religious authorities to draw out and facilitate true confessions. But I think the scene does more than that: it suggests that remorse is a fiction, one whose existence depends on the imagination of the spectator.

Seeing Is Believing, Believing Is Seeing

The sleepwalking scene is less concerned with showing the state of Lady Macbeth's salvation than with the way spectators get to actively and imaginatively participate in the construction of her remorse. In this respect, the scene builds a case against the law's silence around the participatory nature of legal emotions and on the particular fictions underscoring the very notion of sincere remorse. Remorse – at least the detection of remorse – is a function of the communal imagination, or so the scene suggests.

Remorse, according to legal scholars, is an "interpersonal" emotion that reveals the extent of the offender's regret for their action and empathy for the victim of the crime or the victim's (or their own) family.[82] Psychologists call remorse a "retractive" emotion: as contrition eats away at the offender's psyche, he or she will try to withdraw from the painful memory of the crime. Sometimes, remorse might be verbalized as "'I wish I had not done that' or 'I wish I was not like that.'"[83] This aversion to the memory of the act constitutes a form of "rejected action"; it is rejected in the sense that the memory triggers acute pain for the offender. But the offender cannot actually or fully "retract" from the memory because the impulse to banish the memory of the crime inevitably reinforces the painful memory and vice versa. Each attempt to bury the feeling of remorse only serves to drive the pain deeper. That aptly captures Lady Macbeth's condition.

There is a well-established tradition in *Macbeth* criticism that sees Lady Macbeth as thoroughly mad as opposed to sleepwalking. The text allows for that possibility, and the actor has tremendous leeway in negotiating the scene. For my part, I read Lady Macbeth as sleepwalking because that brings her tragic narrative full circle. In her first soliloquy, Lady Macbeth calls on the "spirits that tend on mortal thoughts" to "stop up th'access and passage to remorse, / That no compunctious visitings of nature / Shake my fell purpose" (1.5.3–4, 7–8). Abraham Stoll observes that the word "compunction" is synonymous with "regret"; it also "carries within it the metaphor of the prick of conscience: reflecting its etymology, the first definition of 'compunction' in the *OED* is 'Pricking or stinging of the conscience or heart.'"[84] The sleepwalking scene reveals the fatal consequences of those "compunctious visitings of nature" on Lady Macbeth's mind.

Throughout the play, Shakespeare has carefully avoided the word "conscience." Yet the play, and this scene in particular, is deeply concerned with the psychological and somatic effects of the afflicted conscience. The decision to skirt around the expected words of conscience recalls the relationship between power and language: a sacred word can lose its intended power through negligent usage. When Macbeth falsely and insincerely exclaims in the presence of

Malcolm, Macduff, Lennox, and the others "O, yet I do repent me of my fury, / That I did kill them [the groomsmen]" (2.3.98–9), he empties the word "repent" of its spiritual essence. By avoiding the word "conscience" in a play centrally concerned with the psychological and physical damage wrought by the afflicted conscience, Shakespeare encourages audiences to conjure remorse into existence by using the power of their own imagination. Using theatrical objects and costumes, remorse appears within the playgoer's visual field. Objects silently cue Lady Macbeth's conscience. It begins with that stage direction, "*Enter Lady [Macbeth] with a taper*" (5.1.14.1). The taper, as we recall from Eleanor's penance, was a symbol for repentance.[85] If the taper visually echoes the public penance, so too does Lady Macbeth's nightgown. While sixteenth- and seventeenth-century nightgowns were dyed in a variety of colours, inventories and paintings from the period suggest that many nightgowns or dresses were constructed from light-coloured linen.[86] The actor could have worn a pale nightgown, one resembling the penitent's white sheet. These elements of the *mise en scene* – the taper, the nightgown – urge audiences to see contrition and remorse. Genuine remorse, the scene insists, is perceptible when the faculty of conscience operates independently of the conscious mind. By implication, the sleepwalking scene casts doubt on one of the law's fundamental promises: the magistrate's capacity to detect remorse or true repentance in the words, gestures, and looks of the accused. Indeed, the scene's rejection of that legal commonplace also discloses the law's ritualized character. The law's rigid adherence to ceremonies and forms recalls the so-called "empty formalism" of Catholic sacraments.[87]

The overall impression of the sleepwalking scene is one of irrefutable authenticity. There can be no question of Lady Macbeth feigning emotions because she is not in control of her body. Artifice requires deliberation, consciousness, and awareness. Although Lady Macbeth's remorse is, technically, a performance by an actor exploiting the standard gestures for playing contrition – a point of fact that Shakespeare slyly acknowledges when he has the Doctor say, "besides her walking and other actual *performances*, what, at any time, have you heard her say?" (5.1.8–9, my emphasis) – the scene resists the impression of theatricality. Thus, on a basic level, her performance is manifestly fake and scripted – it takes place on stage and every word was written in advance by the playwright. But on an affective level, an emotional one achieved by the audience's participation in blurring the real and the imagined, the theatricality of the stage and the "truth" audiences find in the performance, Lady Macbeth's remorse comes across as more authentic than any courtroom confession could possibly be. The upshot of this performance is a rebuke of the law's orthodoxies – an exposé of its futile effort to access the private conscience of the criminal subject. Within the larger context of anti-Catholic polemics against ceremonies, Shakespeare's analysis of law's customs – customs that reveal it to be an institution addicted to rituals of penance and absolution – is provocative, if not seditious.

Remorse beyond Shakespeare

In recent years, legal scholars have questioned courts' dependency on remorse. Children and adolescents, as Martha Grace Duncan points out, do not display expected signs of contrition because those expectations are based on studies of adult psychology.[88] Susan A. Bandes argues that "there is *no* good evidence that remorse can be evaluated based on facial expression, body language, or other nonverbal behavior," yet that sobering knowledge has not dampened judges and juries' confidence in "believ[ing] [that] they know remorse when they see it."[89] In the interrelated fields of criminology and psychology, scholars discover that age, gender, race, and ethnicity influence how jurors interpret signs of contrition. In the face of such strong empirical evidence, legal scholars have cautioned against reliance on a universal model of remorse. They argue instead that neither professionals nor laypeople – neither judges nor jury – are able to accurately discern guilt. One person's reading of remorse differs from another's. The advances in critical legal studies do not seem to have reformed the day-to-day operation of the courts: judges, jurors, and the public at large continue to place trust in their capacity to competently read faces.

It may be that the compulsion to detect remorse is too ingrained in our nature and therefore can never be entirely suppressed. It is not enough that a court convicts an offender of a crime and punishes the offender as the law demands. The community also needs to feel that the offender is sincerely sorry. Yet, paradoxically, the performance of remorse often divides interpretations, producing uncertainty as to whether the prisoner's signs of contrition can be trusted. The very process of displaying remorse, in the legal setting, threatens to hollow it of meaning. When the prisoner generates visible signs of remorse (a mournful look, a sigh, a shedding of tears, etc.) or verbalizes remorse by taking the stand at sentencing, these signs are prone to be anxiously treated to paranoid over-reading. Austin Sarat observes that Anglo-American legal culture "both demands remorse and feels anxious in its presence."[90] His conclusion links to Peter Brooks's discussion of confession. Confession, Brooks muses, is "a difficult and slippery notion" because once it is articulated, it immediately elicits suspicion: "[w]e want confessions, yet we are suspicious of them."[91] The cultural anxiety surrounding remorse (and confession) is not new, as early modern texts remind us. If any legal emotion stands to benefit from a historically grounded analysis, it is remorse.

In *Macbeth*, Shakespeare uses the condition of the theatre to highlight the contingent and fictive nature of remorse. We see Lady Macbeth in a remorseful state because we have collectively immersed ourselves in that fiction, one written and performed in such a way as to almost disguise its own fictiveness. The scene carefully avoids the usual signifiers of remorse. It persuades us to believe that what we see is Lady Macbeth in a wholly unscripted moment. In the sleepwalking scene, the fathomless nature of human remorse is signified by the breakdown of language, textually represented by Lady Macbeth's "O, o, o" (5.1.41). This expression of sorrow seems to arise from the innermost recess of her soul. Like Lear's despairing "O, o, o, o" (in the quarto *King Lear*), Lady Macbeth's wails exceed language itself. The reactions of the Doctor and the Gentlewoman lend further weight to the impression of an unrehearsed expression of remorse. The sleepwalking scene implies that remorse is a fiction that belongs to the communal imagination. This rewriting of remorse as an ineluctable collective fantasy challenges the integrity of the law, which relies on language to aggressively assert its dominion over an individual's emotions. Early modern magistrates extended their jurisdictional control over both the internal and external forums, over crime and sin, over the body and soul of the individual. But *Macbeth*'s sleepwalking scene suggests that if spectators see remorse it is because they have *chosen* to see it – because they have empathetically felt with the penitent, because they have recognized themselves in her. Remorse does not have an existence, an ontology or a reality, beyond what exists in the inward eye of the spectator.

With all this in mind, I have several more thoughts on Nathaniel Rogers's "An Exhortacion to Prisoners Condemned." While the text traces the expectations and rules for the magistrate and prisoners, it falls short of capturing its culture's anxieties surrounding remorse. It does not consider how a magistrate's demand to see legible signs of the prisoner's "true repentance" elides the question of sincerity and authenticity. It assumes that inward states such as contrition may be represented. It hides theological debates about the privacy of remorse as an emotion experienced only by the individual and shared with God. It does not register the rich literature on conscience that insists on the secret, private nature of conscience. It contains none of drama's understanding of the communal nature of remorse and other legal emotions. All these blind spots in "An Exhortacion" are arguably symptomatic of the law that it mirrors, and attending to them matters because that law – the common law of Shakespeare's England – continues to shape Anglo-American legal forms, customs, and practices. Still, at present, in spite of good evidence pointing to the contrary, judges and juries assume that remorse has a semiotics, an expression, a signifier, and a "right" or "wrong" form. But a play like *Macbeth* fundamentally challenges that assumption by showing remorse to be an emotion that exists because spectators believe it exists – a belief that is conditioned on affective contagion spreading from the penitent to the audience. Remorse, like any enduring fiction, is a product of our ungovernable imagination. And if this key legal emotion of communal justice is socially, culturally, and theatrically constructed, then does it not suggest that communal justice itself hinges on the communal imagination?

Postscript

No official legal literature in the early modern period speaks at any length about the lay magistrate. This omission is unsurprising given the professional bias of those authors. Lawyers, judges, and jurists prized expert knowledge. The legal characters they were interested in were those who shared their professional sensibility. Yet we know that lay magistrates existed – that ordinary people carried much of the burden of the law, especially when it came to criminal justice. As in birdwatching, then, once we train our eyes to register the presence of lay magistrates, suddenly they appear everywhere in the archive. This book has been just that exercise in attentive looking. Using early modern drama as a primary archive, it has traced the literary representation of lay magistrates engaged in various forms of communal justice. Studying such dramatic representations has clarified the role of popular authors in shaping the public's understanding of law – what law meant symbolically and emotionally during the rise of the common law. The literature of communal justice was written during a unique period of struggle and competition between the defenders of professionalism and the critics of it. Attuned to the public's anti-professionalism sentiment, playwrights – along with moralists and preachers – helped to define magistracy as the collective action of conscientious individuals. The discursive battles between these camps, fought over the nature of legal authority and the people's place in a legal order, shaped cultural expectations around issues of individual and communal legal responsibility.

The goal of *Communal Justice* has been to reconstruct that watershed moment by examining the work of popular literature – early modern drama, in particular, but also religious and moral literature – both in idealizing communal justice and in interrupting institutional logics about legal administration. The drama of communal justice served many purposes. It critiqued emergent, professional standards of legal authority and expertise, it encouraged a renewal of neighbourly relations in the face of economic scarcity, it explored the deforming as well as reparative power of individual and collective legal action, it recognized the limits of communal legal knowledge, and it generated a profound respect for the privacy of the individual conscience.

As a space dedicated to sustaining the public's imagination and emotions, early modern theatre accommodated near-boundless creative explorations of legal concepts and legal feelings. Theatre's communal nature mirrored and accentuated the narrative of communal justice. One is hard pressed to find another medium so perfectly suited to the message. Some plays, such as the domestic tragedies analysed in chapter 3, unabashedly staged hyper-romantic images of communal justice. Other plays, such as Shakespeare's *King Lear*, discussed in chapter 4, revealed the reparative potential of communal witnessing, inviting audiences to reflect on the ethics of spectatorship. Still others, such as *Macbeth*, examined in chapter 5, celebrated lay magistracy by relocating legal punishment from the law to the individual conscience. Whatever their strategies of representation of communal justice and lay magistracy, these plays addressed audiences' desire to see not only dramatic depictions of justice, retribution, and order but also versions of themselves and their communities placed at the centre of a legal cosmos. Early modern drama did not invent the character of the citizen-sleuth or the conscientious bystander – these figures also appear in Athenian tragedies, for example – but it did much to centre these lay magistrates in the popular legal imagination.[1] Early modern theatre made the language, emotions, and actions of lay magistrates undertaking the at times self-endangering labour of communal justice at once more visible and more heroic.

The closing of the playhouses in 1642 shut down a popular venue for the production of dramatic works that touched on matters of law. Other genres swiftly emerged as outlets for communal legal knowledge-making. During the revolutionary decades of the 1640s and 1650s, anonymous authors furnished the public with familiar tales – like those examined in chapter 2 – featuring bad lawyers and corrupt lawmen to drive home the value of lay legal participation. These prose tracts blended several genres: complaint, satire, and religious parable. In the anonymously authored *Every Mans Right: Or, Englands Perspective-Glasse* (1646), for example, the author complains that the "commonalty" has been

> inslaved ... unto the arbitrary will and power of a few mercinarie Lawyers whose profession and gayne inslaves them to the will and disposition of the very worst and skum of men and women, and ingages them (as hirelings) to maintaine their cause at any barre of justice (so called) for the price of iniquity; I mean for their fee of ten or twenty shillings, be the cause never so bace [base] and unjust, so by them mayntained.[2]

The attack on "mercinarie Lawyers" slavishly devoted to "the very worst and skum of men and women" takes place against a complex background of political and jurisdictional struggle between the English crown and its parliament. But the author's grievance is a timeless one. Modernize the spelling and punctuation and it could find a receptive mass audience today.

It was during the violent upheavals of the mid-seventeenth century that the idea of lay magistracy came closest to becoming a political movement. Religious moderates, as well as more radical groups such as the Levellers, the Quakers, and the Diggers, agitated for greater legal representation and less legal mediation.[3] In *The Lawyers Bane* (1647), after rehearsing the many abuses perpetuated on unsuspecting laypeople by lawyers, Benjamin Nicholson recommends cutting out the intermediaries: translate and publish law "in the English tongue, and not in Latin, French, or any other language whatsoever, and in a stile so easie, plaine and familiar, that all may know them, and be enabled to understand them."[4] In *Juries Justified* (1651), William Walwyn asks, "[w]hat more fundamental liberty than the trial of causes by Juries of twelve men? What more constant, more glorious administration of justice and Righteousness?" The answer, he trusted his readers to surmise, was that trial by a jury of one's peers was the only guarantor of English "liberty."[5] In the polemic, Walwyn traces the jury to the pre-Norman era, before the "yoke" and "superstition" of Norman rule. Knowing what we know about the origins of the assize (discussed in chapter 1), we might note that he conveniently ignores the fact that the jury of presentment, the trial jury, and the coroner's jury were legal innovations of Angevin royal justice. These cherished English institutions were never strictly "English," but like the English language itself, combinations of different European legal traditions.

But for all its intensity and fire, the movement for radical law reform was short-lived. It did not ultimately affect the law's relentless production of its institutional memory. After the Restoration, a second phase of professionalization took hold. The common law society returned with renewed confidence. Just as the Stuarts were restored to power, so the great tradition of legal writing founded by Sir Edward Coke, Sir Francis Bacon, Sir William Lambarde, and other Elizabethan and Jacobean jurists was revitalized. For example, in *The History of the Common Law of England* (published posthumously in 1713), by the judge Sir Matthew Hale, a mention of "the People" of England appears in the fourth chapter. Hale does not explore their role in law in any sustained way.[6] The final chapter of Hale's text is devoted to the English jury trial, which Hale celebrates as "the best Trial in the World," and the character of the lay judge – in the form of the trial juror – briefly emerges from the margins. Hale observes that the jury trial allows the juror to assess, and at times, to reject, witness testimony "for the Jurors are not only Judges of the Fact, but many Times of the Truth of Evidence; and if there be just Cause to disbelieve what a Witness swears, they [the jurors] are not bound to give their Verdict according to the Evidence or Testimony of that Witness."[7] This statement would seem to place some trust in the lay judge's keen sense of the truth of testimony. Yet in the very next paragraph, Hale undercuts the value of lay judgment by emphasizing that it is the professional, the judge, whose presence at the trial, "is able in Matters of Law emerging upon the Evidence to direct them [the jurors]; and also, in Matters of Fact, to give them a great Light and Assistance by his weighing the Evidence before them, and observing where the Question and Knot of the Business lies, and by shewing them his Opinion even in Matter of Fact."[8] In other words, Hale suggests that when the judge "shew[s]" the jury "his Opinion even in Matter of Fact," he is not overstepping his role or overextending the power of the Bench, but merely doing what he needs to do to ensure that the truth is not perverted by false testimony.[9] The message is clear: lay judges cannot be trusted to know matters of fact, let alone matters of law. The curtailing of lay legal authority that one sees in the passage is mirrored in other notable seventeenth-century histories of the common law. In his *Origines Juridiciales* (1671), the antiquarian Sir William Dugdale traces the history of the English "courts of justice" to a biblical past, one evacuated of lay judges:

> For when by the multiplying of People, iniquity so increased, as that contentions and differences did daily more and more abound; it was impossible, that any one person should hear and determine all their Causes ... Hence was it therefore, that *Jethro* advised *Moses*, whom God had set over the *Israelites*[,] the first people of the World unto whom any Written *Laws* were delivered as their chief Ruler, to commit the distribution of Justice, under himself, unto several persons, and in sundry places, as in the *xviii*. Chapt. of the Book of *Exodus* appeareth.[10]

Dugdale goes on to describe the rise of professional judges, from medieval itinerant justices to Tudor justices of the assize. Barely a word is spared for the common law's *communal* past – and there is little mention of lay magistracy or the power of individuals to do justice by virtue of the authority and knowledge granted them by conscience.

Although *Communal Justice* has been chiefly concerned with literary and historical problems, it is a project that has settled into its present form as popular distrust of legal institutions has grown to epic proportions. Many people in my community – in yours too, perhaps – believe that the law courts are unjust, that racial and socio-economic privilege, not the facts, shapes the outcome of legal interactions, from traffic stops to criminal indictments. Members of our communities feel terrorized by the law. Protection means self-reliance. What is the value of studying the literature or history of a bygone era when we are daily confronted by existential questions about the law's fairness and effectiveness? For some people, the answer is simple: there is no point. The problems that demand our individual and collective attention now have no solutions in the past. I respect that reality.

But for me, there is value – emotional as well as intellectual value – in excavating the past. The people of the early modern era were endlessly creative and resourceful in combining discursive and imaginative tools – from conscience writing to theatrical performance – to claim legal authority for themselves and to assert themselves as agents capable of determining just outcomes. Early modern authors cared deeply about justice and community. They idealized communality, sometimes to the point of absurd improbability, in order to sustain a doctrine of participatory justice and shared legal responsibility. This aspect of their culture fascinates me and it is, I argue, worth remembering, preserving, and analysing.

In closing, I want to reflect on what it means to me to undertake research in early modern law and literature. In a searing analysis of feminist labour in higher education, Sara Ahmed argues that "in queer, feminist, and antiracist work, self-care is about the creation of community, fragile communities ... assembled out of the experience of being shattered. We reassemble ourselves through the ordinary, everyday, and often painstaking work of looking after ourselves; looking after each other."[11] Ahmed's definition of self-care takes the form of tending to one's emotional, psychological, intellectual, or physical needs, and that work is inextricable from the care that one extends to – or receives from – one's community. For Ahmed, it is not only the people whom one invites into one's life but also the texts and objects that one places within one's field of vision that help fulfil this "painstaking work" of mutual care.

Some of the early modern texts, and the inspiring scholarship on those texts that appear in the notes and bibliography of this book, have done that important work for me. They have sustained me. I invite these texts and their authors into my legality, one that uniquely suits my embodied condition, because they remind me that individuals, working with others, have the ability to change the course of justice. Having these texts in my visual field, in my emotional orbit, has fine-tuned my understanding of the legal power – constructive as well as destructive – of communities. The early moderns knew perfectly well that sometimes living in an intimate community meant dealing with neighbours who were petty, insincere, prejudicial, and apathetic. But they consistently chose to write, stage, and applaud affirming stories of neighbourly love and care. To me, that redemptive narrative of communal justice has lost none of its potency despite the passage of time.

Acknowledgments

Working on this book has allowed me to connect with a wonderful community of scholars, teachers, and students. My first thanks go out to Rebecca Lemon. She has supported this project and my study of the Renaissance from the moment we met. Rebecca, Will Fisher, Steve Hindle, Derek Dunne, Leila Watkins, Jessica Apolloni, Elizabeth E. Tavares, and Aaron Shapiro read the manuscript with the greatest of care. They are generous readers. I hope they find their feedback accurately reflected in the book. Frances E. Dolan read my chapters-in-progress with speedy efficiency and told me to send out the proposal without further delay. Cynthia B. Herrup gave me books from her library and entertained my observations about literary representations of participatory justice. Bruce R. Smith, Joseph A. Dane, and Heather James offered judicious comments on early drafts. Will Fisher got me to the finish line. He organized summer writing workshops for the project, giving me a concrete deadline to work toward. I am grateful to him, Rebecca Lemon, Derek Dunne, Heidi Brayman, Marjorie Rubright, Andrew Fleck, and Tiffany Werth for participating in the workshops and sharing their wealth of knowledge and experience. I am grateful, too, to Juan Gomez for finding a quiet room for us to gather in.

Sharon Oster, Kadin Henningsen, Mark Eaton, April Davidauskis, Brennan Parks, Arunima Paul, Dhiraj Goel, Matthew and Christine Carillo-Vincent, Gino Conti, Megan Herrold, Lauren Weindling, Seth Lerer, Kate Flint, Alice Echols, Daniel Reeve, Colby Gordon, Catherine Chou, Jennifer Park, Dagmar Van Engen, Laura Aydelotte, Trisha Tucker, Rick Ross, Sophie Lesinska, Larry Allen, the late Marilyn Morgan, Nina Berkin, Mark Edelbrock, and the rest of what I think of as my California people ensured that each research trip was special. When I was teaching, I relied on my online writing groups for accountability and support. Wendy Hyman, Brooke Conti, Marissa Greenberg, Lina Perkins Wilder, Claire M. L. Bourne, Kim Hedlin, Dianne Mitchell, and Jessie Hock were generous in sharing their knowledge of the manuscript-to-publication process over Slack and email.

The Huntington Library is where I conducted much of the research and writing. I am grateful to the staff and librarians for their extraordinary professionalism and courtesy. Steve Hindle, Mary Robertson, and Vanessa Wilkie know the collections inside and out and I benefited from their knowledge. The remainder of my research was conducted at the British Library, Lambeth Palace Library, Centre for Reformation and Renaissance Studies at the University of Toronto, Folger Shakespeare Library, Macalester Library, and Library of Congress, and I am grateful to all the librarians and curators who helped me with my queries. My research travel was made possible through USC–Huntington EMSI Fellowships, Huntington Library Francis Bacon Foundation Fellowships, Macalester College Wallace Scholarly Activity Grants, and an Academy for the Advanced Study in the Renaissance Fellowship.

The audiences at the conferences of the Modern Language Association, Shakespeare Association of America, Renaissance Society of America, Law, Culture and the Humanities, and North American Conference on British Studies – and those at the Macalester Humanities Colloquium, the Carleton College Medieval and Renaissance Colloquium, and Bryn Mawr College – all helped me to finesse the argument of the project. On these and other occasions for scholarly conversation, I benefited from talking to Marissa Greenberg, Todd Butler, Paul Yachnin, Emma Whipday, Christopher Foley, Edward Gieskes, James Hirsh, Brendan John Gillis, Edward Muir, Regina Schwartz, Randall Martin, Bradin Cormack, Lorna Hutson, Rachel E. Holmes, Matthew J. Smith, Karen Cunningham, Constance Jordan, Harry Keyishian, András Kiséry, Stephanie Elsky, Cristina León Alfar, Cathy Yandell, Jamie K. Taylor, and Alexis Lothian.

An earlier version of chapter 2 was published as "On Judges and the Art of Judicature: Shakespeare's *Henry IV, Part 2,*" *Studies in Philology* 114.1 (2017): 97–123 and a sliver of chapter 1 appeared in "Jurisprudence by Aphorisms: Francis Bacon and the 'Uses' of Small Forms," first published on 31 January 2019, https://doi.org/10.1177/1743872119826455 (print version and issue assignment forthcoming), and both are reprinted by permission of the publishers, the University of North Carolina Press and SAGE, respectively.

Suzanne Rancourt, my editor at the University of Toronto Press, shared my vision for the book from the moment we spoke at an MLA conference in Chicago. She shepherded the project through various stages of review and production. She made sure things moved along even when the pandemic struck. An author could not ask for more in an editor. The readers of the press offered detailed, incisive, and encouraging comments on the manuscript. They shaped the book in myriad ways, and I am deeply grateful to them for their generous engagement with the project. I am grateful to Anne Laughlin for her help with the copy editing, Christine Robertson for managing the production schedule, and Victoria Baker for creating the index. The beautiful book jacket, based on a painting by Edwin Austin Abbey, was designed by the UTP marketing team.

·   At Macalester College, and in the Twin Cities at large, I have found a welcoming community of teachers and scholars whose work (in the classroom and in the profession) raises the bar for what is possible. Daylanne K. English, Andrea Kaston Tange, Amy E. Elkins, James Dawes, Matthew Burgess, Peter Bognanni, Emma Törzs, Michael Prior, Marlon James, Jan Beebe, Lori Ziegelmeier, Leah Witus, Dennis Cao, Mark Mazullo, Rivi Handler-Spitz, Satoko Suzuki, Sam Asarnow, Rebecca Grossman-Kahn, Arthur Mitchell, Susanna Drake, Beth Severy-Hoven, Colin Agur, and Valerie Belair-Gagnon are among those whose company and conversation I treasure. I benefited from the long-term research assistance of Sam Greenstein and Amy Vandervelde and the short-term assistance of Rachel Wilson, Leon Swerdel-Rich, Josh Weiner, and Amanda Zimmerman. Teaching has improved the way I think and write about early modern literature and law and justice. I am grateful to my students for the time we spent together pouring over early modern texts. Some of the things we discovered have made it into the book.

To Laura Chesne, for years of friendship, laughter, care, and inspiration, my heartfelt gratitude.

My final thanks go out to my family. My parents – Li-ping Geng and Liya Gu – shared their love of literature with me and were unstintingly supportive of my decision to pursue English studies. Their passion for the arts is matched by that of my Vermont family, Rob, Elaine, Erin, and Andrew McIntyre. During the writing process, Andrew kept me grounded in a gentler reality. He assured me there were no limits to what I could accomplish. Andrew, I am delighted to be able to present this finished book to you.

Notes

Preface

1 Robert Yarington, *Two Lamentable Tragedies*, ed. Chiaki Hanabusa (Manchester: Manchester University Press for the Malone Society, 2013), sig. D3r.
2 Edward Coke, *Le second part des reportes del Edward Coke* (London: Printed by Adam Islip in ædibus Thomæ Wight, 1602), sig. ¶5v.
3 Patricia Ewick and Susan S. Silbey, *The Common Place of Law: Stories from Everyday Life* (Chicago: University of Chicago Press, 1998), 17.
4 Ibid.

Introduction

1 Chapter 1 provides a fuller account of the assize. The distinction between "superior" and "inferior" magistrates was a common one; see, for example, *A Solace for This Hard Season: Published by Occasion of Continuance of the Scarcitie of Corne, and Excessive Prices of All Other Kind of Provision* (London: Printed for John Legate, 1595), sig. C2r. Also William Barlow, *The Sermon Preached at Paules Crosse, the Tenth Day of November, Being the next Sunday after the Discoverie of This Late Horrible Treason. / Preached by the Right Reverend Father in God William Lord Bishop of Rochester* (London: Printed for Mathew Lawe, 1606), sig. D2v. The division between superior and inferior, however, was also relative. Hence, Michael Dalton identifies constables as the justice of the peace's "inferior Minister." Michael Dalton, *The Countrey Justice, Conteyning the Practise of the Justices of the Peace out of Their Sessions* (London: Printed for the Societie of Stationers, 1618), sig. B3v.
2 Francis Bacon, *The Works of Francis Bacon*, ed. James Spedding, Robert Leslie Ellis, and Douglas Denon Heath, vol. 5 (London: Longman, 1858), 89.
3 "Visne, n.," *OED.*
4 Cynthia B. Herrup, *The Common Peace: Participation and the Criminal Law in Seventeenth-Century England* (Cambridge: Cambridge University Press, 1987), 4.

5 Pierre Bourdieu, *The Field of Cultural Production: Essays on Art and Literature*, ed. Randal Johnson (New York: Columbia University Press, 1993), 5. One of the most cogent explanations of "habitus" in my memory comes from an introduction to the writings of Norbert Elias; habitus is a kind of "'second nature.' It refers to those levels of our personality makeup which are not inherent or innate but are very deeply habituated in us by learning through social experience from birth onward – so deeply habituated, in fact, that they feel 'natural' or inherent even to ourselves." Norbert Elias, *Norbert Elias on Civilization, Power, and Knowledge: Selected Writings*, ed. Stephen Mennell and Johan Goudsblom (Chicago: University of Chicago Press, 1998), 15.

6 William Sheppard, *The Touch-Stone of Common Assurances. Or, A Plain and Familiar Treatise, Opening the Learning of the Common Assurances or Conveyances of the Kingdome* (London: Printed by M. F. for W. Lee, M. Walbancke, D. Pakeman, and G. Bedell, 1648), sig. A4v. Sheppard, Oliver Cromwell's jurist, was perhaps "the greatest legal publicist in English history." Christopher W. Brooks, "Paradise Lost? Law, Literature, and History in Restoration England," in *The Oxford Handbook of English Law and Literature, 1500–1700* (Oxford: Oxford University Press, 2017), 207. On his life and career, see Nancy L. Matthews, *William Sheppard, Cromwell's Law Reformer* (Cambridge: Cambridge University Press, 1984).

7 Sheppard, *The Touch-Stone*, sig. A4v.

8 Wilfrid R. Prest, *The Rise of the Barristers: A Social History of the English Bar, 1590–1640* (Oxford: Clarendon, 1986), 7.

9 Prest, 8. See "Table 1.1. Bar calls 1518–1639 (decennial totals)."

10 "Table 7.8: Quinquennial English population total 1541–1871," in E.A. Wrigley and R.S. Schofield, *The Population History of England, 1541–1871: A Reconstruction* (London: Arnold, 1981), 208–9. For another vivid account of how the "increase in the size of the profession was beginning to outrun the increase in the number of suits," see Christopher W. Brooks, *Pettyfoggers and Vipers of the Commonwealth: The "Lower Branch" of the Legal Profession in Early Modern England* (Cambridge: Cambridge University Press, 2004), 116.

11 Louis A. Knafla, "The Matriculation Revolution and Education at the Inns of Court in Renaissance England," in *Tudor Men and Institutions*, ed. Arthur Slavin (Baton Rouge: Louisiana State University Press, 1972), 238. For more context, Knafla writes: "one can conclude that the period 1560–78 had a constant rate of matriculation, and that the years 1579–84 comprised the first period of highly accelerated growth. Likewise, the years 1585–93 can be interpreted as years of consolidation, from which a second period of accelerated growth began in 1594" (237).

12 For an account of Elizabethan and Jacobean anti-lawyer satire, see Edward Gieskes, *Representing the Professions: Administration, Law, and Theater in Early Modern England* (Newark: University of Delaware Press, 2006), 119–20. For a

survey of anti-law and anti-lawyer satire (not limited to the early modern period), see Edward F.J. Tucker, *Intruder into Eden: Representations of the Common Lawyer in English Literature, 1350–1750* (Columbia: Camden House, 1984).

13 Michel Foucault, "Of Other Spaces," trans. Jay Miskowiec, *Diacritics* 16, no. 1 (1986): 24.

14 Paul Yachnin, "Performing Publicity," *Shakespeare Bulletin* 28, no. 2 (2010): 210.

15 Sarah Beckwith, *Shakespeare and the Grammar of Forgiveness* (Ithaca: Cornell University Press, 2011), 5.

16 Beckwith, 4.

17 Bruce R. Smith, *The Acoustic World of the Renaissance: Attending to the O-Factor* (Chicago: University of Chicago Press, 1999), 271.

18 Pierre Bourdieu, *Distinction: A Social Critique of the Judgement of Taste*, trans. Richard Nice (Cambridge, MA: Harvard University Press, 1984), 57.

19 Pierre Bourdieu, "The Force of Law: Towards a Sociology of the Juridical Field," *Hastings Law Journal* 38 (July 1986): 817, original emphasis.

20 Bourdieu, 817.

21 Bourdieu, 817.

22 See my preface for a discussion of Ewick and Silbey's concept of legality.

23 Patricia Ewick and Susan S. Silbey, *The Common Place of Law: Stories from Everyday Life* (Chicago: University of Chicago Press, 1998), 78.

24 Ewick and Silbey, 77.

25 Cultural theorists have repeatedly demonstrated that common sense (what Aristotle calls *endoxa*) is a social construction – a myth that masquerades as incontrovertible fact. Aristotle, *On Rhetoric: A Theory of Civic Discourse*, trans. George A. Kennedy (New York: Oxford University Press, 1991), 11.

26 Roland Barthes, "Myth Today," in *Mythologies*, ed. Annette Lavers (London: Vintage, 2000), 120.

27 For a brief account of how communal justice exists in tension with private prosecution, see J.H. Baker, *An Introduction to English Legal History*, 4th ed. (Oxford: Oxford University Press, 2007), 3–8. From the Old French *apeler*, "to call or name, in the sense of naming (that is, accusing) someone as the culprit who had committed a certain crime," the appeal was a legally sanctioned form of private prosecution that phased out over the course of the sixteenth and seventeenth centuries. John H. Langbein, Renée Lettow Lerner, and Bruce P. Smith, eds., *History of the Common Law: The Development of Anglo-American Legal Institutions* (New York: Aspen, 2009), 29.

28 Tom Lambert, *Law and Order in Anglo-Saxon England* (Oxford: Oxford University Press, 2017), 353.

29 Lambert, 353. Lambert observes that the "ideal" of communal justice was often at odds with everyday practice: "bribes and threats in the laws designed to persuade individuals to participate suggest that – as we would have been wise to suspect anyway – reality was often more apathetic" (353).

30 The "first finder" was duty-bound to raise hue and cry; see R.F. Hunnisett, *The Medieval Coroner* (Cambridge: Cambridge University Press, 1961), 10.

31 Hunnisett, 12.

32 Regina M. Schwartz, *Loving Justice, Living Shakespeare* (Oxford: Oxford University Press, 2016), 120.

33 Langbein, Lerner, and Smith, *History of the Common Law*, 27.

34 "Hue and cry, n.," *OED*. For a discussion of how hue and cry and other "policing duties" formed the basis of the post-Conquest frankpledge system, see Langbein, Lerner, and Smith, 27. The Athenian state had a similar provision for the call to arms known as the "'run to the shout' or *boēthein*." Rachel Hall Sternberg, *Tragedy Offstage: Suffering and Sympathy in Ancient Athens* (Austin: University of Texas Press, 2006), 80.

35 Great Britain, *The Statutes of the Realm*, vol. 4, pt. 1 (London, 1819), 721.

36 Herrup, *The Common Peace*, 68.

37 Christopher W. Brooks, *Law, Politics, and Society in Early Modern England* (Cambridge: Cambridge University Press, 2008), 14.

38 Malcolm Gaskill, *Crime and Mentalities in Early Modern England* (Cambridge: Cambridge University Press, 2000), 242.

39 On church courts and their procedures, see Laura Gowing, *Common Bodies: Women, Touch and Power in Seventeenth-Century England* (New Haven: Yale University Press, 2003); Martin Ingram, *Church Courts, Sex and Marriage in England, 1570–1640* (Cambridge: Cambridge University Press, 1987). "Romano-canonic" (or Roman Canon) refers to judicial procedures of the Roman church, which contained elements of "imperial Roman practice, reworked in the Middle Ages for the needs of the church." Langbein, Lerner, and Smith, *History of the Common Law*, 126.

40 "The Common Pleas, usually known to contemporaries as the Bench (*curia domini regis de Banco*) or 'Common Place', though inferior to the King's Bench in the sense that its judgments were subject to review there by writ of error, was the pre-eminent court of law and had by far the largest share of all common-law business throughout our period." J.H. Baker, *The Oxford History of the Laws of England, Volume VI 1483–1558*, ed. J.H. Baker, vol. 6 (Oxford: Oxford University Press, 2003), 125.

41 J.A. Sharpe, "'Such Disagreement Betwyx Neighbours': Litigation and Human Relations in Early Modern England," in *Disputes and Settlements: Law and Human Relations in the West*, ed. John Bossy (Cambridge: Cambridge University Press, 1983), 168.

42 Gowing, *Common Bodies*, 13.

43 Timothy Stretton, *Women Waging Law in Elizabethan England* (Cambridge: Cambridge University Press, 1998), 65.

44 For a concise account of the different jurisdictions and the popular use of them (especially women's use), see Lotte Fikkers, "Early Modern Women in the English Courts of Law," *Literature Compass* (2018): 1–10.

45 Christopher W. Brooks, "Professions, Ideology and the Middling Sort in the
    Late Sixteenth and Early Seventeenth Centuries," in *The Middling Sort of People:
    Culture, Society, and Politics in England, 1550–1800*, ed. Jonathan Barry and
    Christopher W. Brooks (Houndmills: Macmillan, 1994), 123.

46 Steve Hindle, *The State and Social Change in Early Modern England, 1550–1640*
    (Houndmills: Palgrave, 2002), 23, original emphasis.

47 William Blackstone, *Commentaries on the Laws of England: Book III Of Private
    Wrongs*, ed. Thomas P. Gallanis (Oxford: Oxford University Press, 2016), 237. On
    the career of Blackstone and his impact on legal historiography, see Kathryn D.
    Temple, *Loving Justice: Legal Emotions in William Blackstone's England* (New York:
    New York University Press, 2019).

48 Frederic Maitland and Frederick Pollock, *The History of English Law before the
    Time of Edward I*, 2nd ed., vol. 1 (Cambridge: Cambridge University Press, 1898),
    37–40.

49 See, for example, Hunnisett, *The Medieval Coroner*; J.S. Cockburn, *A History
    of English Assizes, 1558–1714* (Cambridge: Cambridge University Press, 1972);
    Herrup, *The Common Peace*.

50 Keith Wrightson, *English Society, 1580–1680* (London: Hutchinson, 1982), 1982.
    For a critique of social history particularly as it pertains to accounting for crime
    in early modern England, see Matthew Lockwood, *The Conquest of Death:
    Violence and the Birth of the Modern English State* (New Haven: Yale University
    Press, 2017), 8.

51 Jonathan Barry and Christopher W. Brooks, eds., *The Middling Sort of People:
    Culture, Society, and Politics in England, 1550–1800* (Houndmills: Macmillan,
    1994), 1.

52 K.J. Kesselring, *Making Murder Public: Homicide in Early Modern England,
    1480–1680* (Oxford: Oxford University Press, 2019), 9.

53 See Frances E. Dolan, *True Relations: Reading, Literature, and Evidence in
    Seventeenth-Century England* (Philadelphia: University of Pennsylvania Press,
    2013); Natalie Zemon Davis, *Fiction in the Archives: Pardon Tales and Their Tellers
    in Sixteenth-Century France* (Stanford: Stanford University Press, 1987).

54 For an introduction to the field of law and literature, see Elizabeth S. Anker and
    Bernadette Meyler, eds., *New Directions in Law and Literature* (Oxford: Oxford
    University Press, 2017). On the state of law and literature in early modern
    literary studies, see the introduction by Lorna Hutson in Lorna Hutson, ed., *The
    Oxford Handbook of English Law and Literature, 1500–1700* (Oxford: Oxford
    University Press, 2017), 1–19. Law and Shakespeare constitutes a subfield within a
    subfield. For an introduction, see Karen Cunningham, "The Shakespearean Legal
    Imaginary," in *The Shakespearean World*, ed. Jill Levenson and Robert Ormsby
    (London: Routledge, 2017), 622–37; Bradin Cormack, Martha C. Nussbaum, and
    Richard Strier, eds., *Shakespeare and the Law: A Conversation among Disciplines
    and Professions* (Chicago: University of Chicago Press, 2013); Karen Cunningham

and Constance Jordan, eds., *The Law in Shakespeare* (Basingstoke: Palgrave, 2010).

55 Julia Reinhard Lupton, *Citizen-Saints: Shakespeare and Political Theology* (Chicago: University of Chicago Press, 2005), 5.

56 In new historicist analysis, "[t]here is simply no room ... for any understanding of the workings of criminal justice as being thought of, historically, as a communal responsibility, dependent on lay instigation and lay participation in judgment." Lorna Hutson, *The Invention of Suspicion: Law and Mimesis in Shakespeare and Renaissance Drama* (Oxford: Oxford University Press, 2007), 66. For another critique of new historicism, see Patricia Fumerton, "Introduction: A New New Historicism," in *Renaissance Culture and the Everyday*, ed. Patricia Fumerton and Simon Hunt (Philadelphia: University of Pennsylvania Press, 2009), 1–17. On the relationship between new historicism, historicism (without the new), and historical methods, see Dolan, *True Relations*, 18.

57 Derek Dunne, *Shakespeare, Revenge Tragedy and Early Modern Law: Vindictive Justice* (London: Palgrave, 2016), 5.

58 Kevin Curran, *Shakespeare's Legal Ecologies: Law and Distributed Selfhood* (Evanston: Northwestern University Press, 2017), 4.

59 Susan A. Bandes, ed., *The Passions of Law* (New York: New York University Press, 1999), 2.

60 See Melissa Gregg and Gregory J. Seigworth, eds., *The Affect Theory Reader* (Durham, NC: Duke University Press, 2010).

61 Martha Nussbaum, *Hiding from Humanity: Disgust, Shame, and the Law* (Princeton: Princeton University Press, 2004), 5.

62 Nussbaum, 9. As Nussbaum puts it, "law ... does not just describe existing emotional norms; it is itself normative, playing a dynamic and educational role" (12). Similarly, Brian Bornstein and Richard Wiener point out the existence of a "double standard" in law with respect to emotions: "[d]espite the legitimacy of emotion in many legal situations, the law has a double standard with respect to emotion. In many situations, the law presumes that legal decision makers can set their emotions aside and behave as cool, dispassionate, rational actors." Brian H. Bornstein and Richard L. Wiener, eds., *Emotion and the Law: Psychological Perspectives* (New York: Springer, 2010), 5.

63 Kathryn D. Temple, *Loving Justice*; Rachel E. Holmes and Toria Johnson, "In Pursuit of Truth," *Forum for Modern Language Notes* 54, no. 1 (2018): 1–16; Merridee L. Bailey and Kimberley-Joy Knight, "Writing Histories of Law and Emotion," *Journal of Legal History* 38, no. 2 (2017): 117–29. The editors' introductions offer excellent summaries of the scholarship in law and emotions (by Susan A. Bandes, Martha Nussbaum, and others with primary affiliation in law) and in the history of law and emotions (by William Reddy, Barbara Rosenwein, and others with affiliations in history and literature).

64 Robert Harris, "Saint Paul's Exercise : A Sermon Preached before the Judges at Assize," in *Two Sermons: The One Preached before the Judges of Assize at Oxford. The Other to the Universities* (London: Printed [at Eliot's Court Press] for J. Bartlet, and are to be sold at his shop in Cheape-side, at the signe of the gilded Cup, 1628), sig. D4r.

65 *A Warning for Faire Women* (London: Printed at London by Valentine Sims for William Aspley, 1599), sig. H2r.

66 The "pan-European common law or *jus commune* … was a combination of medieval canon law and ancient Roman civil law." Henry Ansgar Kelly, *Inquisitions and Other Trial Procedures in the Medieval West* (Aldershot: Ashgate, 2001), xi–xii. See also Harold J. Berman, *Law and Revolution II: The Impact of the Protestant Reformations on the Western Legal Tradition* (Cambridge, MA: Harvard University Press, 2003), 35.

67 Wilfrid R. Prest, *The Professions in Early Modern England* (London: Croom Helm, 1987), 64–5.

68 Bradin Cormack, *A Power to Do Justice: Jurisdiction, English Literature, and the Rise of Common Law, 1509–1625* (Chicago: University of Chicago Press, 2007), 27.

69 Christopher W. Brooks and Kevin Sharpe, "History, English Law and the Renaissance," *Past & Present* 72 (1976): 137. For a more recent analysis of the intellectual exchange between English and continental jurists, see Christopher Warren, *Literature and the Law of Nations, 1580–1680* (Oxford: Oxford University Press, 2015).

70 Christopher W. Brooks, "The Common Lawyers in England c. 1558–1642," in *Lawyers in Early Modern Europe and America*, ed. Wilfrid R. Prest (London: Helm, 1981), 42.

71 Although his study focuses on seventeenth-century political constitutional thought, Pocock backdates seventeenth-century common law–mindedness to the Elizabethan period. As he explain, "for its formulation in the version which was to dominate the seventeenth-century we should no doubt look to that recrudescence of inns-of-court and parliamentary activity, intellectual as well as practical, which marks the later Tudor period." J.G.A. Pocock, *The Ancient Constitution and the Feudal Law: A Study of English Historical Thought in the Seventeenth Century: A Reissue with a Retrospect* (Cambridge: Cambridge University Press, 1987), 31.

72 Jessica Winston, *Lawyers at Play: Literature, Law, and Politics at the Early Modern Inns of Court, 1558–1581* (Oxford: Oxford University Press, 2016), 51.

73 Cormack, *A Power to Do Justice*, 1.

74 Michelle O'Callaghan, *The English Wits: Literature and Sociability in Early Modern England* (Cambridge: Cambridge University Press, 2007), 2.

75 Brian P. Levack, *The Civil Lawyers in England, 1603–1641: A Political Study* (Oxford: Clarendon, 1973), 3. See also Daniel R. Coquillette, *The Civilian*

Writers of Doctors' Commons, London: Three Centuries of Juristic Innovation in Comparative, Commercial, and International Law (Berlin: Duncker & Humblot, 1988).

76 J.H. Baker, *The Legal Profession and the Common Law* (London: Hambledon, 1986), 314.

77 Jane Elisabeth Archer, Elizabeth Goldring, and Sarah Knight, eds., *The Intellectual and Cultural World of the Early Modern Inns of Court* (Manchester: Manchester University Press, 2011).

78 Winston, *Lawyers at Play*, 219.

79 Winston, 12.

80 William Fulbecke, *A Direction or Preparative to the Study of the Lawe* (London: Printed by Thomas Wight, 1600), sig. B5v.

81 George Buck, *The Third Universitie of England*, in *The Annales, or Generall Chronicle of England, Begun First by Maister John Stow, and after Him Continued and Augmented with Matters Forreyne, and Domestique, Auncient and Moderne, unto the Ende of This Present Yeere 1614. by Edmond Howes, Gentleman* (London, 1615), sig. Mmmm1r. Buck (also spelled Buc in some sources) was a member of the Middle Temple and a one-time Master of Revels.

82 "To Sir Edward Coke," in Ben Jonson, *The Complete Poems*, ed. George Parfitt (London: Penguin, 1996), 402.

83 Francis Bacon, *The Works of Francis Bacon [...] The Letters and the Life*, ed. James Spedding, Robert Leslie Ellis, and Douglas Denon Heath, vol. 13 (London: Longman, 1872), 65.

84 For an analysis of Coke's theory of "artificial reason," see Charles Gray, "Reason, Authority, and Imagination: The Jurisprudence of Sir Edward Coke," in *Culture and Politics: From Puritanism to the Enlightenment*, ed. Perez Zagorin (Berkeley: University of California Press, 1980), 30; John U. Lewis, "Sir Edward Coke: His Theory of Artificial Reason as a Context for Modern Basic Legal Theory," *Law Quarterly Review* 84 (1968): 330–42. Coke's emphasis on artificial reason of the law even extended to a critique of the sovereign's legal knowledge. This position eventually led to his clash with James I and James's counsellors including Thomas Egerton and Francis Bacon. See Richard Helgerson, *Forms of Nationhood: The Elizabethan Writing of England* (Chicago: University of Chicago Press, 1992), chapter 2.

85 Edward Coke, *Les reports de Edward Coke L'attorney generall le Roigne* (London: [Printed by Adam Islip] in ædibus Thomæ Wight, 1600), sig. π3v.

86 Edward Coke, *The First Part of the Institutes* (London, 1628), sig. S3r.

87 Hobbes qtd. in Lewis, "Sir Edward Coke," 335. For a fuller quotation (from Hobbes's *A Dialogue between a Philosopher and a Student of the Common Laws of England*, see Helgerson, *Forms of Nationhood*, 319n.57.

88 Fulbecke, *A Direction or Preparative*, sig. B8v. For a brief biography of Fulbecke, see D.R. Woolf, "William Fulbecke (1560–1603?)," in *Dictionary of*

Literary Biography: Sixteenth-Century British Nondramatic Writers, ed. David A. Richardson, vol. 172, 4th ser. (Detroit: Gale, 1996), 91–5.

89 Fulbecke, sig. B5v.

90 Ibid.

91 Sheppard, *The Touch-Stone*, sig. A3r–v. The general dislike of scriveners is expressed by the idiom, "A Scrivener is a Christian Canniball that devoures men alive." Peter Beal, *A Dictionary of English Manuscript Terminology 1450–2000* (Oxford: Oxford University Press, 2008), 367.

92 Edward Coke, *Le second part des reportes del Edward Coke* (London, 1602), sig. ¶5r–v. I am grateful to Amy Vandervelde for improving my translation.

93 "Imperite, n. and adj.," *OED*.

94 Marcia L. Colish, *The Stoic Tradition from Antiquity to the Early Middle Ages*, vol. 1 (Leiden: Brill, 1985), 350.

95 Colish, 1:351.

96 Colish, 1:350.

97 In the *Corpus Juris Civilis*, jurisconsults are called "public interpreters of the law, to whom the power of expounding of the law was given by the emperor … The unanimous decisions and opinions of these persons had such weight that it was settled by a constitution that the judge should not be at liberty to decide otherwise." Justinian and Gaius, *The Institutes of Gaius and Justinian, The Twelve Tables, and the CXVIIIth and CXXVIIth Novels*, trans. T. Lambert Mears (London: Stevens, 1882), 1.2.§8.

98 Donald R. Kelley, "*Vera Philosophia*: The Philosophical Significance of Renaissance Jurisprudence," *Journal of the History of Philosophy* 14, no. 3 (1976): 268.

99 James A. Brundage, *The Medieval Origins of the Legal Profession: Canonists, Civilians, and Courts* (Chicago: University of Chicago Press, 2008), 3.

100 Paul Raffield, "The Inner Temple Revels (1561–62) and the Elizabethan Rhetoric of Signs: Legal Iconography at the Early Modern Inns of Court," in *The Intellectual and Cultural World of the Early Modern Inns of Court*, ed. Jane Elisabeth Archer, Elizabeth Goldring, and Sarah Knight (Manchester: Manchester University Press, 2011), 43. The standard modern edition remains John Fortescue, *De Laudibus Legum Anglie*, ed. S.B. Chrimes (Cambridge: Cambridge University Press, 1942). A paperback edition of this essential text has been available since 2011.

101 Virginia Lee Strain, "*The Winter's Tale* and the Oracle of the Law," *ELH* 78, no. 3 (2011): 557.

102 Sheppard, *The Touch-Stone*, sig. A3r.

103 For further discussion of professionals' suspicion toward lay judgment, see Derek Dunne, "Re-Assessing Trial by Jury in Early Modern Law and Literature," *Literature Compass* 12, no. 10 (2015): 519.

104 Ephraim Huit, *The Anatomy of Conscience or the Summe of Pauls Regeneracy. Wherein Are Handled the Palces of Conscience, Worship, and Scandall, with Diverse Rules of Christian Practise; Very Profitable for the Weake Christian* (London: Printed by J. D. for William Sheffard, and are to be sold at his Shop at the entrance in out of Lumbard streete into Popes-head Alley, 1626), sig. E5r.

105 Huit, sig. E10r.

106 Martin Luther, *A Treatise, Touching the Libertie of a Christian*, trans. James Bell (London, 1579), sig. H6v.

107 Diarmaid MacCulloch, *The Reformation: A History* (New York: Penguin, 2003), 156. On the radical nature of Protestant humanism, see Richard Strier, "Faithful Servants: Shakespeare's Praise of Disobedience," in *The Historical Renaissance: New Essays on Tudor and Stuart Literature and Culture*, ed. Heather Dubrow and Richard Strier (Chicago: University of Chicago Press, 1988), 104–33. For lucid accounts of the co-development of Reformation theology and law, see Berman, *Law and Revolution II*; John Witte Jr., *Law and Protestantism: The Legal Teachings of the Lutheran Reformation* (Cambridge: Cambridge University Press, 2002).

108 Martin Luther, *Luther's Reply to King Henry VIII*, trans. E.S. Buchanan (New York: Swift, 1928), 5.

109 Martin Luther, *Temporal Authority: To What Extent It Should Be Obeyed*, in *Selected Writings of Martin Luther: 1520–1523*, ed. Theodore Tappert, trans. J.J. Schindel and Walther I. Brandt (Minneapolis: Fortress, 2007), 273.

110 Luther, 274.

111 Luther, 306.

112 Philip Melanchthon, *A Faithfull Admonycion of a Certen Trewe Pastor and Prophete Sent unto the Germanes at Such Tyme as Certen Great Princes Went Abowt to Bring in Alienes in to Germany ... Now Translated in to Inglyssh for a Lyte Admonycyon unto All Trewe Inglyssh Hartes Whereby Thei May Lerne and Knowe How to Consyder and Receive the Procedings of the Inglyssh Magistrates and Bisshops. With a Preface of M. Philip Melancthon* (Greenwich?, 1554), sig. A2r. Melanchthon's text is a translation of a text by Eusebius.

113 Melanchthon, sig. A5v.

114 Thomas Smith, *De Republica Anglorum*, ed. Mary Dewar (Cambridge: Cambridge University Press, 1982), 124.

115 See the introduction of Ceri Sullivan, *The Rhetoric of the Conscience in Donne, Herbert and Vaughan* (Oxford: Oxford University Press, 2008).

116 John Calvin, *The institution of Christian religion* (London: Printed by H. Midleton, for W. Norton, 1587), sig. Nn7v–Nn8r. This is from book 3, chapter 19. For a modern translation of the same passage, see John Calvin, *Institutes of the Christian Religion. Vol. 1: Books I.i to III.Xix*, ed. John T. McNeill, trans. Ford Lewis Battles, vol. 1 (Philadelphia: Westminster, 1960), 848.

117 *The Geneva Bible* (London: Christopher Barker, 1582), sig. Sss1v. On the different English translations of the Bible available before the publication of the

King James Bible, see Naseeb Shaheen, *Biblical References in Shakespeare's History Plays* (Newark: University of Delaware Press, 1989), 13–25.

118 The Geneva Bible, sig. Rrr61 (Acts 23:1), sig. Tttlv (1 Cor. 8:12), sig. Xxx4r (1 Tim. 3:9).

119 According to the Renaissance study of forensic rhetoric, "liveliness" is a function of *narratio*, which could be achieved through the artful manipulation of "brevity, clarity (or 'openness'), and probability (or 'credibility'), to which Quintillian adds 'vividness' (*enargeia*) and, when appropriate, 'grandeur' (*magnificentia*)." Hutson, *The Invention of Suspicion*, 121.

120 Calvin had a *licentié ès loix and* was associated with the Université de Bourges. John Calvin, *Calvin's Commentary on Seneca's* De Clementia, trans. Ford Lewis Battles and André Malan Hugo (Leiden: Brill, 1969), 3.

121 Alec Ryrie, *Being Protestant in Reformation Britain* (Oxford: Oxford University Press, 2013), 6. "The patterns set by the earliest reformers endured at least until the Civil War era" (5). Ryrie has also explored the question of why Calvinism, and not Lutheranism, spread in early modern England. See Alec Ryrie, "The Strange Death of Lutheran England," *Journal of Ecclesiastical History* 53, no. 1 (2002): 64–92.

122 John Stachniewski, *The Persecutory Imagination: English Puritanism and the Literature of Religious Despair* (Oxford: Clarendon, 1991), 17, 8.

123 Kristen Poole, *Supernatural Environments in Shakespeare's England: Spaces of Demonism, Divinity, and Drama* (Cambridge: Cambridge University Press, 2011), 150.

124 On the employment of "hirelings" for bit parts, see Tiffany Stern, *Documents of Performance in Early Modern England* (Cambridge: Cambridge University Press, 2009), 212.

125 Michelle M. Dowd, *The Dynamics of Inheritance on the Shakespearean Stage* (Cambridge: Cambridge University Press, 2015), 3.

126 Allison P. Hobgood, *Passionate Playgoing in Early Modern England* (Cambridge: Cambridge University Press, 2014), 10.

127 Chapter 4 discusses the scholarship on empathy and intersubjective witnesses at more length.

128 In his analysis of "minor jurisprudences" – inspired by Deleuze and Guattari's concept of "minor literature" (*literature mineure*) – Peter Goodrich writes that "a minor jurisprudence" poses "a challenge to the science of law and a threat to its monopoly of legal knowledge." Peter Goodrich, *Law in the Courts of Love: Literature and Other Minor Jurisprudences* (London: Routledge, 1996), 2.

1 From *Assise* to the Assize at Home

1 Shoshana Felman, *The Juridical Unconscious: Trials and Traumas in the Twentieth Century* (Cambridge, MA: Harvard University Press, 2002), 6.

2 J.S. Cockburn, *A History of English Assizes, 1558–1714* (Cambridge: Cambridge University Press, 1972), 24. On the thirteenth-century origins of the assize, see Cockburn, 15–22.

3 "Selection and Summoning of Jury Panels," 28 U.S.C. § 1866 (c), https://www .law.cornell.edu/uscode/text/28/1866. For an account of the gradual changes in English jurisprudence concerning the jurors' knowledge, see John H. Langbein, Renée Lettow Lerner, and Bruce P. Smith, eds., *History of the Common Law: The Development of Anglo-American Legal Institutions* (New York: Aspen, 2009), 245–6. It was not until the mid-eighteenth century that the modern "legal norm" of the "ignorant" jury came to be (245).

4 "There was no requirement that jurors banish such things from their minds – quite the opposite. Jury self-informing was a lawful fact of legal life." Thomas A. Green, "A Retrospective on the Criminal Trial Jury: 1200–1800," in *The Criminal Trial Jury in England, 1200–1800*, ed. J.S. Cockburn and Thomas A. Green (Princeton: Princeton University Press, 1988), 370.

5 Julia Reinhard Lupton, *Citizen-Saints: Shakespeare and Political Theology* (Chicago: University of Chicago Press, 2005), 5.

6 Michel Foucault, *Discipline and Punish: The Birth of the Prison*, trans. Alan Sheridan (New York: Random, 1977), 138.

7 J.H. Baker, *An Introduction to English Legal History*, 4th ed. (Oxford: Oxford University Press, 2007), 6.

8 Baker, 4.

9 "Mōt," Joseph Bosworth, *An Anglo-Saxon Dictionary*, ed. T. Northcote Toller (Oxford: Clarendon, 1898), 699, http://ebeowulf.uky.edu/BT/Bosworth-Toller .htm.

10 Baker, 4.

11 Paul R. Hyams, *Rancor and Reconciliation in Medieval England* (Ithaca: Cornell University Press, 2003), 27.

12 *Beowulf*, trans. Seamus Heaney (New York: Norton, 2000), 86, 105–6. All numbers are references to lines.

13 *Beowulf*, 144.

14 *Beowulf*, 78.

15 *Beowulf*, 87–91.

16 Karl Shoemaker, "Punishment," in *Law and the Humanities*, ed. Austin Sarat, Matthew Anderson, and Cathrine O. Frank (Cambridge: Cambridge University Press, 2010), 518.

17 *Beowulf*, 154–6.

18 For an introduction to the astonishing life of the Empress Matilda, see Marjorie Chibnall, "Matilda [Matilda of England] (1102–1167), empress, consort of Heinrich V," *ODNB*.

19 Hyams, *Rancor and Reconciliation*, 157.

20 R.C. van Caenegem, "Public Prosecution of Crime in Twelfth-Century England," in *Legal History: A European Perspective* (London: Hambledon, 1991), 3.

21 In the civil context, "assize" denoted the writ issued by jurors after a hearing of the claimant's arguments for the rightful possession of land. Four types of writs were available to jurors at this time, the most common being the writ of *novel disseisin* concerning the recovery (or restoration) of lands and tenements of which the plaintiff claimed to have been unlawfully dispossessed. The issuance of the writ terminated a man's seisin (or possession) in law of the estate or freehold. *Novel disseisin* comes from the French, meaning recent dispossession; see John Rastell, *Exposiciones terminorum legum Anglorum* (London, 1525), in *Lexicons of Early Modern English*, ed. Ian Lancashire (Toronto: University of Toronto Library and University of Toronto Press, 2006), leme.library.utoronto .ca/lexicon/entry.cfm?ent=836-24. The expansion of the assize from civil to criminal cases was a consequence of the violent nature of property dispute. To quote Paul R. Hyams, "the questions of title and tenure were frequently the basis for violence and retribution. The strong passions that prick individuals to do violence – envy, resentment, anger, hatred – often arise from disputes over land, property, or the title over the two." Hyams, *Rancor and Reconciliation*, 157.

22 van Caenegem, "Public Prosecution," 3.

23 *Glanvill* qtd. in K.J. Kesselring, *Making Murder Public: Homicide in Early Modern England, 1480–1680* (Oxford: Oxford University Press, 2019), 21.

24 "Assize, n.," *OED*.

25 Alexander Mansfield Burrill, *A Law Dictionary and Glossary*, 2nd ed., vol. 1 (New York: Baker, 1871), 149.

26 "Assises, (or assizes)," Burrill, 1:107.

27 Burrill, 1:104.

28 Burrill 1:147. See also Baker, *An Introduction*, 73.

29 Finbarr McAuley, "Canon Law and the End of the Ordeal," *Oxford Journal of Legal Studies* 26, no. 3 (2006): 473.

30 See Robert Bartlett, *Trial by Fire and Water: The Medieval Judicial Ordeal* (Oxford: Clarendon, 1986).

31 See Henry Ansgar Kelly, *Inquisitions and Other Trial Procedures in the Medieval West* (Aldershot: Ashgate, 2001).

32 "The true trial jury first appears at Westminster during the 1219–21 interim, specifically at the end of Hilary term 1220. It began in approvers' appeals, a specialized kind of prosecution with a specialized non-convicting jury procedure, the inquest *de fidelitate*. The first convicting juries grew out of this inquest." Roger D. Groot, "The Early-Thirteenth-Century Criminal Jury," in *Twelve Good Men and True: The Criminal Trial Jury in England, 1200–1800*, ed. J.S. Cockburn and Thomas A. Green (Princeton: Princeton University Press, 1988), 3.

33 Ranulf de Glanvill, *The Treatise on the Laws and Customs of England Commonly Called Glanvill*, ed. G.D.H. Hall (London: Nelson, 1965), 28. *Glanvill*, attributed

to the jurist of that name, "was written, probably between 1187 and 1189, by a man learned in the law and in the current practice and usage of the king's court at the Exchequer" (xi).

34 Glanvill, 28.

35 Andrew Horn, *The Booke Called, the Mirrour of Justices*, ed. William Joseph Whittaker (London: Selden Society, 1895), 145. The text is dated to 1290, did not circulate during the Middle Ages, and was subsequently unearthed by early modern antiquarians and finally published in 1642. For more on the nature of this, "the most fantastic work in our legal literature," see Theodore F.T. Plucknett, *A Concise History of the Common Law*, 2nd ed. (Rochester: Lawyers Co-Operative, 1936), 267.

36 Horn, *The Booke Called, the Mirrour of Justices*, 145.

37 Note that scholars interchangeably use "jury of presentment," the "presenting jury," and the "presentment jury." On the grand jury: the Assize of Clarendon of 1166 and the Assize of Northampton of 1176 laid the foundation for the criminal jury trial and these statutes "mark[ed] the ultimate origin of the grand juries and indictment that have characterized public prosecution of crime in the Anglo-American common law into the modern age." Hyams, *Rancor and Reconciliation*, 159.

38 Groot, "The Early-Thirteenth-Century Criminal Jury," 5.

39 John Fortescue, *De Laudibus Legum Anglie*, ed. S.B. Chrimes (Cambridge: Cambridge University Press, 1942), 53–4. The term "hundred" "originally may have meant that the unit had about 100 men." Langbein, Lerner, and Smith, *History of the Common Law*, 18.

40 Hyams, *Rancor and Reconciliation*, 160. Note that the legal term "rogue" designated a person who had "committed any one of four categories of serious offense (expanded to six in 1176 and further thereafter)." Ibid.

41 Hyams, 159–60.

42 In medieval England, a presentment juror could reappear as a trial juror: "many trial jurors in the early period had served as presenters in the same case." Green, "A Retrospective," 370. See also Thomas A. Green, *Verdict According to Conscience: Perspectives on the English Criminal Trial Jury, 1200–1800* (Chicago: University of Chicago Press, 1985). Eventually, there would be a separation between the presentment and trial jury: "by 1328 the separation between presenters (the later grand jury) and trial jurors was well advanced but by no means completed. The former were of decidedly higher status than the latter." Green, "A Retrospective," 365.

43 Green, "A Retrospective," 370.

44 Groot, "The Early-Thirteenth-Century Criminal Jury," 4.

45 Green, "A Retrospective," 367.

46 Green, 359.

47 Langbein, Lerner, and Smith, *History of the Common Law*, 17.

48 Craig Muldrew, *The Economy of Obligation: The Culture of Credit and Social Relations in Early Modern England* (Houndmills: Palgrave, 1998), 149.

49 Patricia Orr, *"Non Potest Appellum Facere*: Criminal Charges Women Could Not – But Did – Bring in Thirteenth-Century English Royal Courts of Justice," in *The Final Argument: The Imprint of Violence on Society in Medieval and Early Modern Europe*, ed. Donald J. Kagay and L.J. Villalon (Woodbridge: Boydell, 1998), 141–60; Laura Gowing, *Common Bodies: Women, Touch and Power in Seventeenth-Century England* (New Haven: Yale University Press, 2003).

50 Green, "A Retrospective," 366.

51 Groot, "The Early-Thirteenth-Century Criminal Jury," 17–18.

52 John H. Langbein, "Bifurcation and the Bench: The Influence of the Jury on English Conceptions of the Judiciary," in *Judges and Judging in the History of the Common Law and Civil Law: From Antiquity to Modern Times*, ed. Paul Brand and Joshua Getzler (Cambridge: Cambridge University Press, 2012), 76–7. Langbein is supported by Green, "A Retrospective," 360.

53 Matthew Lockwood, *The Conquest of Death: Violence and the Birth of the Modern English State* (New Haven: Yale University Press, 2017), 150.

54 Lockwood, 181.

55 Langbein, Lerner, and Smith, *History of the Common Law*, 230.

56 Langbein, Lerner, and Smith, 262n.139.

57 For the Marian Bail and Committal Statutes (1 & 2 Phil. & M., c. 13 and 2 & 3 Phil. & M., c. 10, respectively), see Great Britain, *The Statutes of the Realm*, vol. 4, pt. 1 (London, 1819), 259, 286. On how these statutes "greatly augmented the pretrial role of the JPs," see Langbein, Lerner, and Smith, *History of the Common Law*, 578. For further comment on how the statutes formalized a trend begun in the medieval period, see K.J. Kesselring, *Mercy and Authority in the Tudor State* (Cambridge: Cambridge University Press, 2003), 10.

58 Francis Bacon, *The Works of Francis Bacon*, ed. James Spedding, Robert Leslie Ellis, and Douglas Denon Heath, vol. 7 (London: Longman, 1859), 779.

59 J.H. Gleason, *The Justices of the Peace in England, 1558 to 1640* (Oxford: Clarendon, 1969), 47.

60 Gleason, 83–4.

61 Gleason, 87.

62 Prest notes that "self-help manuals ... constituted a large, flexible, and relatively inexpensive medium of legal instruction, aimed predominantly (if by no means exclusively) at a non-professional market." Wilfrid R. Prest, "Lay Legal Knowledge in Early Modern England," in *Learning the Law: Teaching and the Transmission of English Law, 1150–1900*, ed. Jonathan Bush and Alain Wijffels (London: Hambledon, 1999), 310.

63 William Lambarde, *Eirenarcha: Or of The Office of the Justices of Peace, in Two Bookes* (London: Imprinted by Ra: Newbery, and H. Bynneman, by the ass. of

Ri. Tot. & Chr. Bar., 1581), sig. A2v. For an introduction to early modern legal publishing, see Richard J. Ross, "The Commoning of Common Law: Debates over Printing English Law, 1520–1640," *University of Pennsylvania Law Review* 146 (1998): 323–462.

64 Michael Dalton, *The Countrey Justice, Conteyning the Practise of the Justices of the Peace out of Their Sessions* (London: Printed for the Societie of Stationers, 1618), title page.

65 The Huntington Library's copy of Dalton's book (RB 243254) contains marginalia by an early owner, probably a magistrate, who was especially energized by the chapter on the regulation of "Labourers" (sig. F6r, sig. F7r–v).

66 The diary of the seventeenth-century Puritan JP Sir John Newdigate has been invaluable to social historians; see Richard Cust, "Reading for Magistracy: The Mental World of Sir John Newdigate," in *The Monarchical Republic of Early Modern England: Essays in Response to Patrick Collinson*, ed. John F. McDiarmid (Aldershot: Ashgate, 2007), 181–99; Steve Hindle, "Self-Image and Public Image in the Career of a Jacobean Magistrate: Sir John Newdigate in the Court of Star Chamber," in *Popular Culture and Political Agency in Early Modern England and Ireland: Essays in Honour of John Walter*, ed. Michael J. Braddick and Phil Withington (Woodbridge: Boydell & Brewer, 2017), 123–43.

67 William Lambarde, *The Duties of Constables, Borsholders, Tithingmen, and Such Other Low Ministers of the Peace* (London: By Rafe Newberie and Henrie Middleton, 1583), sig. B3r.

68 Lambarde, sig. B3r.

69 For example, with regards to the maintenance of highways, "Every Justice of Peace (upon his owne knowledge) may present in open generall Sessions, any High-way not sufficiently repaired." Dalton, *The Countrey Justice*, sig. F2r.

70 Kesselring, *Making Murder Public*, 8.

71 Cockburn explains that "twice yearly, normally in the Lent vacation during late February and March and the Trinity vacation during July and early August, two common law judges, a judge and a serjeant, or, infrequently, two serjeants, literally rode each circuit, hearing pleas and delivering gaols in the county town or an important centre in every shire. Occasionally a single judge or serjeant rode the circuit alone." Cockburn, *A History of English Assizes*, 24.

72 Cockburn, 59–60. For a brief and lucid explanation of *nisi prius*, see Cockburn, 17.

73 Philip Julius, "Diary of the Journey of the Most Illustrious Philip Julius, Duke of Stettin-Pomerania ... through ... England, ... 1602," ed. Gottfried von Bülow, *Transactions of the Royal Historical Society* 6 (1892): 59.

74 William Shakespeare, *Measure for Measure*, in *The Riverside Shakespeare*, ed. G. Blakemore Evans et al. (Boston: Houghton, 1974), 2.2.82–3.

75 William Shakespeare, *The Two Noble Kinsmen*, in *The Riverside Shakespeare*, ed. G. Blakemore Evans et al. (Boston: Houghton, 1974), 3.6.6–7.

76 Cockburn, *A History of English Assizes*, 298.

77 Barbara J. Shapiro, "Political Theology and the Courts: A Survey of Assize Sermons c. 1600–1688," *Law and Humanities* 2, no. 1 (2008): 5. For two additional analyses of assize sermons and their political uses, see Hugh Adlington, "Restoration, Religion, and Law: Assize Sermons, 1660–1685," in *The Oxford Handbook of the Early Modern Sermon*, ed. Peter McCullough, Hugh Adlington, and Emma Rhatigan (Oxford: Oxford University Press, 2011), 423–59; Juliet Amy Ingram, "The Conscience of the Community: The Character and Development of Clerical Complaint in Early Modern England" (PhD thesis, University of Warwick, 2004).

78 William Overton, *A Godlye, and Pithie Exhortation, Made to the Judges and Justices of Sussex, and the Whole Countie, Assembled Togither, at the Generall Assises. By William Overton, Doctor of Divinitie, and One of the Queenes Majesties Justices Appoynted for the Peace Within the Same Countie* (London: R. Newbery and H. Bynneman, 1579), sig. A2r.

79 "Sheriff's Duties and Ceremonial at Carlisle Assizes 1661–2," qtd. in Cockburn, *A History of English Assizes*, 298.

80 George Macey, *A Sermon Preached at Charde in the Countie of Somerset, the Second of March 1597. Being the First Day of the Assises There Holden* (London: [by R. Bradock?] for R. D[exter]. and are to be soulde by Michaell Hart bookseller in the city of Exceter, 1601), sig. A3v.

81 Anthony Cade, *A Sermon of the Nature of Conscience Which May Well Be Tearmed, a Tragedy of Conscience in Her. First, a Wakning. Secondly, Wrastling. Thirdly, Scourging. Preached before the Right Honourable Sir Henry Hobart Knight and Baronet, Lord Chiefe Justice of the Common Pleas: And Sir Edward Bromley Knight, One of the Barons of the Exchequer, at the Assises at Leicester. 1620. July, 25. By Anthony Cade Batchelour in Divinity* (London: Bernard Alsop for Thomas Jones, and are to be solde at his shop in Chancery Lane, and in Westminster hall, 1621), sig. D2r, original emphasis. For further discussion of the testifying conscience, see Ceri Sullivan, *The Rhetoric of the Conscience in Donne, Herbert and Vaughan* (Oxford: Oxford University Press, 2008).

82 Wolfgang Musculus, *The Temporysour (That Is to Saye: The Observer of Tyme, or He That Chaungeth with the Tyme.) Compyled in Latyn by the Excellent Clarke Wolfangus Musculus, and Translated into Frenche by M. Vallerain Pullain. And out of Frenche into Inglishe by R. P.*, trans. R.P. (Zurich? Geneva?, 1555), sig. A7r.

83 George Closse, *The Parricide Papist, or, Cut-Throate Catholicke. A Tragicall Discourse of a Murther Lately Committed at Padstow in the Countie of Cornewall by a Professed Papist, Killing His Owne Father, and Afterwardes Himselfe, in Zeale of His Popish Religion. The 11 of March Last Past. 1606. Written by G Closse, Preacher of the Word of God at Blacke Torrington in Devon* (London: Printed at London for Christopher Hunt, dwelling in Pater-noster-row, neere the Kings head, 1606).

84 For an account of George Closse's rocky career, see Arnold Hunt, *The Art of Hearing: English Preachers and Their Audiences, 1590–1640* (Cambridge: Cambridge University Press, 2010), 315–16; Mary Morrissey, *Politics and the Paul's Cross Sermons, 1558–1642* (Oxford: Oxford University Press, 2011), 81; Ian W. Archer, *The Pursuit of Stability: Social Relations in Elizabethan London* (Cambridge: Cambridge University Press, 1991), 53. I am grateful to Arnold Hunt for telling me about Closse's highly entertaining sermon, portions of which are transcribed in Hunt's book, in this chapter, and in chapter 2.

85 See Jacqueline Eales, "Robert Abbot (fl. c. 1589–1652), Church of England clergyman and religious writer," *ODNB*.

86 Robert Abbot, *A Hand of Fellowship, to Helpe Keepe out Sinne and Antichrist. In Certaine Sermons Preached upon Severall Occasions* (London, 1623), sig. E8r, original emphasis.

87 Cockburn, *A History of English Assizes*, 24.

88 Abbot, *A Hand of Fellowship*, sig. E8v.

89 Abbot, sig. F8v, original emphasis.

90 Martha Tuck Rozett, *The Doctrine of Election and the Emergence of Elizabethan Tragedy* (Princeton: Princeton University Press, 1984), 49.

91 John Lightfoot, "Sermon. The Text Psalm I. 5, 'Therefore Shall Not the Wicked Rise up in Judgement'" (n.d.), BL Sloane MS 1926, fol. 48v. The sermon was preserved by his nephew, who entered the following headnote: "The sermon was preached by the revererant devine m^r John Lightfoott, my worthy good uncle" (fol. 47). This sermon does not appear in John Lightfoot, *The Works of the Reverend and Learned John Lightfoot D. D.* (London: Printed by William Rawlins, for Richard Chiswell at the Rose and Crown in St. Paul's Church-yard, 1684), 1033–121.

92 Coke was incensed by Closse's sermon and brought a formal complaint against him to King James; see Hunt, *The Art of Hearing*, 316.

93 George Closse, *A Looking Glasse for Lawers, & Lawiers. A Sermon Preached before the Judges of Assize for the Countie of Devon, in the Cathedrall Church of St Peter in Exon on the 8th Day of August: 1603: By George Closse Maister of Artes, a Preacher of the Worde of God at Blacktorrington*, Lambeth MS 113, fol. 59v. Closse's manuscript shows the work of two hands. The main text is written in an elegant professional script. Emendations are entered in a crabbier hand. My guess is that this was a copy prepared by a professional scribe and edited by the author.

94 Closse, fol. 59v–60r.

95 Closse, fol. 57v.

96 Closse, fol. 56v.

97 According to St. German, man's "reason" is evidence of God's law: "the law of reason is nothing else than the participation or knowledge of eternal law in a rational creature, revealed to him by the natural light of reason, whereby he has a natural inclination to act duly, and to a due end" (Christopher St. German, *Doctor*

and Student, ed. Theodore F.T. Plucknett and J.L. Barton (London: Selden Society, 1974), 13. Furthermore, St. German maintained that "all actes and dedes of man be called right wyse & juste when they be done accordynge to the lawe of god and be conformable to it" (21).

98 John Rous, *Diary of John Rous, Incumbent of Santon Downham, Suffolk, from 1625 to 1642*, ed. Mary Anne Everett Green (London: Camden Society, 1856), 50.

99 Rous, 50.

100 Rous, 50–1. For more on this incident, see Cockburn, *A History of English Assizes*, 66.

101 George Wither, *Britain's Remembrancer Containing a Narration of the Plague Lately Past; a Declaration of the Mischiefs Present; and a Prediction of Judgments to Come; (If Repentance Prevent Not.) It Is Dedicated (for the Glory of God) to Posteritie; and, to These Times (If They Please)* (London: Imprinted for Great Britaine, and are to be sold by John Grismond in Ivie-Lane, 1628), sig. I2v, original emphasis.

102 William Drummond, *The Poetical Works of William Drummond of Hawthornden*, ed. William Barclay Turnbull (London: John Russell Smith, 1856), 268.

103 Thomas Browne, *Religio Medici* (London: Andrew Crooke, 1642), sig. K7r–v.

104 Browne, sig. K7r.

105 For additional examples of literary representations of the assize, see Virginia Lee Strain, *Legal Reform in English Renaissance Literature* (Edinburgh: Edinburgh University Press, 2018), chapter 4. Strain compares the arrival of the Duke in the final act of *Measure for Measure* to the visitation of an assize judge.

2 Judicature in Crisis

1 Aristotle, *The Nicomachean Ethics*, trans. H. Rackham (Cambridge, MA: Harvard University Press, 1926), 5.4.7 (277). This passage appears just before the famous discussion of the judge (*dikast*) as a "*dichast* (halver)" or one who "restores equality" (ibid.).

2 Christy Desmet, *Reading Shakespeare's Characters: Rhetoric, Ethics, and Identity* (Amherst: University of Massachusetts Press, 1992), 36–7.

3 William Gascoigne lived six years into the reign of Henry V. Born in Gawthorpe, Yorkshire, Gascoigne graduated from Cambridge, and later the Inner Temple, and enjoyed a respectable career from the time he was appointed to the bench (15 November 1400) to the time of Henry IV's death. Henry V paid the Chief Justice due respect by rewarding him "four bucks and does out of the Forest of Pontefract annually for the term of his natural life." F. Solly-Flood, "The Story of Prince Henry of Monmouth and Chief-Justice Gascoign," *Transactions of the Royal Historical Society*, New Ser. 3, 3 (1886): 65. See also Edward Powell, "Gascoigne, Sir William (c. 1350–1419)," *ODNB*.

4 M.C. Bradbrook, *Shakespeare and Elizabethan Poetry* (Cambridge: Cambridge University Press, 1951), 201.

5 John Manningham, *The Diary of John Manningham of the Middle Temple, 1602–1603*, ed. Robert Parker Sorlien (Hanover: University Press of New England, 1976), 78.

6 George Closse, *A looking Glasse for lawers, & lawiers. A sermon preached before the Judges of Assize for the countie of Devon, in the Cathedrall church of St Peter in Exon on the 8th day of August:1603: by George Closse maister of Artes, a preacher of the worde of God at Blacktorrington.* Lambeth MS 113, fol. 57v. For my introduction to Closse, see chapter 1.

7 Closse, *A looking Glasse for lawers, & lawiers*, fol. 58r.

8 Hugh Adlington, "Restoration, Religion, and Law: Assize Sermons, 1660–1685," in *The Oxford Handbook of the Early Modern Sermon*, ed. Peter McCullough, Hugh Adlington, and Emma Rhatigan (Oxford: Oxford University Press, 2011), 427. Subha Mukherji has examined other popular images of law, including the image of law as a Hydra's head, a waxen nose, and a labyrinth; see Subha Mukherji, *Law and Representation in Early Modern Drama* (Cambridge: Cambridge University Press, 2006), 233–48. For additional examples of common legal iconography, satirical or otherwise, see Peter Goodrich, *Legal Emblems and the Art of Law*: Obiter Depicta *as the Vision of Governance* (Cambridge: Cambridge University Press, 2014).

9 See the introduction for a fuller discussion.

10 Edward Coke, *Le second part des reportes del Edward Coke* (London, 1602), sig. ¶4v.

11 Francis Bacon, *The Essayes or Counsels, Civill and Morall*, ed. Michael Kiernan, vol. 15, *The Oxford Francis Bacon* (Oxford: Clarendon, 2000), 166. In an ironic reversal, Bacon himself would be indicted for taking bribes while serving as the Lord Chancellor and judge of the Chancery court.

12 An early but seminal text in this genre is *A Mirror for Magistrates* (written sometime in the 1550s); see Lily B. Campbell, ed., *The Mirror for Magistrates: Edited from Original Texts in the Huntington Library* (New York: Barnes and Noble, 1938). Occasionally, lawyers acknowledged the complaints of the people. For example, in his legal treatise *Archeion, or Commentaries on the Courts of England* (composed in 1591, possibly begun earlier, and ultimately published in 1635), Sir William Lambarde raises the possibility of judicial corruption. The Harvard Law School Library possesses a manuscript copy of Lambarde's book under the title of "Against Auricular Information of Judges: 1590: W. La." When Wilfrid R. Prest compared the manuscript to the printed copy, he discovered that the manuscript copy "lists some of the more subtle ways in which a case law can be prejudiced." Wilfrid R. Prest, "William Lambarde, Elizabethan Law Reform, and Early Stuart Politics," *Journal of British Studies* 34, no. 4 (1995): 71–2. Throughout his critique, Lambarde

carefully omits details that could connect his observations to a specific place, time, or person.

13 Robert Harris, "Saint Paul's Exercise. A Sermon Preached before the Judges at Assize," in *Two Sermons: The One Preached before the Judges of Assize at Oxford. The Other to the Universities* (London: Printed [at Eliot's Court Press] for J. Bartlet, and are to be sold at his shop in Cheape-side, at the signe of the gilded Cup, 1628), sig. D4r.

14 On the day-to-day operations of the Star Chamber, see Steve Hindle, *The State and Social Change in Early Modern England, 1550–1640* (Houndmills: Palgrave, 2002). On the Court of Requests, particularly as it was used by female litigants, see Timothy Stretton, *Women Waging Law in Elizabethan England* (Cambridge: Cambridge University Press, 1998).

15 Popham was Chief Justice between 1592 and 1607. See Douglas Walthew Rice, *The Life and Achievements of Sir John Popham, 1531–1607: Leading to the Establishment of the First English Colony in New England* (Madison, NJ: Fairleigh Dickinson University Press, 2005), 102–3.

16 On the problem of legal mediation, see Holger Schott Syme, *Theatre and Testimony in Shakespeare's England: A Culture of Mediation* (Cambridge: Cambridge University Press, 2012).

17 Joseph Hall, *Characters of Vertues and Vices. In Two Bookes* (London, 1608), sig. E5v. Hall quotes nearly verbatim from Pierre de Charron's *De la sagesse* (*On Wisdom*): "Le Magistrat doibt estre de facile acces, prest a ouyr & entendre toutes plaintes & requestes, tenant sa porte ouverte a tous, & ne s'absenter point, se souvenant qu'il n'est à foy, mais à tous; & serviteur du public." *De la Sagesse* (Paris, 1607), 685.

18 According to Hugh Adlington, "approximately three-fifths of printed assize sermons were preached on Old Testament texts, with Psalms, Proverbs, and Exodus being the favourite sources. Acts, Romans, and Hebrews were the most popular sources of New Testament texts." Adlington, "Restoration, Religion, and Law," 427.

19 Henry Smith, "A Memento for Magistrates," in *The Poore-Mans Teares* (London: Printed by John Wolfe, & are to be sold by William Wright, 1592), sig. E8r.

20 Samuel Garey, *Jentaculum Judicum: Or, A Breake-Fast for the Bench: Prepared, Presented, and Preached in Two Sacred Services, or Sermons, the Morning Sacrifice before the Two Assizes: At Thetford, at Norwich: 1619. Containing Monitory Meditations, to Execute Justice and Law-Businesse with a Good Conscience* (London: B[ernard]. A[lsop]. for Matthew Law, and are to be sold by Edmond Casson at Norwich in the market-place, at the signe of the Bible, 1623), sig. B3r, original emphasis.

21 Kim Hedlin, "The Book of Job in Early Modern England" (PhD diss., University of California, Los Angeles, 2018).

22 Richard Carpenter, *The Conscionable Christian: Or, The Indevour of Saint Paul, to Have and Discharge a Good Conscience Alwayes towards God, and Men: Laid Open and Applyed in Three Sermons. Preached before the Honourable Judges of the Circuit, at Their Severall Assises, Holden in Chard and Taunton, for the County of Somerset. 1620. By Richard Carpenter, Doctor of Divinity, and Pastor of Sherwell in Devon* (London: F[elix] K[ingston] for John Bartlet, and are to be sold at the signe of the gilded Cup, in the Goldsmiths Rowe in Cheapside, 1623), sig. D1r.

23 Harris, "Saint Paul's Exercise," sig. D2v, original emphasis.

24 *The Holy Bible, Conteyning the Old Testament, and the New* (London: Robert Barker, 1611), sig. 3A4r. (Job 29:14–17). On assize preachers' frequent citation of Job's magistracy, see Adlington, "Restoration, Religion, and Law," 429.

25 Harris, "Saint Paul's Exercise," sig. D4r.

26 Samuel Ward, *Jethro's Justice of Peace. A Sermon Preached at the Generall Assises Held at Bury St Edmunds for the Countie of Suffolke* (London: Printed by Augustine Mathewes, for John Marriot and Iohn Grismand, and are to be sold at their shops in Saint Dunstones Church-yard, and in Pauls Alley at the signe of the Gunne, 1621), sig. B7r–v.

27 Henry Smith, "The Magistrates Scripture," in *The Sermons of Maister Henrie Smith, Gathered into One Volume. Printed According to His Corrected Copies in His Life Time* (London, 1593), sig. Yy8v, original emphasis.

28 Smith, "A Memento for Magistrates," sig. F1r.

29 Regina M. Schwartz, *Loving Justice, Living Shakespeare* (Oxford: Oxford University Press, 2016), 20.

30 Alastair J.L. Blanshard and Tracey A. Sowerby, "Thomas Wilson's Demosthenes and the Politics of Tudor Translation," *International Journal of the Classical Tradition* 12, no. 1 (2005): 46–80.

31 Christopher? Yelverton, "Notes of Sermons," 1592–1621, BL Additional MS 48016, fol. 31r.

32 Dodderidge qtd. in Paul Raffield, "The Ancient Constitution, Common Law and the Idyll of Albion: Law and Lawyers in *Henry IV, Parts 1 and 2*," *Law and Literature* 22, no. 1 (2010): 20.

33 Croke qtd. in G.W. Keeton, *Shakespeare's Legal and Political Background* (New York: Barnes and Noble, 1967), 6.

34 Edward Coke, *Le tierce part des reports del Edward Coke* (London: [Printed by Adam Islip] in ædibus Thomæ Wight, 1602), sig. E1r.

35 Edward Coke, *The First Part of the Institutes* (London, 1628), sig. Ggggg2v–3r.

36 Coke, sig. ¶¶v.

37 Coke, sig. A2r.

38 Artificial reason, or *lex ratio*, is defined by Coke in the following passage: "*Ratio est anima legis*; for then are we said to know the law, when we apprehend the reason of the law; that is, when we bring the reason of the law so to our owne reason, that wee perfectly understand it as our owne." Edward Coke, *The First*

Part of the Institutes of the Lawes of England or a Commentary upon Littleton (London: Printed by L. Hansard & sons for E. Brooke; W. Clarke and Sons, 1809), §395a. Further discussion of Coke's understanding of the difference between natural and artificial reason may be found in Allen D. Boyer, "Sir Edward Coke, Ciceronianus: Classical Rhetoric and the Common Law Tradition," *International Journal for the Semiotics of Law* 10, no. 28 (1997): 6; J.G.A. Pocock, *The Ancient Constitution and the Feudal Law: A Study of English Historical Thought in the Seventeenth Century: A Reissue with a Retrospect* (Cambridge: Cambridge University Press, 1987), 35; Charles Gray, "Reason, Authority, and Imagination: The Jurisprudence of Sir Edward Coke," in *Culture and Politics: From Puritanism to the Enlightenment*, ed. Perez Zagorin (Berkeley: University of California Press, 1980), 30; John U. Lewis, "Sir Edward Coke: His Theory of Artificial Reason as a Context for Modern Basic Legal Theory," *Law Quarterly Review* 84 (1968): 337.

39 Bacon, "Speech … before the Summer Circuits," qtd. in Bacon, *The Essayes*, 15:307n.10. For more on the context behind Bacon's admonishment, see J.S. Cockburn, *A History of English Assizes, 1558–1714* (Cambridge: Cambridge University Press, 1972), 58–9.

40 Jeffrey S. Doty, "*Measure for Measure* and the Problem of Popularity," *English Literary Renaissance* 42, no. 1 (2012): 33.

41 William Lambarde, *Archeion* (London, 1635), sig. G1v, original emphasis.

42 Edward Coke, *The Lord Coke His Speech and Charge. With a Discoverie of the Abuses and Corruption of Officers*, ed. Robert Pricket (London: Printed for Nathaniell Butter, 1607), sig. B4r.

43 C.L. Barber, "The Trial of Carnival in *Part 2*," in *William Shakespeare's Henry IV, Part 2*, ed. Harold Bloom (New York: Chelsea House Publishers, 1987), 23.

44 Paul Raffield observes that the Chief Justice is a "model of governance" who upholds the "ancient constitution" by ultimately teaching Hal the lesson of "accountable kingship and limited monarchy." Raffield, "The Ancient Constitution," 41. See also Lorna Hutson, "Not the King's Two Bodies: Reading the 'Body Politic' in Shakespeare's *Henry IV, Parts 1 and 2*," in *Rhetoric and Law in Early Modern Europe*, ed. Lorna Hutson and Victoria Kahn (New Haven: Yale University Press, 2001), 167. While I too believe that this important scene shines a positive light on the Chief Justice's office, I seek to nuance the understanding of the function of this scene within the context of competing discourses on judicature.

45 Thomas Elyot, *The Boke Named the Governour* (London, 1531), sig. P7v–P8r, my emphasis. The line divisions are in the original text.

46 Barbara Hodgdon, ed., *The Famous Victories of Henry the Fifth*, in *The First Part of King Henry the Fourth: Texts and Contexts* (Boston: Bedford, 1997), 4.1.

47 William Shakespeare, *Henry IV, Part 2*, ed. René Weis (Oxford: Clarendon, 1998). Subsequent quotations will be cited parenthetically in the chapter.

48 "Purse, n., 1.1 and 7a.," *OED*.

49 Proponents of restorative justice argue that it remedies the excessively retributive aspects of the legal systems. Whereas retributive justice is "revenge formalized by the state" (*retributio*: recompense, punishment), restorative justice attempts to restore the relationship between the duelling parties. In theory, all members of the community may take part in restorative justice: "victims, offenders and other 'stakeholders' in a criminal case should be allowed to encounter one another outside highly formal, professional-dominated settings such as the courtroom." Gerry Johnstone and Daniel W. Van Ness, "The Meaning of Restorative Justice," in *Handbook of Restorative Justice*, ed. Gerry Johnstone and Daniel Van Ness (Cullompton: Willan, 2007), 9.

50 Martin Wright, *Justice for Victims and Offenders: A Restorative Response to Crime*, 2nd ed. (Winchester: Waterside Press, 1996), iv.

51 Carpenter, *The Conscionable Christian*, sig. D1r.

52 Marissa Greenberg, "Signs of the Crimes: Topography, Murder, and Early Modern Domestic Tragedy," *Genre* 40, nos. 1–2 (2007): 4. See also chapter 3 for a discussion of London's topography of crime.

53 The failure of Shallow as a justice of the peace – and how it could be seen to reflect the government's complaints against wayward JPs – is illuminated in Colin Burrow, "Reading Tudor Writing Politically: The Case of *2 Henry IV*," *Yearbook of English Studies* 38 (2008): 234–50. See also John Kerrigan, "*Henry IV* and the Death of Old Double," *Essays in Criticism* 40, no. 1 (1990): 24–53.

54 18 Edw. 3 (sess. 2), c. 2, qtd. in J.H. Baker, *An Introduction to English Legal History*, 4th ed. (Oxford: Oxford University Press, 2007), 25.

55 William Lambarde, *Eirenarcha: Or of The Office of the Justices of Peace, in Two Bookes* (London: Imprinted by Ra: Newbery, and H. Bynneman, by the ass. of Ri. Tot. & Chr. Bar., 1581), sig. C8v.

56 J.H. Gleason, *The Justices of the Peace in England, 1558 to 1640* (Oxford: Clarendon, 1969), 53.

57 Lambarde's and Fuller's notebooks are available in modern editions: William Lambarde, *William Lambarde and Local Government: His "Ephemeris" and Twenty-Nine Charges to Juries and Commissions*, ed. Conyers Read (Ithaca: Cornell University Press for the Folger Shakespeare Library, 1962); Bostock Fuller, "Note Book of a Surrey Justice," in *Surrey Archæological Collections, Relating to the History and Antiquities of the County*, ed. Granville Leveson-Gower, vol. 9 (London: The Surrey Archæological Society, 1888), 161–232. William Dove's inquest book exists only in manuscript; see Dove, "Gravesend Inquests: Casebook (1673–76)," BL Harleian MS 6749. For more on this inquest or casebook, see Syme, *Theatre and Testimony*, 37.

58 Lambarde, *William Lambarde*, 27.

59 Fuller, "Note Book of a Surrey Justice," 217.

60 William Shakespeare, *The Merry Wives of Windsor*, in *The Riverside Shakespeare*, ed. G. Blakemore Evans (Boston: Houghton, 1974), 1.1.6–7.

61 Burrow explains that "Wo'ncot and the 'Hill' are Gloucestershire places, corresponding to Woodmancote and Stinchcombe Hill." Burrow, "Reading Tudor Writing Politically," 243.

62 "Knave, n., 1 and 3," *OED*.

63 "Visor, vizor, n., 1 and 2," *OED*.

64 The scholarship on equity in early modern literature is vast. See Mark Fortier, *The Culture of Equity in Early Modern England* (Aldershot: Ashgate, 2005).

65 William Shakespeare, *The First Part of Henry the Fourth*, in *The Riverside Shakespeare*, ed. G. Blakemore Evans et al. (Boston: Houghton, 1974), 1.2.83–4. Subsequent quotations will be cited parenthetically in the chapter.

66 The Great Bible qtd. in Naseeb Shaheen, *Biblical References in Shakespeare's History Plays* (Newark: University of Delaware Press, 1989), 138. According to Shaheen, "in this passage, Shakespeare appears to be closest to the Great Bible and to the translations that preceded it (Coverdale, Matthew, Taverner), and is least like the Geneva" (138).

67 Chrimes's preface in John Fortescue, *De Laudibus Legum Anglie*, ed. S.B. Chrimes (Cambridge: Cambridge University Press, 1942), xiii.

68 "Sessions, 1613: 4 and 6 August," in *County of Middlesex. Calendar to the Sessions Records: New Series, Vol. 1: 1612–14*, ed. William Le Hardy, British History Online, http://www.british-history.ac.uk/report.aspx?compid=82310.

69 A.C. Bradley, *Oxford Lectures on Poetry* (London: Macmillan, 1934), 251.

70 *Digital Facsimile of the Bodleian First Folio of Shakespeare's plays*, Bodleian Arch. G c.7., http://firstfolio.bodleian.ox.ac.uk/book.html.

71 "Tenor, n.1 and adj.," *OED*.

72 Baker, *An Introduction*, 223.

73 William Shakespeare, *The Life of Henry V*, in *The Riverside Shakespeare*, ed. G. Blakemore et al. (Boston: Houghton, 1974), 1.2.54.

74 William Shakespeare, *Henry VI, Part 2*, ed. Roger Warren (Oxford: Oxford University Press, 2003), 1.3.208–10.

75 Robert Bartlett, *Trial by Fire and Water: The Medieval Judicial Ordeal* (Oxford: Clarendon, 1986), 115.

76 Richard Strier, "Shakespeare and Legal Systems: The Better the Worse (But Not Vice Versa)," in *Shakespeare and the Law*, ed. Bradin Cormack, Martha Nussbaum, and Richard Strier (Chicago: University of Chicago Press, 2013), 174.

77 On the concept of "legality," see my preface and introduction.

78 This list of moral qualities comes from Garey, *Jentaculum Judicum*, sig. B3r–v.

79 John Dodderidge, "Charge, 1620," in *Collection of Justices' Charges* (1610–42), BL Harleian MS 583, fol. 9v.

80 Aristotle, *Ethics*, 1.4.2–3 (11).

81 Justinian and Gaius, *The Institutes of Gaius and Justinian, The Twelve Tables, and the CXVIIIth and CXXVIIth Novels*, trans. T. Lambert Mears (London: Stevens, 1882), Just. 1.1.

3 Neighbourliness and the Coroner's Inquest in English Domestic Tragedies

1 Edward Arber, ed., *A Transcript of the Registers of the Company of Stationers of London, 1554–1640*, vol. 2 (London: Privately Printed, 1875), 311b–3312. For more on these lost texts, see Robert Yarington, *Two Lamentable Tragedies*, ed. Chiaki Hanabusa (Manchester: Manchester University Press for the Malone Society, 2013), xxiv.

2 On Haughton and Day's lost play, which is entered in Henslowe's "diary" as both "The Tragedy of Merry" and "Beech's Tragedy," see Emma Whipday and Freyja Cox Jensen, "'Original Practices,' Lost Plays, and Historical Imagination: Staging 'The Tragedy of Merry,'" *Shakespeare Bulletin* 35, no. 2 (2017): 289; Robert Adger Law, "Yarington's 'Two Lamentable Tragedies,'" *Modern Language Review* 5 (1910): 168.

3 The play was likely written sometime after the murders of Beech and his boy Winchester (in August 1594) and before its eventual publication in 1601. Anne Weston Patenaude suggests a composition date of "late 1594 to 1595," reasoning that "Yarington may well have been inspired to write the Merry plot at this time by the notoriety of the London crime, and possibly he sought to capitalize on a market which had already supported the publication of five ballads and a 'booke' on the same event." Anne Weston Patenaude, "A Critical Old-Spelling Edition of Robert Yarington's *Two Lamentable Tragedies*" (PhD diss., University of Michigan, 1978), 15. Patenaude's conclusion is endorsed by Chiaki Hanabusa in the Malone edition. Yarington, *Two Lamentable Tragedies*, xxvii. The absence of legal documentation is frustrating but not unusual. As Ian Archer notes, "[f]or the Elizabethan period we lack any sessions material for the City proper; that surviving for the Middlesex suburbs is extremely fragmentary." Ian W. Archer, *The Pursuit of Stability: Social Relations in Elizabethan London* (Cambridge: Cambridge University Press, 1991), 3.

4 I considered replacing every mention of *Two Lamentable Tragedies* with "The Tragedy of Merry." In the end, I did not do so because, while it is true I have far more to say about the Merry plot than the Italian one, my sustained discussion of the choric-presenter Truth (a character who appears in both plots) warranted the use of the play's full title.

5 See Lena Cowen Orlin, "Yarington [Yarrington], Robert (fl. 1601), putative playwright," *ODNB*. See also Yarington, *Two Lamentable Tragedies*, xxiv–xxix.

6 Chiaki Hanabusa, the editor of the Malone Society edition of the play, argues that "on the basis of the requirement of a sufficient large and wide stage, some awkward and comical staging effects, a lack of expository structure to inform the audience of personal names, and the use of extremely rare and exceptional locutions for the stage directions, two observations can be made: one is that the author may have had less theatrical experience than his colleagues amongst professional playwrights; the other is that the play as it stands was never

performed" (Yarington, xv). However, her conclusion has been disputed: see
Whipday and Cox Jensen, "'Original Practice,'" 294–5.

7 For an introduction to the genre – and the problems related to the term "domestic
tragedy" – see Lena Cowen Orlin, "Domestic Tragedy: Private Life on the Public
Stage," in *A Companion to Renaissance Drama*, ed. Arthur F. Kinney (Malden:
Blackwell, 2002), 367–83.

8 Philip Brophy, "Horrality – The Textuality of Contemporary Horror Films,"
Screen 27, no. 1 (1986): 10. Body horror is related to "gross-out horror," which,
to quote Linda Williams, focuses on "ecstatic excesses." Linda Williams, "Film
Bodies: Gender, Genre, and Excess," *Film Quarterly* 44, no. 4 (1991): 3.

9 Brophy, "Horrality," 8.

10 Robert Yarington, *Two Lamentable Tragedies*, ed. Chiaki Hanabusa (Manchester:
Manchester University Press for the Malone Society, 2013). Subsequent
quotations will be cited parenthetically in the chapter.

11 For a discussion of the common prosthetics used to stage scenes of
dismemberment, specifically those used by the Lord Admiral's Men, see
Lucy Munro, "'They Eat Each Others' Arms': Stage Blood and Body Parts," in
Shakespeare's Theatres and the Effects of Performance, ed. Farah Karim-Cooper
and Tiffany Stern (London: Bloomsbury, 2015), 73–93.

12 Law, "Yarington's 'Two Lamentable Tragedies,'" 168.

13 Lambeth Hill (also called Lambert Hill in the play) was situated in London, the
north side of the Thames, from Thames Street to the west end of Old Fish Street.
See Edward H. Sugden, *A Topographical Dictionary to the Works of Shakespeare
and His Fellow Dramatists* (Manchester: Manchester University Press, 1925), 296.
See also Janelle Jenstad and Melanie Chernyk, "Lambeth Hill," *The Map of Early
Modern London* (Victoria, BC: University of Victoria), http://mapoflondon.uvic
.ca/LAMB2.htm. For insight on the possible location of Merry's tavern on Thames
Street, see Marissa Greenberg, *Metropolitan Tragedy: Genre, Justice, and the City
in Early Modern England* (Toronto: University of Toronto Press, 2015), 38–9.

14 According to English jurists, whereas in England, the accused had the
opportunity to confront accusers and witnesses in open court and could also
choose to be judged by a jury drawn from the neighbourhood, the unfortunate
citizens of Romano-canonic jurisdictions had few protections against secret
inquisitions. The chancellor in Sir John Fortescue's dialogue reports that many
in France are "thrust into a sack without any form of trial, and … thrown by
the officers of the provost-marshal into the river at night and drowned." John
Fortescue, *De Laudibus Legum Anglie*, ed. S.B. Chrimes (Cambridge: Cambridge
University Press, 1942), 85.

15 Lena Cowen Orlin, *Private Matters and Public Culture in Post-Reformation
England* (Ithaca: Cornell University Press, 1994), 10.

16 On the term the "middling sort," see Keith Wrightson, "'Sorts of People' in
Tudor and Stuart England," in *The Middling Sort of People: Culture, Society, and*

Politics in England, 1550–1800, ed. Jonathan Barry and Christopher W. Brooks (Houndmills: Macmillan, 1994), 28–51, 227–33. For examples of how critics have used the genre of the domestic tragedy to explore facets of English cultural values, see Emma Whipday, *Shakespeare's Domestic Tragedies: Violence in the Early Modern Home* (Cambridge: Cambridge University Press, 2019); Greenberg, *Metropolitan Tragedy*; Catherine Richardson, *Domestic Life and Domestic Tragedy in Early Modern England: The Material Life of the Household* (Manchester: Manchester University Press, 2006); Frances E. Dolan, *Dangerous Familiars: Representations of Domestic Crime in England 1550–1700* (Ithaca: Cornell University Press, 1994).

17 John Calvin, *The Institution of Christian Religion* (London: By Arnold Hatfield, for Bonham Norton, 1599), sig. O6v.

18 Golding's authorship of this pamphlet is discussed in *A Warning for Fair Women: A Critical Edition*, ed. Charles Dale Cannon (The Hague: Mouton, 1975), 64–5; Louis Thorn Golding, *An Elizabethan Puritan: Arthur Golding* (New York: Smith, 1937), 68. In addition to Golding's pamphlet and *A Warning for Fair Women*, the murder of George Sanders was recounted in a ballad: see "The Wofull Lamentacon of Mrs. Anne Saunders, Which She Wrote with Her Own Hand, Being Prisoner in Newgate, Justly Condemned to Death," in *Old English Ballads: 1553–1625*, ed. Hyder Rollins (Cambridge: Cambridge University Press, 1920), 340–8. The story was featured in Anthony Munday, *A View of Sundry Examples. Reporting Many Straunge Murthers, Sundry Persons Perjured, Signes and Tokens of Gods Anger towards Us* (London: J. Charlewood] for William Wright, and are to be sold [by J. Allde] at the long shop, adjoyning unto S. Mildreds Church in the Poultrie, 1580). Munday's title page advertises the book as containing "all memorable murthers since the murther of Maister Saunders by George Browne to this present"; this is a measure of the historical importance of the Sanders case. For a complete list of sixteenth- and seventeenth-century media related to the Sanders case, see Greenberg, *Metropolitan Tragedy*, 25.

19 Golding, *An Elizabethan Puritan: Arthur Golding*, 149.

20 Alan H. Nelson, *Monstrous Adversary: The Life of Edward de Vere, 17th Earl of Oxford* (Liverpool: Liverpool University Press, 2003), 90. Edward de Vere (1550–1604), the seventeenth Earl of Oxford, was Cecil's son-in-law and Golding's nephew-in-law.

21 Cecil qtd. in Nelson, 89. Nelson notes that Browne was not Irish but had temporarily served in Ireland as a "Captain" (90).

22 George Sanders "was first cousin to Sir Edward Sanders, Chief Baron of the Exchequer, and the same relation to Alice Sanders, mother of Sir Christopher Hatton, who later became Lord Chancellor. Sanders' father, William, married the mother of the celebrated legal scholar, Walter Haddon, the friend of Cheke and Ascham; Walter Haddon and George Sanders were therefore stepbrothers." Joseph

H. Marshburn, "'A Cruell Murder Donne in Kent' and Its Literary Manifestations," *Studies in Philology* 46, no. 2 (1949): 136.

23 E. St. John Brooks, "A Pamphlet by Arthur Golding. The Murder of George Saunders," *Notes and Queries* 174, no. 11 (1938): 183–4.

24 Arthur Golding, "A Briefe Discourse," in *A Warning for Fair Women: A Critical Edition*, ed. Charles Dale Cannon (The Hague: Mouton, 1975), 216–30. Subsequent quotations will be cited parenthetically in the chapter.

25 Alan H. Nelson dates the arrest to 30 March. Nelson, *Monstrous Adversary*, 90. Browne is arraigned at the Queen's Bench – perhaps on account of the Sanders' family's court connections – on 17 April (219). The original indictment against Browne is contained in LMA MJ/SR/0179/21. See Randall Martin, *Women, Murder, and Equity in Early Modern England* (New York: Routledge, 2008), 222n.3.

26 Gibbeting was a multi-step process: "after he [the condemned] was dead and cut down from the gibbet, a stout canvas dress was put on the body, well saturated with tar; the face, hands, and feet were likewise daubed with it, and then a light frame of hoop-iron was fitted round the legs, body, and arms, with the object of causing the ghastly remains to hang together as long as possible. At the top of this framework, was an iron loop, which went over the head, and to this was secured the chain, by which the corpse was finally suspended to a lofty gibbet made of oak, and studded with tenterhooks, to prevent any one from climbing up to remove the body." William Lennox de Ros, *Memorials of the Tower of London* (London: Murray, 1866), 88. Another notorious murderer, Arnold Cosby, was "hanged till he was dead, and nowe remaineth in the placed [*sic*] hanged up in chaines." *The Manner of the Death and Execution of Arnold Cosbie* (London: [John Wolfe?] for William Wright, 1591), sig. A2v.

27 Marshburn, "'A Cruell Murder,'" 137.

28 Marshburn, 137.

29 Randall Martin identifies Mr. Yong as Matthew Yonge. Martin, *Women, Murder, and Equity*, 92. William Charke was the lecturer at Gray's Inn from 1575 to 1580. Wilfrid R. Prest, *The Inns of Court Under Elizabeth I and the Early Stuarts, 1590–1640* (London: Longman, 1972), 191. Alexander Nowell was the Dean of St. Paul's from 1560 to the time of his death in 1602. Stanford Lehmberg, "Nowell, Alexander (c. 1516/17–1602), dean of St Paul's," *ODNB*.

30 William Fulbecke, *A Direction or Preparative to the Study of the Lawe* (London, 1600), sig. C4r.

31 On 22 July1566/7, a George Mell published *A Proper New Balad of the Bryber Gehesie. Taken out of the Fourth Booke of Kinges, the v. Chapter; to the Tune of Kynge Salomon* (London: In fletestreate beneath the Conduit, at the signe of S. John Evangelist by Thomas Colwell, 1567). This may have been the same Mell mentioned in Golding's pamphlet. Marshburn, "'A Cruell Murder,'" 132. Given

the theme of anti-bribery in the ballad, the arrest of Mell for attempted bribery is particularly ironic.

32   Martin Ingram, "Shame and Pain: Themes and Variations in Tudor Punishments," in *Penal Practice and Culture, 1500–1900: Punishing the English*, ed. Simon Devereaux and Paul Griffiths (New York: Palgrave, 2004), 43.

33   It is impossible to precisely date *A Warning for Fair Women*. Charles Dale Cannon argues that the play could have been written and staged in the mid-1580s based on the following internal evidence: "because the 'custom of smoking tobacco in pipes' became established around the mid-1580s, the play's reference to a 'tobacco pipe' suggests it was performed around that time." *A Warning* [Ed. Cannon], 46. Other scholars have suggested a date of between 1593 and 1599; see, for example, Andrew Clark, "An Annotated List of Sources and Related Material for Elizabethan Domestic Tragedy, 1591–1625," *Research Opportunities in Renaissance Drama* 18 (1974): 28.

34   Rebecca Lemon, *Addiction and Devotion in Early Modern England* (Philadelphia: University of Pennsylvania Press, 2018), 136–52.

35   *A Warning for Faire Women* (London: Printed at London by Valentine Sims for William Aspley, 1599). Subsequent quotations will be cited parenthetically in the chapter.

36   J.H. Gleason further observes that Kent is "very much within the London metropolitan region even in 1558, yet also essentially rural." J.H. Gleason, *The Justices of the Peace in England, 1558 to 1640* (Oxford: Clarendon, 1969), 6.

37   Paris Garden was "[a] manor on the S. bank of the Thames, W. of the Liberty of the Clink ... It was surrounded by a stream, called the P[aris] G[arden] Ditch, and was in the 16th cent. 'so dark with trees that one man cannot see another' (Letter of Fleetwood 1578) ... It was approached from the Thames by way of the P[aris] G[arden] Stairs, a few yards E[ast] of the present Blackfriars B[ri]dge ... [it] was best known through the huge amphitheatre erected there for bull- and bear-baiting early in the reign of Henry VIII." Sugden, *A Topographical Dictionary*, 391.

38   John Davies, *The Poems of Sir John Davies*, ed. Robert Krueger (Oxford: Clarendon, 1975).

39   K.J. Kesselring, *Making Murder Public: Homicide in Early Modern England, 1480–1680* (Oxford: Oxford University Press, 2019), 39.

40   *The Compleat Justice. Being an Exact and Compendious Collection out of Such as Have Treated of the Office of Justices of the Peace, but Principally out of Mr. Lambert, Mr. Crompton, and Mr. Dalton ... Whereunto Are Added The Resolutions of the Judges of Assises in the Year 1633* (London: Printed by James Flesher for William Lee and Daniel Pakeman, and are to be sold at their Shops in Fleetstreet, 1661), sig. D8v.

41   Early coroners were known as "'keepers of the pleas of the crown' ... The articles of the 1194 eyre ordered that 'in each county are to be chosen three knights

and one cleric as keepers of the pleas of the crown,' and this order does seem to mark the general establishment of the position at county level." John Hudson, *The Oxford History of the Laws of England, Volume 2: 871–1216*, vol. 2 (Oxford: Oxford University Press, 2012), 508. For more on the history of this office, see Matthew Lockwood, *The Conquest of Death: Violence and the Birth of the Modern English State* (New Haven: Yale University Press, 2017); Carol Loar, "'Go and Seek the Crowner': Coroners' Inquests and the Pursuit of Justice in Early Modern England" (PhD diss., Northwestern University, 1998).

42 For a succinct description of the function and form of the coroners' rolls, see Reginald R. Sharpe, *Calendar of Coroners Rolls of the City of London, A.D. 1300–1378* (London: Clay, 1913).

43 John Dodderidge, *The History of the Ancient and Moderne Estate of the Principality of Wales, Dutchy of Cornewall, and Earldome of Chester. Collected out of the Records of the Tower of London, and Divers Ancient Authours. By Sir John Dodridge Knight, Late One of His Majesties Judges in Th[e] Kings Bench. And by Himselfe Dedicated to King James of Ever Blessed Memory* (London: printed by Tho. Harper, for Godfrey Emondson, and Thomas Alchorne, 1630), sig. G2r.

44 In the fourteenth century, the coroner was more typically a "substantial landowner," making him just "only slightly below" the knightly class. R.F. Hunnisett, *The Medieval Coroner* (Cambridge: Cambridge University Press, 1961), 174. Hunnisett explains that the requirement about the coroner's wealth was a function of two considerations. First, because the office was unpaid, the coroner had to be independently wealthy in order to put up with the "great inconvenience and expense" of running an inquest. Second, because the crown could financially penalize the coroner for conducting a faulty inquest, it was in the crown's interest to insure that the coroner had "lands in order to be able to account to the king … if necessary" (175).

45 Great Britain, *The Statutes of the Realm*, vol. 1 (London, 1810), 29.

46 Hunnisett, *The Medieval Coroner*, 173.

47 Johann Boemus, *The Manners, Lawes, and Customes of All Nations*, trans. Edward Aston (London: Printed by G. Eld and are to bee sold by Francis Burton, 1611), sig. Dd5r, my emphasis.

48 Thomas Smith, *De Republica Anglorum*, ed. Mary Dewar (Cambridge: Cambridge University Press, 1982), 42.

49 Michael Dalton, *The Countrey Justice, Conteyning the Practise of the Justices of the Peace out of Their Sessions* (London: Printed for the Societie of Stationers, 1618), sig. B1v.

50 Malcolm Gaskill, *Crime and Mentalities in Early Modern England* (Cambridge: Cambridge University Press, 2000), 246.

51 Lockwood, *The Conquest of Death*, 128.

52 John Rastell, *An Exposition of Certaine Difficult and Obscure Words, and Termes of the Lawes of This Realme* (London: Printed by Thomas Wight, 1602), sig. G7v.

Rastell's book was published in 1579. Rastell cites the Statute of Westminster I of 1275, which indeed decreed that only the "most wise and discreet knights which best knewe could & would attend this Office." Ibid.

53 For all "[e]nquests for the Death of man … all being Twelve Years of Age ought to appear, unless they have reasonable cause of absence." Great Britain, *Statutes*, 1:25. For a further discussion of this requirement, see Kesselring, *Making Murder Public*, 50n.58. The practice of the coroner's jury continued in the United States well into the twentieth century. For example, in the jurisdiction of Newport News, Virginia, the coroner's jury was only abolished in 1926. See "A Guide to the Newport News (Va.) Coroners' Inquisitions, 1879–1944," Library of Virginia, http://ead.lib.virginia.edu /vivaxtf/view?docId=lva/vi03636.xml. I am grateful to Jessica Apolloni for this reference.

54 Hunnisett, *The Medieval Coroner*, 15.

55 Sara M. Butler, *Forensic Medicine and Death Investigation in Medieval England* (New York: Routledge, 2015), 2.

56 Lockwood, *The Conquest of Death*, 124.

57 Holger Schott Syme, *Theatre and Testimony in Shakespeare's England: A Culture of Mediation* (Cambridge: Cambridge University Press, 2012), 69.

58 Smith, *De Republica Anglorum*, 108.

59 Ibid.

60 Dodderidge, *The History…. of Wales*, sig. G2r.

61 For a further comment on the confusion surrounding *"corona populi"* see Michael MacDonald, "Suicide and the Rise of the Popular Press in England," *Representations* 22 (1988): 37.

62 In contrast, the anonymously authored domestic tragedy *A Yorkshire Tragedy* features a "Knight" and a "Master of the College." *A Yorkshire Tragedy. Not so New as Lamentable and True. Acted by His Majesties Players at the Globe* (London: Printed by R. B. for Thomas Pavier and are to bee sold at his shop on Cornhill, neere the exchange, 1608). These characters are based on the single figure of the "Gentleman" in the play's source text *Two Most Unnaturall and Bloodie Murthers: The One by Maister Caverley, a Yorkshire Gentleman, Practised upon His Wife, and Committed Uppon His Two Children, the Three and Twentie of April 1605. The Other by Mistris Browne, and Her Servant Peter, Upon Her Husband, Who Were Executed in Lent Last Past at Bury in Suffolke. 1605* (London: By V. S[immes] for Nathanael Butter dwelling in Paules churchyard neere Saint Austens gate, 1605). In the pamphlet, the gentleman who shelters the victims is named as Sir Henry Savill (sig. C2r).

63 The relationship between Merry and Harry Williams is never explicitly addressed but the text implies one of service; Master Cowley refers to Merry as Harry's "maister" (sig. H3r). Yet, confusingly, Merry calls Harry his "carefull" companion (sig. A3v).

64 Tiffany Stern, *Documents of Performance in Early Modern England* (Cambridge: Cambridge University Press, 2009), 212.

65 Archer, *The Pursuit of Stability*, 11.

66 Ibid.

67 Paul Slack, *Poverty and Policy in Tudor and Stuart England* (London, Longman, 1988), 49. See also J.A. Sharpe, "Social Strain and Social Dislocation, 1585-1603," in *The Reign of Elizabeth I: Court and Culture in the Last Decade*, ed. John Guy (Cambridge: Cambridge University Press, 1995), 196.

68 Steve Hindle, "Dearth, Fasting, and Alms: The Campaign for General Hospitality in Late Elizabethan England," *Past & Present* 172 (2001): 48.

69 On anti-alien rhetoric, see Eric Griffin, "Shakespeare, Marlowe, and the Stranger Crisis of the Early 1590s," in *Shakespeare and Immigration*, ed. Ruben Espinosa and David Ruiter (Farnham: Ashgate, 2014), 13-36.

70 The Geneva Bible (London: Christopher Barker, 1582), sig. Ooo2v.

71 Ibid.

72 Geneva Bible, sig. Ooo3r.

73 My understanding of Beech builds on previous readings of domestic tragedy that underscore the ambivalent depiction of the murdered householder. For example, critics point out that Arden of *Arden of Faversham* is a "new man" who straddles the line between being a "loving husband and … rapacious landlord." Catherine Belsey, *The Subject of Tragedy: Identity and Difference in Renaissance Drama* (London: Methuen, 1985), 131-2.

74 England and Wales, *By the Queene. A Proclamation for the Dearth of Corne* (London: By the deputies of Christopher Barker, Printer to the Queenes most excellent Majestie, 1596).

75 Keith Wrightson, *Earthly Necessities: Economic Lives in Early Modern Britain* (New Haven: Yale University Press, 2000), 159. For an account of how literary authors grappled with these economic shocks, see Patricia Fumerton, *Unsettled: The Culture of Mobility and the Working Poor in Early Modern England* (Chicago: University of Chicago Press, 2006); William C. Carroll, *Fat King, Lean Beggar: Representations of Poverty in the Age of Shakespeare* (Ithaca: Cornell University Press, 1996).

76 Wrightson, *Earthly Necessities*, 159.

77 Archer, *The Pursuit of Stability*, 198.

78 In his study of the relationship between the 1596 Oxford rising and the grain shortage, John Walter explains that "[p]rices at local markets paralleled the trajectory of prices nationally. Wheat prices at Oxford doubled over the average of the four preceding years in the harvest year 1594. In the year of the intended rising wheat was selling at 5s. a bushel on Lady Day (25 March). Some six months later at Michaelmas it was 8s. a bushel, a near threefold increase on the earlier average." John Walter, "A 'Rising of the People'? The Oxfordshire Rising of 1596," *Past & Present* 107, no. 1 (1985): 95.

79 William Lambarde, "Charges to Juries and Commissions," in *William Lambarde and Local Government: His "Ephemeris" and Twenty-Nine Charges to Juries and Commissions*, ed. Conyers Read (Ithaca: Cornell University Press, 1962), 128.

80 "Engrosser, n.," *OED*.

81 T.W., *The Office of the Clerk of Assize: Containing the Form and Method of the Proceedings at the Assizes, and General Gaol-Delivery, as Also on the Crown and Nisi Prius Side* (London: printed for Henry Twyford in Vine Court, Middle Temple, 1676), sig. I1v.

82 England and Wales, *Proclamation*, 1596.

83 England and Wales, *By the Queene. The Queenes Majesties Proclamation, 1. For Observation of Former Orders against Ingrossers, & Regraters of Corne, 2. And to See the Markets Furnished with Corne. 3. And Also against the Carying of Corne out of the Realme. 4. And a Prohibition to Men of Hospitalitie from Remooving from Their Habitation in the Time of Dearth. 5. And Finally a Strait Commandement to All Officers Having Charge of Forts to Reside Thereon Personally, and No Inhabitant to Depart from the Sea Coast* (London: By the deputies of Christopher Barker, printer to the Queenes most excellent Majestie, 1596), 1.

84 England and Wales, 2.

85 "Instructions to the Judges of Assize upon going their Circuits, to be delivered to all Justices of the Peace temp. Eliz. concerning the hoarding of Corn, & the suppressing Vagabonds & Thieves," BL Harleian MS 6846, fol. 19r–v. The Lord Keeper would have given the circuit charge.

86 Henry Cocke, "Sir Henry Cocke, to Lord Burghley; on Sinking the Excessive Price of Grain, and Forbidding to Make Strong Ale and Beer, July 25, 1594" (1594), BL Lansdowne MS 76, fol. 85r. Cocke was Lord Burghley's neighbour. On Cocke's political career, see "Cocke, Henry (1538–1610), of Broxbourne, Herts.," Roger Virgoe, *The History of Parliament: The House of Commons, 1558–1603*, ed. P.W. Hasler (History of Parliament Trust, 1981), http://www.historyofparliamentonline.org/volume/1558-1603/member/cocke-henry-1538-1610.

87 Henry Cocke, "Sir H[enry] Cocke, to Lord Burghley; to Regulate the Price of Grain; and That Justices of Peace Produce Their Armour on Demand, Sept. 13, 1594" (1594), BL Lansdowne MS 76, fol. 133r.

88 On the distinction between the deserving and undeserving poor, see Carroll, *Fat King, Lean Beggar*, 24. On the emergence of a national policy on poverty, see Slack, *Poverty and Policy in Tudor and Stuart England*; Steve Hindle, *On the Parish? The Micro-Politics of Poor Relief in Rural England, c. 1550–1750* (Oxford: Clarendon, 2004).

89 Arber, *A Transcript*, 2:313b.

90 A recent analysis revealed that "the works least likely to survive were clearly ballads and fiction." Alexandra Hill, "Lost Print in England: Entries in the

Stationers' Company Register," in *Lost Books: Reconstructing the Print World of Pre-Industrial Europe*, ed. Flavia Bruni and Andrew Pettegree (Leiden: Brill, 2016), 153.

91 Stephen Slany, "The Lord Mayor of London, to Lord Burghley; Concerning Thomas Delonie, Who Composed a Seditious Ballad, on the Scarcity of Corn, July 26, 1596" (1596), BL Lansdowne MS 81, fol. 76r. For a modern transcription of the mayor's letter, see Thomas Deloney, *Jack of Newbury*, ed. Peter C. Herman (Peterborough, ON: Broadview, 2015), 160.

92 Hugh Plat, *Sundrie New and Artificiall Remedies against Famine* (London: Printed by P[eter] S[hort] dwelling on Breadstreet hill, at the signe of the Starre, 1596), sig. A4v–B1r. For more on Plat's establishment of a "dearth science" see Ayesha Mukherjee, *Penury into Plenty: Dearth and the Making of Knowledge in Early Modern England* (New York: Routledge, 2015).

93 *A Solace for This Hard Season: Published by Occasion of Continuance of the Scarcitie of Corne, and Excessive Prices of All Other Kind of Provision* (London: Printed for John Legate, 1595), sig. C7r.

94 Edward Coke, *The Third Part of the Institutes of the Laws of England Concerning High Treason, and Other Pleas of the Crown, and Criminall Causes* (London: Printed by M. Flesher, for W. Lee, and D. Pakeman, 1644), sig. Ee4r.

95 Linda Hutcheon, *A Theory of Adaptation*, 2nd ed. (London: Routledge, 2013), 8.

96 With any adaptation, there are bound to be audiences who have seen or read the original text and those who have not. Hutcheon uses the term "knowing" – as opposed to "learned or competent" – to describe audiences who experience the adaptation "*as an adaptation*" (Hutcheon, 120, original emphasis). I follow her practice.

97 Douglas Bruster and Robert Weimann, *Prologues to Shakespeare's Theatre: Performance and Liminality in Early Modern Drama* (Abingdon: Routledge, 2004), viii.

98 Bruster and Weimann, 2.

99 On the sound of the prologue, see Bruce R. Smith, *The Acoustic World of the Renaissance: Attending to the O-Factor* (Chicago: University of Chicago Press, 1999), 271.

100 "Rap, v.², 2," *OED*.

101 Alec Ryrie, *Being Protestant in Reformation Britain* (Oxford: Oxford University Press, 2013), 22.

102 On providentialism in popular media, see Alexandra Walsham, *Providence in Early Modern England* (Oxford: Oxford University Press, 1999).

103 Thomas Heywood in *An Apology for Actors* (1612 but likely composed around 1608) tells this story: "At *Lin* in *Norfolke*, the then Earle of *Sussex* players acting the old History of Fryer *Francis*, & presenting a woman, who insatiately doting on a yong gentleman, had (the more securely to enjoy his affection) mischievously and secretly murdered her husband, whose ghost haunted her, and at divers times

in her most solitary and private contemplations, in most horrid and fearefull shapes, appeared, and stood before her. As this was acted, a townes-woman (till then of good estimation and report) finding her conscience (at this presentment) extremely troubled, suddenly skritched and cryd out Oh my husband, my husband! I see the ghost of my husband fiercely threatning and menacing me. At which shrill and u[n]expected out-cry, the people about her, moov'd to a strange amazement, inquired the reason of her clamour, when presently un-urged, she told them, that seven yeares ago, she, to be possest of such a Gentleman (meaning him) had poysoned her husband, whose fearefull image personated it selfe in the shape of that ghost: whereupon the murdresse was apprehended, before the Justices further examined, & by her voluntary confession after condemned. That this is true, as well by the report of the Actors as the records of the Towne, there are many eyewitnesses of this accident yet living, vocally to confirme it." Thomas Heywood, *An Apology for Actors* (London: Printed by Nicholas Okes, 1612), sig. G1v–G2r. On the composition date of *An Apology*, see Ellen MacKay, *Persecution, Plague, and Fire: Fugitive Histories of the Stage in Early Modern England* (Chicago: University of Chicago Press, 2011), 25n.5.

104 MacKay, 97.

105 William Shakespeare, *The Tragedy of Hamlet, Prince of Denmark*, in *The Riverside Shakespeare*, ed. G. Blakemore Evans et al. (Boston: Houghton, 1974), 2.2.605. The intertextuality between *A Warning for Fair Women* and *Hamlet* has long been a source of critical fascination; see Naseeb Shaheen, "*A Warning for Fair Women* and the *Ur-Hamlet*," *Notes and Queries* 30, no. 2 (1983): 126–7.

106 Thomas Rymer, *Tragedies of the Last Age* (London: Printed for Richard Tonson at his Shop under Grays-Inn Gate, next Grays-Inn, 1678), sig. C5r.

107 Hutcheon, *A Theory of Adaptation*, 8.

4 Repairing Community

1 "Testimony," in Alexander Mansfield Burrill, *A Law Dictionary and Glossary*, 2nd ed., vol. 2 (New York: Baker, 1871), 526. For a concise discussion of the use of testimony in English and continental courts, see Barbara J. Shapiro, "Law and the Evidentiary Environment," in *The Oxford Handbook of English Law and Litearture, 1500–1700*, ed. Lorna Hutson (Oxford: Oxford University Press, 2017), 257–76.

2 Holger Schott Syme points out that depositions "foreground the act of speaking" and physical "presence" (the presence of the witness) but the recorded "voice" that reaches the ears of the auditors has been put "through multiple representational layers." Holger Schott Syme, *Theatre and Testimony in Shakespeare's England: A Culture of Mediation* (Cambridge: Cambridge University Press, 2012), 70. Frances E. Dolan emphasizes that "[d]epositions are not polyvocal as much as they are univocal: written in a consistent clerical style that erases the prompts to which the

deponent responds and casts the deponent as a third person." Frances E. Dolan, *True Relations: Reading, Literature, and Evidence in Seventeenth-Century England* (Philadelphia: University of Pennsylvania Press, 2013), 139.

3 J.H. Baker, *The Oxford History of the Laws of England, Volume VI, 1483–1558*, ed. J.H. Baker, vol. 6 (Oxford: Oxford University Press, 2003), 518, my emphasis.

4 Jamie K. Taylor, *Fictions of Evidence: Witnessing, Literature, and Community in the Late Middle Ages* (Columbus: Ohio State University Press, 2013), 14.

5 Sara M. Butler, *Forensic Medicine and Death Investigation in Medieval England* (New York: Routledge, 2015), 17.

6 United States Federal Rules of Evidence, Rule 602, "Need for Personal Knowledge," https://www.law.cornell.edu/rules/fre/rule_602.

7 United States Federal Rules of Evidence, Rule 603, "Oath or Affirmation to Testify Truthfully," https://www.law.cornell.edu/rules/fre/rule_603, my emphasis. Although law courts assume an ontologically stable "I" in testimony, scholars have consistently problematized that premise. Notably, Jacques Derrida argues that the "I" in first-person testimonies is a fictional construct. In *Demeure*, Derrida challenges the (European) juridical norm of treating eyewitness testimony as objective evidence, arguing, "there is no testimony that does not structurally imply in itself the possibility of fiction, simulacra, dissimulation, lie, and perjury ... the possibility of literature." Jacques Derrida, *Demeure: Fiction and Testimony*, trans. Elizabeth Rottenberg (Stanford: Stanford University Press, 2000), 8.

8 "Witan," in Joseph Bosworth, *An Anglo-Saxon Dictionary*, ed. T. Northcote Toller (Oxford: Clarendon, 1898), 1243, http://ebeowulf.uky.edu/BT/Bosworth-Toller .htm.

9 I am grateful to Brian Lush and Nanette Goldman for their help with the Greek translation.

10 Devin Jacobsen, "The Testimony of Martyr: A Word History of Martyr in Anglo-Saxon England," *Studies in Philology* 115, no. 3 (2018): 418–19.

11 Hobbes qtd. in "martyr, n., 3," *OED*.

12 If one looks up "witness, n." in the *OED*, one finds the religious definition (a witness as "[one who] testifies for Christ or the Christian faith, esp. by death; a martyr") at the bottom of the entry; see "witness, n., 8.a.," *OED*.

13 Taylor, *Fictions of Evidence*, 3.

14 John N. King, *Foxe's Book of Martyrs and Early Modern Print Culture* (Cambridge: Cambridge University Press, 2006).

15 The literature on Foxe is vast but see Andrew Pettegree, *Marian Protestantism: Six Studies* (Aldershot: Scolar, 1996); David Loades, ed., *John Foxe: An Historical Perspective* (Aldershot: Ashgate, 1999), 199; King, *Foxe's Book of Martyrs*.

16 John D. Staines, "Radical Pity: Responding to Spectacles of Violence in *King Lear*," in *Staging Pain, 1580–1800: Violence and Trauma in British Theatre*, ed. James Robert Allard and Matthew R. Martin (Fanshaw: Ashgate, 2009), 75–92; David

K. Anderson, "The Tragedy of Good Friday: Sacrificial Violence in *King Lear*," *ELH* 78, no. 2 (2011), 277. On conscientious "non-obedience" in *King Lear*, see Richard Strier, "Faithful Servants: Shakespeare's Praise of Disobedience," in *The Historical Renaissance: New Essays on Tudor and Stuart Literature and Culture*, ed. Heather Dubrow and Richard Strier (Chicago: University of Chicago Press, 1988), 108.

17   William Shakespeare, *A Midsummer Night's Dream*, in *The Riverside Shakespeare*, ed. G. Blakemore Evans et al. (Boston: Houghton, 1974), 5.1.14–15. There is a wonderful irony in that it is Theseus – a ruler who prides himself in his mastery over Athenian laws and logic, who mocks poets for their runaway imagination – who speaks those silky lines of verse; Theseus actively resists poetry yet speaks as a poet.

18   Following its initial publication in 1563, *Acts and Monuments* underwent three more editions in 1570, 1576, and 1583. Subsequent quotations will be cited parenthetically in the chapter as "Foxe [year of the edition] page." In his own words, Foxe set out to "collect and set forth the actes, fame and memorie of these our Martyrs of this latter tyme of the churche ... against the importunitie of the malignaunt." Foxe [1563] 8. The bulk of the text is devoted to the affliction of Protestants during the reigns of Henry VIII and Mary I and Philip II.

19   This law was based on previous iterations: 5 Rich. 2, st. 2, c. 5 (1382), 2 Hen. 4, c. 15 (1400–1, also known as *De haeretico comburendo*), 2 Hen. 5, st. 1, c. 7 (1414), and 25 Hen. 8, c. 14 (1534).

20   For an analysis of the rhetoric and structural pattern of martyrdom in Foxe, see John R. Knott, *Discourses of Martyrdom in English Literature, 1563–1694* (Cambridge: Cambridge University Press, 1993).

21   In reality, the majority of the persecuted evangelicals were "gentry, professionals, yeomen farmers, and, above all, artisans," with an overall demographics that was "socially top-heavy." Christopher Haigh, *English Reformations: Religion, Politics, and Society under the Tudors* (Oxford: Clarendon, 1993), 196.

22   Foxe and his collaborators kept written records and transcriptions of prison writings, royal letters to heresy commissioners, and other legal materials related to trials and examinations. Their exhaustive research stemmed in part from a sensitivity toward criticism. Foxe states that in publishing the book, he "exposes [himself] to the hatred, hissings, ill will and censure of many people." Foxe [1563] 9. On Foxe as a historian, see Patrick Collinson, "Truth and Legend: The Veracity of John Foxe's *Book of Martyrs*," in *Elizabethan Essays* (London: Hambledon, 1994), 155.

23   Despite writing a popular history of the Reformation, Foxe was not a populist. Like many of his humanist contemporaries, he mistrusted the masses. For example, Foxe inveighs against "the vulgare sort" and "simple flocke of Christ" who harboured an "ignoraunce of history, not knowing the course of times, and true descent of the Church." Foxe [1570] 2. Patrick Collinson observes that

"nowhere does [Foxe] suggest that death at the stake conferred infallibility on the mental capacities of poorly educated people. Their deaths were edifying, their opinions not always correct." Collinson, "Truth and Legend," 168.

24 Ralph Houlbrooke, *Church Courts and the People during the English Reformation, 1520–1570* (Oxford: Oxford University Press, 1979), 218.

25 John H. Langbein, *Prosecuting Crime in the Renaissance: England, Germany, France* (Cambridge, MA: Harvard University Press, 1974), 1. For a more succinct summary of the prosecutorial role of the Tudor JP, see John H. Langbein, "The Origins of Public Prosecution at Common Law," *American Journal of Legal History* 17 (1973): 313–35.

26 Langbein, *Prosecuting Crime in the Renaissance*, 31.

27 Houlbrooke, *Church Courts*, 233.

28 Her last name is also spelled "Lewis" and "Lewys." Foxe [1563] 1700.

29 John Glover underwent his conversion during the latter part of the reign of Henry VIII. In Foxe's account, after an initial taste of "knowledge of the gospel," and upon learning that those who "fall away" from "the heavenly gift" are damned, Glover began to "misdoubt hymselfe." He looked obsessively for signs of his redemption. Finding none, he experienced "terrors, boylings, & convulsions" in "his wofull brest." Glover soon succumbed to "intollerable griefes of mynd" and he began to wither physically: so "worne" and devoid of "senses" he seemed more dead than alive. Then, inexplicably, Glover began to revive. Foxe does not explain how, when, or why the wracking of conscience ceases. Foxe simply states the "Lord" removed Glover's "discomfort" so that he could spend the rest of his days in "godly study" and "Saboth rest." Foxe [1583] 1733. For a concise account of Glover's conversion, see Susannah Brietz Monta, *Martyrdom and Literature in Early Modern England* (Cambridge: Cambridge University Press, 2005), 18.

30 Historically, apparitors were frequently maltreated by the people they summoned. For examples from the early Middle Ages – including an incident in 1299 in which William de Bredon "forced the archbishop's messenger to eat the citation" – see Dave Postles, "Penance and the Market Place: A Reformation Dialogue with the Medieval Church (c. 1250–c. 1600)," *Journal of Ecclesiastical History* 54, no. 3 (2003): 464.

31 "Friend, n. and adj., 3 and 4c.," *OED*.

32 The second edition of 1570 names the second man as Augustine Bernher, once in the service of Latimer. Susannah Brietz Monta, "Foxe's Female Martyrs and the Sanctity of Transgression," *Renaissance and Reformation* 25, no. 1 (2001): 22n.46.

33 The word "communion" derives from the Anglo-Norman *communiun* signifying "fellowship or mutual relationship between people who profess the same belief." "Communion, n.," *OED*.

34 For an account of the behaviour of crowds at executions across the early modern and Enlightenment periods, see Thomas W. Laqueur, "Crowds, Carnival and the

State in English Executions, 1604–1868," in *The First Modern Society: Essays in English History in Honour of Lawrence Stone*, ed. A.L. Beier, David Cannadine, and James M. Rosenheim (Cambridge: Cambridge University Press, 1989), 305–55.

35 Gilles Deleuze and Félix Guattari, *A Thousand Plateaus: Capitalism and Schizophrenia*, trans. Brian Massumi (Minneapolis: University of Minnesota Press, 1987), 400.

36 The Geneva Bible (London: Christopher Barker, 1582), sig. Sss5r.

37 Patrick Collinson explains that Foxe frequently highlights his subjects' *apatheia*, "the true courage which is a mean between foolish temerity and despicable cowardice." Collinson, "Truth and Legend," 174.

38 I use "intersubjective" in the way it is used in human rights and trauma studies: as an exchange of empathy between individuals, one that contains the possibility of transcending the Hegelian notion of self v. other; see Kelly Oliver, "Witnessing and Testimony," *Parallex* 10, no. 1 (2004): 79–88; Kelly Oliver, *Witnessing: Beyond Recognition* (Minneapolis: University of Minnesota Press, 2001).

39 *Concordance of Shakespeare's Complete Works* (Fairfax: George Mason University, 2020), https://www.opensourceshakespeare.org/concordance/.

40 In his influential essay, first published in 1967, Stanley Cavell (wading into a debate between Robert Heilman and Paul J. Alpers) argues that *King Lear* is ultimately a tragedy centred on "acknowledgment." Stanley Cavell, *Disowning Knowledge in Seven Plays of Shakespeare*, updated ed. (Cambridge: Cambridge University Press, 1987). For Cavell, the play's tragic action hinges on the characters' avoidance of the sources of their shame. Cavell does not find "hope" in an allegorical reading of the play but rather in the irreducibility of witnessing in the face of duress, torture, and annihilation. Gloucester's blinding reveals the limitations of "evil's" effort to erase its presence; "evil has to turn upon him because it cannot bear him to witness. As long as that is true, evil does not have *free* sway over the world" (80, original emphasis). For a reply to Cavell's essay, see both Sarah Beckwith, *Shakespeare and the Grammar of Forgiveness* (Ithaca: Cornell University Press, 2011), and Richard C. McCoy, "'Look upon Me, Sir': Relationships in *King Lear*," *Representations* 81 (2003): 46–60.

41 William Shakespeare, *King Lear: A Parallel Text Edition*, ed. René Weis (London: Longman, 1993). Subsequent quotations will be cited parenthetically in the chapter. Unless indicated otherwise, quotations are based on the folio *King Lear*. Occasionally, I will quote from Q1, the first quarto of 1608, the Pied Bull quarto.

42 For more on the similarities between *King Lear* and the Old Testament story of Abraham, Isaac, and Ishmael, see Barbara A. Mowat, "Shakespeare Reads the Geneva Bible," in *Shakespeare, the Bible, and the Form of the Book: Contested Scriptures*, ed. Travis DeCook and Alan Galey (New York: Routledge, 2012), 31.

43 The resemblance between Gloucester and Leonato of *Much Ado about Nothing* is very strong in this scene. See Hutson's analysis of Leonato's "great haste" and "fatal

deviation" from the forensic method. Lorna Hutson, *The Invention of Suspicion: Law and Mimesis in Shakespeare and Renaissance Drama* (Oxford: Oxford University Press, 2007), 341.

44 "Abhor, v.," and "whore, n.," *OED*.

45 The scene positions Gloucester's character offstage. We know this because Edmund tells Edgar "My father watches" and that "I hear my father coming" (2.1.20, 28), which indicate that Gloucester is absent in the scene and therefore does not see any of the exchange between Edmund and Edgar. Thus, Gloucester's trust in Edmund's narrative is entirely based on the single-witness testimony of Edmund.

46 Garthine Walker, "Imagining the Unimaginable: Parricide in Early Modern England and Wales, c. 1600–1760," *Journal of Family History* 41, no. 3 (2016): 271.

47 Walker, 273.

48 Dalton qtd. in Walker, 283.

49 Thomas Middleton, William Rowley, and Thomas Heywood?, *An/The Old Law*, ed. Jeffrey Masten, in *The Collected Works of Thomas Middleton*, Gary Taylor and John Lavagnino, eds. (Oxford: Clarendon, 2007), 5.1.225–6.

50 The two-witness rule was used in church courts which followed Romano-canonic procedures. For a discussion of the two-witness rule in civil procedure, see John H. Langbein, Renée Lettow Lerner, and Bruce P. Smith, eds., *History of the Common Law: The Development of Anglo-American Legal Institutions* (New York: Aspen, 2009), 133. Although the two-witness rule was in use in English common law, some lawyers such as Sir John Fortescue associated it with the supposedly inferior form of civil law. Fortescue writes that in "the truth of such issue ought, by the civil laws, to be proved by the deposition of witnesses, and for that two suitable witnesses suffice. But by the laws of England, the truth cannot be settled for the judge, unless by the oath of twelve men of the neighbourhood where the fact is supposed to have been located." John Fortescue, *De Laudibus Legum Anglie*, ed. S.B. Chrimes (Cambridge: Cambridge University Press, 1942), 43. To reinforce his argument about the evidentiary weakness of the two-witness rule, Fortescue cites the story of Jezebel and Naboth and that of Susanna and the Elders: "Thus the wicked Jezebel procured two witnesses, sons of Belial, against Naboth in proceedings by which he lost his life, and Ahab his king took possession of his vineyard. So Susanna, a most chaste wife, would have been put to death for adultery by the testimony of two old men, themselves judges, if the Lord had not miraculously freed her by means of an inconceivable wisdom unnatural to a youth not yet advanced in years." Fortescue, 45. Notwithstanding Fortescue's critique, the two-witness rule was widely adopted in England, in both procedural and substantive law.

51 The Geneva Bible, sig. K7r.

52 5 & 6 Edw. 6, c. 11 (1551–2), Great Britain, *The Statutes of the Realm*, vol. 4, pt. 1 (London, 1819), 146. See also L.M. Hill, "The Two-Witness Rule in English

Treason Trials: Some Comments on the Emergence of Procedural Law," *The American Journal of Legal History* 12, no. 2 (1968): 101.

53 Andrea Frisch, *The Invention of the Eyewitness: Witnessing and Testimony in Early Modern France* (Chapel Hill: University of North Carolina Press, 2004), 34.

54 At his treason trial in 1603, Sir Walter Raleigh cited the two-witness rule, which had been revived by Elizabeth I's treason act of 1571; it had been repealed during Mary's reign. His prosecutor, Lord Chief Justice Popham, however, rejected Raleigh's arguments. Hill, "The Two-Witness Rule," 108.

55 Hill, 95.

56 On drama and the dissemination of treason law and cases in the public imagination, see Rebecca Lemon, *Treason by Words: Literature, Law, and Rebellion in Shakespeare's England* (Ithaca: Cornell University Press, 2008); Karen Cunningham, *Imaginary Betrayals: Subjectivity and the Discourses of Treason in Early Modern England* (Philadelphia: University of Pennsylvania Press, 2002).

57 For a helpful summary of the two-witness rule in the Bible, see Peter R. Moore, "*Hamlet* and the Two Witness Rule," *Notes and Queries* 44, no. 4 (1997): 498–505.

58 *A Manuell, or A Justice of Peace His Vade-Mecum. : A Table Containing the Substance of All Statutes Whereby One or More Justices Are Inabled and Authorized to Order Matters out of the Sessions of the Peace* (Cambridge: Printed by Roger Daniel, Printer to the Universitie of Cambridge, 1641), sig. C2r, original emphasis. Citations are to Thomas Birch's personal annotated copy (Folger MS V.a.395).

59 R.H. Helmholz, *The Oxford History of the Laws of England Volume 1: The Canon Law and Ecclesiastical Jurisdiction from 597 to the 1640s*, ed. J.H. Baker, vol. 1 (Oxford: Oxford University Press, 2004), 609.

60 Helmholz, 1:609–10. "*Ribaldus*" refers to a "person of low social status, esp. regarded as worthless or good-for-nothing; a rascal, vagabond," and "a wicked, dissolute, or licentious person; a villain." See "ribald, n. and adj., 1.a. and 4," *OED*.

61 R.C. van Caenegem, "Public Prosecution of Crime in Twelfth-Century England," in *Legal History: A European Perspective* (London: Hambledon, 1991), 8. For a longer discussion of the concept of *tihtbysig* ("charge-laden") in Anglo-Saxon England, see Tom Lambert, *Law and Order in Anglo-Saxon England* (Oxford: Oxford University Press, 2017), 257.

62 One might ask the same question of Othello, who also refuses to let in the wider community and whom Iago keeps forcing to witness spectacles of his betrayal (or what he takes to be proof). I am grateful to Rebecca Lemon for this point.

63 William Shakespeare, *Much Ado about Nothing*, in *The Riverside Shakespeare*, ed. G. Blakemore Evans et al. (Boston: Houghton, 1974), 3.2.128–9.

64 William Shakespeare, *The Tragedy of Othello, the Moor of Venice*, in *The Riverside Shakespeare*, ed. G. Blakemore Evans et al. (Boston: Houghton, 1974), 3.3.360.

65 Suzanne Keen, *Empathy and the Novel* (Oxford: Oxford University Press, 2007), xx–xxi, original emphasis.

66 For example, the line is glossed by Weis as "Gloucester compares himself to a baited bear who will have to endure the onslaught (*course*) of dogs" (208n.51).

67 William Shakespeare, *Macbeth: Texts and Contexts*, ed. William C. Carroll (New York: Bedford, 1999), 5.7.1–2.

68 For a description of the "spectacle" of bear and bull baiting, see Horace Walpole, trans., *Paul Hentzner's Travels in England, During the Reign of Queen Elizabeth* (Strawberry Hill, 1797), 29–30.

69 Anderson, "The Tragedy of Good Friday," 268. The image of Regan plucking Gloucester's "white beard" could have reminded audiences of a famous scene in *Acts of Monuments* when Bishop Edmund Bonner plucks the beard of Thomas Tomkins, the first lay Protestant martyr. A flowing beard was "an evangelical trademark." Eamon Duffy, *Fires of Faith: Catholic England under Mary Tudor* (New Haven: Yale University Press, 2009), 100.

70 Dennis Kennedy, ed., *The Oxford Companion to Theatre and Performance* (Oxford: Oxford University Press, 2010), 154.

71 The phrase "ingrateful fox" potentially evokes the memory of Guy Fawkes, who, along with other conspirators of the Gunpowder Plot, was captured, examined, tortured, and executed between late 1605 and early 1606. (I am grateful to Sam Greenstein for this point.) Cornwall and the sisters' verbal tactic is consistent with the playbook of torturers who use dehumanizing language (for example, calling a person a beast or an insect) to take away their victims' humanity. Cornwall, Regan, and Goneril's rough diction is tonally at odds with Gloucester's ornate verse. The verbal contrast between the "traitor's" high verse and the authorities' degrading prose is one of the play's many dramatic uses of language to underscore the illegitimacy of the latter's action.

72 The Geneva Bible, sig. Zzz2v. In his study of John Rogers's performance of martyrdom, John Knott observes that "the linkage between prophet and martyr was an old one, going back to apocryphal accounts of the martyrdom of Old Testament prophets and the New Testament association of martyrdom with vision and inspiration by the Holy Spirit." Knott, *Discourses of Martyrdom*, 21.

73 Coke defines petty treason as "when a servant slayeth his Master, or a wife her husband, or when a man secular or religious slayeth his Prelate to whom he oweth faith and obedience." Edward Coke, *The Third Part of the Institutes of the Laws of England Concerning High Treason, and Other Pleas of the Crown, and Criminall Causes* (London: Printed by M. Flesher, for W. Lee, and D. Pakeman, 1644), sig. D4r–v. Male traitors were hanged and then hung in chains while female ones (whether petty or grand) were burned. See Frances E. Dolan, *Dangerous Familiars: Representations of Domestic Crime in England 1550–1700* (Ithaca: Cornell University Press, 1994).

74 For a striking interpretation of this scene, see Strier, "Faithful Servants: Shakespeare's Praise of Disobedience."

75 According to one such household remedy for "Hurt in the eye," a "Pultess" of "Yolks and Whites of three Eggs well beaten" and "well mixed" should be "applied warm every seventh hour" to the wound. John Hall, *Select Observations on English Bodies of Eminent Persons in Desperate Diseases* (London: Printed by J[ohn]. D[arby]. for Benjamin Shirley, under the Dial of St. Dunstan's Church in Fleet-street, 1679), sig. P2r.

76 The characters of the Second Servant and Third Servant, who only appear in the quarto *King Lear*, are replaced by the character of the Old Man in the folio. The image of the aged tenant leading his master into the countryside anticipates the meeting of Gloucester and Lear at Dover.

77 Albany is a divisive character. Jeffrey Kahan calls Albany a "hen-pecked cuckold." Jeffrey Kahan, ed., *King Lear: New Critical Essays* (New York: Routledge, 2008), 61. Others, however, have observed how the character changes from a passive witness to an active participant in the action. See, for example, Leo Kirshbaum, "Albany," *Shakespeare Studies* 13 (1960): 20–9; Peter Mortenson, "The Role of Albany," *Shakespeare Quarterly* 16, no. 2 (1965): 217–25.

78 Mortenson observes that "Albany is the only major figure in *King Lear* who loses neither moral rectitude nor high temporal position." Mortenson, "The Role of Albany," 224.

79 "Albany" denotes both a person, a hereditary title, and, geographically, Scotland. Mary, Queen of Scots revived the title and bestowed it on her second husband, Lord Darnley; King James gave the title to his son, Prince Charles. "To speak of Albany was to speak of Scotland (James himself had previously been Duke of Albany, as had his father)." James Shapiro, *The Year of Lear: Shakespeare in 1606* (New York: Simon & Schuster, 2015), 40. As Victor Kiernan explains, at the time of the 1606 performance at Whitehall palace, "[James's] elder son Henry was now, as heir apparent, duke of Cornwall; the younger, Charles, still a boy, had until that year borne the Scottish royal title of duke of Albany – once a region of Scotland, whose name now vaguely covered all Scotland. Thus the two magnates of Shakespeare's play represent (very indistinct though its geography is) the two extremities of Lear's kingdom of Britain, whose two realms were now governed by James." Victor Kiernan, *Eight Tragedies of Shakespeare: A Marxist Study* (London: Verso, 1996), 104–5.

80 Weis notes in his introduction that "F's Albany is a greatly impoverished character" on account of the multiple cuts to his speeches and the assignment of the final lines of the play to Edgar. Shakespeare, *King Lear*, 11.

81 Nina Taunton and Valerie Hart, "'King Lear,' King James and the Gunpowder Treason of 1605," *Renaissance Studies* 17, no. 4 (2003): 714.

82 Attributed to Francis Bacon, *The Elements of the Common Lawes of England* (London, 1630), sig. B4r.

83 Doug Eskew, "'Soldiers, Prisoners, Patrimony': *King Lear* and the Place of the Sovereign," *Cahiers Élisabéthains* 78 (2010): 31.

84 Shannon McSheffrey, *Seeking Sanctuary: Crime, Mercy, and Politics in English Courts, 1400–1550* (Oxford: Oxford University Press, 2017), 7.

85 Christy Desmet, *Reading Shakespeare's Characters: Rhetoric, Ethics, and Identity* (Amherst: University of Massachusetts Press, 1992), 130, 131.

86 Simon Palfrey, *Poor Tom: Living* King Lear (Chicago: University of Chicago Press, 2014), 172.

87 Johnson qtd. in Bert O. States, "Standing on the Extreme Verge in 'King Lear' and Other High Places," *Georgia Review* 36, no. 2 (1982): 418.

88 States, 423.

89 I am grateful to Michael Prior for this insight.

90 "Samphire, n., 1.a." refers to "the plant *Crithmum maritimum* (growing on rocks by the sea), the aromatic saline fleshy leaves of which are used in pickles. Also called *rock samphire*." *OED*.

91 John Gerard, *The Herball or Generall Historie of Plantes* (London: by [Edm. Bollifant] for [Bonham Norton and] John Norton, 1597), sig. Dd6v.

92 Sharon Marcus, Heather Love, and Stephen Best, "Building a Better Description," *Representations* 135, no. 1 (2016): 14, original emphasis.

93 Mark Doty, *The Art of Description: World into Word* (Minneapolis: Graywolf, 2010), 65, original emphasis.

94 Doty, 106, original emphasis.

95 James I, *The Workes of the Most High and Mighty Prince, James … King of Great Britaine, France and Ireland* (London, 1616), sig. R6r.

96 "To exercise sovereignty is to exercise control over mortality and to define life as the deployment and manifestation of power." Achille Mbembe, "Necropolitics," trans. Libby Meintjes, *Public Culture* 15, no. 1 (2003): 11. For a discussion of how this concept of sovereignty figures in Roman jurisprudence, see Giorgio Agamben, *Homo Sacer: Sovereign Power and Bare Life*, trans. Daniel Heller-Roazen (Stanford: Stanford University Press, 1998).

97 Jan Kott decries redemptive readings of *King Lear*: "all that remains at the end of this gigantic pantomime is the earth, empty and bleeding." Jan Kott, *Shakespeare Our Contemporary* (New York: Norton, 1964), 147.

98 David Loewenstein, "Agnostic Shakespeare? The Godless World of *King Lear*," in *Shakespeare and Early Modern Religion*, ed. David Loewenstein and Michael Witmore (Cambridge: Cambridge University Press, 2015), 155. To be clear, Loewenstein does not argue that Shakespeare was an agnostic playwright, but that the world of *King Lear* promotes an agnostic reading of life devoid of providentialism.

99 I am grateful to Frances E. Dolan for this insight. On the erasure of female presence, see Ann Thompson, "Are There Any Women in *King Lear*?," in *The Matter of Difference: Materialist Feminist Criticism of Shakespeare*, ed. Valerie Wayne (Ithaca: Cornell, 1991), 117–28; Coppélia Kahn, "The Absent Mother in *King Lear*," in *Rewriting the Renaissance: The Discourses of Sexual Difference*

in Early Modern Europe, ed. Margaret W. Ferguson, Maureen Quilligan, and Nancy Vickers (Chicago: University of Chicago Press, 1986), 33–49; Kathleen McLuskie, "The Patriarchal Bard: Feminist Criticism and Shakespeare: *King Lear* and *Measure for Measure*," in *Political Shakespeare: New Essays in Cultural Materialism*, ed. Jonathan Dollimore and Alan Sinfield, 2nd ed. (Manchester: Manchester University Press, 1994), 88–108.

5 Communal Shaming and the Limitations of Legal Forms

1 Charles Baxter, "Rhyming Action," *Michigan Quarterly Review* 35, no. 4 (1996): 620–1.

2 See chapter 1 for an explanation of the early modern assize.

3 See "Sheriff's Duties and Ceremonial at Carlisle Assizes, 1661–2," in J.S. Cockburn, *A History of English Assizes, 1558–1714* (Cambridge: Cambridge University Press, 1972), 298.

4 Literary scholars have long recognized the laconic nature of legal reports, trial transcripts, and other legal documents. Subha Mukherji emphasizes that "where legal documentation is insufficient or non-existent, there is a case to be made for using literary material to reconstruct certain aspects of the experience of law." Subha Mukherji, *Law and Representation in Early Modern Drama* (Cambridge: Cambridge University Press, 2006), 16.

5 "An Exhortacion" appears in Nathaniel Rogers, "A book of presidents for a Justice of Peace his Clarke," 1606?, BL Harleian MS 1603, fol. 30v–31r. Note that the item is also available as BL Harleian MS 1829. Little is known of Nathaniel Rogers and his formulary, a portion of which I have transcribed and excerpted. Christopher W. Brooks identifies Rogers as an attorney who was professionally active during the early seventeenth century. Christopher W. Brooks, *Law, Politics, and Society in Early Modern England* (Cambridge: Cambridge University Press, 2008), 161. It is unlikely this was the same Nathaniel Rogers, a Puritan preacher, who emigrated to New England in 1636. John L. Blake, *A Biographical Dictionary ... Lives of the Most Distinguished Persons ... American Biography* (Philadelphia: Cowperthwait, 1859), 1075.

6 John Bulwer, *Chirologia: Or the Naturall Language of the Hand. Composed of the Speaking Motions, and Discoursing Gestures Thereof. Whereunto Is Added Chironomia; Or, the Art of Manuall Rhetoricke* (London: Printed by Tho. Harper, and are to be sold by R. Whitaker, at his shop in Pauls Church-yard, 1644), sig. B4v, sig. B7v.

7 Cockburn, *A History of English Assizes*, 109.

8 Martin Ingram, *Carnal Knowledge: Regulating Sex in England, 1470–1600* (Cambridge: Cambridge University Press, 2017), 12.

9 "When offences became a matter of scandal and an affront to the Christian community, they were punishable in the 'external forum' of the spiritual courts.

They were supposed to operate both *pro salutate animæ* and *procorrectione* (or *reformatione*) *morum* – for the health of the soul and for the reformation of manners." Ingram, 13.

10 Martin Ingram, "Shame and Pain: Themes and Variations in Tudor Punishments," in *Penal Practice and Culture, 1500–1900: Punishing the English*, ed. Simon Devereaux and Paul Griffiths (New York: Palgrave, 2004), 37. For examples of public penances (as recorded in act books), see Paul Edward Hedley Hair, ed., *Before the Bawdy Courts: Selections from Church Court and Other Records Relating to the Correction of Moral Offences in England, Scotland and New England, 1300–1800* (London: Elek, 1972).

11 R.H. Helmholz, *The Oxford History of the Laws of England Volume 1: The Canon Law and Ecclesiastical Jurisdiction from 597 to the 1640s*, ed. J.H. Baker, vol. 1 (Oxford: Oxford University Press, 2004), 622.

12 On the "creativity" of early and mid-Tudor courts, see Ingram, "Shame and Pain," 37.

13 Ingram, "Shame and Pain," 39.

14 Ingram, 39–40.

15 Mary C. Mansfield, *The Humiliation of Sinners: Public Penance in Thirteenth-Century France* (Ithaca: Cornell University Press, 1995), viii.

16 Ingram, *Carnal Knowledge*, 13.

17 *Sir Gawain and the Green Knight*, trans. Simon Armitage (New York: Norton, 2007), Fitt 3, 1880–4. But as readers know, Gawain is not rendered "pure" by his confession to the priest. At the Green Chapel, the Green Knight (Lord Bertilak) forces Gawain to confess again and the shamefaced Gawain confesses his sin of "cowardice and covetousness" (Fitt 3, 2374, 2393). The doubling of confession and absolution prompts the reader to contrast the spiritual authority of the Green Knight to that of the priestly confessor.

18 Heather Hirschfeld, *The End of Satisfaction: Drama and Repentance in the Age of Shakespeare* (Ithaca: Cornell University Press, 2014), 30–1.

19 Hirschfeld, 2.

20 See Dave Postles, "Penance and the Market Place: A Reformation Dialogue with the Medieval Church (c. 1250–c. 1600)," *Journal of Ecclesiastical History* 54, no. 3 (2003): 441–68.

21 By the "early eighteenth century the public dimension of this punishment [penance] had thus been almost entirely removed." Robert Shoemaker, "Streets of Shame? The Crowd and Public Punishments in London, 1700–1820," in *Penal Practice and Culture, 1500–1900: Punishing the English*, ed. Simon Devereaux and Paul Griffiths (New York: Palgrave, 2004), 237.

22 W.J.B. Owen and Jane Worthington Smyser, eds., *The Prose Works of William Wordsworth*, vol. 3 (Oxford: Clarendon, 1974), 371. Wordsworth tells this story to his nephew as part of his "Autobiographical Memoranda" dictated in 1847.

23 Shoemaker, "Streets of Shame?," 236.

24 Craig Muldrew, *The Economy of Obligation: The Culture of Credit and Social Relations in Early Modern England* (Houndmills: Palgrave, 1998), 126.

25 The early modern market depended on "a sort of competitive piety in which householders sought to construct and preserve their reputation for religious virtue, belief and honesty in order to bolster the credit of their households so that they could be trusted." Muldrew, 148–9.

26 "London's households were full of young women in the less protected conditions of domestic service … They were probably both freer than their rural counterparts, and more vulnerable." Laura Gowing, *Domestic Dangers: Women, Words, and Sex in Early Modern London* (Oxford: Oxford University Press, 1996), 15.

27 William Shakespeare, *The Tragedy of Othello, the Moor of Venice*, in *The Riverside Shakespeare*, ed. G. Blakemore Evans et al. (Boston: Houghton, 1974), 2.3.252.

28 Regarding the composition and performance history of *Edward IV* – and issues of authorship – Richard Rowland in his introduction suggests the two parts of *Edward IV* were "planned and composed together, in the course of 1599." Thomas Heywood, *The First and Second Parts of King Edward IV*, ed. Richard Rowland (Manchester: Manchester University Press, 2005), 56. Subsequent quotations will be cited parenthetically in the chapter.

29 Samuel Daniel, *The First Fowre Bookes of the Civil Wars between the Two Houses of Lancaster and Yorke* (London: Printed by P. Short for Simon Waterson, 1595), sig. B1r.

30 Daniel, sig. B1v.

31 On the reduction of orders for public penance in the late sixteenth century, see Postles, "Penance and the Market Place."

32 Throughout this chapter, I use "Eleanor" and "Jane" to signify Shakespeare's and Heywood's characters. When I talk about the historical persons, I employ their full names, "Eleanor Cobham" and "Jane Shore." For a discussion of the influence of Boccaccio on fifteenth- and sixteenth-century literary representations of York and Lancaster queens, peeresses, and mistresses, see Kavita Mudan Finn, *The Last Plantagenet Consorts: Gender, Genre, and Historiography, 1440–1627* (New York: Palgrave, 2012), 2–5.

33 Lily B. Campbell, ed., *The Mirror for Magistrates: Edited from Original Texts in the Huntington Library* (Cambridge: Cambridge University Press, 1938), 373–86 ("Shores Wife"), 432–41 ("Elianor Cobham"). On the influence of Thomas Churchyard's *Shore's Wife* and Michael Drayton's *Englands Heroicall Epistles,* see Richard Rowland, ed., "Introduction," in *The First and Second Parts of King Edward IV* (Manchester: Manchester University Press, 2005), 43–7. On Churchyard's life and career, see Matthew Woodcock, *Thomas Churchyard: Pen, Sword, and Ego* (Oxford: Oxford University Press, 2016). On Ferrer's tragedy of "Elianor," see Cathy Shrank, "'Hoysted High upon the Rolling Wheele': Elianor

Cobham's *Lament*," in *A Mirror for Magistrates in Context: Literature, History, and Politics in Early Modern England*, ed. Harriet Archer and Andrew Hadfield (Cambridge: Cambridge University Press, 2016), 109–25.

34 Rossell Hope Robbins, ed., *Historical Poems of the XIVth and XVth Centuries* (New York: Columbia University Press, 1959), 176–80.

35 Richard Helgerson, "Weeping for Jane Shore," *South Atlantic Quarterly* 98, no. 3 (1999): 456. Helgerson argues that Thomas More's *History of King Richard III* was influential in introducing a sympathetic portrait of Jane Shore. In the eighteenth century, Sarah Siddons's portrayal of Jane in a revival of Nicholas Rowe's *The Tragedy of Jane Shore* (1714) drew hysterical tears from playgoers.

36 For an introduction and overview of the history of the female complaint genre, see Susan Wiseman and Alison Thorne, eds., *The Rhetoric of Complaint: Ovid's Heroides in the Renaissance and Restoration* (Oxford: Blackwell, 2008); Shirley Sharon-Zisser, ed., *Critical Essays on Shakespeare's* A Lover's Complaint: *Suffering Ecstasy* (Aldershot: Ashgate, 2006); John Kerrigan, *Motives of Woe: Shakespeare and "Female Complaint": A Critical Anthology* (Oxford: Clarendon, 1991).

37 This scene echoes those of empathetic witnessing discussed in chapter 4.

38 Lauren Berlant, *The Female Complaint: The Unfinished Business of Sentimentality in American Culture* (Durham, NC: Duke University Press, 2008), 11.

39 G.L. Harriss, "Eleanor [Née Eleanor Cobham], Duchess of Gloucester (c. 1400–1452), Alleged Sorcerer," *ODNB*. On representations of Eleanor in late medieval and Tudor literature, see also Sally Fisher, "Eleanor, Duchess of Gloucester: Chronicles and Ideas of Exile and Imprisonment in Fifteenth-Century England," *Parergon* 34, no. 2 (2017): 73–97.

40 Eleanor Cobham was examined on 24 and 25 July 1441. G.L. Harriss counts eighteen charges against her but Ralph A. Griffiths counts twenty-eight. The uncertainty may be a reflection of biases in the historical sources. See Harriss, "Eleanor." See also Ralph A. Griffiths, "The Trial of Eleanor Cobham: An Episode in the Fall of Duke Humphrey of Gloucester," *Bulletin of the John Rylands Library* 51, no. 2 (1969): 389.

41 The Duchess's case was the impetus for a statutory change in the prosecution of high treason: "the Commons petitioned that all doubt and ambiguity about the trial and judgement of peeresses for treason and felony be removed. It was accordingly resolved and made statutory that peeresses should be so judged by the judges and peers of the realm, just like English peers." Griffiths, "The Trial of Eleanor Cobham," 398.

42 Griffiths, 394.

43 On the various documentary evidence, see Fisher, "Eleanor."

44 Charles Lethbridge Kingsford, ed., *The Chronicles of London* (Oxford: Clarendon, 1905), 149.

45 John Page, John Lydgate, and William Gregory, *The Historical Collections of a Citizen of London in the Fifteenth Century. Containing: I. John Page's Poem on the*

Siege of Rouen. II. Lydgate's Verses on the Kings of England. III. William Gregory's Chronicle of London, ed. James Gairdner (London: Camden Society, 1876), 184.

46 Foxe [1570] 851.

47 William Shakespeare, *Henry VI, Part 2*, ed. Roger Warren (Oxford: Oxford University Press, 2003). Subsequent quotations will be cited parenthetically in the chapter. The play exists in two different forms: the quarto edition printed in 1594 (Q) and the folio edition printed in 1623 (F). Q is "roughly a third shorter than F, and differs from it in most of its readings." Warren, 75. The scene that I am most concerned with – Eleanor's penitential walk – is nearly the same in both Q and F, barring slight differences in stage directions. The stage direction in Warren's edition combines lines from Q and F. The stage direction in Q reads: "*Enter Dame El[ea]nor Cobham bare-foote, and a white sheete about her, with a waxe Candle in her hand, and verses written on her backe and pind on, and accompanied with the Sheriffes of London, and Sir John Standly, and Officers, with billes and holbards.*" William Shakespeare, *The First Part of the Contention Betwixt the Two Famous Houses of York and Lancaster, with the Death of the Good Duke Humphrey: And the Banishment and Death of the Duke of Suffolke, and the Tragicall End of the Proud Cardinall of Winchester, with the Notable Rebellion of Jacke Cade: And the Duke of Yorkes First Claime unto the Crowne* (London: Printed by Thomas Creed, for Thomas Millington, and are to be sold at his shop under Saint Peters Church in Cornwall, 1594), sig. D2r. In F, the stage direction is: "*Enter the Duchesse in a white Sheet, and a Taper burning in her hand, with the Sherife and Officers.*" *The Workes of William Shakespeare* (London, 1623), sig. n1r.

48 Lawrence Manley points out that although "in neither version [Q or F] is Eleanor particularly innocent … Q … accepts the argument that Eleanor's prophecy by witchcraft was a state crime, whereas F questions whether a capital state sentence was being improperly imposed for a spiritual offense, an offense that may in any case have been committed through entrapment." Lawrence Manley, "From Strange's Men to Pembroke's Men: *2 Henry VI* and *The First Part of the Contention*," *Shakespeare Quarterly* 54, no. 3 (2003): 265–6; Manley goes on to argue that these changes mark Q as a "distinct *version* of a play whose meaning changed as it passed from one company to another." Manley, 259, original emphasis.

49 On More's sympathetic portrayal of Jane, see Helgerson, "Weeping for Jane Shore," 453.

50 The play's authorship is uncertain but most scholars believe Heywood to have been the principal author. Rowland, "Introduction," 11.

51 Rebecca Tomlin, "'I Trac'd Him Too and Fro': Walking the Neighbourhood on the Early Modern Stage," *Early Theatre* 19, no. 2 (2016): 200.

52 Mansfield, *The Humiliation of Sinners*, 5.

53 On the concept of the knowing audience, which I borrow from Linda Hutcheon's theory of adaptation, see chapter 3.

54 Melissa Gregg and Gregory J. Seigworth, eds., *The Affect Theory Reader* (Durham, NC: Duke University Press, 2010), 8.

55 Eve Kosofsky Sedgwick, *Touching Feeling: Affect, Pedagogy, Performativity* (Durham, NC: Duke University Press, 2003), 64.

56 Sara Ahmed, *The Promise of Happiness* (Durham, NC: Duke University Press, 2010), 39.

57 Ahmed, 39.

58 As Wilco W. van Dijk and Jaap W. Ouwerkerk explain, the German compound loanword *Schadenfreude* (from the "German words *Schaden*, meaning harm, and *Freude*, meaning joy") is a moral emotion – and one that carries the weight of centuries (if not millennia) of controversy. The word "schadenfreude" entered the English lexicon in 1852, relatively late in the long history of the English language. Wilco W. van Dijk and Jaap W. Ouwerkerk, eds., *Schadenfreude: Understanding Pleasure at the Misfortune of Others* (Cambridge: Cambridge University Press, 2014), 1.

59 Tiffany Watt Smith, *Schadenfreude: The Joy of Another's Misfortune* (New York: Little, Brown, 2018), 17.

60 Aaron Ben-Ze'ev, "The Personal Comparative Concern in Schadenfreude," in *Schadenfreude: Understanding Pleasure at the Misfortune of Others*, ed. Wilco W. van Dijk and Jaap W. Ouwerkerk (Cambridge: Cambridge University Press, 2014), 81.

61 Jean E. Howard, "Crossdressing, the Theatre, and Gender Struggle in Early Modern England," *Shakespeare Quarterly* 39, no. 4 (1988): 423.

62 Timothy Bright, *A Treatise of Melancholie. Containing the Causes Thereof, & Reasons of the Strange Effects It Worketh in Our Minds and Bodies: With the Phisicke Cure, and Spirituall Consolation for Such as Have Thereto Adjoyned an Afflicted Conscience* (London: By Thomas Vautrollier, dwelling in the Black-Friers, 1586), sig. N4r. Similarly, William Perkins writes, "[a]ll men are wholly corrupted with sinne through Adams fall, and so are become slaves of Sathan, and guiltie of eternall damnation." William Perkins, *The foundation of Christian religion: gathered into sixe principles* (London: Printed [by John Orwin] for John Porter and J[ohn]. L[egat], 1595), sig. A3v.

63 A Globe production of *Macbeth* (2013) uses doubling to heighten a sense of poetic justice: the same actors who had earlier portrayed Duncan and Lady Macduff (Gawn Granger and Finty Williams, respectively) assume the roles of the Doctor and the Gentlewoman. The murder victims become, through doubling, Lady Macbeth's witnesses.

64 William Shakespeare, *Macbeth: Texts and Contexts*, ed. William C. Carroll (New York: Bedford, 1999). Subsequent quotations will be cited parenthetically in the chapter.

65 "Dignity, n.," *OED*.

66 Robert Bolton, *Instructions for a Right Comforting Afflicted Conciences: With Speciall Antidotes against Some Grievous Temptations. Delivered for the Most Part*

in the Lecture at Kettering in Northamptonshire (London: Imprinted by Felix Kyngston for Thomas Weaver, and are to be sold at his shop at the great north-dore of Saint Pauls Church, 1631), sig. C3r.

67 Laura Mulvey, "Visual Pleasure and Narrative Cinema," *Screen* 16, no. 3 (1975): 8.

68 Philip Brophy, "Horrality – The Textuality of Contemporary Horror Films," *Screen* 27, no. 1 (1986): 5.

69 Rebecca Lemon, *Treason by Words: Literature, Law, and Rebellion in Shakespeare's England* (Ithaca: Cornell University Press, 2008), 1.

70 For a riveting account of the Gunpowder plot, see James Shapiro, *The Year of Lear: Shakespeare in 1606* (New York: Simon & Schuster, 2015), 155–99.

71 Shapiro, 99.

72 Anne James, *Poets, Players, and Preachers: Remembering the Gunpowder Plot in Seventeenth-Century England* (Toronto: University of Toronto Press, 2016).

73 *A True and Perfect Relation of the Whole Proceedings against the Late Most Barbarous Traitors, Garnet a Jesuite, and His Confederats: Contayning Sundry Speeches Delivered by the Lords Commissioners at Their Arraignments, for the Better Satisfaction of Those That Were Hearers, as Occasion Was Offered; the Earle of Northamptons Speech Having Bene Enlarged upon Those Grounds Which Are Set Downe. And Lastly All That Passed at Garnets Execution* (London: by Robert Barker, printer to the Kings most Excellent Majestie, 1606), sig. D3r–v.

74 Allison P. Hobgood, *Passionate Playgoing in Early Modern England* (Cambridge: Cambridge University Press, 2014), 44.

75 Garnet "wrote but apparently never published 'A Treatise of Equivocation' to support his friend and colleague Robert Southwell's defense of equivocation at his trial in 1595." Henry Garnet, "A Treatise of Equivocation," in *Recusancy and Conformity in Early Modern England: Manuscript and Printed Sources in Translation*, ed. Ginevra Crosignani, Thomas M. McCoog, and Michael C. Questier (Toronto: Pontifical Institute of Mediaeval Studies, 2010), 298–9.

76 Pierre Janelle, *Robert Southwell the Writer: A Study in Religious Inspiration* (London: Sheed & Ward, 1935), 82, original emphasis.

77 *A True and Perfect Relation*, sig. H4v–I1r.

78 *A True and Perfect Relation*, sig. I2v.

79 *A True and Perfect Relation*, sig. T2v–3r.

80 *A True and Perfect Relation*, sig. Bb4v. Note that throughout this section, Garnet's replies and reactions are typographically set off in italics.

81 *A True and Perfect Relation*, sig. K2v.

82 Michael Proeve and Steven Tudor, *Remorse: Psychological and Jurisprudential Perspectives* (Farnham: Ashgate, 2010), 3.

83 Proeve and Tudor, 31. Not all of Lady Macbeth's lines point to the "retractive" nature of remorse. For example, when she says, "here's the smell of the blood still. All the perfumes of Arabia will not sweeten this little hand. O, o, o" (5.1.40–1),

her characterization of her hand as "little" brings to mind a childlike horror, one that directs pity inwardly to the self.

84 Abraham Stoll, "Macbeth's Equivocal Conscience," in *Macbeth: New Critical Essays*, ed. Nick Moschovakis (London: Routledge, 2008), 148.

85 The taper could also serve as a visual reminder of Lady Macbeth's imminent death. Candles, in early modern stage imagery, were a "traditional symbol of the shortness of human life." R. Chris Hassel Jr., *Shakespeare's Religious Language: A Dictionary* (New York: Continuum, 2005), 48. The metaphor of life as a candle or taper appears elsewhere in Shakespeare. In *Henry IV, Part 2*, the Lord Chief Justice mockingly compares Falstaff to a "candle, the better part burnt out." William Shakespeare, *Henry IV, Part 2*, ed. René Weis (Oxford: Clarendon, 1998), 1.2.156.

86 Eleri Lynn, *Tudor Fashion* (New Haven: Yale University Press, 2017), 48.

87 Sarah Beckwith, *Shakespeare and the Grammar of Forgiveness* (Ithaca: Cornell University Press, 2011), 20. To be clear, my comment about Catholic sacraments' "theatricality" does not reflect my own views but paraphrases the polemics of the Protestant reformers such as Tyndale and Foxe. For a summary of the Protestant attacks on Catholic ritual, see Beckwith, 20–1.

88 Martha Grace Duncan, "'So Young and so Untender': Remorseless Children and the Expectations of the Law," *Columbia Law Review* 102, no. 6 (2002): 1469–526.

89 Susan A. Bandes, "Remorse and Criminal Justice," *Emotion Review* 8, no. 1 (2015): 1–2, my emphasis. Bandes points out that "remorse is likely even harder to recognize from outward manifestations, as it describes an unfolding internal process of soul-searching and reevaluation" (4). For a fuller analysis of remorse, including how courts within major common law jurisdictions (Canada, England and Wales, the United States, etc.) have acknowledged remorse as a mitigating factor, see Proeve and Tudor, *Remorse: Psychological and Jurisprudential Perspectives*, 136–8. For another perspective, see Rocksheng Zhong et al., "So You're Sorry? The Role of Remorse in Criminal Law," *Journal of the American Academy of Psychiatry and the Law* 42, no. 1 (2014): 39–48.

90 Austin Sarat, "Remorse, Responsibility, and Criminal Punishment: An Analysis of Popular Culture," in *The Passions of Law*, ed. Susan A. Bandes (New York: New York University Press, 1999), 170.

91 Peter Brooks, *Troubling Confessions: Speaking Guilt in Law and Literature* (Chicago: University of Chicago Press, 2000), 3.

Postscript

1 For an account of Athenian representation of bystander responsibility, see Rachel Hall Sternberg, *Tragedy Offstage: Suffering and Sympathy in Ancient Athens* (Austin: University of Texas Press, 2006), chapter 3.

2 *Every Mans Right: Or, Englands Perspective-Glasse*, 1646, sig. A4v.

3   Donald Veall, *The Popular Movement for Law Reform, 1640–1660* (Oxford: Oxford University Press, 1970), 99. See also Thomas A. Green, *Verdict According to Conscience: Perspectives on the English Criminal Trial Jury, 1200–1800* (Chicago: University of Chicago Press, 1985), chapter 5. For literary scholars' perspective on the late-sixteenth and seventeenth-century law reform movement, see Virginia Lee Strain, *Legal Reform in English Renaissance Literature* (Edinburgh: Edinburgh University Press, 2018).

4   Benjamin Nicholson, *The Lawyers Bane. Or, the Lawes Reformation, and New Modell: Wherein the Errours and Corruptions Both of the Lawyers and of the Law It Selfe Are Manifested and Declared. And Also, Some Short and Profitable Considerations Laid down for the Redresse of Them* (London: printed for George Whittington, at the blew Anchor in Cornehill, neer the Royall Exchange, 1647), sig. A2v. Parliament did indeed abolish the use of Law French. "November [22] 1650: An Act for turning the Books of the Law, and all Proces and Proceedings in Courts of Justice, into English," in *Acts and Ordinances of the Interregnum, 1642–1660* (London, 1911), 455–6, http://www.british-history.ac.uk/report .aspx?compid=56426), but it would not be until 1731 that English became the language of law by an act of parliament (4 Geo. 2., c. 26). See John H. Langbein, Renée Lettow Lerner, and Bruce P. Smith, eds., *History of the Common Law: The Development of Anglo-American Legal Institutions* (New York: Aspen, 2009), 153.

5   William Walwyn, *Juries Justified: Or, A Word of Correction to Mr. Henry Robinson; for His Seven Objections Against the Trial of Causes, by Juries of Twelve Men. By William Walwin. Published by Authority* (London: Printed by Robert Wood, 1651), sig. A4v.

6   Matthew Hale, *The History of the Common Law of England*, ed. Charles M. Gray (Chicago: University of Chicago Press, 1971), 39.

7   Hale, 164.

8   Hale, 164–5.

9   Ibid.

10 William Dugdale, *Origines Juridiciales, or, Historical Memorials of the English Laws, Courts of Justice, Forms of Tryal, Punishment in Cases Criminal, Law-Writers, Law-Books, Grants and Settlements of Estates, Degree of Serjeant, Innes of Court and Chancery* (London: Printed by Tho. Newcomb, for Abel Roper, John Martin, and Henry Herringman, 1671), sig. D3v, original emphasis.

11 Sara Ahmed, *Living a Feminist Life* (Durham, NC: Duke University Press, 2017), 240.

Bibliography

Manuscript

Birch, Thomas. Marginalia in *A Manuell, or A Justice of Peace His Vade-Mecum*. Cambridge: Printed by Roger Daniel, Printer to the Universitie of Cambridge, 1641. Folger MS V.a.395.

Closse, George. *A looking Glasse for lawers, & lawiers. A sermon preached before the Judges of Assize for the countie of Devon, in the Cathedrall church of St Peter in Exon on the 8th day of August:1603: by George Closse maister of Artes, a preacher of the worde of God at Blacktorrington*. 1603. Lambeth MS 113. Fol. 53r–60v.

Cocke, Henry. "Sir Henry Cocke, to Lord Burghley; on Sinking the Excessive Price of Grain, and Forbidding to Make Strong Ale and Beer, July 25, 1594." 1594. BL Lansdowne MS 76. Fol. 85r.

– "Sir H[enry] Cocke, to Lord Burghley; to Regulate the Price of Grain; and That Justices of Peace Produce Their Armour on Demand, Sept. 13, 1594." 1594. BL Lansdowne MS 76. Fol. 133r.

Dodderidge, John. "Charge, 1620." In *Collection of Justices' Charges*. 1610–42. BL Harleian MS 583. Fol. 9v.

Dove, William. "Gravesend Inquests: Casebook." 1673–6. BL Harley MS 6749.

"Instructions to the Judges of Assize upon going their Circuits, to be delivered to all Justices of the Peace temp. Eliz. concerning the hoarding of Corn, & the suppressing Vagabonds & Thieves." N.d. BL Harleian MS 6846. Fol. 19r–20v.

Lightfoot, John. "Sermon. The Text Psalm I. 5, 'Therefore Shall Not the Wicked Rise up in Judgement.'" N.d. BL Sloane MS 1926. Fol. 47–66.

Rogers, Nathaniel. "A book of presidents for a Justice of Peace his Clarke." 1606?. BL Harleian MS 1603 (alternatively catalogued as BL Harleian MS 1829). Fol. 30v–31r.

Slany, Stephen. "The Lord Mayor of London, to Lord Burghley; Concerning Thomas Delonie, Who Composed a Seditious Ballad, on the Scarcity of Corn, July 26, 1596." 1596. BL Lansdowne MS 81. Fol. 76r.

Yelverton, Christopher?. "Notes on Sermons." 1592–1621. BL Additional MS 48016.

Online

Bosworth, Joseph. *An Anglo-Saxon Dictionary*. Ed. T. Northcote Toller. Oxford: Clarendon, 1898. http://ebeowulf.uky.edu/BT/Bosworth-Toller.htm.

Chibnall, Marjorie. "Matilda [Matilda of England] (1102–1167), empress, consort of Heinrich V." *ODNB*.

Clergy of the Church of England Database. http://theclergydatabase.org.uk/.

Coke, Edward. *Part Eight of the Reports. The Selected Writings and Speeches of Sir Edward Coke*. Ed. Steve Sheppard. http://oll.libertyfund.org/titles/911#lf0462-01 _footnote_nt_705_ref.

Concordance of Shakespeare's Complete Works. Fairfax: George Mason University, 2020. https://www.opensourceshakespeare.org/concordance/.

Digital Facsimile of the Bodleian First Folio of Shakespeare's Plays, Bodleian Arch. G c.7. Oxford University Library. http://firstfolio.bodleian.ox.ac.uk/book.html.

Eales, Jacqueline. "Robert Abbot (fl. c. 1589–1652), Church of England Clergyman and Religious Writer." *ODNB*.

Foxe, John. *The Unabridged Acts and Monuments Online*. HRI Online Publications, Sheffield, 2011. http//www.johnfoxe.org.

"A Guide to the Newport News (Va.) Coroners' Inquisitions, 1879–1944." Library of Virginia. http://ead.lib.virginia.edu/vivaxtf/view?docId=lva/vi03636.xml.

Harriss, G.L. "Eleanor [Née Eleanor Cobham], Duchess of Gloucester (c. 1400–1452), Alleged Sorcerer." *ODNB*.

"Lambeth Hill." *The Map of Early Modern London*. Victoria: University of Victoria. http://mapoflondon.uvic.ca/LAMB2.htm.

Lehmberg, Stanford. "Nowell, Alexander (c. 1516/17–1602), dean of St Paul's." *ODNB*.

Lexicons of Early Modern English. Toronto: University of Toronto Library and University of Toronto Press, 2006. leme.library.utoronto.ca.

"November 1650: An Act for turning the Books of the Law, and all Process and Proceedings in Courts of Justice, into English." *Acts and Ordinances of the Interregnum, 1642–1660*. Ed. C.H. Firth and R.S. Rait. London: His Majesty's Stationery Office, 1911. 455–6. *British History Online*. http://www.british-history .ac.uk/no-series/acts-ordinances-interregnum/pp455-456.

Orlin, Lena Cowen. "Yarington [Yarrington], Robert (fl. 1601), putative playwright." *ODNB*.

Oxford Dictionary of National Biography. Oxford: Oxford University Press, 2019. http:// www.oxforddnb.com/.

Oxford English Dictionary. Oxford: Oxford University Press, 2019. http://www .oed.com.

Powell, Edward. "Gascoigne, Sir William (c. 1350–1419), justice." *ODNB*.

"Selection and Summoning of Jury Panels." 28 U.S.C. § 1866 (c). https://www.law.cornell .edu/uscode/text/28/1866.

"Sessions, 1613: 4 and 6 August." *County of Middlesex. Calendar to the Sessions Records: New Series, Vol. 1: 1612–14*. Ed. William Le Hardy. British History Online. http://www.british-history.ac.uk/report.aspx?compid=82310.

United States Federal Rules of Evidence. Rule 602 "Need for Personal Knowledge." https://www.law.cornell.edu/rules/fre/rule_602.

– Rule 603. "Oath or Affirmation to Testify Truthfully." https://www.law.cornell.edu/rules/fre/rule_603.

Virgoe, Roger. "Cocke, Henry (1538–1610), of Broxbourne, Herts." *The History of Parliament: The House of Commons 1558–1603*. Ed. P.W. Hasler. http://www.historyofparliamentonline.org/volume/1558-1603/member/cocke-henry-1538-1610.

Print

Abbey, Charles J., and John H. Overton. *The English Church in the Eighteenth Century*. Vol. 2. London: Longman, 1878.

Abbot, Robert. *A Hand of Fellowship, to Helpe Keepe out Sinne and Antichrist. In Certaine Sermons Preached upon Severall Occasions*. London, 1623.

Adlington, Hugh. "Restoration, Religion, and Law: Assize Sermons, 1660–1685." In *The Oxford Handbook of the Early Modern Sermon*, ed. Peter McCullough, Hugh Adlington, and Emma Rhatigan, 423–59. Oxford: Oxford University Press, 2011.

Agamben, Giorgio. *Homo Sacer: Sovereign Power and Bare Life*. Trans. Daniel Heller-Roazen. Stanford: Stanford University Press, 1998.

Ahmed, Sara. *Living a Feminist Life*. Durham, NC: Duke University Press, 2017.

– *The Promise of Happiness*. Durham, NC: Duke University Press, 2010.

Anderson, David K. "The Tragedy of Good Friday: Sacrificial Violence in *King Lear*." *ELH* 78. 2 (2011): 259–86.

Anker, Elizabeth S., and Bernadette Meyler, eds. *New Directions in Law and Literature*. Oxford: Oxford University Press, 2017.

Arber, Edward, ed. *A Transcript of the Registers of the Company of Stationers of London, 1554–1640*. Vol. 2. London: Privately Printed, 1875.

Archer, Ian W. *The Pursuit of Stability: Social Relations in Elizabethan London*. Cambridge: Cambridge University Press, 1991.

Archer, Jane Elisabeth, Elizabeth Goldring, and Sarah Knight, eds. *The Intellectual and Cultural World of the Early Modern Inns of Court*. Manchester: Manchester University Press, 2011.

Aristotle. *The Nicomachean Ethics*. Trans. H. Rackham. Cambridge: Harvard University Press, 1926.

– *On Rhetoric: A Theory of Civic Discourse*. Trans. George A. Kennedy. Oxford: Oxford University Press, 1991.

Bacon, Francis. *The Elements of the Common Lawes of England*. London, 1630.

– *The Essayes or Counsels, Civill and Morall*. Ed. Michael Kiernan. Vol. 15. *The Oxford Francis Bacon*. Oxford: Clarendon, 2000.

– *The Works of Francis Bacon*. Ed. James Spedding et al. Vol. 5. London: Longman, 1858.
– *The Works of Francis Bacon [...] The Letters and the Life*. Ed. James Spedding et al. Vol. 13. London: Longman, 1872.
Bailey, Merridee L., and Kimberley-Joy Knight. "Writing Histories of Law and Emotion." *Journal of Legal History* 38, no. 2 (2017): 117–29.
Baker, J.H. *An Introduction to English Legal History*. 4th ed. Oxford: Oxford University Press, 2007.
– *The Legal Profession and the Common Law*. London: Hambledon, 1986.
– *The Oxford History of the Laws of England, Volume VI, 1483–1558*. Ed. J.H. Baker. · Vol. 6. Oxford: Oxford University Press, 2003.
Bandes, Susan A. "Remorse and Criminal Justice." *Emotion Review* 8, no. 1 (2015): 1–6.
Barber, C.L. "The Trial of Carnival in *Part 2*." In *William Shakespeare's* Henry IV, Part 2, ed. Harold Bloom, 21–8. New York: Chelsea House Publishers, 1987.
Barlow, William. *The Sermon Preached at Paules Crosse, the Tenth Day of November, Being the next Sunday after the Discoverie of This Late Horrible Treason. / Preached by the Right Reverend Father in God William Lord Bishop of Rochester*. London: Printed for Mathew Lawe, 1606.
Barry, Jonathan, and Christopher W. Brooks, eds. *The Middling Sort of People: Culture, Society, and Politics in England, 1550–1800*. Houndmills: Macmillan, 1994.
Barthes, Roland. "Myth Today." In *Mythologies*, ed. Annette Lavers, 109–59. London: Vintage, 2000.
Bartlett, Robert. *Trial by Fire and Water: The Medieval Judicial Ordeal*. Oxford: Clarendon, 1986.
Baxter, Charles. "Rhyming Action." *Michigan Quarterly Review* 35, no. 4 (1996): 616–30.
Beal, Peter. *A Dictionary of English Manuscript Terminology, 1450–2000*. Oxford: Oxford University Press, 2008.
Beckwith, Sarah. *Shakespeare and the Grammar of Forgiveness*. Ithaca: Cornell University Press, 2011.
Belsey, Catherine. *The Subject of Tragedy: Identity and Difference in Renaissance Drama*. London: Methuen, 1985.
Ben-Ze'ev, Aaron. "The Personal Comparative Concern in Schadenfreude." In *Schadenfreude: Understanding Pleasure at the Misfortune of Others*, ed. Wilco W. van Dijk and Jaap W. Ouwerkerk, 77–90. Cambridge: Cambridge University Press, 2014.
Beowulf. Trans. Seamus Heaney. New York: Norton, 2000.
Berlant, Lauren. *The Female Complaint: The Unfinished Business of Sentimentality in American Culture*. Durham, NC: Duke University Press, 2008.
Berman, Harold J. *Law and Revolution II: The Impact of the Protestant Reformations on the Western Legal Tradition*. Cambridge, MA: Harvard University Press, 2003.
The Bible (The Geneva Bible). London: Christopher Barker, 1582.
Blake, John L. *A Biographical Dictionary ... Lives of the Most Distinguished Persons ... American Biography*. Philadelphia: Cowperthwait, 1859.

Blanshard, Alastair J.L., and Tracey A. Sowerby. "Thomas Wilson's Demosthenes and the Politics of Tudor Translation." *International Journal of the Classical Tradition* 12, no. 1 (2005): 46–80.

Boemus, Johann. *The Manners, Lawes, and Customes of All Nations*. Trans. Edward Aston. London: Printed by G. Eld and are to bee sold by Francis Burton, 1611.

Bolton, Robert. *Instructions for a Right Comforting Afflicted Conciences: With Speciall Antidotes against Some Grievous Temptations. Delivered for the Most Part in the Lecture at Kettering in Northamptonshire*. London: Imprinted by Felix Kyngston for Thomas Weaver, and are to be sold at his shop at the great north-dore of Saint Pauls Church, 1631.

– *Mr. Boltons Last and Learned Worke of the Foure Last Things, Death, Judgement, Hell, and Heaven. With His Assise Sermons, and Notes on Justice Nicholls His Funerall*. Ed. Edward Bagshaw. 4th ed. London: George Miller, 1639.

Bornstein, Brian H., and Richard L. Wiener, eds. *Emotion and the Law: Psychological Perspectives*. New York: Springer, 2010.

Bourdieu, Pierre. *Distinction: A Social Critique of the Judgement of Taste*. Trans. Richard Nice. Cambridge: Harvard University Press, 1984.

– *The Field of Cultural Production: Essays on Art and Literature*. Ed. Randal Johnson. New York: Columbia University Press, 1993.

– "The Force of Law: Towards a Sociology of the Juridical Field." *Hastings Law Journal* 38 (1986): 805–53.

Boyer, Allen D. "Sir Edward Coke, Ciceronianus: Classical Rhetoric and the Common Law Tradition." *International Journal for the Semiotics of Law* 10, no. 28 (1997): 3–36.

Bradbrook, M.C. *Shakespeare and Elizabethan Poetry*. Cambridge: Cambridge University Press, 1951.

Bradley, A.C. *Oxford Lectures on Poetry*. London: Macmillan, 1934.

Bright, Timothy. *A Treatise of Melancholie. Containing the Causes Thereof, & Reasons of the Strange Effects It Worketh in Our Minds and Bodies: With the Phisicke Cure, and Spirituall Consolation for Such as Have Thereto Adjoyned an Afflicted Conscience*. London: By Thomas Vautrollier, dwelling in the Black-Friers, 1586.

Brooks, Christopher W. "The Common Lawyers in England c. 1558–1642." In *Lawyers in Early Modern Europe and America*, ed. Wilfrid R. Prest, 42–64. London: Helm, 1981.

– *Law, Politics, and Society in Early Modern England*. Cambridge: Cambridge University Press, 2008.

– "Paradise Lost? Law, Literature, and History in Restoration England." In *The Oxford Handbook of English Law and Literature, 1500–1700*, ed. Lorna Hutson. Oxford: Oxford University Press, 2017.

– *Pettyfoggers and Vipers of the Commonwealth: The "Lower Branch" of the Legal Profession in Early Modern England*. Cambridge: Cambridge University Press, 2004.

– "Professions, Ideology and the Middling Sort in the Late Sixteenth and Early Seventeenth Centuries." In *The Middling Sort of People: Culture, Society, and Politics in England, 1550–1800*, ed. Jonathan Barry and Christopher W. Brooks, 113–40. Houndmills: Macmillan, 1994.

Brooks, Christopher W., and Kevin Sharpe. "History, English Law and the Renaissance." *Past & Present* 72 (1976): 133–42.

Brooks, Peter. *Troubling Confessions: Speaking Guilt in Law and Literature*. Chicago: University of Chicago Press, 2000.

Brophy, Philip. "Horrality – The Textuality of Contemporary Horror Films." *Screen* 27, no. 1 (1986): 2–13.

Browne, Thomas. *Religio Medici*. London: Andrew Crooke, 1642.

Bruster, Douglas, and Robert Weimann. *Prologues to Shakespeare's Theatre: Performance and Liminality in Early Modern Drama*. Abingdon: Routledge, 2004.

Buck, George. *The Third Universitie of England*. In *The Annales, or Generall Chronicle of England, Begun First by Maister John Stow, and after Him Continued and Augmented with Matters Forreyne, and Domestique, Auncient and Moderne, unto the Ende of This Present Yeere 1614. by Edmond Howes, Gentleman*. London, 1615.

Bulwer, John. *Chirologia*. London, 1644.

Burrill, Alexander Mansfield. *A Law Dictionary and Glossary*. 2nd ed. 2 vols. New York: Baker, 1871.

Burrow, Colin. "Reading Tudor Writing Politically: The Case of *2 Henry IV*." *Yearbook of English Studies* 38 (2008): 234–50.

Burton, Robert. *The Anatomy of Melancholy*. Oxford, 1651.

Butler, Sara M. *Forensic Medicine and Death Investigation in Medieval England*. New York: Routledge, 2015.

Cade, Anthony. *A Sermon of the Nature of Conscience Which May Well Be Tearmed, a Tragedy of Conscience in Her*. London: Bernard Alsop for Thomas Jones, and are to be solde at his shop in Chancery Lane, and in Westminster hall, 1621.

Caenegem, R.C. van. "Public Prosecution of Crime in Twelfth-Century England." In *Legal History: A European Perspective*, 1–36. London: Hambledon, 1991.

Calvin, John. *Calvin's Commentary on Seneca's* De Clementia. Trans. Ford Lewis Battles and André Malan Hugo. Leiden: Brill, 1969.

– *The institution of Christian religion*. London: Printed by H. Midleton, for W. Norton, 1587.

– *The Institution of Christian Religion*. London: By Arnold Hatfield, for Bonham Norton, 1599.

– *Institutes of the Christian Religion*. Vol. 1: Books I.i to III.Xix. Ed. John T. McNeill. Trans. Ford Lewis Battles. Vol. 1. Louisville, KY: Westminster, 1960.

Campbell, Lily B., ed. *The Mirror for Magistrates: Edited from Original Texts in the Huntington Library*. Cambridge: Cambridge University Press, 1938.

Carpenter, Richard. *The Conscionable Christian: Or, The Indevour of Saint Paul, to Have and Discharge a Good Conscience Always towards God, and Men: Laid Open and Applyed in Three Sermons. Preached before the Honourable Judges of the Circuit, at Their Severall Assises, Holden in Chard and Taunton, for the County of Somerset*.

1620. By Richard Carpenter, Doctor of Divinity, and Pastor of Sherwell in Devon. London: F[elix] K[ingston] for John Bartlet, and are to be sold at the signe of the gilded Cup, in the Goldsmiths Rowe in Cheapside, 1623.

Carroll, William C. Fat King, Lean Beggar: Representations of Poverty in the Age of Shakespeare. Ithaca: Cornell University Press, 1996.

Cavell, Stanley. Disowning Knowledge in Seven Plays of Shakespeare. Cambridge: Cambridge University Press, 1987.

Charron, Pierre de. De la Sagesse. Paris, 1607.

– Of Wisdom. Three Books. Trans. George Stanhope. London, 1697.

Clark, Andrew. "An Annotated List of Sources and Related Material for Elizabethan Domestic Tragedy, 1591–1625." Research Opportunities in Renaissance Drama 18 (1974): 25–33.

Closse, George. The Parricide Papist, or, Cut-Throate Catholicke. A Tragicall Discourse of a Murther Lately Committed at Padstow in the Countie of Cornewall by a Professed Papist, Killing His Owne Father, and Afterwardes Himselfe, in Zeale of His Popish Religion. The 11 of March Last Past. 1606. Written by G Closse, Preacher of the Word of God at Blacke Torrington in Devon. London: Printed at London for Christopher Hunt, dwelling in Pater-noster-row, neere the Kings head, 1606.

Cockburn, J.S. A History of English Assizes, 1558–1714. Cambridge: Cambridge University Press, 1972.

Coke, Edward. The First Part of the Institutes. London, 1628.

– The Lord Coke His Speech and Charge. With a Discoverie of the Abuses and Corruption of Officers. Ed. Robert Pricket. London: Printed for Nathaniell Butter, 1607.

– Les reports de Edward Coke L'attorney generall le Roigne. London: [Printed by Adam Islip] in ædibus Thomæ Wight, 1600.

– Le second part des reportes del Edward Coke. London, 1602.

– The Third Part of the Institutes of the Laws of England Concerning High Treason, and Other Pleas of the Crown, and Criminall Causes. London: Printed by M. Flesher, for W. Lee, and D. Pakeman, 1644.

– Le tierce part des reportes del Edward Coke. London: [Printed by Adam Islip] in ædibus Thomæ Wight, 1602.

Colish, Marcia L. The Stoic Tradition from Antiquity to the Early Middle Ages. Vol. 1. Leiden: Brill, 1985.

Collinson, Patrick. "Truth and Legend: The Veracity of John Foxe's Book of Martyrs." In Elizabethan Essays, 151–77. London: Hambledon, 1994.

Collinson, Patrick, Arnold Hunt, and Alexandra Walsham. "Religious Publishing in England 1557–1640." In The Cambridge History of the Book in Britain, vol. 4, ed. John Barnard, D.F. McKenzie, and Maureen Bell, 29–66. Cambridge: Cambridge University Press, 2002.

The Compleat Clark, and Scriveners Guide. Containing Exact Draughts and Presidents of All Manner of Assurances and Instruments Now in Use: As They Were Penned and

Perfected by Divers Learned Judges, Eminent Lawyers, and Great Conveyancers, Both Ancient and Modern. London: Printed by T.R. for H. Twyford, and are to be sold at his Shop in Vine-Court Middle Temple, N. Brookes at the Angell in Cornhill, J. Place at Furnivals Inne Gate in Holborne, and R. Wingate, at the Golden Hind in Chancery-Lane, 1655.

The Compleat Justice. London: Printed by James Flesher for William Lee and Daniel Pakeman, and are to be sold at their Shops in Fleetstreet, 1661.

Coquillette, Daniel R. *The Civilian Writers of Doctors' Commons, London: Three Centuries of Juristic Innovation in Comparative, Commercial, and International Law.* Berlin: Duncker & Humblot, 1988.

Cormack, Bradin. *A Power to Do Justice: Jurisdiction, English Literature, and the Rise of Common Law, 1509–1625.* Chicago: University of Chicago Press, 2007.

Cunningham, Karen. "The Shakespearean Legal Imaginary." In *The Shakespearean World*, ed. Jill Levenson and Robert Ormsby, 622–37. London: Routledge, 2017.

Curran, Kevin. *Shakespeare's Legal Ecologies: Law and Distributed Selfhood.* Evanston: Northwestern University Press, 2017.

Cust, Richard. "Reading for Magistracy: The Mental World of Sir John Newdigate." In *The Monarchical Republic of Early Modern England: Essays in Response to Patrick Collinson*, ed. John F. McDiarmid, 181–99. Aldershot: Ashgate, 2007.

Dalton, Michael. *The Countrey Justice, Conteyning the Practise of the Justices of the Peace out of Their Sessions.* London: Printed for the Societie of Stationers, 1618.

Daniel, Samuel. *The First Fowre Bookes of the civil wars between the two houses of Lancaster and Yorke.* London: Printed by P. Short for Simon Waterson, 1595.

Davies, John. *The Poems of Sir John Davies.* Ed. Robert Krueger. Oxford: Clarendon, 1975.

Davis, Natalie Zemon. *Fiction in the Archives: Pardon Tales and Their Tellers in Sixteenth-Century France.* Stanford: Stanford University Press, 1987.

Deleuze, Gilles, and Félix Guattari. *A Thousand Plateaus: Capitalism and Schizophrenia.* Trans. Brian Massumi. Minneapolis: University of Minnesota Press, 1987.

Deloney, Thomas. *Jack of Newbury.* Ed. Peter C. Herman. Peterborough, ON: Broadview, 2015.

Derrida, Jacques. *Demeure: Fiction and Testimony.* Trans. Elizabeth Rottenberg. Stanford: Stanford University Press, 2000.

Desmet, Christy. *Reading Shakespeare's Characters: Rhetoric, Ethics, and Identity.* Amherst: University of Massachusetts Press, 1992.

Dijk, Wilco W. van, and Jaap W. Ouwerkerk, eds. *Schadenfreude: Understanding Pleasure at the Misfortune of Others.* Cambridge: Cambridge University Press, 2014.

Dodderidge, John. *The History of the Ancient and Moderne Estate of the Principality of Wales, Dutchy of Cornewall, and Earldome of Chester. Collected out of the Records of the Tower of London, and Divers Ancient Authours. By Sir John Dodridge Knight, Late One of His Majesties Judges in Th[e] Kings Bench. And by Himselfe Dedicated to*

King James of Ever Blessed Memory. London: Printed by Tho. Harper, for Godfrey Emondson, and Thomas Alchorne, 1630.

Dolan, Frances E. *Dangerous Familiars: Representations of Domestic Crime in England, 1550–1700*. Ithaca: Cornell University Press, 1994.

– *True Relations: Reading, Literature, and Evidence in Seventeenth-Century England*. Philadelphia: University of Pennsylvania Press, 2013.

Doty, Jeffrey S. "*Measure for Measure* and the Problem of Popularity." *English Literary Renaissance* 42, no. 1 (2012): 32–57.

Doty, Mark. *The Art of Description: World into Word*. Minneapolis: Graywolf, 2010.

Dowd, Michelle M. *The Dynamics of Inheritance on the Shakespearean Stage*. Cambridge: Cambridge University Press, 2015.

Drummond, William. *The Poetical Works of William Drummond of Hawthornden*. Ed. William Barclay Turnbull. London: John Russell Smith, 1856.

Duffy, Eamon. *Fires of Faith: Catholic England under Mary Tudor*. New Haven: Yale University Press, 2009.

Dugdale, William. *Origines Juridiciales, or, Historical Memorials of the English Laws, Courts of Justice, Forms of Tryal, Punishment in Cases Criminal, Law-Writers, Law-Books, Grants and Settlements of Estates, Degree of Serjeant, Innes of Court and Chancery*. London: Printed by Tho. Newcomb, for Abel Roper, John Martin, and Henry Herringman, 1671.

Duncan, Martha Grace. "'So Young and so Untender': Remorseless Children and the Expectations of the Law." *Columbia Law Review* 102, no. 6 (2002): 1469–526.

Dunne, Derek. "Re-Assessing Trial by Jury in Early Modern Law and Literature." *Literature Compass*, 12 (2015): 517–26.

– *Shakespeare, Revenge Tragedy and Early Modern Law: Vindictive Justice*. London: Palgrave, 2016.

Elias, Norbert. *Norbert Elias on Civilization, Power, and Knowledge: Selected Writings*. Ed. Stephen Mennell and Johan Goudsblom. Chicago: University of Chicago Press, 1998.

Elyot, Thomas. *The Boke Named the Governour*. London, 1531.

England and Wales. *By the Queene. A Proclamation for the Dearth of Corne*. London: By the deputies of Christopher Barker, Printer to the Queenes most excellent Majestie, 1596.

– *By the Queene. The Queenes Majesties Proclamation, 1. For Observation of Former Orders against Ingrossers, & Regraters of Corne, 2. And to See the Markets Furnished with Corne. 3. And Also against the Carying of Corne out of the Realme. 4. And a Prohibition to Men of Hospitalitie from Remooving from Their Habitation in the Time of Dearth. 5. And Finally a Strait Commandement to All Officers Having Charge of Forts to Reside Thereon Personally, and No Inhabitant to Depart from the Sea Coast*. London: By the deputies of Christopher Barker, printer to the Queenes most excellent Majestie, 1596.

Eskew, Doug. "'Soldiers, Prisoners, Patrimony': *King Lear* and the Place of the Sovereign." *Cahiers Élisabéthains* 78 (2010): 29–38.

Ewick, Patricia, and Susan S. Silbey. *The Common Place of Law: Stories from Everyday Life*. Chicago: University of Chicago Press, 1998.

The Famous Victories of Henry the Fifth. In *The First Part of King Henry the Fourth: Texts and Contexts*, ed. Barbara Hodgdon, 291–308. Boston: Bedford, 1997.

Felman, Shoshana. *The Juridical Unconscious: Trials and Traumas in the Twentieth Century*. Cambridge, MA: Harvard University Press, 2002.

Fikkers, Lotte. "Early Modern Women in the English Courts of Law." *Literature Compass* (2018): 1–10.

Finn, Kavita Mudan. *The Last Plantagenet Consorts: Gender, Genre, and Historiography, 1440–1627*. New York: Palgrave, 2012.

Fisher, Sally. "Eleanor, Duchess of Gloucester: Chronicles and Ideas of Exile and Imprisonment in Fifteenth-Century England." *Parergon* 34, no. 2 (2017): 73–97.

Fortescue, John. *De Laudibus Legum Anglie*. Ed. S.B. Chrimes. Cambridge: Cambridge University Press, 1942.

Fortier, Mark. *The Culture of Equity in Early Modern England*. Aldershot: Ashgate, 2005.

Foucault, Michel. *Discipline and Punish: The Birth of the Prison*. Trans. Alan Sheridan. New York: Random, 1977.

– "Of Other Spaces." Trans. Jay Miskowiec. *Diacritics* 16, no. 1 (1986) 22–7.

Frisch, Andrea. *The Invention of the Eyewitness: Witnessing and Testimony in Early Modern France*. Chapel Hill: University of North Carolina Press, 2004.

Fulbecke, William. *A Direction or Preparative to the Study of the Lawe*. London: Printed by Thomas Wight, 1600.

Fuller, Bostock. "Note Book of a Surrey Justice." In *Surrey Archæological Collections, Relating to the History and Antiquities of the County*, ed. Granville Leveson-Gower, 161–232. London: Surrey Archæological Society, 1888.

Fumerton, Patricia. *Unsettled: The Culture of Mobility and the Working Poor in Early Modern England*. Chicago: University of Chicago Press, 2006.

– "Introduction: A New New Historicism." In *Renaissance Culture and the Everyday*, ed. Patricia Fumerton and Simon Hunt, 1–17. Philadelphia: University of Pennsylvania Press, 2009.

Garey, Samuel. *Jentaculum Judicum: Or, A Breake-Fast for the Bench: Prepared, Presented, and Preached in Two Sacred Services, or Sermons, the Morning Sacrifice before the Two Assizes: At Thetford, at Norwich: 1619. Containing Monitory Meditations, to Execute Justice and Law-Businesse with a Good Conscience*. London: B[ernard]. A[lsop]. for Matthew Law, and are to be sold by Edmond Casson at Norwich in the market-place, at the signe of the Bible, 1623.

– *A Manuall for Magistrates: Or a Lanterne for Lawyers: A Sermon Preached before Judges and Justices at Norwich Assizes, 1619*. London: printed by B[ernard]. A[lsop].

for Matthew Law, and are to be sold by Edmond Casson at Norwich in the market-place, at the signe of the Bible, 1623.

Garnet, Henry. "A Treatise of Equivocation." In *Recusancy and Conformity in Early Modern England: Manuscript and Printed Sources in Translation*, ed. Ginevra Crosignani, Thomas M. McCoog, and Michael C. Questier, 298–343. Toronto: Pontifical Institute of Mediaeval Studies, 2010.

Gaskill, Malcolm. *Crime and Mentalities in Early Modern England*. Cambridge: Cambridge University Press, 2000.

Gerard, John. *The Herball or Generall Historie of Plantes*. London: By [Edm. Bollifant] for [Bonham Norton and] John Norton, 1597.

Gieskes, Edward. *Representing the Professions: Administration, Law, and Theater in Early Modern England*. Newark: University of Delaware Press, 2006.

Glanvill, Ranulf de. *The Treatise on the Laws and Customs of England Commonly Called Glanvill*. Ed. G.D.H. Hall. London: Nelson, 1965.

Gleason, J.H. *The Justices of the Peace in England, 1558 to 1640*. Oxford: Clarendon, 1969.

Golding, Arthur. *A briefe discourse of the late murther of master George Saunders. A Warning for Fair Women: A Critical Edition*. Ed. Charles Dale Cannon. The Hague: Mouton, 1975.

Goodrich, Peter. *Law in the Courts of Love: Literature and Other Minor Jurisprudences*. London: Routledge, 1996.

– *Legal Emblems and the Art of Law*: Obiter Depicta *as the Vision of Governance*. Cambridge: Cambridge University Press, 2014.

Gowing, Laura. *Common Bodies: Women, Touch and Power in Seventeenth-Century England*. New Haven: Yale University Press, 2003.

– *Domestic Dangers: Women, Words, and Sex in Early Modern London*. Oxford: Oxford University Press, 1996.

Gray, Charles. "Reason, Authority, and Imagination: The Jurisprudence of Sir Edward Coke." In *Culture and Politics: From Puritanism to the Enlightenment*, ed. Perez Zagorin, 25–66. Berkeley: University of California Press, 1980.

Great Britain. *The Statutes of the Realm*. Vol. 1. London, 1810.

– *The Statutes of the Realm*. Vol. 4, Pt. 1. London, 1819.

Green, Thomas A. "A Retrospective on the Criminal Trial Jury: 1200–1800." In *The Criminal Trial Jury in England, 1200–1800*, ed. J.S. Cockburn and Thomas A. Green, 358–400. Princeton: Princeton University Press, 1988.

– *Verdict According to Conscience: Perspectives on the English Criminal Trial Jury, 1200–1800*. Chicago: University of Chicago Press, 1985.

Greenberg, Marissa. *Metropolitan Tragedy: Genre, Justice, and the City in Early Modern England*. Toronto: University of Toronto Press, 2015.

– "Signs of the Crimes: Topography, Murder, and Early Modern Domestic Tragedy." *Genre* 40, no. 1–2 (2007): 1–29.

Gregg, Melissa, and Gregory J. Seigworth, eds. *The Affect Theory Reader*. Durham, NC: Duke University Press, 2010.

Griffin, Eric. "Shakespeare, Marlowe, and the Stranger Crisis of the Early 1590s."
    In *Shakespeare and Immigration*, ed. Ruben Espinosa and David Ruiter, 13–36.
    Farnham: Ashgate, 2014.

Griffiths, Ralph A. "The Trial of Eleanor Cobham: An Episode in the Fall of Duke
    Humphrey of Gloucester." *Bulletin of the John Rylands Library* 51, no. 2 (1969):
    381–99.

Groot, Roger D. "The Early-Thirteenth-Century Criminal Jury." In *Twelve Good Men
    and True: The Criminal Trial Jury in England, 1200–1800*, ed. J.S. Cockburn and
    Thomas A. Green, 3–35. Princeton: Princeton University Press, 1988.

Guéroult, Guillaume. *Le Premier livre des Emblèmes*. Lyon, 1550.

Haigh, Christopher. *English Reformations: Religion, Politics, and Society under the
    Tudors*. Oxford: Clarendon, 1993.

Hale, Matthew. *The History of the Common Law of England*. Ed. Charles M. Gray.
    Chicago: University of Chicago Press, 1971.

Hall, John. *Select Observations on English Bodies of Eminent Persons in Desperate
    Diseases*. London: Printed by J[ohn]. D[arby]. for Benjamin Shirley, under the Dial
    of St. Dunstan's Church in Fleet-street, 1679.

Hall, Joseph. *Characters of Vertues and Vices. In Two Bookes*. London, 1608.

Harding, A. "The Revolt against the Justices." In *The English Rising of 1381*, ed. R.H.
    Hilton and T.H. Aston, 165–93. Cambridge: Cambridge University Press, 1981.

Harris, Robert. "Saint Paul's Exercise: A Sermon Preached before the Judges at
    Assize." In *Two Sermons: The One Preached before the Judges of Assize at Oxford.
    The Other to the Universities*, 1–26. London: Printed [at Eliot's Court Press] for
    J. Bartlet, and are to be sold at his shop in Cheape-side, at the signe of the gilded
    Cup, 1628.

Hassel Jr., R. Chris. *Shakespeare's Religious Language: A Dictionary*. New York:
    Continuum, 2005.

Hedlin, Kim. "The Book of Job in Early Modern England." PhD diss., University of
    California, Los Angeles, 2018.

Helgerson, Richard. *Forms of Nationhood: The Elizabethan Writing of England*.
    Chicago: University of Chicago Press, 1992.

– "Weeping for Jane Shore." *South Atlantic Quarterly* 98, no. 3 (1999): 451–76.

Helmholz, R.H. *The Oxford History of the Laws of England Volume 1: The Canon Law
    and Ecclesiastical Jurisdiction from 597 to the 1640s*. Ed. J.H. Baker. Vol. 1. 12 vols.
    Oxford: Oxford University Press, 2004.

Herrup, Cynthia B. *The Common Peace: Participation and the Criminal Law in
    Seventeenth-Century England*. Cambridge: Cambridge University Press, 1987.

Heywood, Thomas. *An Apology for Actors*. London: Printed by Nicholas Okes, 1612.

– *The First and Second Parts of King Edward IV*. Ed. Richard Rowland. Manchester:
    Manchester University Press, 2005.

Hickerson, Megan L. *Making Women Martyrs in Tudor England*. Houndmills: Palgrave,
    2005.

Hill, Alexandra. "Lost Print in England: Entries in the Stationers' Company Register." In *Lost Books: Reconstructing the Print World of Pre-Industrial Europe*, ed. Flavia Bruni and Andrew Pettegree, 144–60. Leiden: Brill, 2016.

Hill, L.M. "The Two-Witness Rule in English Treason Trials: Some Comments on the Emergence of Procedural Law." *American Journal of Legal History* 12, no. 2 (1968): 95–111.

Hindle, Steve. "Dearth, Fasting, and Alms: The Campaign for General Hospitality in Late Elizabethan England." *Past & Present* 172 (2001): 44–86.

– *On the Parish? The Micro-Politics of Poor Relief in Rural England, c. 1550–1750*. Oxford: Clarendon, 2004.

– "Self-Image and Public Image in the Career of a Jacobean Magistrate: Sir John Newdigate in the Court of Star Chamber." In *Popular Culture and Political Agency in Early Modern England and Ireland: Essays in Honour of John Walter*, ed. Michael J. Braddick and Phil Withington, 123–43. Woodbridge: Boydell & Brewer, 2017.

– *The State and Social Change in Early Modern England, 1550–1640*. Houndmills: Palgrave, 2002.

Hirschfeld, Heather. *The End of Satisfaction: Drama and Repentance in the Age of Shakespeare*. Ithaca: Cornell University Press, 2014.

Hobgood, Allison P. *Passionate Playgoing in Early Modern England*. Cambridge: Cambridge University Press, 2014.

Holmes, Rachel E., and Toria Johnson. "In Pursuit of Truth." *Forum for Modern Language Notes* 54, no. 1 (2018): 1–16.

The Holy Bible, Conteyning the Old Testament, and the New. London: Robert Barker, 1611.

Horn, Andrew. *The Booke Called, the Mirrour of Justices*. Ed. William Joseph Whittaker. London: Selden Society, 1895.

Houlbrooke, Ralph. *Church Courts and the People during the English Reformation, 1520–1570*. Oxford: Oxford University Press, 1979.

Howard, Jean E. "Crossdressing, the Theatre, and Gender Struggle in Early Modern England." *Shakespeare Quarterly* 39, no. 4 (1988): 418–40.

Hudson, John. *The Oxford History of the Laws of England Volume 2: 871–1216*. Vol. 2. Oxford: Oxford University Press, 2012.

Huit, Ephraim. *The Anatomy of Conscience or the Summe of Pauls Regeneracy. Wherein Are Handled the Palces of Conscience, Worship, and Scandall, with Diverse Rules of Christian Practise; Very Profitable for the Weake Christian*. London: Printed by I. D. for William Sheffard, and are to be sold at his Shop at the entrance in out of Lumbard streete into Popes-head Alley, 1626.

Hunnisett, R.F. *The Medieval Coroner*. Cambridge: Cambridge University Press, 1961.

Hunt, Arnold. *The Art of Hearing: English Preachers and Their Audiences, 1590–1640*. Cambridge: Cambridge University Press, 2010.

Hutcheon, Linda. *A Theory of Adaptation*. 2nd ed. London: Routledge, 2013.

Hutson, Lorna. "From Penitent to Suspect: Law, Purgatory, and Renaissance Drama." *Huntington Library Quarterly* 65, nos. 3/4 (2002): 295–319.

– *The Invention of Suspicion: Law and Mimesis in Shakespeare and Renaissance Drama.* Oxford: Oxford University Press, 2007.
– "Not the King's Two Bodies: Reading the 'Body Politic' in Shakespeare's *Henry IV, Parts 1 and 2*." In *Rhetoric and Law in Early Modern Europe*, ed. Lorna Hutson and Victoria Kahn, 166–89. New Haven: Yale University Press, 2001.
–, ed. *The Oxford Handbook of English Law and Literature, 1500–1700.* Oxford: Oxford University Press, 2017.
Hyams, Paul R. *Rancor and Reconciliation in Medieval England.* Ithaca: Cornell University Press, 2003.
Ingram, Juliet Amy. "The Conscience of the Community: The Character and Development of Clerical Complaint in Early Modern England." PhD thesis, University of Warwick, 2004.
Ingram, Martin. *Carnal Knowledge: Regulating Sex in England, 1470–1600.* Cambridge: Cambridge University Press, 2017.
– *Church Courts, Sex and Marriage in England, 1570–1640.* Cambridge: Cambridge University Press, 1987.
– "Shame and Pain: Themes and Variations in Tudor Punishments." In *Penal Practice and Culture, 1500–1900: Punishing the English*, ed. Simon Devereaux and Paul Griffiths, 36–62. New York: Palgrave, 2004.
Jacobsen, Devin. "The Testimony of Martyr: A Word History of Martyr in Anglo-Saxon England." *Studies in Philology* 115, no. 3 (2018): 417–32.
James, Anne. *Poets, Players, and Preachers: Remembering the Gunpowder Plot in Seventeenth-Century England.* Toronto: University of Toronto Press, 2016.
James I. *The Workes of the Most High and Mighty Prince, James ... King of Great Britaine, France and Ireland.* London, 1616.
Janelle, Pierre. *Robert Southwell the Writer: A Study in Religious Inspiration.* London: Sheed & Ward, 1935.
Johnstone, Gerry, and Daniel W. Van Ness. "The Meaning of Restorative Justice." In *Handbook of Restorative Justice*, ed. Gerry Johnstone and Daniel Van Ness, 5–23. Cullompton: Willan, 2007.
Jonson, Ben. *The Complete Poems.* Ed. George Parfitt. London: Penguin, 1996.
Jordan, Constance and Karen Cunningham, eds. *The Law in Shakespeare.* Basingstoke: Palgrave, 2010.
Julius, Philip. "Diary of the Journey of the Most Illustrious Philip Julius, Duke of Stettin-Pomerania ... through ... England, ... 1602." Ed. Gottfried von Bülow. *Transactions of the Royal Historical Society* 6 (1892): 1–67.
Justinian, and Gaius. *The Institutes of Gaius and Justinian, The Twelve Tables, and the CXVIIIth and CXXVIIth Novels.* Trans. T. Lambert Mears. London: Stevens. 1882.
Kahan, Jeffrey, ed. King Lear: *New Critical Essays.* New York: Routledge, 2008.
Kahn, Coppélia. "The Absent Mother in *King Lear*." In *Rewriting the Renaissance: The Discourses of Sexual Difference in Early Modern Europe*, ed. Margaret W. Ferguson,

Maureen Quilligan, and Nancy Vickers, 33–49. Chicago: University of Chicago Press, 1986.

Keen, Suzanne. *Empathy and the Novel*. Oxford: Oxford University Press, 2007.

Keeton, G.W. *Shakespeare's Legal and Political Background*. New York: Barnes and Noble, 1967.

Kelley, Donald R. "*Vera Philosophia*: The Philosophical Significance of Renaissance Jurisprudence." *Journal of the History of Philosophy* 14, no. 3 (1976): 267–79.

Kelly, Henry Ansgar. *Inquisitions and Other Trial Procedures in the Medieval West*. Aldershot: Ashgate, 2001.

Kennedy, Dennis, ed. *The Oxford Companion to Theatre and Performance*. Oxford: Oxford University Press, 2010.

Kerrigan, John. "*Henry IV* and the Death of Old Double." *Essays in Criticism* 40, no. 1 (1990): 24–53.

– *Motives of Woe: Shakespeare and 'Female Complaint': A Critical Anthology*. Oxford: Clarendon, 1991.

Kesselring, K.J. *Making Murder Public: Homicide in Early Modern England, 1480–1680*. Oxford: Oxford University Press, 2019.

– *Mercy and Authority in the Tudor State*. Cambridge: Cambridge University Press, 2003.

Kiernan, Victor. *Eight Tragedies of Shakespeare: A Marxist Study*. London: Verso, 1996.

King, John N. *Foxe's* Book of Martyrs *and Early Modern Print Culture*. Cambridge: Cambridge University Press, 2006.

Kirshbaum, Leo. "Albany." *Shakespeare Studies* 13 (1960): 20–9.

Knafla, Louis A. "The Matriculation Revolution and Education at the Inns of Court in Renaissance England." In *Tudor Men and Institutions*, ed. Arthur Slavin, 232–64. Baton Rouge: Louisiana State University Press, 1972.

Knott, John R. *Discourses of Martyrdom in English Literature, 1563–1694*. Cambridge: Cambridge University Press, 1993.

Lambarde, William. *Archeion*. London, 1635.

– *The Duties of Constables, Borsholders, Tithingmen, and Such Other Low Ministers of the Peace*. London: By Rafe Newberie and Henrie Middleton, 1583.

– *Eirenarcha: Or of The Office of the Justices of Peace, in Two Bookes*. London: Imprinted by Ra: Newbery, and H. Bynneman, by the ass. of Ri. Tot. & Chr. Bar., 1581.

– *William Lambarde and Local Government: His "Ephemeris" and Twenty-Nine Charges to Juries and Commissions*. Ed. Conyers Read. Ithaca: Cornell University Press for the Folger Shakespeare Library, 1962.

Lambert, Tom. *Law and Order in Anglo-Saxon England*. Oxford: Oxford University Press, 2017.

Langbein, John H. "The Origins of Public Prosecution at Common Law." *American Journal of Legal History* 17, no. 4 (1973): 313–35.

– *Prosecuting Crime in the Renaissance: England, Germany, France*. Cambridge: Harvard University Press, 1974.

Langbein, John H., Renée Lettow Lerner, and Bruce P. Smith, eds. *History of the Common Law: The Development of Anglo-American Legal Institutions*. New York: Aspen, 2009.

Laqueur, Thomas W. "Crowds, Carnival and the State in English Executions, 1604–1868." In *The First Modern Society: Essays in English History in Honour of Lawrence Stone*, ed. A.L. Beier, David Cannadine, and James M. Rosenheim, 305–55. Cambridge: Cambridge University Press, 1989.

Law, Robert Adger. "'Yarington's 'Two Lamentable Tragedies.'" *Modern Language Review* 5 (1910): 167–77.

Lemon, Rebecca. *Addiction and Devotion in Early Modern England*. Philadelphia: University of Pennsylvania Press, 2018.

– *Treason by Words: Literature, Law, and Rebellion in Shakespeare's England*. Ithaca: Cornell University Press, 2008.

Levack, Brian P. *The Civil Lawyers in England, 1603–1641: A Political Study*. Oxford: Clarendon, 1973.

Lewis, John U. "Sir Edward Coke: His Theory of Artificial Reason as a Context for Modern Basic Legal Theory." *Law Quarterly Review* 84 (1968): 330–42.

Lightfoot, John. *The Works of the Reverend & Learned John Lightfoot D. D. Late Master of Katherine Hall in Cambridge. The Second Volume. Part II*. London: Printed by William Rawlins, for Richard Chiswell at the Rose and Crown in St. Paul's Church-yard, 1684.

Loades, David, ed. *John Foxe: An Historical Perspective*. Aldershot: Ashgate, 1999.

Loar, Carol. "'Go and Seek the Crowner': Coroners' Inquests and the Pursuit of Justice in Early Modern England." PhD diss., Northwestern University, 1998.

Lockwood, Matthew. *The Conquest of Death: Violence and the Birth of the Modern English State*. New Haven: Yale University Press, 2017.

Loewenstein, David. "Agnostic Shakespeare? The Godless World of *King Lear*." *Shakespeare and Early Modern Religion*, ed. David Loewenstein and Michael Witmore, 155–71. Cambridge: Cambridge University Press, 2015.

Lupton, Julia Reinhard. *Citizen-Saints: Shakespeare and Political Theology*. Chicago: University of Chicago Press, 2005.

Luther, Martin. *Luther's Reply to King Henry VIII*. Trans. E. S. Buchanan. New York: Swift, 1928.

– *Temporal Authority: To What Extent It Should Be Obeyed*. In *Selected Writings of Martin Luther: 1520–1523*, ed. Theodore Tappert, trans. J.J. Schindel and Walther I. Brandt, 267–319. Minneapolis: Fortress, 2007.

– *A Treatise, Touching the Libertie of a Christian*. Trans. James Bell. London, 1579.

Lynn, Eleri. *Tudor Fashion*. New Haven: Yale University Press, 2017.

MacCulloch, Diarmaid. *The Reformation: A History*. New York: Penguin, 2003.

MacDonald, Michael. "Suicide and the Rise of the Popular Press in England." *Representations* 22, no. 2 (1988): 36–55.

Macey, George. *A Sermon Preached at Charde in the Countie of Somerset, the Second of March 1597. Being the First Day of the Assises There Holden.* London: [by R. Bradock?] for R. D[exter]. and are to be soulde by Michaell Hart bookseller in the city of Exceter, 1601.

MacKay, Ellen. *Persecution, Plague, and Fire: Fugitive Histories of the Stage in Early Modern England.* Chicago: University of Chicago Press, 2011.

Maitland, Frederic, and Frederick Pollock. *The History of English Law before the Time of Edward I.* 2nd ed. Vol. 1. Cambridge: Cambridge University Press, 1898.

Manley, Lawrence. "From Strange's Men to Pembroke's Men: *2 Henry VI* and *The First Part of the Contention.*" *Shakespeare Quarterly* 54, no. 3 (2003): 253–87.

The Manner of the Death and Execution of Arnold Cosbie. London: [John Wolfe?] for William Wright, 1591.

Manningham, John. *The Diary of John Manningham of the Middle Temple, 1602–1603.* Ed. Robert Parker Sorlien. Hanover: University Press of New England, 1976.

Marcus, Sharon, Heather Love, and Stephen Best. "Building a Better Description." *Representations* 135 (2016): 1–21.

Marshburn, Joseph H. "'A Cruell Murder Donne in Kent' and Its Literary Manifestations." *Studies in Philology* 46, no. 2 (1949): 131–40.

Martin, Randall. *Women, Murder, and Equity in Early Modern England.* New York: Routledge, 2008.

Matthews, Nancy L. *William Sheppard, Cromwell's Law Reformer.* Cambridge University Press, 1984.

Maus, Katharine Eisaman. *Inwardness and Theater in the English Renaissance.* Chicago: University of Chicago Press, 1995.

Mbembe, Achille. "Necropolitics." Trans. Libby Meintjes. *Public Culture* 15, no. 1 (2003): 11–40.

McAuley, Finbarr. "Canon Law and the End of the Ordeal." *Oxford Journal of Legal Studies* 26, no. 3 (2006): 473–513.

McCoy, Richard C. "'Look upon Me, Sir': Relationships in *King Lear.*" *Representations* 81 (2003): 46–60.

McLuskie, Kathleen. "The Patriarchal Bard: Feminist Criticism and Shakespeare: *King Lear* and *Measure for Measure.*" In *Political Shakespeare: New Essays in Cultural Materialism,* ed. Jonathan Dollimore and Alan Sinfield, 88–108. Manchester: Manchester University Press, 1985.

McSheffrey, Shannon. *Seeking Sanctuary: Crime, Mercy, and Politics in English Courts, 1400–1550.* Oxford: Oxford University Press, 2017.

Melanchthon, Philip. *A Faithfull Admonycion of a Certen Trewe Pastor and Prophete Sent unto the Germanes at Such Tyme as Certen Great Princes Went Abowt to Bring in Alienes in to Germany … Now Translated in to Inglyssh for a Lyte Admonycyon unto All Trewe Inglyssh Hartes Whereby Thei May Lerne and Knowe How to Consyder and Receive the Procedings of the Inglyssh Magistrates and Bisshops. With a Preface of M. Philip Melancthon.* Greenwich?, 1554.

Mell, George. *A Proper New Balad of the Bryber Gehesie. Taken out of the Fourth Booke of Kinges, the v. Chapter; to the Tune of Kynge Salomon.* London: In fletestreate beneath the Conduit, at the signe of S. John Evangelist by Thomas Colwell, 1567.

Middleton, Thomas, William Rowley, and Thomas Heywood?. *An/The Old Law.* Ed. Jeffrey Masten. In *The Collected Works of Thomas Middleton,* Gary Taylor and John Lavagnino, eds. 1335–96. Oxford: Clarendon, 2007.

Monta, Susannah Brietz. "Foxe's Female Martyrs and the Sanctity of Transgression." *Renaissance and Reformation* 25, no. 1 (2001): 3–22.

– *Martyrdom and Literature in Early Modern England.* Cambridge: Cambridge University Press, 2005.

Moore, Peter R. "*Hamlet* and the Two Witness Rule." *Notes and Queries* 44, no. 4 (1997): 498–505.

More, Thomas. *Utopia.* Ed. S.J. Surtz. New Haven: Yale University Press, 1964.

Morrissey, Mary. *Politics and the Paul's Cross Sermons, 1558–1642.* Oxford: Oxford University Press, 2011.

Mortenson, Peter. "The Role of Albany." *Shakespeare Quarterly* 16, no. 2 (1965): 217–25.

Mowat, Barbara A. "Shakespeare Reads the Geneva Bible." In *Shakespeare, the Bible, and the Form of the Book: Contested Scriptures,* ed. Travis DeCook and Alan Galey, 25–39. Abingdon: Routledge, 2012.

Mukherjee, Ayesha. *Penury into Plenty: Dearth and the Making of Knowledge in Early Modern England.* New York: Routledge, 2015.

Mukherji, Subha. *Law and Representation in Early Modern Drama.* Cambridge: Cambridge University Press, 2006.

Muldrew, Craig. *The Economy of Obligation: The Culture of Credit and Social Relations in Early Modern England.* Houndmills: Palgrave, 1998.

Mulvey, Laura. "Visual Pleasure and Narrative Cinema." *Screen* 16, no. 3 (1975): 6–18.

Munday, Anthony. *A View of Sundry Examples. Reporting Many Straunge Murthers, Sundry Persons Perjured, Signes and Tokens of Gods Anger towards Us.* London: J. Charlewood for William Wright, and are to be sold [by J. Allde] at the long shop, adjoyning unto S. Mildreds Church in the Poultrie, 1580.

Munro, Lucy. "'They Eat Each Others' Arms': Stage Blood and Body Parts." In *Shakespeare's Theatres and the Effects of Performance,* ed. Farah Karim-Cooper and Tiffany Stern, 73–93. London: Bloomsbury, 2012.

Musculus, Wolfgang. *The Temporysour (That Is to Saye: The Observer of Tyme, or He That Chaungeth with the Tyme.) Compyled in Latyn by the Excellent Clarke Wolfangus Musculus, and Translated into Frenche by M. Vallerain Pullain. And out of Frenche into Inglishe by R. P.* Trans. R. P. Zurich? Geneva?, 1555.

Musson, Anthony. *Medieval Law in Context: The Growth of Legal Consciousness from Magna Carta to the Peasants' Revolt.* Manchester: Manchester University Press, 2001.

Nelson, Alan H. *Monstrous Adversary: The Life of Edward de Vere, 17th Earl of Oxford.* Liverpool: Liverpool University Press, 2003.

Nicholson, Benjamin. *The Lawyers Bane. Or, the Lawes Reformation, and New Modell: Wherein the Errours and Corruptions Both of the Lawyers and of the Law It Selfe Are Manifested and Declared. And Also, Some Short and Profitable Considerations Laid down for the Redresse of Them.* London: Printed for George Whittington, at the blew Anchor in Cornehill, neer the Royall Exchange, 1647.

Nussbaum, Martha. *Hiding from Humanity: Disgust, Shame, and the Law.* Princeton: Princeton University Press, 2004.

O'Callaghan, Michelle. *The English Wits: Literature and Sociability in Early Modern England.* Cambridge: Cambridge University Press, 2007.

Oliver, Kelly. *Witnessing: Beyond Recognition.* Minneapolis: University of Minnesota Press, 2001.

– "Witnessing and Testimony." *Parallex* 10, no. 1 (2004): 79–88.

Orlin, Lena Cowen. "Domestic Tragedy: Private Life on the Public Stage." In *A Companion to Renaissance Drama*, ed. Arthur F. Kinney, 367–83. Malden: Blackwell, 2002.

– *Private Matters and Public Culture in Post-Reformation England.* Ithaca: Cornell University Press, 1994.

Orr, Patricia. "*Non Potest Appellum Facere*: Criminal Charges Women Could Not – But Did – Bring in Thirteenth-Century English Royal Courts of Justice." In *The Final Argument: The Imprint of Violence on Society in Medieval and Early Modern Europe*, ed. Donald J. Kagay and L. J. Villalon, 141–60. Woodbridge: Boydell, 1998.

Owen, W.J.B., and Jane Worthington Smyser, eds. *The Prose Works of William Wordsworth.* Vol. 3. 3 vols. Oxford: Clarendon, 1974.

Page, John, John Lydgate, and William Gregory. *The Historical Collections of a Citizen of London in the Fifteenth Century. Containing: I. John Page's Poem on the Siege of Rouen. II. Lydgate's Verses on the Kings of England. III. William Gregory's Chronicle of London.* Ed. James Gairdner. London: Camden Society, 1876.

Palfrey, Simon. *Poor Tom: Living King Lear.* Chicago: University of Chicago Press, 2014.

Patenaude, Anne Weston. "A Critical Old-Spelling Edition of Robert Yarington's *Two Lamentable Tragedies*." PhD diss., University of Michigan, 1978.

Perkins, William. *The foundation of Christian religion: gathered into sixe principles.* London: Printed [by John Orwin] for John Porter and J[ohn]. L[egat], 1595.

Pettegree, Andrew. *Marian Protestantism: Six Studies.* Aldershot: Scolar, 1996.

Plat, Hugh. *Sundrie New and Artificiall Remedies against Famine.* London: Printed by P[eter] S[hort] dwelling on Breadstreet hill, at the signe of the Starre, 1596.

Pocock, J.G.A. *The Ancient Constitution and the Feudal Law: A Study of English Historical Thought in the Seventeenth Century: A Reissue with a Retrospect.* Cambridge: Cambridge University Press, 1987.

Poole, Kristen. *Supernatural Environments in Shakespeare's England: Spaces of Demonism, Divinity, and Drama.* Cambridge: Cambridge University Press, 2011.

Postles, Dave. "Penance and the Market Place: A Reformation Dialogue with the Medieval Church (c. 1250–c. 1600)." *Journal of Ecclesiastical History* 54, no. 3 (2003): 441–68.

Prest, Wilfrid R. "Lay Legal Knowledge in Early Modern England." In *Learning the Law: Teaching and the Transmission of English Law 1150–1900*, ed. Jonathan Bush and Alain Wijffels, 302–13. London: Hambledon: 1999.

– *The Professions in Early Modern England*. London: Croom Helm, 1987.

– *The Rise of the Barristers: A Social History of the English Bar, 1590–1640*. Oxford: Clarendon, 1986.

– "William Lambarde, Elizabethan Law Reform, and Early Stuart Politics." *Journal of British Studies* 34, no. 4 (1995): 464–80.

Proeve, Michael, and Steven Tudor. *Remorse: Psychological and Jurisprudential Perspectives*. Farnham: Ashgate, 2010.

Raffield, Paul. "The Ancient Constitution, Common Law and the Idyll of Albion: Law and Lawyers in *Henry IV, Parts 1 and 2*." *Law and Literature* 22, no. 1 (2010): 18–47.

– "The Inner Temple Revels (1561–62) and the Elizabethan Rhetoric of Signs: Legal Iconography at the Early Modern Inns of Court." In *The Intellectual and Cultural World of the Early Modern Inns of Court*. ed. Jane Elisabeth Archer, Elizabeth Goldring, and Sarah Knight, 32–50. Manchester: Manchester University Press, 2011.

Rastell, John. *Exposiciones terminorum legum Anglorum*. London, 1525.

– *An Exposition of Certaine Difficult and Obscure Words, and Termes of the Lawes of This Realme*. London: Printed by Thomas Wight, 1602.

Rice, Douglas Walthew. *The Life and Achievements of Sir John Popham, 1531–1607: Leading to the Establishment of the First English Colony in New England*. Madison, NJ: Fairleigh Dickinson University Press, 2005.

Richardson, Catherine. *Domestic Life and Domestic Tragedy in Early Modern England: The Material Life of the Household*. Manchester: Manchester University Press, 2006.

Ros, William Lennox de. *Memorials of the Tower of London*. London: Murray, 1866.

Ross, Richard J. "The Commoning of Common Law: Debates over Printing English Law, 1520–1640." *University of Pennsylvania Law Review* 146 (1998): 323–462.

Rous, John. *Diary of John Rous, Incumbent of Santon Downham, Suffolk, from 1625 to 1642*. Ed. Mary Anne Everett Green. Camden Society, 1856.

Rowland, Richard, ed. "Introduction." In *The First and Second Parts of King Edward IV*, by Thomas Heywood, 1–77. Manchester: Manchester University Press, 2005.

Rozett, Martha Tuck. *The Doctrine of Election and the Emergence of Elizabethan Tragedy*. Princeton: Princeton University Press, 1984.

Rymer, Thomas. *Tragedies of the Last Age*. Printed for Richard Tonson at his Shop under Grays-Inn Gate, next Grays-Inn, 1678.

Ryrie, Alec. *Being Protestant in Reformation Britain*. Oxford: Oxford University Press, 2013.

– "The Strange Death of Lutheran England." *Journal of Ecclesiastical History* 53, no. 1 (2002): 64–92.

Sarat, Austin. "Remorse, Responsibility, and Criminal Punishment: An Analysis of Popular Culture." In *The Passions of Law*, ed. Susan A. Bandes, 168–90. New York: New York University Press, 1999.

Schwartz, Regina M. *Loving Justice, Living Shakespeare*. Oxford: Oxford University Press, 2016.

Sedgwick, Eve Kosofsky. *Touching Feeling: Affect, Pedagogy, Performativity*. Durham, NC: Duke University Press, 2003.

Shaheen, Naseeb. *Biblical References in Shakespeare's History Plays*. Newark: University of Delaware Press, 1989.

– "*A Warning for Fair Women* and the *Ur-Hamlet*." *Notes and Queries* 30, no. 2, (1983): 126–7.

Shakespeare, William. *The First Part of the Contention Betwixt the Two Famous Houses of York and Lancaster*. London: Printed by Thomas Creed, for Thomas Millington, and are to be sold at his shop under Saint Peters Church in Cornwall, 1594.

– *The First Part of Henry the Fourth*. In *The Riverside Shakespeare*. Ed. G. Blakemore Evans et al. Boston: Houghton, 1974.

– *Henry IV, Part 2*. Ed. René Weis. Oxford: Clarendon, 1998.

– *King Lear: A Parallel Text Edition*. Ed. René Weis. London: Longman, 1993.

– *The Life of Henry V*. In *The Riverside Shakespeare*. Ed. G. Blakemore Evans et al. Boston: Houghton, 1974.

– *Measure for Measure*. In *The Riverside Shakespeare*. Ed. G. Blakemore Evans et al. Boston: Houghton, 1974.

– *The Merry Wives of Windsor*. In *The Riverside Shakespeare*. Ed. G. Blakemore Evans et al. Boston: Houghton, 1974.

– *A Midsummer Night's Dream*. In *The Riverside Shakespeare*. Ed. G. Blakemore Evans et al. Boston: Houghton, 1974.

– *Much Ado about Nothing*. In *The Riverside Shakespeare*. Ed. G. Blakemore Evans et al. Boston: Houghton, 1974.

– *The Tragedy of Hamlet, Prince of Denmark*. In *The Riverside Shakespeare*. Ed. G. Blakemore Evans et al. Boston: Houghton, 1974.

– *The Tragedy of Othello, the Moor of Venice*. In *The Riverside Shakespeare*. Ed. G. Blakemore Evans et al. Boston: Houghton, 1974.

– *The Two Noble Kinsmen*. In *The Riverside Shakespeare*. Ed. G. Blakemore Evans et al. Boston: Houghton, 1974.

– *The Workes of William Shakespeare*. London. 1623.

Shapiro, Barbara J. "Law and the Evidentiary Environment." In *The Oxford Handbook of English Law and Literature, 1500–1700*, ed. Lorna Hutson, 257–76. Oxford: Oxford University Press, 2017.

– "Political Theology and the Courts: A Survey of Assize Sermons c. 1600–1688." *Law and Humanities* 2, no. 1 (2008): 1–28.

Shapiro, James. *The Year of Lear: Shakespeare in 1606*. New York: Simon & Schuster, 2015.

Sharon-Zisser, Shirley, ed. *Critical Essays on Shakespeare's "A Lover's Complaint":* *Suffering Ecstasy*. Aldershot: Ashgate, 2006.

Sharpe, J.A. *Crime in Early Modern England, 1550–1750*. 2nd ed. Harlowe: Longman, 1984.

– "Social Strain and Social Dislocation, 1585–1603." In *The Reign of Elizabeth I: Court and Culture in the Last Decade*, ed. John Guy, 192–211. Cambridge: Cambridge University Press, 1995.

– "'Such Disagreement Betwyx Neighbours': Litigation and Human Relations in Early Modern England." In *Disputes and Settlements: Law and Human Relations in the West*, ed. John Bossy, 167–87. Cambridge: Cambridge University Press, 1983.

Sharpe, Reginald R. *Calendar of Coroners Rolls of the City of London, A.D. 1300–1378*. London: Clay, 1913.

Sheppard, William. *The Touch-Stone of Common Assurances. Or, A Plain and Familiar Treatise, Opening the Learning of the Common Assurances or Conveyances of the Kingdome*. London: Printed by M. F. for W. Lee, M. Walbancke, D. Pakeman, and G. Bedell, 1648.

Shoemaker, Karl. "Punishment." In *Law and the Humanities*, ed. Austin Sarat, Matthew Anderson, and Cathrine O. Frank, 517–29. Cambridge: Cambridge University Press, 2010.

Shoemaker, Robert. "Streets of Shame? The Crowd and Public Punishments in London, 1700–1820." In *Penal Practice and Culture, 1500–1900: Punishing the English*, ed. Simon Devereaux and Paul Griffiths, 232–57. New York: Palgrave, 2004.

Shrank, Cathy. "'Hoysted High upon the Rolling Wheele': Elianor Cobham's *Lament*." In *"A Mirror for Magistrates" in Context: Literature, History, and Politics in Early Modern England*, ed. Harriet Archer and Andrew Hadfield, 109–25. Cambridge: Cambridge University Press, 2016.

Sir Gawain and the Green Knight. Trans. Simon Armitage. New York: Norton, 2007.

Slack, Paul. *Poverty and Policy in Tudor and Stuart England*. London: Longman, 1988.

Smith, Bruce R. *The Acoustic World of the Renaissance*. Chicago: University of Chicago Press, 1999.

Smith, Henry. *The Magistrates Scripture. The Sermons of Maister Henrie Smith, Gathered into One Volume. Printed According to His Corrected Copies in His Life Time*. London, 1593.

– *A Memento for Magistrates. The Poore-Mans Teares*. London: Printed by John Wolfe, & are to be sold by William Wright, 1592.

Smith, Thomas. *De Republica Anglorum*. Ed. Mary Dewar. Cambridge: Cambridge University Press, 1982.

Smith, Tiffany Watt. *Schadenfreude: The Joy of Another's Misfortune*. New York: Little, Brown, 2018.

A Solace for This Hard Season: Published by Occasion of Continuance of the Scarcitie of Corne, and Excessive Prices of All Other Kind of Provision. London: Printed for John Legate, 1595.

Solly-Flood, F. "The Story of Prince Henry of Monmouth and Chief-Justice Gascoign." *Transactions of the Royal Historical Society*, new. ser. 3, no. 3 (1886): 47–152.

St. German, Christopher. *Doctor and Student*. Ed. Theodore F.T. Plucknett and J.L. Barton. London: Selden Society, 1974.

Stachniewski, John. *The Persecutory Imagination: English Puritanism and the Literature of Religious Despair*. Oxford: Clarendon, 1991.

Staines, John D. "Radical Pity: Responding to Spectacles of Violence in *King Lear*." In *Staging Pain, 1580–1800: Violence and Trauma in British Theatre*, ed. James Robert Allard and Matthew R. Martin, 75–92. Fanshaw: Ashgate, 2009.

Stern, Tiffany. *Documents of Performance in Early Modern England*. Cambridge: Cambridge University Press, 2009.

Sternberg, Rachel Hall. *Tragedy Offstage: Suffering and Sympathy in Ancient Athens*. Austin: University of Texas Press, 2006.

Stoll, Abraham. "Macbeth's Equivocal Conscience." In *Macbeth: New Critical Essays*, ed. Nick Moschovakis, 132–50. London: Routledge, 2008.

Strain, Virginia Lee. *Legal Reform in English Renaissance Literature*. Edinburgh: Edinburgh University Press, 2018.

– "*The Winter's Tale* and the Oracle of the Law." *ELH* 78, no. 3 (2011): 557–84.

Stretton, Timothy. *Women Waging Law in Elizabethan England*. Cambridge: Cambridge University Press, 1998.

Strier, Richard. "Faithful Servants: Shakespeare's Praise of Disobedience." In *The Historical Renaissance: New Essays on Tudor and Stuart Literature and Culture*, ed. Heather Dubrow and Richard Strier, 104–33. Chicago: University of Chicago Press, 1988.

– "Shakespeare and Legal Systems: The Better the Worse (But Not Vice Versa)." In *Shakespeare and the Law*, ed. Bradin Cormack, Martha Nussbaum, and Richard Strier, 174–200. Chicago: University of Chicago Press, 2013.

Sugden, Edward H. *A Topographical Dictionary to the Works of Shakespeare and His Fellow Dramatists*. Manchester: Manchester University Press, 1925.

Sullivan, Ceri. *The Rhetoric of the Conscience in Donne, Herbert and Vaughan*. Oxford: Oxford University Press, 2008.

Syme, Holger Schott. *Theatre and Testimony in Shakespeare's England: A Culture of Mediation*. Cambridge: Cambridge University Press, 2012.

Taunton, Nina, and Valerie Hart. "'King Lear,' King James and the Gunpowder Treason of 1605." *Renaissance Studies* 17, no. 4 (2003): 695–715.

Taylor, Jamie K. *Fictions of Evidence: Witnessing, Literature, and Community in the Late Middle Ages*. Columbus: Ohio State University Press, 2013.

Temple, Kathryn D. *Loving Justice: Legal Emotions in William Blackstone's England*. New York: New York University Press, 2019.

Thompson, Ann. "Are There Any Women in *King Lear*?" In *The Matter of Difference: Materialist Feminist Criticism of Shakespeare*, ed. Valerie Wayne, 117–28. Ithaca: Cornell University Press, 1991.

Tomlin, Rebecca. "'I Trac'd Him Too and Fro': Walking the Neighbourhood on the Early Modern Stage." *Early Theatre* 19, no. 2 (2016): 197–208.

A True and Perfect Relation of the Whole Proceedings against the Late Most Barbarous Traitors, Garnet a Jesuite, and His Confederats. London: by Robert Barker, printer to the Kings most Excellent Majestie, 1606.

Tucker, Edward F.J. *Intruder into Eden: Representations of the Common Lawyer in English Literature, 1350–1750*. Columbia, SC: Camden House, 1984.

Two Most Unnaturall and Bloodie Murthers: The One by Maister Caverley, a Yorkshire Gentleman, Practised upon His Wife, and Committed Uppon His Two Children. London: By V. S[immes] for Nathanael Butter dwelling in Paules churchyard neere Saint Austens gate, 1605.

Veall, Donald. *The Popular Movement for Law Reform, 1640–1660*. Oxford: Oxford University Press, 1970.

W., T. *The Office of the Clerk of Assize: Containing the Form and Method of the Proceedings at the Assizes, and General Gaol-Delivery, as Also on the Crown and Nisi Prius Side*. London: Printed for Henry Twyford in Vine Court, Middle Temple, 1676.

Walker, Garthine. "Imagining the Unimaginable: Parricide in Early Modern England and Wales, c. 1600–1760." *Journal of Family History* 41, no. 3 (2016): 271–93.

Walpole, Horace, trans. *Paul Hentzner's Travels in England, During the Reign of Queen Elizabeth*. Strawberry Hill, 1797.

Walsham, Alexandra. *Providence in Early Modern England*. Oxford: Oxford University Press, 1999.

Walter, John. "A 'Rising of the People'? The Oxfordshire Rising of 1596." *Past & Present* 107, no. 1 (1985): 90–143.

Walwyn, William. *Juries Justified: Or, A Word of Correction to Mr. Henry Robinson; for His Seven Objections Against the Trial of Causes, by Juries of Twelve Men. By William Walwin. Published by Authority*. London: Printed by Robert Wood, 1651.

Ward, Samuel. *Jethro's Justice of Peace. A Sermon Preached at the Generall Assises Held at Bury St Edmunds for the Countie of Suffolke*. London: Printed by Augustine Mathewes, for John Marriot and John Grismand, and are to be sold at their shops in Saint Dunstones Church-yard, and in Pauls Alley at the signe of the Gunne, 1621.

A Warning for Faire Women. London: Valentine Sims for William Aspley, 1599.

A Warning for Fair Women: A Critical Edition. Ed. Charles Dale Cannon. The Hague: Mouton, 1975.

Warren, Christopher. *Literature and the Law of Nations, 1580–1680*. Oxford: Oxford University Press, 2015.

Whipday, Emma. *Shakespeare's Domestic Tragedies: Violence in the Early Modern Home*. Cambridge: Cambridge University Press, 2019.

Whipday, Emma, and Freyja Cox Jensen. "'Original Practices,' Lost Plays, and Historical Imagination: Staging 'The Tragedy of Merry.'" *Shakespeare Bulletin* 35, no. 2 (2017): 289–308.

Williams, Linda. "Film Bodies: Gender, Genre, and Excess." *Film Quarterly* 44, no. 4 (1991): 2–13.

Winston, Jessica. *Lawyers at Play: Literature, Law, and Politics at the Early Modern Inns of Court, 1558–1581*. Oxford: Oxford University Press, 2016.

Wiseman, Susan, and Alison Thorne, eds. *The Rhetoric of Complaint: Ovid's Heroides in the Renaissance and Restoration*. Oxford: Blackwell, 2008.

Wither, George. *Britain's Remembrancer Containing a Narration of the Plague Lately Past; a Declaration of the Mischiefs Present; and a Prediction of Judgments to Come; (If Repentance Prevent Not.) It Is Dedicated (for the Glory of God) to Posteritie; and, to These Times (If They Please)*. London: Imprinted for Great Britaine, and are to be sold by John Grismond in Ivie-Lane, 1628.

Witte, John, Jr. *Law and Protestantism: The Legal Teachings of the Lutheran Reformation*. Cambridge: Cambridge University Press, 2002.

"The Wofull Lamentacon of Mrs. Anne Saunders, Which She Wrote with Her Own Hand, Being Prisoner in Newgate, Justly Condemned to Death." In *Old English Ballads: 1553–1625*, ed. Hyder Rollins, 340–8. Cambridge: Cambridge University Press, 1920.

Woolf, D.R. "William Fulbecke (1560–1603?)." In *Dictionary of Literary Biography: Sixteenth-Century British Nondramatic Writers*, 4th series, ed. David A. Richardson, 172:91–95. Detroit: Gale, 1996.

Wright, Martin. *Justice for Victims and Offenders: A Restorative Response to Crime*. 2nd ed. Winchester: Waterside Press, 1996.

Wrightson, Keith. *Earthly Necessities: Economic Lives in Early Modern Britain*. New Haven: Yale University Press, 2000.

– *English Society, 1580–1680*. London: Hutchinson, 1982.

– "'Sorts of People' in Tudor and Stuart England." In *The Middling Sort of People: Culture, Society, and Politics in England, 1550–1800*, ed. Jonathan Barry and Christopher W. Brooks, 28–51, 227–33. Houndmills: Macmillan, 1994.

Wrigley, E.A., and R.S. Schofield. *The Population History of England, 1541–1871: A Reconstruction*. London: Arnold, 1981.

Yachnin, Paul. "Performing Publicity." *Shakespeare Bulletin* 28, no. 2 (2010): 201–19.

Yarington, Robert. *Two Lamentable Tragedies*. Ed. Chiaki Hanabusa. Manchester: Manchester University Press for the Malone Society, 2013.

A Yorkshire Tragedy. Not so New as Lamentable and True. Acted by His Majesties Players at the Globe. London: Printed by R. B. for Thomas Pavier and are to bee sold at his shop on Cornhill, neere the exchange, 1608.

Zhong, Rocksheng, et al. "So You're Sorry? The Role of Remorse in Criminal Law." *Journal of the American Academy of Psychiatry and the Law* 42, no. 1 (2014): 39–48.

Index

NOTE: Page numbers in *italics* denote illustrations or their captions. The abbreviation "JP" stands for Justice of the Peace. Anonymous works are indexed by their titles, all other works are indexed by their authors (exception to this rule is works by Shakespeare).

Laqueur, Thomas W., 193–4n34
law: agreement on superiority of English
law, 52; diversity of, 12–13, 161n66;
heteropatriarchal double standards
and, 34; as juridical field, 6; legality
distinguished from, xiii; and new
historicism, 10–11, 160n56. *See also*
law and emotions; law and literature,
field of; law reform; law study; legal
literature; statutes
law and emotions: overview, 11–12; and
the antiemotion program in law, 11–12,
59, 160n62; magistrate's management of
emotions in the courtroom, 123–4.
See also remorse; shame
law and literature, field of: overview, xiii–
xiv, 13–14; communal justice and, 10–
11; social history and establishment of,
10. *See also* law and emotions
Law French, 147, 208n4
law reform, communal justice and, 26,
147, 208n4
law study: diversity of outlooks in, 12;
doubt cast on the layman's capacity for,
16; law manuals/preparatives for, 13
lawyers: popular critiques of, 51–2; as
satirized figure, 50
lay judges, the medieval assize and, 31–2
lay legal commentators, injustices
attributed to moral failings, 52–3
lay magistracy: assize sermons and,
28, 41–2, 47, 49, 123; community
as indivisible from, 7; definition of,
xi, 36; Golding's *A brief discourse*
and, 77; in *King Lear*, 111–12; as
political movement, 26, 147. *See
also* communal justice; conscience;
coroner's jury; jury of presentment
lay magistrates: Athenian state and the
figure of, 146; citizen-sleuth as figure
of, 23, 74, 146; disambiguation of JPs
from "lay magistrates" as term, 36; as

heroic figures, 25, 74; model of the
self as, 21, 23, 41–2, 49, 123; moral
seriousness of, 77; omission from the
writings of legal profession, 145
legal emotions. *See* law and emotions
legality: concepts of communal justice
as deeply embedded in, 49; definition
of, xiii, 128; *Henry IV, Part 2* as raising
questions of, 71; historicity of, 7, 26,
157n25; literature's role in shaping,
xiii, 11, 95, 128, 148–9; as narrative of
disempowerment, 6–7
legal literature: overview, 13; on the
coroner, 81, 82, 84, 185–6n52;
emotional and physical distance in
law, 50, 56, 58; and hegemony of the
common law, 13; justicing manuals of
JPs, 36–7, 169n62, 170n65; lay judges
acknowledged in, 31–2; marginalia/
readers' marks in, 37, 170n65;
professional bias against communal
justice buried in writing style of, 32;
reconstructing the experience of law
with, xiii, 123, 200n4; and rhetoric
of expertise, 14; two-witness rule in,
106–7. *See also* justicing manuals;
literature of magistracy
legal personhood, defined as state of
communal belonging, 29–30
legal profession: focus on reason,
knowledge, and disavowal of the
passions, 50, 51, 53, 56–8, 59, 64–9;
and friendship as source of judicial
corruption, 58; popular critiques of
legal persons, not the law itself, 51–3;
and problem of popularity of judges,
57–8. *See also* professionalization of
the common law
legislators, denigration of, 17
Lemon, Rebecca, 139, 196n56
Lerner, Renée Lettow, 157n27, 158nn34,39,
166n3, 168n39, 169n57, 195n50, 208n4

Privy Council interest in the murder of, 74–5, 182–3nn20–2,25. *See also* Golding, Arthur, *A briefe discourse*; *A Warning for Fair Women* (anon.)

Sarat, Austin, 143

Saunders, Laurence, 100, *101*, 103, 113

Savill, Sir Henry, 186n62

scapegoating, 34

schadenfreude, 135, 205n58

Schwartz, Regina M., 8, 55

Scotland, 198n79

scriveners, general dislike of, 16, 17, 163n91

Sedgwick, Eve Kosofsky, 11, 134

self: model of the self as lay magistrate, 21, 23, 41–2, 49, 123; social model of, 8

Shaheen, Naseeb, 164–5n117, 179n66, 190n105

Shakespeare, William: unauthorized publishing of "bad quartos," 40; version of the Bible quoted by, 179n66. Works: *Hamlet*, 94, 137, 190n105; *Henry IV, Part 1*, 60, 64, 67; *Measure for Measure*, 40, 45, 106, 173n105; *The Merchant of Venice*, 7; *A Midsummer Night's Dream*, 98, 192n17; *Much Ado About Nothing*, 107, 194–5n43; *Othello*, 107, 127, 196n62; *The Two Noble Kinsmen*, 40. See also *Henry IV, Part 2*; *Henry V*; *Henry VI* plays; *Henry VI, Part 2*; *King Lear*; *Macbeth*

shame: as contagious, 134–5; in *Henry IV, Part 2*, 51, 67–8; in *Henry VI, Part 2*, 124, 130–2, 138–9; the pillory and, 76–7; in *A Warning for Fair Women* (anon.), 78–9. *See also* public penance

Shapiro, Barbara J., 40, 190n1

Shapiro, James, 198n79, 206n70

Sharon-Zisser, Shirley, 203n36

Sharpe, James A., 9

Sharpe, Reginald R., 185n42

Sheppard, William, *The Touch-Stone of Common Assurances*, 3–4, 16, 156n6

sheriffs: choosing jurors for jury of presentment, 28; choosing preachers for assize sermons, 28, 40, 41; jury of presentment reporting to, 33; manuals for, 41

Shoemaker, Karl, 30, 201n21

Shoemaker, Robert, 127–8

Shore, Jane, 129, 132–3, 202n32, 203n35

Shrank, Cathy, 202–3n33

Siddons, Sarah, 203n35

Silbey, Susan S., xiii, 6–7

Sir Gawain and the Green Knight (Armitage, trans.), 127, 201n17

Slack, Paul, 188n88

Slany, Sir Stephen, 89

Smith, Bruce P., 157n27, 158nn34,39, 166n3, 168n39, 169n57, 195n50, 208n4

Smith, Bruce R., 5, 189n99

Smith, Henry, 54, 55, 56

Smith, Sir Thomas, *De Republica Anglorum*, 19, 82, 83

Smith, Tiffany Watt, 135

social belonging. *See* belonging

social credit, 34, 127–8, 202n25. *See also* reputation

social history, 10–11

Solace for This Hard Season, A (anon.), 90

Solly-Flood, F., 173n3

Solon, 51

Sophocles, 97; *Antigone*, 106

Southwell, Father Robert, 139, 206n75

sovereign power: definition of, 199n96; King James I on, 120

Stachniewski, John, 20

Staines, John D., 97–8

States, Bert O., 116–17

statutes: 1 & 2 Phil. & M., c. 6 (1555, aka "An Acte ... for the punishement of

Heresies"), 98; 1 & 2 Phil. & M., c. 13
and 2 & 3 Phil. & M., c. 10 (1554–5,
aka Marian Bail and Committal
Statutes), 36, 82, 100; 2 Hen. 4,
c. 15 (1400–1, aka *De haeretico
comburendo*), 192n19; 2 Hen. 5, st.
1, c. 7 (1414), 192n19; 5 & 6 Edw. 6,
c. 11 (1551–2), 195n52; 5 Rich. 2, st.
2, c. 5 (1382), 192n19; 7 & 8 Wil. 3,
c. 3 (1695–6), 106; 18 Hen. 6, c. 11
(1439), 36; 25 Hen. 8, c. 14 (1534),
192n19; 27 Eliz. 1, c. 13 (1584–5),
8; "assize" as term for, 31; Assize of
Arms (1181), 8; Assize of Bread and
Ale (uncertain date), 31; Assize of
Clarendon (1166), 33, 168n37; Assize
of Northampton (1176), 168n37;
Statute of Marlborough (1267), 82,
186n53; Statute of Westminster I (3
Edw. 1, c. 10) (1275), 81, 185–6n52;
Treason Act of 1571, 196
Stephen of Blois (king), 30
Sternberg, Rachel Hall, 158n34, 207n1
Stern, Tiffany, 165n124
Stoll, Abraham, 141
Strain, Virginia Lee, 18, 173n105, 208n3
Stretton, Timothy, 9, 175n14
Strier, Richard, 69, 97, 159–60n54,
164n107, 191–2n16, 197n73
subjectivity, and model of the self as lay
magistrate, 21
Sullivan, Ceri, 171n81
Syme, Holger Schott, 82, 190–1n2
sympathy: distinguished from empathy,
108; evolving into empathy, 108–9,
112–13
Szymborska, Wisława, 119

taste (Bourdieu), 3, 6
Taunton, Nina, 115
Taylor, Jamie K., 96, 97
Temple, Kathryn D., 159n47

testimony: depositions, 96, 190–1n2;
etymology of term, 96; false, and crisis
of magistracy in *King Lear,* 104–5,
107–8, 194–9n43; familial betrayal
through, 101–2, 103; JPs and, 35; as
legal obligation of subjects, 3; and
the medieval assize, 32; mishandling
of protocols, 103–4; oath taken
prior to, 96–7; oral (*viva voce*), 96;
personal knowledge as privileged in,
96–7, 191n7; *ribaldi* excluded from,
107, 196n60; and royal/professional
legal administration integrated with
communal justice, 123; trial by battle
and, 32; two-witness rule, 105–8,
195nn45,50, 196n54. *See also* fact;
witnessing
testis unus, testis nullus. See two-witness
rule
theatre: as "acoustic field," 5; actors
and performance of remorse, 126;
closing of the playhouses (1642), 6,
146; communal justice depictions
in, and the rise of state-appointed
magistrates, 37; and communal
justice, shaping of, 5–6, 7, 22–3, 95,
145–6; emotional contagion and,
22; and erasure of class differences,
84; fictional community of, 21–2; as
generating intersubjectivity, 22, 117,
136; as healing, 5; as heterotopias/
counter-sites, 5, 11; interstitial scenes,
59, 112; metatheatrical prologue
(induction), 91–4; *mimesis* and
diegesis and, 23; persecutorial poetics
of, 94; as "public making" sites, 5;
resemblance to the courtroom, 124;
and search for community, 5–6; as site
of collective knowledge-making, 5–6,
91, 95. *See also* audience
Theophrastus, *Characters,* 50
Theseus, 98, 192n17